Marina Owners Workshop Manual

by J H Haynes
Associate Member of the Guild of Motoring Writers
and B L Chalmers-Hunt
TEng(CEI), AMIMI, AMIRTE, AMVBRA

Models covered

UK: Marina Saloon (1.8 & 1.8TC), 1798 cc. 1971 on
Marina Coupe (1.8 & 1.8TC), 1798 cc. 1971 on
Marina Estate, 1798 cc. 1972 on
USA: Marina Sedan, 110 cu in. 1973 on
Marina GT Coupe, 110 cu in. 1973 on

ISBN 0 900550 74 0

Printed in England

J H HAYNES AND COMPANY LIMITED
SPARKFORD YEOVIL SOMERSET ENGLAND
distributed in the USA by
HAYNES PUBLICATIONS INC.
9421 WINNETKA AVENUE
CHATSWORTH LOS ANGELES
CALIFORNIA 91311 USA

Acknowledgements

Thanks are due to the British Leyland Motor Corporation (Austin/Morris Division) for their permission to use certain line illustrations in this manual, to Castrol Limited for lubrication details and to Terry Kimpton Esq.

Invaluable assistance was given by Brian Horsfall in preparing the car for photography and the text was arranged and edited by Tim Parker.

About this manual

Its arrangement

The manual is divided into thirteen chapters, each covering a logical sub-division of the vehicle. The chapters are each divided into sections, numbered with single figures, e.g. 5; and the sections into paragraphs (or sub-sections), with decimal numbers following on from the section they are in, e.g. 5.1, 5.2, 5.3, etc.

It freely illustrated, especially in those parts where there is a detailed sequence to be carried out. There are two forms of illustration: figures and photographs. The figures are numbered in sequence with decimal numbers, according to their position in the chapter: e.g. Fig.6.4 is the 4th drawing/illustration in Chapter 6. Photographs are numbers (either individually or in related groups) the same as the section or sub-section of the text where the operation they show is described.

There is an alphabetical index at the back of the manual as well as a contents list at the front.

References to the 'left' or 'right' of the vehicle are in the sense of a person in a seat facing forwards towards the engine.

Chapter 13 is devoted to modifications fitted to cars going to market outside Europe, to North America in particular. In that Chapter are details of all the modifications to meet the special regulations of the USA. The sections within that chapter deal with subjects in the same order as the main chapters. When reading Chapter 1 to 12 also check what relevant material is in Chapter 13.

Modifications

The policy of the manufacturer of these vehicles is one of continuous development, and designs and specifications are frequently being changed as a result. It follows naturally that spares may sometimes be purchased which differ both from the original part removed and from the part referred to in this manual. However, suppliers of genuine British Leyland spare parts can usually settle queries about interchangeability by reference to the latest information issued by the manufacturer. (Read the section, Ordering spare parts).

Every care has been taken to ensure the accuracy of this manual but no liability can be accepted by the authors and publishers for any loss, damage or injury caused by any errors or omissions in the information given.

Contents

Austin Marina 1.8 4 door Super DeLuxe (North American market)

Morris Marina 1.8 TC 2 door Coupe (UK)

Morris Marina 1.8 Super DeLuxe Estate (UK)

Introduction to the Marina

There are two approaches to building a car. A conventional design can be used, and from it can be expected the reliability and dependability that must come from the thorough development of a well proven layout. The unconventional car should give some startling advantages, but in return some penalties must be accepted. In the British Leyland Motor Corporation the ordinary mass produced cars are made by the Austin-Morris Group. Their unconventional cars such as the Mini, the Maxi, and more recently the Allegro, have transverse engines driving the front wheels, and unusual suspension, such as hydroelastic and hydragas. These cars are renowned for their road holding and the large space inside with small overall dimensions. The conventional car is usually cheaper to build and to repair. Its different layout suits some owners who do not take to the transverse engined ones. The Marina is aimed at this large market. The dealer and agency loyalty in the United Kingdom was built originally when Austin and Morris were separate, and rivals. Whilst the Maxi and Allegro use the Austin agency, on the home market the Marina was launched as a Morris.

In the USA local British Leyland arrangements call for the Marina to be an Austin. So the Morris Marina is the home version, and the Austin the North American one.

The Morris Marina is available with three body styles and two engines, only the larger of which is dealt with in this manual. There is the four door Saloon, the two door Coupe, and the five door Estate. There is the ordinary 1.8 engine with one carburettor, and the 1.8 TC with twin carburettors. The TC and the Estate have a brake servo, and the super de luxe trim. The ordinary Coupe and Saloon may be had in a de luxe trim.

The Austin Marina is available in the four door and two door bodies. The two door is the Coupe GT. Only one engine is fitted, and this is a version of the 1.8 engine with single carburettor, and all the necessary equipment to meet the emissions regulations of the USA. It has the brake servo.

Either a manual four speed gear box, or Borg Warner 35 automatic transmission can be fitted. The engine at the front drives a live rear axle mounted on semi-elliptic leaf springs.

At the front the suspension is by longitudinal torsion bars.

The Marina 1,8 engine is the same one that is used in the MG B.

The Marina is simple and straightforward to work on. All the major components have been in use in earlier models so have long development behind them to give reliability.

Main overall dimensions

Length	Saloon	13 ft 10.1/8 in	(4.219 m)	
	Coupe	13 ft 7.1/8 in	(4.143 m)	
	Estate	13 ft 11.5/8 in	(4.255 m)	
Width	Saloon	5 ft 4.1/16 in	(1.640 m)	
	Coupe	5 ft 4.3/8 in	(1.635 m)	
	Estate	5 ft 4.7/8 in	(1.655 m)	
Height	Saloon	4 ft 8.1/8 in	(1.425 m)	TC saloon 4 ft 7.7/8 in (1.419 m)
	Coupe	4 ft 7.3/8 in	(1.406 m)	TC coupe 4 ft 7.1/8 in (1.400 m)
	Estate	4 ft 8.3/8 in	(1.436 m)	
Wheelbase		8 ft	(2.438 m)	
Kerbside weight	Saloon	2126 lb (964 kg)		TC saloon 2136 lb (968 kg)
	Coupe	2060 lb (934 kg)		TC coupe 2070 lb (938 kg)
	Estate	2172 lb (985 kg)		

Front and rear view close-ups of the GT (North American market)

Ordering spare parts

Always try to obtain genuine British Leyland parts from a franchised BLMC garage. Use the Unipart system too, if you can. It obviously makes good sense to go straight to a franchised garage even though you can order parts through any garage for they will be more familiar with your car than most, and there is a better chance that they can supply you ex-stock.

When ordering new parts it is essential that the storeman has full information about your particular model of Marina. He cannot guarantee to supply you with the correct part unless you give him your model and car and body numbers and in the case of engine, gearbox or rear axle parts, their relevant numbers. If possible take the part to be replaced along too.

If you are going to use the extensive BLMC exchange scheme make sure that the component which you wish to exchange is clean and complete before placing it on the parts counter.

The car and body numbers are located on two plates fixed to the left hand bonnet lock platform.

The engine number is afixed to the cylinder block on its right hand side.

The gearbox number is stamped on the right hand side.

The rear axle number is stamped on the outside face of the differential casing joint flange.

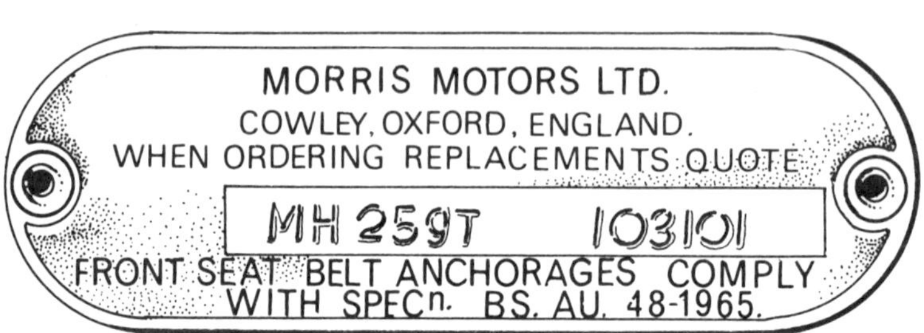

Prefix number

Prefix number	MH 2S 9–10.....................	1.8	2 door Coupe
	MH 4S 9–10.....................	1.8	4 door Saloon
	MH 2S 9T–10..................	1.8TC	2 door Coupe
	MH 4S 9T–10..................	1.8TC	4 door Saloon
	MH 5W9–10	1.8	Estate

M – Morris. H – 'B' series engine. 2S/4S – 2 or 4 door
9 – Model series 10...... – serial number

M – BLMC internal reference suffix

(A typical Marina 1.3 car number could be MA 4S 107618m)

Engine number 18V........ 10.... 1.8 'B' series engine

(Analysis of the engine number is much more complex because of the options available. Check with a BLMC parts list for clarification). The engine cylinder block should have '1800' embossed on it.

Routine maintenance

Maintenance should be regarded as essential for ensuring safety and desirable for the purpose of obtaining economy and performance from the car. By far the largest element of the maintenance routine is visual examination.

The maintenance instructions listed are those recommended by the manufacturer. They are supplemented by additional maintenance tasks which, from practical experience, need to be carried out.

The additional tasks are indicated by an asterisk and are primarily of a preventative nature — they will assist in eliminating the unexpected failure of a component.

Weekly, before a long journey, or every 250 miles (400 km)

1 Remove the dipstick and check the engine oil level which should be up to the 'MAX' mark. Top up the oil in the sump with Castrol GTX. On no account allow the oil to fall below the 'MIN' mark on the dipstick. The distance between the 'MAX' and 'MIN' marks corresponds to the approximately 1.5 pints (0.85litre) Fig.RM1/1.

2 Check the battery electrolyte level and top up as necessary with distilled water. Make sure that the top of the battery is always kept clean and free of moisture. See Chapter 10.

3 Inspect the level of water in the translucent plastic reservoir. This should be maintained at the required level mark by adding soft water, such as rain water, via the cap (Fig.RM2). If the reservoir is empty, remove the radiator filler plug, completely fill the radiator and replace the filler plug. Remove the reservoir screwed cap and half fill the reservoir. Refit the cap. Check for leaks. See Chapter 4.

4 Check the tyre pressure with an accurate gauge and adjust as necessary. Make sure that the tyre walls and treads are free of damage. Remember that the tyre tread should have a minimum of 1 millimetre depth across three quarters of the total width of the tread.

5 Refill the windscreen washer container with soft water. Add an anti-freezing solution satchet in cold weather to prevent freezing (do not use ordinary anti-freeze). Check that the jets operate correctly.

6 Remove the wheel trims and check all wheel nuts for tightness but take care not to overtighten.

Every 6000 miles (10000 km) or 6 months

Complete the service items in the weekly service check as applicable, plus:

1 Run the engine until it is hot and then place a container of 8 pints (4.55 litres) under the engine sump drain plug located on the right hand side at the rear of the sump (Fig.RM1/4). Remove the drain plug and its copper sealing washer. Allow the oil to drain out for 10 minutes. Whilst this is being done unscrew the old oil filter cartridge located on the right hand side of the engine and discard. Smear the rubber seal on a new cartridge with a little oil and refit it to the filter head. Screw it on and tighten hand tight only (Fig.RM1/5). Clean the oil filler cap in petrol and wipe dry. Check the drain plug copper sealing washer and if damaged fit a new one. Refit the drain plug and sealing washer. Refill the engine with 6.375 pints (3.8 litres) of Castrol GTX and clean off any oil which may have been spilt over the engine or its components. Run the engine and check the oil level. The interval between oil changes should be reduced in very hot or dusty conditions or during cool weather with much slow or stop/start driving (Fig.RM1/1).

2 Wipe the top of the carburettor suction chamber and unscrew and withdraw the oil cap. Top up the dashpot with fresh Castrol GTX to raise the level to ½ inch (13mm) above the top of the hollow piston rod. Push the damper assembly back into position and screw the cap firmly into position (Fig.RM1/2).

3 Check the carburettor adjustment as described in Chapter 3.

4 Carefully examine the cooling and heater systems for signs of leaks. Make sure that all hose clips are tight and that none of the hoses have cracked or perished. Do not attempt to repair a leaking hose, always fit new. Generally inspect the exterior of the engine for signs of water leaks or stains. The method of repair will depend on its location. This check is particularly important before filling the cooling system with anti-freeze as it has a greater searching action than pure water and is bound to find any weak spots.

5 The fan belt adjustment must be tight enough to drive the alternator without overloading the bearings, including the water pump bearings too. The method of adjusting the fan belt is described in Chapter 2. It is correct when it can be pressed in ½ inch (13mm) under moderate hand pressure at the mid point of its longest run from the alternator to the crankshaft pulley.

6 Lubricate the accelerator control linkage cable and pedal fulcrum with a little engine oil.

7 Inspect the steering rack rubber boots for signs of leaking which, if evident, must be rectified as described in Chapter 11.

8 Lubricate the two nipples on each of the front swivel pins with several strokes of the grease gun filled with Castrol LM Grease (Fig.RM1/10).

9 Inspect all steering ball joints for signs of wear, leaking rubber boots and securing nuts for tightness. If a ball joint rubber boot has failed the whole assembly should be renewed. See Chapter 11.

10 Check the front wheel alignment. For this special equipment is necessary therefore leave this to the local BLMC garage. See Chapter 11.

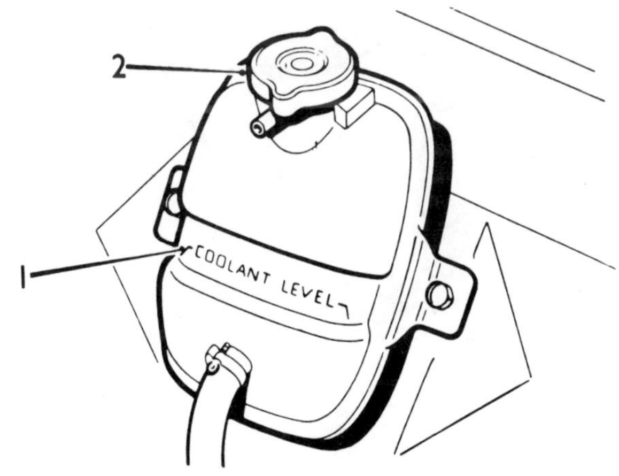

FIG RM2 COOLANT RESERVOIR

1 Level mark 2 Pressure cap

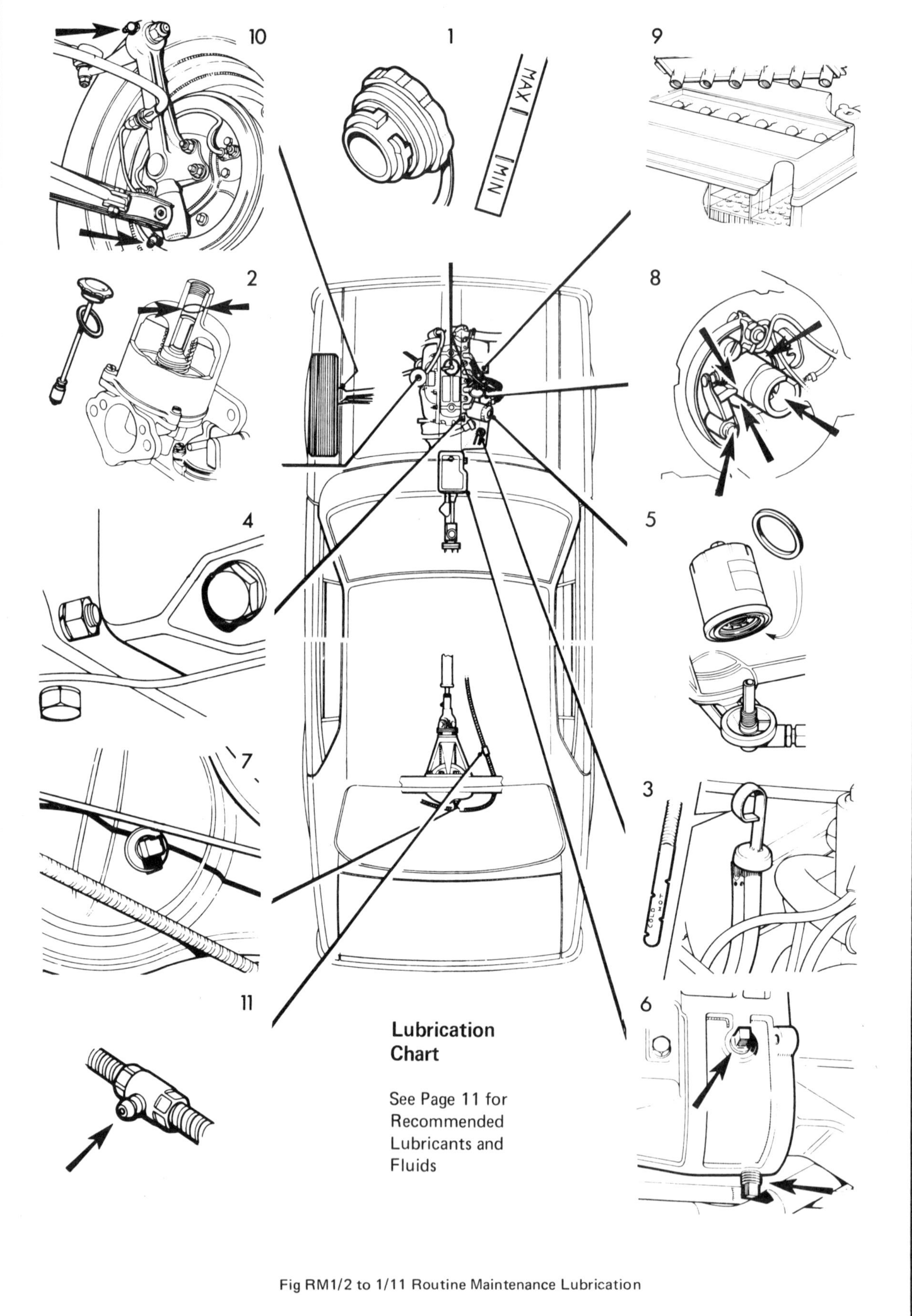

Fig RM1/2 to 1/11 Routine Maintenance Lubrication

11 Wipe the top of the brake and clutch master cylinder and unscrew the caps. Check the level of hydraulic fluid in the reservoirs and top up, if necessary to the marks on the exterior of the reservoir with the recommended fluid. Make sure the cap breather vent is clean and then refit the cap. Take care not to spill any hydraulic fluid on the paintwork as it acts as a solvent. (Fig.RM3).

12 Check the adjustment of the handbrake and footbrake. If travel is excessive refer to Chapter 9 and check the footbrake adjustment and then the handbrake if its travel is still excessive.

13 Refer to Chapter 9 and inspect the brake linings and pads for wear and the front discs and rear drums for scoring.

14 Carefully examine all brake hydraulic pipes and unions for signs of leakage. Check flexible hoses are not in contact with any body or mechanical component when the steering is turned through both locks.

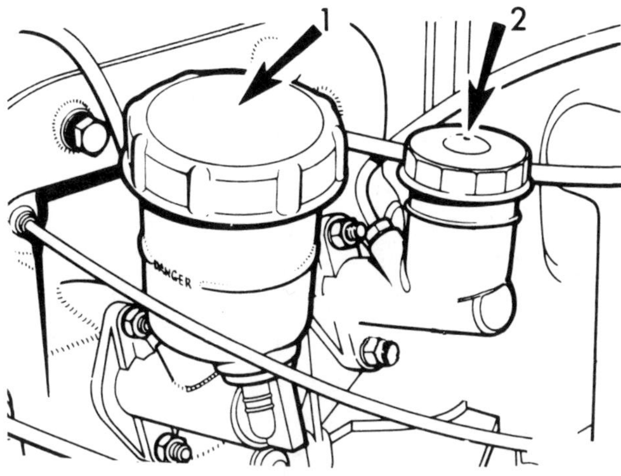

FIG.RM3 BRAKE AND CLUTCH MASTER CYLINDER RESERVOIRS

1 Brake master cylinder reservoir
2 Clutch master cylinder reservoir

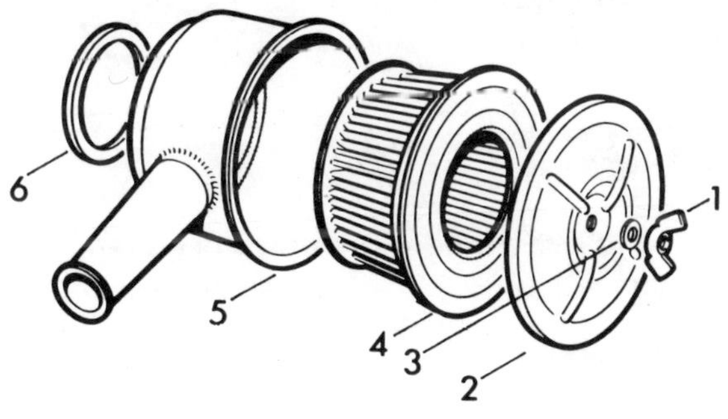

FIG.RM4 AIR CLEANER COMPONENTS

1 Wing nut
2 Top cover
3 Sealing washer
4 Element
5 Body
6 Sealing ring

15 Lubricate the nipple on the handbrake cable using a grease gun filled with Castrol LM Grease (Fig.RM1/11).

16 Lubricate all moving parts of the handbrake system with Castrol GTX.

17 From cars numbered 43892 to 45000 and 48101 and any cars prior to that if fitted with a grease nipple on the propeller shaft front universal joint lubricate the nipple with 3 to 4 strokes of the grease gun filler with Castrol LM Grease.

18 Refer to Chapter 4 and remove the spark plugs. Clean, adjust, if necessary, and replace.

19 Refer to Chapter 4, and clean and adjust the distributor contact breaker points.

20 Spring back the two clips and remove the distributor cap. Lift off the rotor arm. Apply a few drops of thin oil over the screw in the centre of the cam spindle and on the moving contact breaker pivot. Apply a smear of grease to the cam surface. Remove any excess oil or grease with a clean rag. Apply a few drops of oil through the hole in the contact breaker base plate to lubricate the automatic timing control (Fig.RM1/8).

21 Refer to Chapter 4, and check the ignition timing. Adjust if necessary.

22 Wipe the area around the gearbox level/filler plug. Unscrew the plug and check the level of oil which should be up to the bottom of the threads. Top up if necessary using Castrol Hypoy and refit the plug. Wipe away any spilled oil (Fig.RM1/6).

23 Wipe the area around the rear axle level/filler plug. Unscrew the plug and check the level of oil which should be up to the bottom of the threads. Top up if necessary using Castrol Hypoy and refit the plug. Wipe away any spilled oil (Fig.RM1/7).

24 Automatic transmission: With the vehicle standing on level ground, apply the handbrake and move the selector to the 'P' position. Start the engine and allow to run at idle speed for a minimum of 2 minutes. With the engine still running withdraw the dipstick from the filler tube to be found at the rear of the engine compartment. Wipe the dipstick and quickly replace and withdraw the dipstick again. Check the level of oil and top up if necessary with Castrol TQF. Take great care not to overfill (Fig.RM1/3).

25 Generally check the operation of all lights and electrical equipment. Renew any blown bulbs with bulbs of the same wattage rating and rectify any electrical equipment fault. See Chapter 10.

26 Check the battery electrolyte specific gravity as described in Chapter 10. Clean the battery terminals and smear them with vaseline (petroleum jelly) to prevent corrosion.

27 Check the alignment of the headlights and adjust if necessary. See Chapter 10.

28 Check the condition of the windscreen wiper blades and fit new if the blade end has frayed, softened or perished. They should be renewed every 12 months.

Generally check the exhaust system for signs of leaks. Apply a little Holts Silencer Seal or Gum Gum to small blow holes. If badly corroded the system must be renewed. Check all exhaust mountins for tightness.

Carefully examine all clutch and fuel lines and unions for signs of leakage and flexible hoses for signs of perishing. Check the tightness of all unions and renew any faulty lines or hoses.

Lubricate all door, bonnet and boot lid locks, hinges and controls with Castrol Everyman.

Inspect the seat belts for damage to the webbing. Check that all seat and seat belt mountings are tight.

Make sure that the rear view mirror is firm in its mounting and is not crazed or cracked.

Wash the bodywork and chromium fittings and clean out the interior of the car. Wax polish the bodywork including all chromium and bright metal trim. Force wax polish into any joints in the bodywork to prevent rust formation.

If it is wished change over the tyres to equalise wear.

Balance the wheels to eliminate any vibration especially from the steering. This must be done on specialist equipment.

Lubricate the washer around the wiper spindles with several drops of glycerine.

Every 12,000 miles (20,000 km) or 12 months

Complete the service items in the 6000 mile service check as applicable plus:

1 To fit a new air cleaner element, unscrew the wing nut and lift away the cover, body and element which should be discarded. Wipe out the container and fit a new element. Replace the cover. Make sure that the sealing ring between the air cleaner body and carburettor is not damaged or perished. Refit the air cleaner to the carburettor and secure with the fibre washer and nut. During warm weather position the air cleaner intake away from the exhaust manifold or during cold weather move the air intake close to the exhaust manifold (Fig.RM4).

On TC models undo and remove the air manifold securing nuts and bolts, and lift away. Also remove the support securing bolt, spring and plain washers. To gain access to the filter element undo and remove the wing nut and fibre washer. Refitting is the reverse sequence to removal (Fig.RM5).

2 Remove the oil filler cap and filter assembly on the top of the rocker cover and fit a new one.

3 Refer to Chapter 1, and check the valve rocker clearances. Adjust as necessary.

4 Refer to Chapter 11, and adjust the front wheel bearing end float.

5 Inspect the ignition HT leads for cracks or deterioration. Replace as necessary.

6* Examine the dynamo brushes, replace them if worn and clean the commutator. See Chapter 10.

Every 24,000 miles (40,000 km) or 18 months

Complete the service items in the 6000 and 12,000 mile service check as applicable plus:

1* Examine the hub bearings for wear and replace as necessary. See Chapter 11.

2* Check the tightness of the battery earth lead on the body.

3* Renew the condenser in the distributor. See Chapter 4.

4* Remove the starter motor, examine the brushes and replace as necessary. Clean the commutator and starter drive. See Chapter 10.

5* Test the cylinder compressions, and if necessary remove the cylinder head, decarbonise, grind in the valves and fit new valve springs. See Chapter 1 and Chapter 13/14.

6 Completely drain the brake hydraulic fluid from the system. All seals and flexible hoses throughout the braking system should be examined and preferably renewed. The working surfaces of the master cylinder, wheel and caliper should be inspected for signs of wear or scoring and new parts fitted as necessary. Refill the hydraulic system with recommended brake fluid. See Chapter 9.

7 Remove alternator. Clean slip rings. Check bushes. Fit a new drive belt.

Every 36,000 miles (60,000 km) or 3 years

Complete the service items in the 6000 and 12000 mile service as applicable plus:

1 If a brake servo unit is fitted, pull back the filter dust cover and withdraw the end cap. The filter is located in the servo unit housing where the pushrod passes through from the brake pedal. Cut off the old filter element. Cut through the new filter in a diagonal manner to the centre hole and fit it over the pushrod and into the housing. Replace the end cap and dust cover Fig.RM6

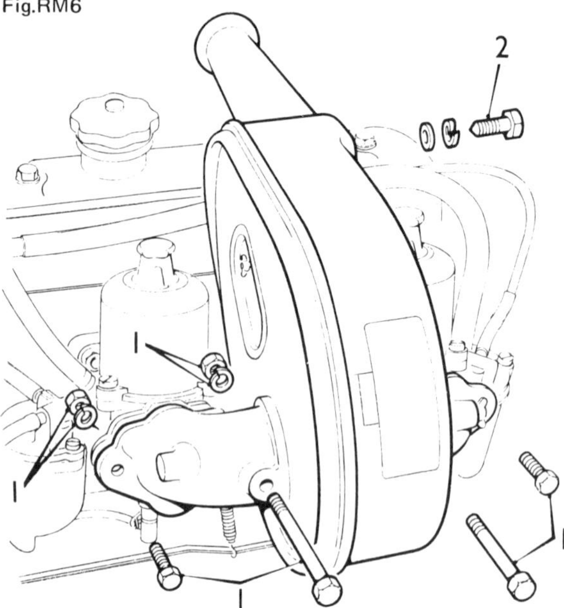

FIG.RM5 AIR CLEANER ASSEMBLY (TC MODELS ONLY)

1 Air manifold attachments
2 Support secuirng bolt, spring and plain washer

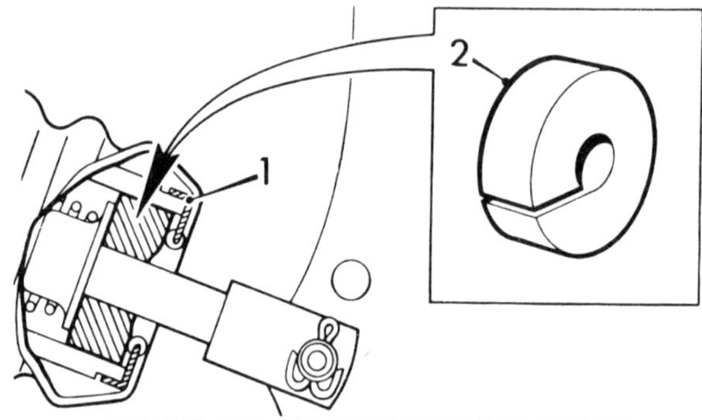

FIG.RM6 BRAKE SERVO UNIT AIR FILTER

1 End cap 2 Filter element

Quick glance capacities and reference

Engine sump capacity (with filter)	6.3/8 pints (3.8 litres)
Manual gearbox capacity	1½ pints
Automatic gearbox (top up from MIN to MAX on dipstick)	1 pint (0.57 litres)
Rear axle capacity	1¼ pints (0.71 litres)
Cooling system (with heater)	9 pints (5.1 litres)
Windscreen washer bottle	3 pints (1.7 litres)
Valve clearances	0.013 in (0.33 mm) COLD
Plug gap	0.025 in (0.64 mm)
Contact breaker gap	0.014 to 0.016 in (0.35 to 0.40 mm)
Firing order	1 3 4 2
These models are NEGATIVE (–) earthed	
Fuel tank capacity	11½ Imp galls (52 litres)

Recommended lubricants and fluids

COMPONENT	TYPE OF LUBRICANT OR FLUID	CORRECT CASTROL PRODUCTS
ENGINE	Multigrade. To API SE specification... ...	Castrol GTX
GEARBOX (MANUAL)	High quality EP90 gear oil to specification MIL-L-2105B and API service GL..	Castrol Hypoy B
AUTOMATIC TRANSMISSION	High quality automatic transmission fluid fluid BLMC type F	Castrol TQF
REAR AXLE	High quality EP90 gear oil	Castrol Hypoy B
GREASE POINTS	Multi-purpose high melting point lithium based grease	Castrol LM Grease
DISTRIBUTOR LUBRICATION	See text for details of application	Vaseline petroleum jelly and Castrol LM Grease
WINDSCREEN WIPER SPINDLES ...	Glycerine	
COOLING SYSTEM	Anti-freeze solution complying with BS 3151 or 3152	Castrol Anti-freeze
BRAKE AND CLUTCH HYDRAULIC SYSTEMS	Hydraulic brake fluid exceeding SAE specification J1703c..	Castrol Girling Brake Fluid

Castrol GRADES

Castrol Engine Oils

Castrol GTX

An ultra high performance SAE 20W/50 motor oil which exceeds the latest API MS requirements and manufacturers' specifications. Castrol GTX with liquid tungsten† generously protects engines at the extreme limits of performance, and combines both good cold starting with oil consumption control. Approved by leading car makers.

Castrol XL 20/50

Contains liquid tungsten†; well suited to the majority of conditions giving good oil consumption control in both new and old cars.

Castrolite (Multi-grade)

This is the lightest multi-grade oil of the Castrol motor oil family containing liquid tungsten†. It is best suited to ensure easy winter starting and for those car models whose manufacturers specify lighter weight oils.

Castrol Grand Prix

An SAE 50 engine oil for use where a heavy, full-bodied lubricant is required.

Castrol Two-Stroke-Four

A premium SAE 30 motor oil possessing good detergency characteristics and corrosion inhibitors, coupled with low ash forming tendency and excellent anti-scuff properties. It is suitable for all two-stroke motor-cycles, and for two-stroke and small four-stroke horticultural machines.

Castrol CR (Multi-grade)

A high quality engine oil of the SAE-20W/30 multi-grade type, suited to mixed fleet operations.

Castrol CRI 10, 20, 30

Primarily for diesel engines, a range of heavily fortified, fully detergent oils, covering the requirements of DEF 2101-D and Supplement 1 specifications.

Castrol CRB 20, 30

Primarily for diesel engines, heavily fortified, fully detergent oils, covering the requirements of MIL-L-2104B.

Castrol R 40

Primarily designed and developed for highly stressed racing engines. Castrol 'R' should not be mixed with any other oil nor with any grade of Castrol.

†Liquid Tungsten is an oil soluble long chain tertiary alkyl primary amine tungstate covered by British Patent No. 882,295.

Castrol Gear Oils

Castrol Hypoy (90 EP)

A light-bodied powerful extreme pressure gear oil for use in hypoid rear axles and in some gearboxes.

Castrol Gear Oils (continued)

Castrol Hypoy Light (80 EP)

A very light-bodied powerful extreme pressure gear oil for use in hypoid rear axles in cold climates and in some gearboxes.

Castrol Hypoy B (90 EP)

A light-bodied powerful extreme pressure gear oil that complies with the requirements of the MIL-L-2105B specification, for use in certain gearboxes and rear axles.

Castrol Hi-Press (140 EP)

A heavy-bodied extreme pressure gear oil for use in spiral bevel rear axles and some gearboxes.

Castrol ST (90)

A light-bodied gear oil with fortifying additives

Castrol D (140)

A heavy full-bodied gear oil with fortifying additives.

Castrol Thio-Hypoy FD (90 EP)

A light-bodied powerful extreme pressure gear oil. This is a special oil for running-in certain hypoid gears.

Automatic Transmission Fluids

Castrol TQF
(Automatic Transmission Fluid)

Approved for use in all Borg-Warner Automatic Transmission Units. Castrol TQF also meets Ford specification M2C 33F.

Castrol TQ Dexron®
(Automatic Transmission Fluid)

Complies with the requirements of Dexron® Automatic Transmission Fluids as laid down by General Motors Corporation.

Castrol Greases

Castrol LM

A multi-purpose high melting point lithium based grease approved for most automotive applications including chassis and wheel bearing lubrication.

Castrol MS3

A high melting point lithium based grease containing molybdenum disulphide.

Castrol BNS

A high melting point grease for use where recommended by certain manufacturers in front wheel bearings when disc brakes are fitted.

Castrol Greases (continued)

Castrol CL

A semi-fluid calcium based grease, which is both waterproof and adhesive, intended for chassis lubrication.

Castrol Medium

A medium consistency calcium based grease.

Castrol Heavy

A heavy consistency calcium based grease.

Castrol PH

A white grease for plunger housings and other moving parts on brake mechanisms. *It must NOT be allowed to come into contact with brake fluid when applied to the moving parts of hydraulic brakes.*

Castrol Graphited Grease

A graphited grease for the lubrication of transmission chains.

Castrol Under-Water Grease

A grease for the under-water gears of outboard motors.

Anti-Freeze

Castrol Anti-Freeze

Contains anti-corrosion additives with ethylene glycol. Recommended for the cooling systems of all petrol and diesel engines.

Speciality Products

Castrol Girling Damper Oil Thin

The oil for Girling piston type hydraulic dampers.

Castrol Shockol

A light viscosity oil for use in some piston type shock absorbers and in some hydraulic systems employing synthetic rubber seals. It must not be used in braking systems.

Castrol Penetrating Oil

A leaf spring lubricant possessing a high degree of penetration and providing protection against rust.

Castrol Solvent Flushing Oil

A light-bodied solvent oil, designed for flushing engines, rear axles, gearboxes and gearcasings.

Castrollo

An upper cylinder lubricant for use in the proportion of 1 fluid ounce to two gallons of fuel.

Everyman Oil

A light-bodied machine oil containing anti-corrosion additives for both general use and cycle lubrication.

Chapter 1 Engine

Contents

Specifications

Manufacturers type number	18V
Number of cylinders	4
Bore	3.160 in (80.26 mm)
Stroke	3.5 in (88.9 mm)
Capacity	109.7 in^3 (1798 cm^3)
Firing order	1 3 4 2
Valve operation	Overhead by pushrod
Compression ratio: High (HC)	9.0 : 1
Low (LC)	8.0 : 1 (single carburettor models only)
Cranking pressure: HC	190 lb/in^2 (13.4 kg/cm^2)
LC	170 lb/in^2 (12 kg/cm^2)
Oversize bores	+ 0.010 in (+ 0.254 mm)
	+ 0.020 in (+ 0.508 mm)
	+ 0.030 in (+ 0.762 mm)
	+ 0.040 in (+ 1.016 mm)
Torque HC	98.5 lb.f.ft at 2000 rpm
LC	95 lb.f.ft at 2000 rpm

Crankshaft

Main journal diameter	2.1265 to 2.127 in (54.01 to 54.02 mm)
Minimum regrind diameter	2.0865 in (52.997 mm)

Crankpin journal diameter	1.8759 to 1.8764 in (47.648 – 47.661 mm)
Minimum regrind diameter	1.836 in (45.632 mm)
Crankshaft end thrust	Taken on thrust washers at centre main bearing
Crankshaft endlfoat	0.002 to 0.003 in (0.051 to 0.076 mm)

Main bearings

Number and type	5, thin wall type
Material	Steel backed copper - lead or reticular tin
Length: front, centre, rear	1.125 in (28.5 mm)
intermediate	0.875 in (22.22 mm)
Diametrical clearance	0.001 to 0.0027 in (0.025 to 0.068 mm
Undersizes:	0.010 in (0.254 mm)
	0.020 in (0.508 mm)
	0.030 in (0.762 mm)
	0.040 in (1.016 mm)

Connecting rods

Type	Horizontal, split big end
Length between centres	6.5 in (165.1 mm)

Big end bearings

Type and material	Steel backed copper lead or VP3
Length	0.775 to 0.785 in (19.68 to 19.44 mm)
Diametrical clearances	0.0015 to 0.0032 in (0.038 to 0.081 mm)
Endfloat on crankpin (nominal)	0.008 to 0.012 in (0.20 to 0.30 mm)
Undersizes:	0.010 (0.254 mm)
	0.020 (0.508 mm)
	0.030 (0.762 mm)
	0.040 (1.016 mm)

Gudgeon pin

Type	Pressed in connecting rod
Fit in piston	Hand push fit at 16°C (60°F)
Outer diameter	0.8124 to 0.8127 in (20.608 to 20.615 mm)

Pistons

Type	Aluminium, solid skirt
Clearance of skirt in cylinder:	
Top	0.0021 to 0.0037 in (0.0535 to 0.0936 mm)
Bottom	0.0018 to 0.0024 in (0.045 to 0.061 mm)
Number of rings	4 (3 compression, 1 oil control)
Width of ring grooves:	
Top and second	0.064 to 0.065 in (1.625 to 1.65 mm)
Oil control	1.578 to 1.588 in (4.01 to 4.033 mm)
Gudgeon pin bore	0.8128 to 0.813 in (20.610 to 20.617 mm)

Piston rings

Compression:	
Type: Top	Plain, sintered alloy
Second and third	Tapered, sintered alloy
Width: Top, second	0.0615 to 0.0625 in (1.562 to 1.587 mm)
Fitted gap: Top	0.012 to 0.017 in (0.304 to 0.431 mm)
Ring to groove clearance:	
Top, second and third	0.0015 to 0.0035 in (0.028 to 0.088 mm)
Oil control: Type	Slotted scraper
Width	0.1552 to 0.1562 in (3.94 to 3.96 mm)
Fitted gap	0.015 to 0.045 in (0.381 to 1.147 mm)
Ring to groove clearance	0.0016 to 0.0036 in (0.04 to 0.01 mm)

Camshaft

Journal diameters: Front	1.78875 to 1.78925 in (45.424 to 45.483 mm)
Centre	1.72875 to 1.72925 in (43.910 to 43.923 mm)
Rear	1.62275 to 1.62325 in (41.218 to 41.230 mm)
Bearing liner inside diameter (finished):	
Front	1.79025 to 1.79075 in (45.472 to 45.485 mm)
Centre	1.73025 to 1.73075 in (43.948 to 43.961 mm)
Rear	1.62425 to 1.62475 in (41.256 to 41.269 mm)
Bearings - type:	White metal lined, steel backed
Diametrical clearance	0.001 to 0.002 in (0.0254 to 0.0508 mm)
End thrust	Taken on locating plate
Endfloat	0.003 to 0.007 in (0.076 to 0.178 mm)
Drive	Chain and sprocket from crankshaft
Timing chain	0.375 in (9.52 mm) pitches x 52 pitches

Tappets

Type	Bucket with radiused base
Outside diameter	0.812 in (20.64 mm)
Length	1.495 to 1.505 in (37.977 to 38.227 mm)

Rocker gear

Rocker shaft: Length	14.032 in (355.6 mm)
Diameter	0.624 to 0.625 in (15.85 to 15.87 mm)
Rocker arm:	
Bore	0.7485 to 0.7495 in (19.01 to 19.26 mm)
Bush internal diameter (finished)	0.6255 to 0.626 in (15.8 to 15.9 mm)

Valves

Seat angle: Inlet	45.5^o
Exhaust	45.5^o
Head diameter:	
Inlet	1.625 to 1.630 in (41.27 to 41.40 mm)
Exhaust	1.343 to 1.348 in (34.11 to 34.23 mm)
Stem diameter:	
Inlet	0.3422 to 0.3427 in (8.692 to 8.704 mm)
Exhaust	0.3417 to 0.3422 in (8.66 to 8.692 mm)
Stem to guide clearance:	
Inlet	0.0015 to 0.0025 in (0.0381 to 0.063 mm)
Exhaust	0.002 to 0.003 in (0.051 to 0.076 mm)
Valve lift: Inlet and Exhaust	0.360 in (9.14 mm)

Valve guides

Length: Inlet	1.875 in (47.63 mm)
Exhaust	2.203 in (55.95 mm)
Outside diameter: Inlet and Exhaust	0.5635 to 0.5640 in (14.30 to 14.32 mm)
Inside diameter: Inlet and Exhaust	0.3442 to 0.3447 in (8.743 to 8.755 mm)
Fitted height above head:	
Inlet	0.75 in (19.05 mm)
Exhaust	0.625 in (15.87 mm)
Interference fit in head:	
Inlet and Exhaust	0.0005 to 0.00175 in (0.012 to 0.044 mm)

Valve springs

Free length	1.92 in (48.77 mm) approx.
Fitted length	1.44 in (36.58 mm)
Load at fitted length	82 lb (37 kg)
Load at top of lift	142 lb (64 kg)
Number of working coils	4.5

Valve timing - timing marks	Dimples in camshaft and crankshaft wheels
Rocker clearance:	
Running (cold)	0.013 in (0.33 mm)
Timing	0.020 in (0.51 mm)
Inlet valve:	
Opens	5° BTDC
Closes	45° ABDC
Exhaust valve:	
Opens	40° BBDC
Closes	10° ATDC

Lubrication

System	Wet sump, pressure fed
Pressure: Running	50 to 70 lb/in^2 (3.5 to 4.9 kg/cm^2)
Idling	15 to 25 lb/in^2 (1.0 to 1.8 kg/cm^2)
Oil pump	Hobourn - later rotor type
Capacity	3.25 gallons (14.8 litres) per minute at 1000 rpm
Oil filter	Full flow: disposable cartridge type
By-pass valve opens	8 to 12 lb/in^2 (0.56 to 0.84 kg/cm^2)
Oil pressure relief valve	70 lb/in^2 (4.9 kg/cm^2)
Relief valve spring:	
Free length	3 in (76 mm)
Fitted length	2.156 in (54.77 mm)
Load at fitted length	15.5 to 16.5 lb (7.0 to 7.4 kg)
Sump capacity	6.375 pints (3.8 litres)

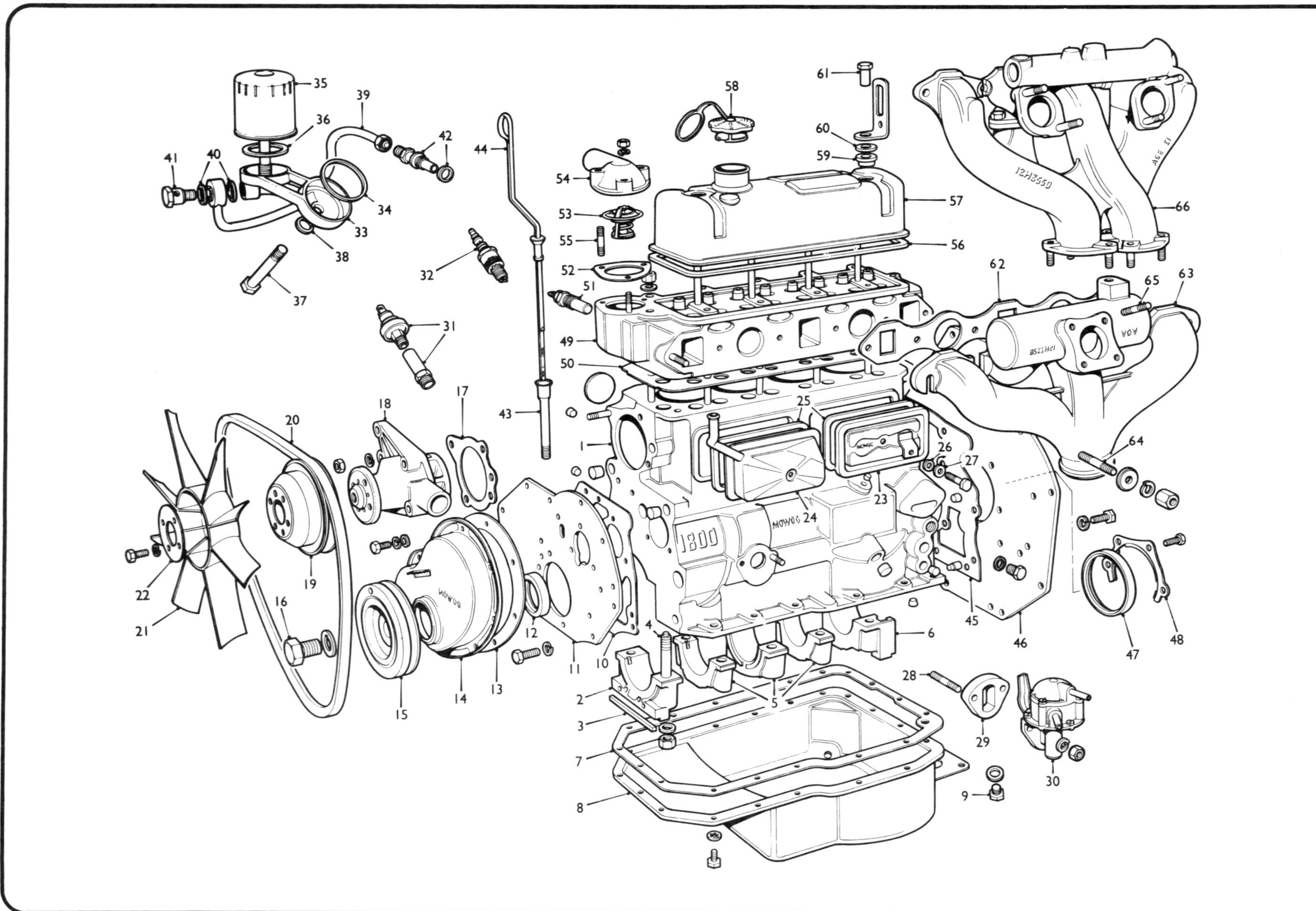
1
2
3
4
5
6
7
8
9
10
11
12
13
14
15
16
17
18
19
20
21
22
23
24
25
26
27
28
29
30
31
32
33
34
35
36
37
38
39
40
41
42
43
44
45
46
47
48
49
50
51
52
53
54
55
56
57
58
59
60
61
62
63
64
65
66
1800
MOWOG
12H3550
AOA

Torque wrench settings

	lb.f.ft.	kg.fm.
Main bearing cap nuts	70	9.7
Big end bearing cap nuts	33	4.6
Gearbox adaptor plate bolts	30	4.15
Crankshaft rear oil seal retainer bolts	25	3.5
Flywheel securing bolts	40	5.5
Oil pump cover bolts	10	1.38
Oil pump securing bolts	14	1.9
Sump securing bolts	6	0.8
Cylinder head nuts	45 to 50	6.2 to 6.9
Rocker shaft bracket nuts	25	3.4
Cylinder side cover	3 to 4	0.41 to 0.55
Timing cover — ¼ in bolts	6	0.83
5/16 in bolts	14	1.94
Water pump retaining bolts	17	2.35
Water outlet elbow	8	1.11
Manifold to cylinder head	15	2.07
Rocker cover fixing bolts	4	0.55
Crankshaft pulley nut	70 to 80	9.68 to 11.06
Camshaft nut	60 to 70	8.30 to 9.68
Distributor clamp bolt	2.5	0.35
Heater outlet adaptor	6 to 8	0.83 to 1.11
Oil release valve dome nut	40 to 45	5.53 to 6.22
Water pump pulley bolts	18	2.49
Thermal transmitter	16	2.21

FIG.1.1. ENGINE EXTERNAL COMPONENTS

1 Cylinder block
2 Front main bearing cap
3 Cap joint
4 Fixing stud
5 Main bearing caps
6 Rear main bearing cap
7 Sump gasket
8 Sump
9 Sump drain plug
10 Front mounting plate gasket
11 Front mounting plate
12 Oil seal
13 Timing cover gasket
14 Timing cover
15 Crankshaft pulley
16 Pulley bolt
17 Water pump gasket
18 Water pump
19 Pulley
20 Fan belt
21 Fan
22 Lock washer
23 Cylinder side cover
24 Oil separator
25 Side cover gaskets
26 Rubber seal
27 Cup washer
28 Petrol pump fixing stud
29 Distance piece
30 Petrol pump
31 Oil pressure switch
32 Sparking plug
33 Oil filter head
34 Oil filter head seal
35 Oil filter cartridge
36 Oil filter cartridge seal
37 Oil filter head bolt
38 Bolt sealing washer
39 Lubrication pipe
40 Sealing washers
41 Banjo bolt
42 Adaptor and seal
43 Dipstick guide tube
44 Dipstick
45 Gasket
46 Engine backplate
47 Oil seal
48 Oil seal retainer
49 Cylinder head
50 Cylinder head gasket
51 Thermal transmitter
52 Thermostat housing gasket
53 Thermostat
54 Water oulet
55 Fixing stud
56 Rocker cover gasket
57 Rocker cover
58 Oil filler cap
59 Rubber seal
60 Cup washer
61 Rocker cover fixing
62 Manifold gasket
63 Manifold – SC
64 Manifold fixing stud
65 Carburettor fixing stud
66 Manifold – TC

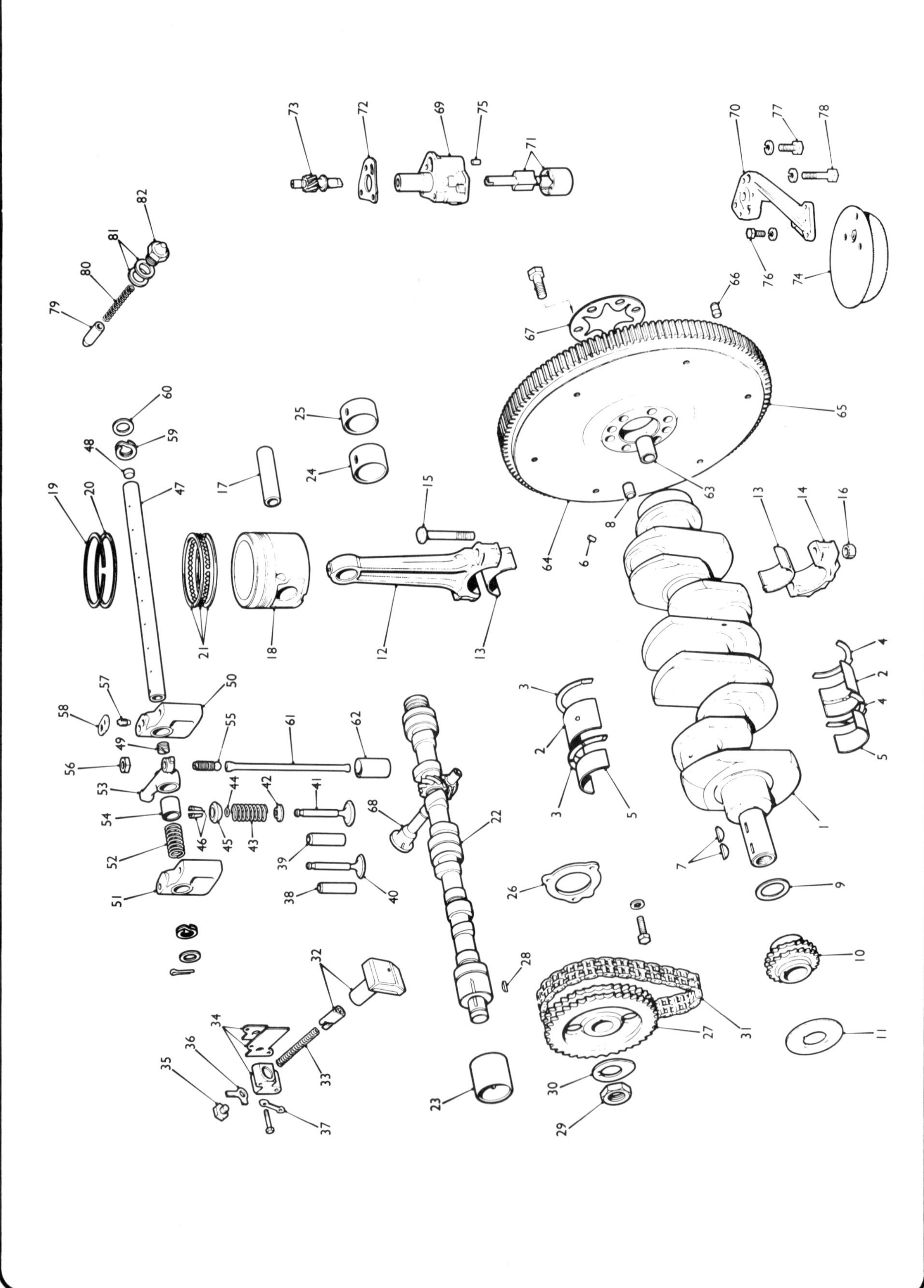

FIG.1.2. ENGINE INTERNAL COMPONENTS

1 Crankshaft
2 Main bearing
3 Thrust washer - upper
4 Thrust washer - lower
5 Main bearing
6 Oil restrictor
7 Key for gear
8 Crankshaft dowel
9 Gear packing washer
10 Timing gear
11 Oil thrower
12 Connecting rod
13 Big end bearing
14 Big end bearing cap
15 Big end bearing cap bolt
16 Big end nuts
17 Gudgeon pin
18 Piston
19 Compression ring - top
20 Compression ring - 2nd
21 Scraper ring
22 Camshaft
23 Camshaft bearing - front
24 Camshaft bearing - centre
25 Camshaft bearing - rear
26 Camshaft locking plate
27 Timing gear
28 Timing gear key
29 Camshaft nut
30 Lock washer
31 Timing chain
32 Slipper head & cylinder
33 Spring
34 Tensioner body,plate & gasket
35 Plug for body
36 Lock washer for plug
37 Lock washer
38 Exhaust valve guide
39 Inlet valve guide
40 Exhaust valve
41 Inlet valve
42 Valve spring collar
43 Valve spring
44 Packing ring
45 Spring cup
46 Valve cotter
47 Valve rocker shaft
48 Plain plug
49 Screwed plug
50 Bracket with tapped hole
51 Plain bracket
52 Spring
53 Valve rocker
54 Bush
55 Adjusting screw
56 Adjusting screw locknut
57 Locking screw
58 Locking plate
59 Spring washer
60 Wahser for rocker shaft
61 Pushrod
62 Tappet
63 Crankshaft spigot bush
64 Flywheel
65 Starter ring
66 Dowel for clutch
67 Lock washer
68 Distributor drive shaft
69 Oil pump body
70 Oil pump cover
71 Oil pump rotors
72 Oil pump gasket
73 Oil pump drive spindle
74 Oil pump strainer
75 Pump cover to body dowel
76 Oil pump cover to strainer screw
77 Oil pump cover screw - short
78 Oil pump cover screw - long
79 Oil pressure relief valve
80 Spring for relief valve
81 Oil pressure relief valve washer
82 Oil pressure cap nut

1 General description

The 1789 cc engine is a four cylinder overhead valve type fitted with either single or twin SU carburettors.

Two valves per cylinder are mounted vertically in the cast iron cylinder head and run in pressed in valve guides. They are operated by rocker arms and pushrods from the camshaft which is located at the base of the cylinder bores in the left hand side of the engine.

The cylinder head has all five inlet and exhaust ports on the left hand side. Cylinders 1 and 2 have a siamised inlet port as have cylinders 3 and 4. Cylinders 1 and 4 have individual exhaust ports and cylinders 2 and 3 share a siamised exhaust port.

The cylinder block and upper half of the crankcase are cast together and a pressed steel oil sump is bolted to the underside. Attached to the rear of the engine backplate is the clutch bell-housing and gearbox.

The dished crown pistons are made from anodised aluminium and they have a solid skirt. Two or three compression and one oil control ring are fitted to each piston depending on type of pistons fitted.

At the front of the engine is a double row chain driving the camshaft via the camshaft and crankshaft sprockets. The chain is tensioned by a spring loaded slipper type tensioner which automatically adjusts for chain stretch. The camshaft is supported by three steel backed white metal bearings. If these are replaced it is necessary to ream the bearings in position.

The overhead valves are operated by means of rocker arms mounted on the rocker shaft running along the top of the cylinder head. The rocker arms are activated by pushrods and tappets which in turn rise and fall in accordance with the lobes on the camshaft. The valves are held closed by small springs.

The static and dynamically balanced forged steel crankshaft is supported by five renewable main bearings. Crankshaft end float is controlled by tour semi-circular thrust washers two of which are located on either side of the centre bearing.

The centrifugal water pump and radiator cooling fan are driven, together with the alternator, from the crankshaft pulley wheel by a rubber/fabric 'fan' belt. The distributor is mounted towards the rear of the right hand side of the cylinder block and advances and retards the ignition timing by mechanical and vacuum means. The distributor is driven at half crankshaft by a short shaft and skew gear from a skew gear on the camshaft. The oil pump is mounted inside the crankcase and driven from the camshaft by a short drive spindle.

Attached to the rear of the crankshaft by six bolts and two dowels is the flywheel which is bolted to the diaphragm spring clutch. Mounted on the circumference of the flywheel is the starter ring gear into which the starter motor drive engages when starting the engine.

2 Major operations with engine in place

The following major operations can be carried out to the engine with it in place in the car:

1 Removal and replacement of the cylinder head assembly.
2 Removal and replacement of the sump.
3 Removal and replacement of the big end bearings.
4 Removal and replacement of the pistons and connecting rods.
5 Removal and replacement of the timing chain and gears.
6 Removal and replacement of the camshaft.

3 Major operations with engine removed

The following major operations must be carried out with the engine out of the car and on a bench or floor.

1 Removal and replacement of the main bearings.
2 Removal and replacement of the crankshaft.
3 Removal and replacement of the oil pump.
4 Removal and replacement of the flywheel.

4 Methods of engine removal

The engine can be removed either attached to the gearbox or disconnected from it, by itself. Both methods are described.

It is easier if a hydraulic type trolley jack is used in conjunction with two pairs of axle stands so that the car can be raised sufficiently to allow easy access underneath the car. Overhead lifting tackle will be necessary in both cases.

Because of the weight consideration and the very steep angle to which the engine must be tilted, the do-it-yourself motorist without the use of a pit or ramp should remove the gearbox first. A third method can be used and this is to detach the engine and gearbox from its mountings and lower the unit onto the floor. The front of the car can then be lifted up and the power unit drawn forwards. Using this method (possibly removing the cylinder head as well) can eliminate the need for an overhead hoist and may be of use in a confined space.

Note: Cars fitted with automatic transmission necessitating engine and transmission removal should have the transmission removed first as described in Chapter 6, Section 9, and then followed by the engine. This is because of the size and weight of the transmission.

FIG.1.3. SUMMARY OF ITEMS TO BE DETACHED – ENGINE REMOVAL WITH GEARBOX

1 Carburettor attachments
2 Heater hoses
3 Engine mounting nuts, bolts and spring washers
4 Gear change lever
5 Gearbox mounting
6 Speedometer cable
7 Front exhaust pipe mounting
8 Exhaust downpipe to manifold clamp
9 Starter motor cables
10 Electrical leads
11 Air cleaner
12 Propeller shaft flange
13 Nut and bolt
14 Mating marks
15 Fuel pipe connection to pump
16 Clutch pipe bracket
17 Clutch pipe to master cylinder union
18 Heater hose to side of cylinder head
19 Engine lifting bracket

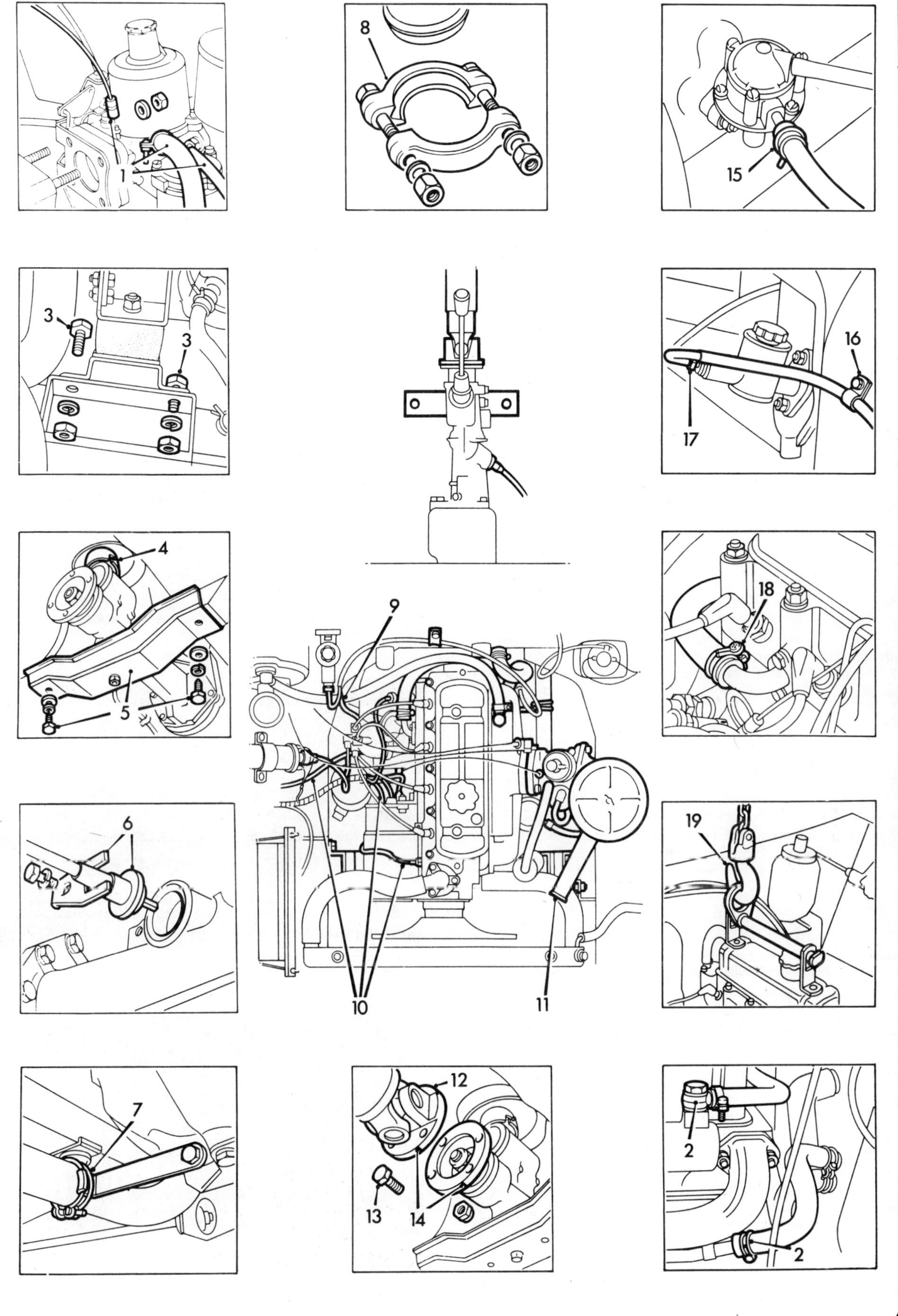
1
8
15
3
3
16
17
4
5
9
18
6
19
10
11
7
12
13
14
2
2

5 Engine removal with gearbox

1 Practical experience has proved that the complete unit can be removed easily in about three hours or less by the following sequence of operations.
2 With the help of an assistant take the weight of the bonnet and undo and remove the four bolts, spring and plain washers (photo). Carefully lift the bonnet up, releasing the prop, and then over the front of the car. Store in a safe place where it will not be scratched (photo).
3 Remove the expansion tank cap and radiator filler plug. Slacken the bottom hose clip and remove the hose from the radiator. Place a container under the hose to catch the coolant especially if anti-freeze is in use. Also remove the cylinder block drain plug (photos).
4 Undo and remove the cylinder block drain plug located towards the rear right hand side of the cylinder block.
5 Disconnect the negative and then the positive battery terminals and tuck the leads to the rear of the battery.
6 Slacken the radiator top hose clip at the thermostat elbow and pull off the hose.
7 Slacken the radiator heater hose at the union to the metal pipe located beneath the exhaust manifold. Pull off the hose (photo). Also remove the hose from the pipe located on the right hand side of the cylinder head.
8 Unwind the expansion tank hose clip at the radiator end and pull off the hose (photo).
9 Slacken the second heater hose clip at the bottom hose and pull off this hose (photo).
10 It will be found easier to work in the engine compartment if the bonnet support is removed. Using a screwdriver ease the clip from the support and unhook the support from its bracket on the front panel (photo).
11 Undo and remove the two bolts, plain and spring washers securing the top radiator supports to the front panel (photo).
12 Undo and remove the two bolts, plain and spring washers that secure the top radiator support brackets to the side panels.
13 Lift away the two top support brackets, carefully detaching the rubber insert from the mounting peg on the radiator.
14 The radiator may now be lifted upwards and away from the car (photo).
15 This photo shows the rubber insert in one of the two lower radiator mounting brackets.
16 Now make sure the total working floor area is clean and dry.
17 Slacken the accelerator cable to linkage clamp bolt and withdraw the accelerator inner cable.
18 Using two open ended spanners slacken the choke control cable nut and withdraw the inner cable.
19 Carefully release the two cables from the outer cable support bracket and withdraw the cables.
20 Detach the accelerator linkage control spring from its lower attachment.
21 Slacken the clip that secures the breather hose to the carburettor and carefully detach the hose.
22 Carefully pull the fuel hose from the union on the carburettor float chamber. Plug the end with a pencil to stop dirt ingress.
23 Slacken the clip that secures the fuel tank feed pipe to the fuel pump. Pull off the hose and plug the end with a pencil (photo).
24 Single carburettor: Undo and remove the wing nut and fibre washer securing the air cleaner body to the carburettor (photo). Lift away the air cleaner lid, element and body.
25 TC: Undo and remove the four nuts and bolts that secure the air cleaner to the carburettors. Lift away the air cleaner assembly.
26 Undo and remove the nuts and spring washers that secure the carburettor(s) to the inlet manifold studs. Ease the carburettor(s) away from the inlet manifold (photos).
27 Lift the metal shield away from the inlet manifold.
28 Undo and remove the four bolts and washers that secure the fan to the water pump hub (photo).

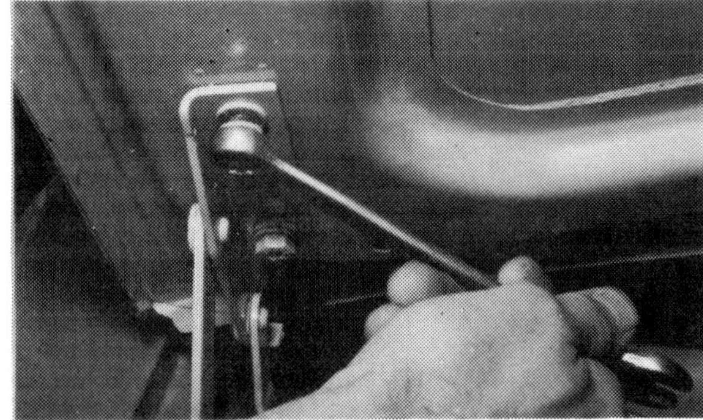

5.2A Bonnet hinge securing bolts

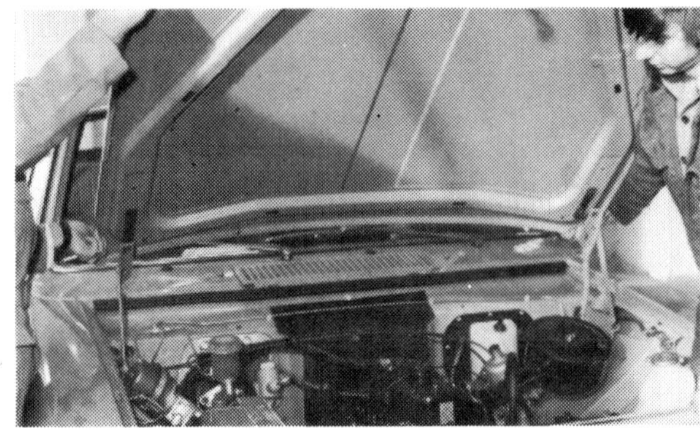

5.2B Lifting away bonnet

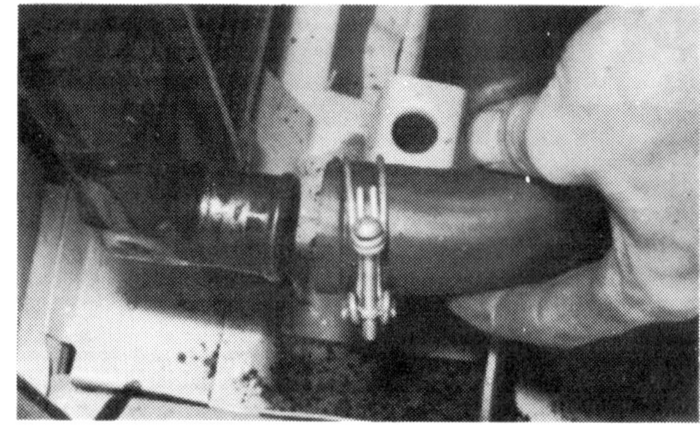

5.3A Bottom hose removal from radiator

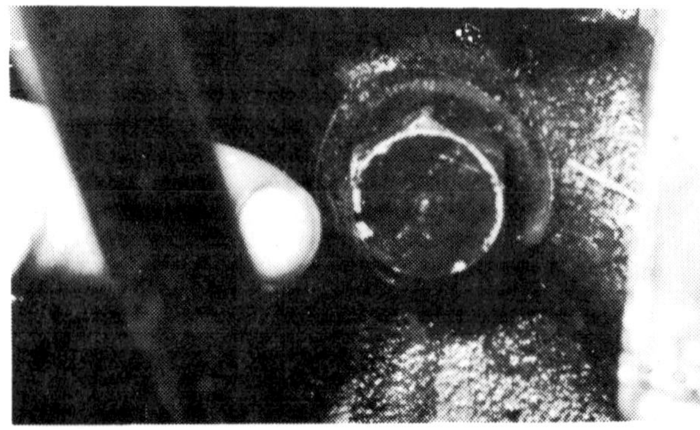

5.3B Cylinder block drain plug

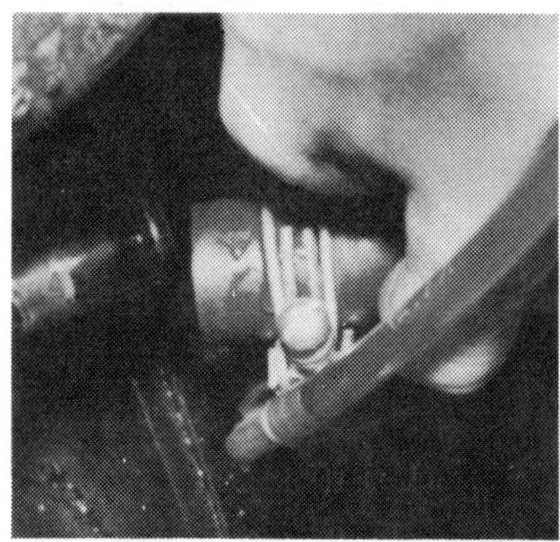
5.7 Heater hose detachment from metal transfer pipe

5.8 Expansion tank hose removal

5.9 Bottom hose connection to metal transfer pipe

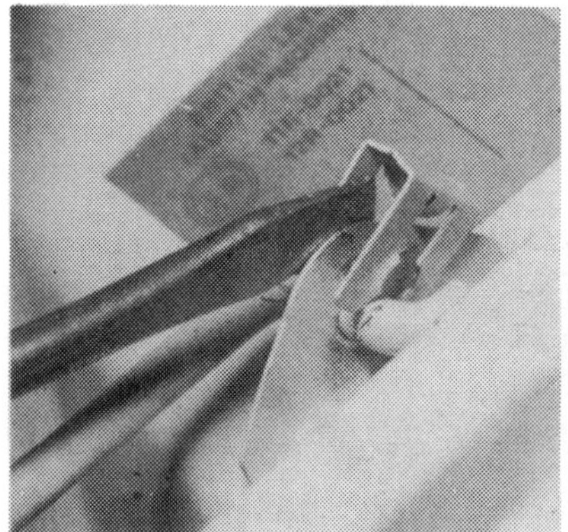
5.10 Bonnet support clip removal

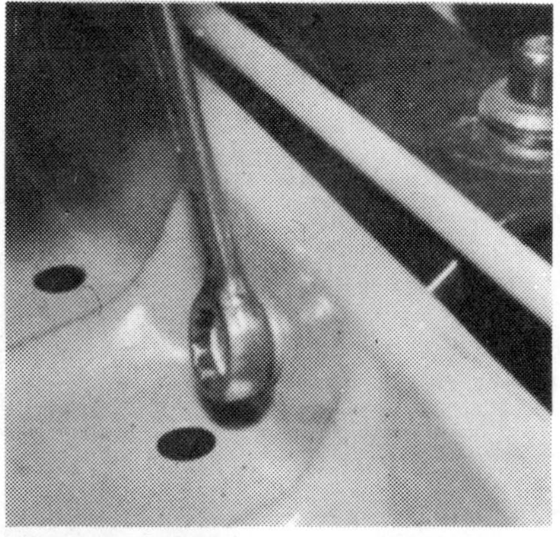
5.11 Radiator top support detachment from front panel

5.14 Lifting away radiator

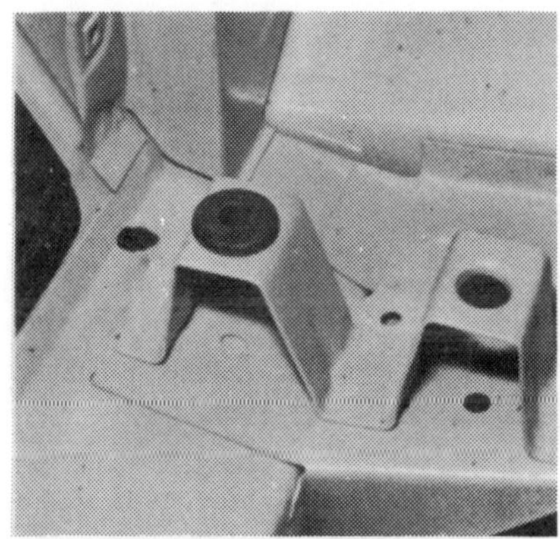
5.15 Radiator lower mounting rubber insert

5.23 Releasing fuel line from pump

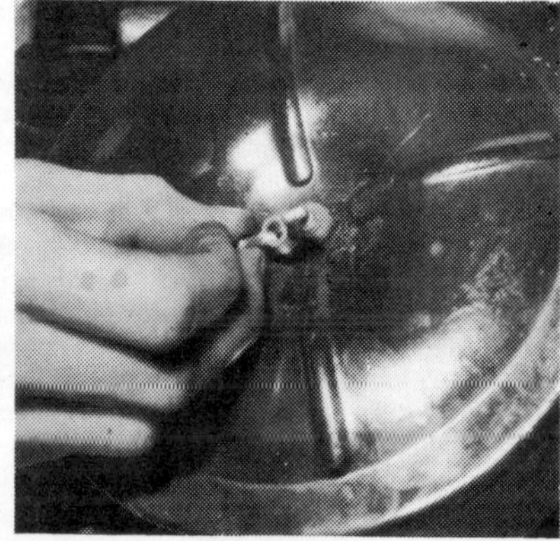
5.24 Air cleaner retaining wing nut removal

5.26A Carburettor securing nuts and spring washers removal

5.26B Lifting away carburettor assembly

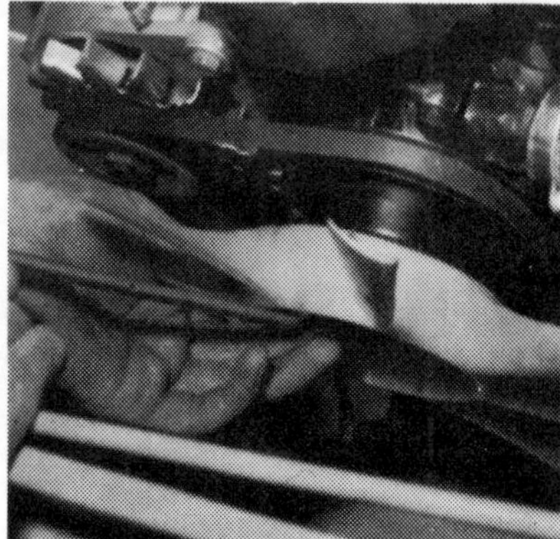
5.28 Removal of fan assembly retaining bolts and washers

29 Lift the metal plate and fan from the front of the water pump (photo).
30 Undo and remove the two exhaust manifold to downpipe clamp nuts and lift away the two halves of the clamp.
31 Slacken the hose clip to the inlet manifold union and ease the vacuum hose.
32 Undo and remove the nuts and washers that secure the manifold assembly to the side of the cylinder head. Lift away the manifold assembly and recover the gasket.
33 Slacken the clip that attaches the downpipe to the gearbox mounted bracket. Unhook the clip (photo).
34 Undo and remove the nut, bolt and spring washer that secures the exhaust mounting bracket to the gearbox (photo). Lift away the bracket. Tie the exhaust downpipe to the left hand wing inner valance.
35 Working under the car, undo and remove the one bolt and plain washer that secures the braided earth cable to the body (photo).
36 Spring back the alternator terminal block securing clip and detach the terminal block (photo).
37 Mark the spark plug HT cable to ensure refitting in the correct order and disconnect from the spark plugs.
38 Release the HT cable from the centre of the ignition coil, spring back the two clips securing the distributor cap to the distributor body and lift away the distributor cap and HT leads (photo).
39 Disconnect the LT wiring to the distributor and ignition coil and the wiring to the oil pressure switch and thermal transmitter (photo).
40 Make a note of the cable connections to the rear of the starter motor solenoid and detach the cables (photo).
41 Working under the car undo and remove the one bolt and spring washer securing the speedometer cable retainer to the gearbox extension housing (photo).
42 Lift away the retainer and withdraw the speedometer cable. Tuck the end of the cable back out of the way so it is not damaged during subsequent operations.
43 Wipe the area around the top of the clutch master cylinder reservoir. Unscrew the cap and place a thin piece of polythene over the top of the reservoir. Replace the cap. This will stop hydraulic fluid syphoning out during subsequent operations.
44 Wipe the area around the clutch slave cylinder hydraulic pipe union and unscrew the union. Wrap a rag around the end of the pipe and tuck back out of the way of the engine (photo).
45 Mark the gearbox and propeller shaft mating flanges so that they may be refitted in their original positions. Undo and remove the four self locking nuts and bolts (photo).
46 Place a piece of wood in the manner shown in this photograph so that the propeller shaft is supported (photo).
47 Using a garage hydraulic jack support the weight of the gearbox and then undo and remove the two bolts, spring and plain washers securing the gearbox mounting bracket to the underside of the body (photo).
48 Undo and remove the one bolt and spring washer securing the mounting bracket to the underside of the gearbox. Lift away the mounting.
49 Unscrew and remove the self tapping screws securing each carpet finisher to the door sill. Lift away the finisher and carpeting so exposing the gear change lever rubber moulding retaining plate (photos).
50 Undo and remove the six self tapping screws securing the gear change lever rubber moulding retaining plate to the floor panel (photo).
51 Slide the plate and moulding and foam sleeve up the gear change lever (photo). Note that sealer is used under the rubber moulding flange.
52 Turn the gear change lever retaining cup in an anti-clockwise direction so releasing the bayonet fixing (photo).
53 Ease the gear change lever up, at the same time being prepared to depress the plunger and spring in the fulcrum ball (photo).
54 Recover the plunger and spring from the fulcrum ball.
55 Place a rope sling or chain around the engine and support its

5.29 Lifting away metal plate and fan

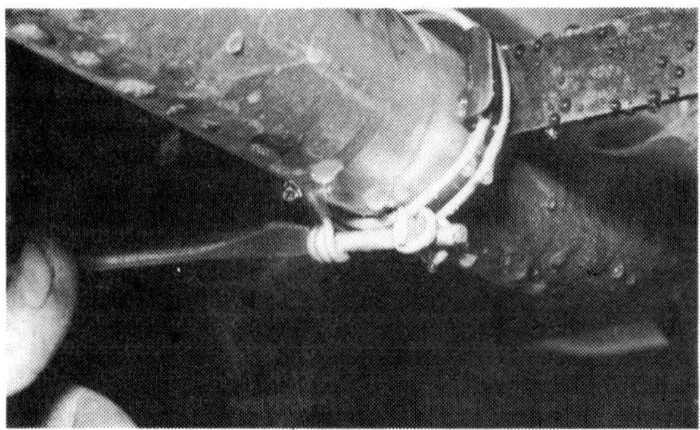
5.33 Slackening exhaust downpipe to bracket clip

5.34 Detaching exhaust downpipe bracket from clutch bellhousing

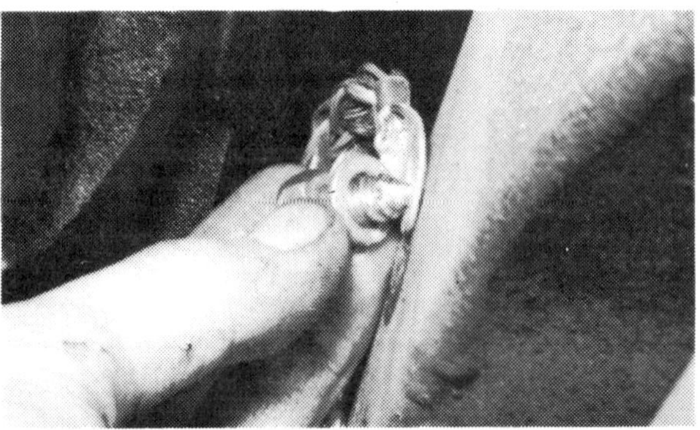
5.35 Removal of bolt securing earth cable to body

5.36 Detaching terminal block from rear of alternator

5.38 Removing distributor cap and HT leads

5.39A Detaching cable from oil pressure switch

5.39B Thermal transmitter located in side of cylinder head

5.40 Electric cable connections at rear of starter motor solenoid

5.41 Speedometer cable retainer removal

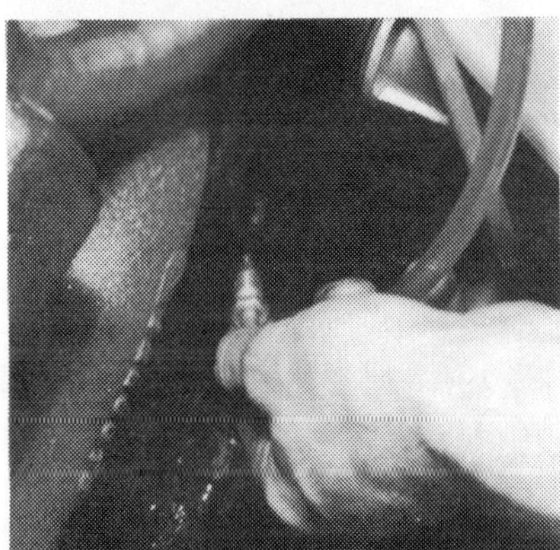
5.44 Clutch hydraulic pipe detached fork slave cylinder

5.45 Propeller shaft detachment from drive flange

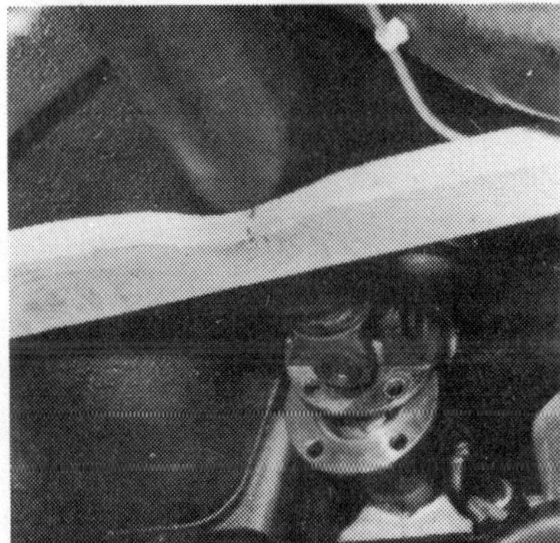
5.46 Propeller shaft supported by length of wood

5.47 Gearbox mounting bracket detachment from body

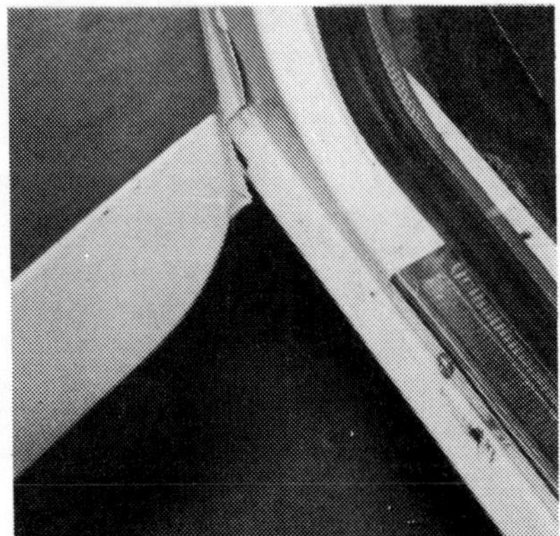
5.49A Front carpet finisher

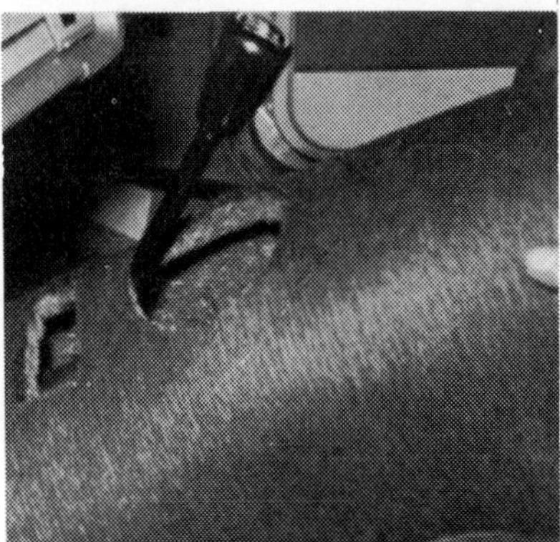
5.49B Front carpet removal

5.50 Removal of rubber moulding self tapping screws

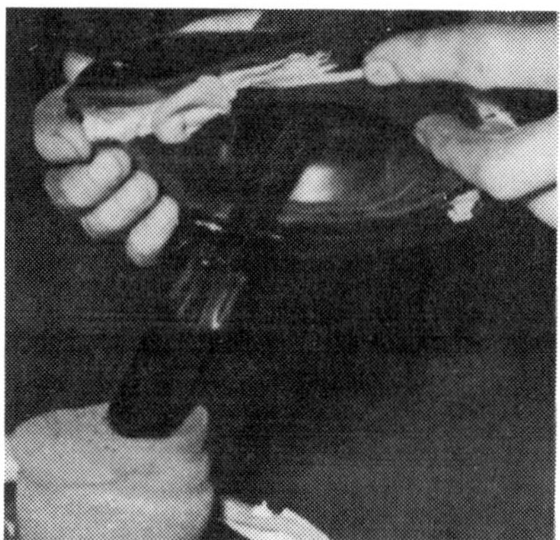
5.51 Sliding moulding and sleeve up gear change lever

5.52 Releasing gear change lever retaining cup

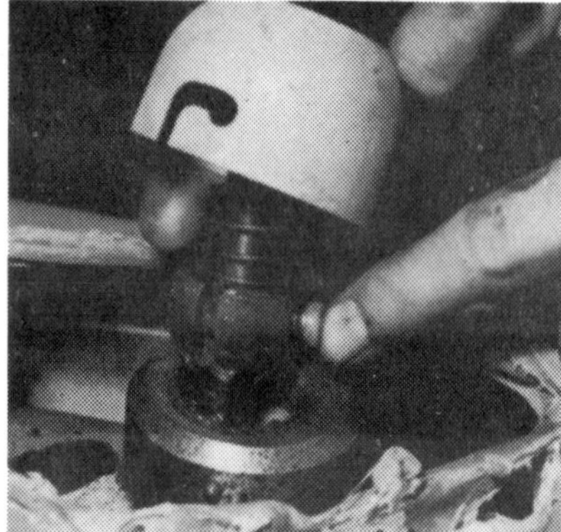
5.53 Plunger and spring located in gear change lever fulcrum ball

5.56 Engine mounting release

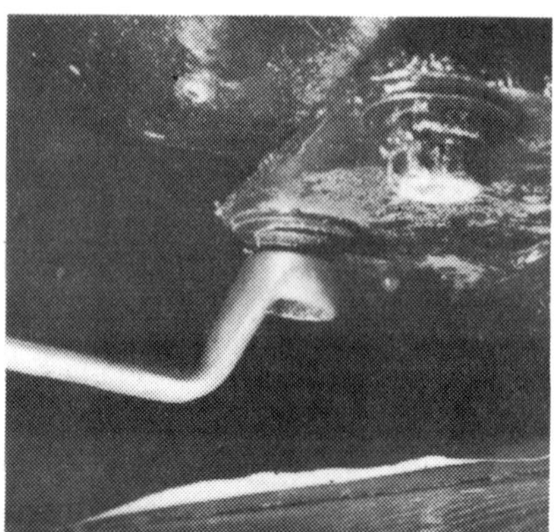
5.57 Sump extension bracket detachment from clutch bellhousing

weight using an overhead hoist. Make sure that there is no possibility of these slipping when the unit is being removed as it has to be lifted out at rather a steep angle.

56 Undo and remove the two nuts, bolts and spring washers securing the engine mounting to the main body member brackets (photo).

57 If the gearbox is to be separated from the engine when away from the vehicle undo and remove the two bolts and spring washers securing the sump extension bracket to the underside of the clutch bellhousing (photo).

58 Check that no controls, cables or pipes have been left connected to the engine or gearbox and that they are safely tucked to one side where they will not be caught as the unit is being removed.

59 Lower the jack supporting the weight of the gearbox and commence raising the engine. Continue lifting the engine until the rear of the sump is clear of the front cross member. The rear of the gearbox can now be lifted by hand over this cross member as either the car is pushed rearwards or the hoist is drawn away from the engine compartment.

60 Lower the unit to the ground. To complete the job, clear out any loose nuts and bolts and tools from the engine compartment and place them where they will not be lost.

6 Engine removal less gearbox

1 If it is necessary to remove only the engine leaving the gearbox in position, the following sequence will enable the engine to be removed.

2 Follow the instructions given in Section 5, paragraphs 2 - 40 inclusive.

3 Using a garage hydraulic jack support the weight of the gearbox.

4 Undo and remove the two nuts, bolts and spring washers that secure the starter motor to the engine backplate and gearbox bell housing and lift away the starter motor.

5 Place a rope sling or chains around the engine and support its weight using an overhead hoist.

6 Undo and remove the remaining nuts, bolts and spring washers that secure the engine back plate to the gearbox bell housing.

7 Undo and remove the two nuts, bolts and spring washers securing the engine mounting to the main body member brackets.

8 Check that no controls, cables or pipes have been left connected to the engine and that they are safely tucked to one side where they will not be caught as the unit is being removed.

9 Raise the engine slightly to enable the engine mounting to clear their mounting brackets and move it forwards until the clutch is clear of the first motion shaft.

10 Continue lifting the unit, taking care not to damage the front valance and grille. Draw it forwards or push the car rearwards and lower to the ground.

11 To complete the job clear out any loose nuts, and bolts and tools from the engine compartment and place them where they will not be lost.

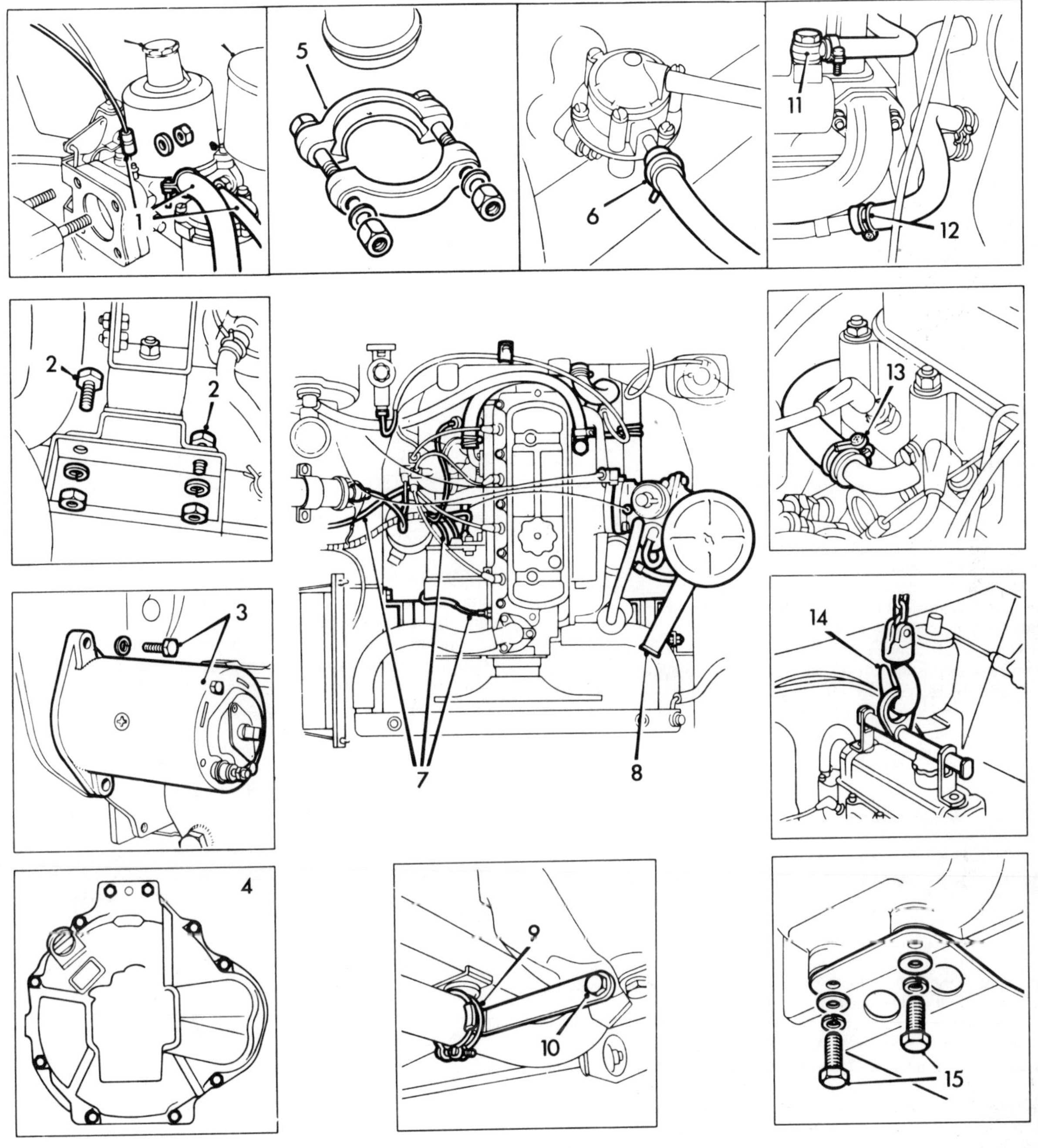

FIG.1.4. SUMMARY OF ITEMS TO BE DETACHED – ENGINE REMOVAL LESS GEARBOX

1 Carburettor attachments
2 Engine mounting nuts, bolts and spring washers
3 Starter motor
4 Clutch bellhousing to engine backplate attachments
5 Exhaust downpipe to manifold clamp
6 Fuel pipe connection –pump
7 Electrical leads
8 Air cleaner
9 Front exhaust pipe mounting
10 Mounting bracket attachment
11 Servo unit pipe at inlet manifold
12 Heater hose
13 Heater hose
14 Engine lift bracket
15 Sump bracket to clutch bellhousing bolts, spring and plain washers

7 Engine removal with gearbox (from underside)

1 Follow the instructions given in Section 5, paragraphs 2 – 58 inclusive.
2 Remove the nuts, bolts and spring washers that secure the body mounted engine brackets and completely remove the brackets (photo).
3 Place some wood on the floor of at least the complete length of the engine and gearbox.
4 Carefully lower the complete power unit through the engine compartment until it is resting on the previously placed wood (photo).
5 Release the rope or chains from the engine and transfer these to the two brackets on the inner faces at the front of the longitudinal members (photo).
6 Lift up the front of the body to a sufficient height to clear the front valance and support the body on firmly based axle stands (photo).
7 The complete power unit may now be slid forwards and from under the car (photo).
8 To complete the job clear out any loose nuts and bolts and tools from the engine compartment and place them where they will not be lost.

8 Separating the engine from the gearbox

1 With the engine and gearbox on the floor undo and remove the one remaining nut, bolt and spring washer securing the starter motor to the engine backplate and gearbox bell housing. Lift away the starter motor (photo).
2 Undo and remove the two bolts and spring washers securing the sump extension bracket to the underside of the clutch bell housing if they are still in place.
3 Undo and remove the remaining nuts, bolts and spring washers securing the clutch bell housing to the engine backplate.
4 Carefully draw the gearbox rearwards, detaching it from the dowels located at the top rear of the engine cylinder block. It is important that the weight of the gearbox is not allowed to hang on the first motion shaft as it can easily be bent (photo).

9 Dismantling the engine - general

1 It is best to mount the engine on a dismantling stand, but if one is not available, stand the engine on a strong bench, to be at a comfortable working height. It can be dismantled on the floor but it is not easy.
2 During the dismantling process greatest care should be taken to keep the exposed parts free from dirt. As an aid to achieving this, thoroughly clean down the outside of the engine, removing all traces of oil and congealed dirt.
3 Use paraffin or Gunk. The latter compound will make the job much easier for, after the solvent has been applied and allowed to stand for a time, a vigorous jet of water will wash off the solvent with all the grease and dirt. If the dirt is thick and deeply embedded, work the solvent into it with a wire brush.
4 Finally wipe down the exterior of the engine with a rag and only then, when it is quite clean, should the dismantling process begin. As the engine is stripped, clean each part in a bath of paraffin or Gunk.
5 Never immerse parts with oilways (for example the crankshaft), in paraffin but to clean wipe down carefully with a petrol dampened cloth. Oilways can be cleaned out with nylon pipe cleaners. If an air line is available, all parts can be blown dry and the oilways blown through as an added precaution.
6 Re-use of old engine gaskets is false economy and will lead to oil and water leaks, if nothing worse. Always use new gaskets throughout.
7 Do not throw the old gasket away, for it sometimes happens that an immediate replacement cannot be found and the old gasket is then very useful as a template. Hang up the old gaskets as they are removed.
8 To strip the engine it is best to work from the top down. The underside of the crankcase when supported on wood blocks acts as a firm base. When the stage is reached, where the crankshaft and connecting rods have to be removed, the engine can be turned on its side and all other work carried out with it in this position.
9 Whenever possible, replace nuts, bolts and washers finger tight from wherever they were removed. This helps avoid loss and muddle later. If they cannot be replaced lay them out in such a fashion that it is clear from whence they came.

10 Removing the ancillary engine components

Before basic engine dismantling begins it is necessary to strip it of ancillary components as follows:

Alternator
Distributor
Thermostat
Oil filter cartridge
Inlet and exhaust manifold and carburettor

It is possible to strip all these items with the engine in the car if it is merely the individual items that require attention. Presuming the engine is to be out of the car and on the bench and that the item mentioned is still on the engine, follow the procedure described below:
1 Slacken off the alternator retaining bolts and nuts and remove the unit together with its adjustment link.
2 To remove the distributor first disconnect the vacuum advance/retard pipe from the side of the distributor. Undo and remove the two screws with spring and plain washers that secure the distributor clamp flange to the cylinder block. Lift away the distributor and clamp flange.
3 Remove the thermostat cover by undoing and removing the three nuts and spring washers which hold it in position. Lift away the cover and gasket, followed by the thermostat itself.
4 Remove the oil filter cartridge by simply unscrewing it from the oil filter head on the side of the cylinder block.
5 Undo and remove the six nuts and washers that secure the inlet and exhaust manifold assembly to the side of the cylinder head. If the carburettor is still mounted on the inlet manifold release it from the petrol feed pipe from the pump. Lift off the manifold assembly and recover the gasket.
6 Remove the mechanical fuel pump by unscrewing the two retaining nuts and spring washers which hold it to the block. Release it from the petrol feed pipe to the carburettor float chamber and lift away the fuel pump.

The engine is now stripped of ancillary components and is ready for major dismantling to begin.

FIG 1.5 ENGINE FRONT MOUNTING (LEFT), GEARBOX BRACKET (RIGHT)

⇨

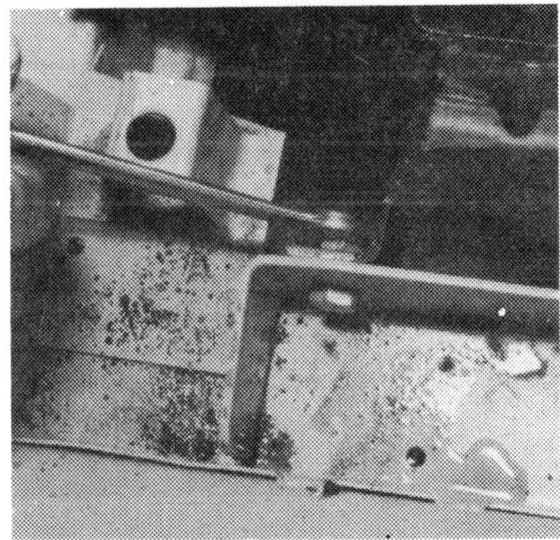
7.2 Engine mountings removed

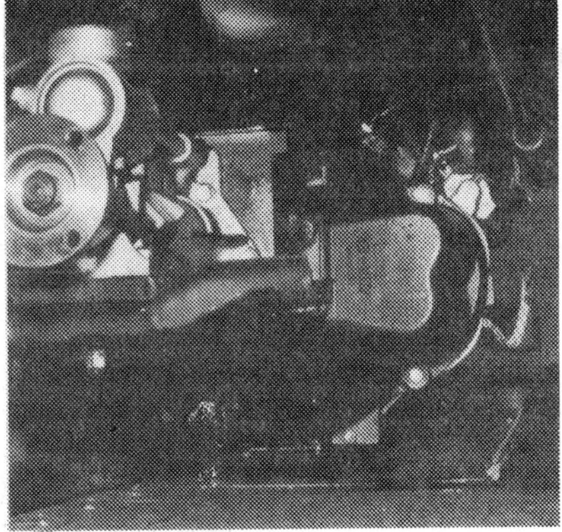
7.4A Lowering engine onto wood

7.4B Engine and gearbox resting on wood

7.5 Lifting front of body

7.6 Body at sufficient height to pull power unit forwards

7.7 Pulling power unit away from body

8.1 Removal of starter motor securing bolts

8.4A Drawing gearbox rearwards from engine

8.4B Dowel located at top of clutch bellhousing

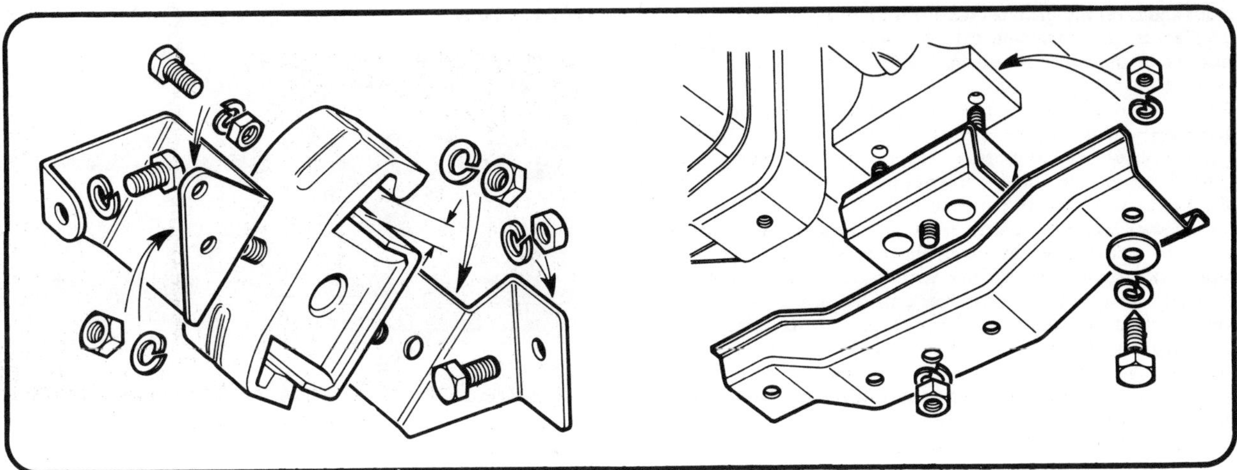

11 Cylinder head removal - engine in car

1 Drain the cooling system as described in Chapter 2.
2 For safety reasons disconnect the negative and then the positive battery terminals and tuck the leads to the rear of the battery (photo).
3 Pull off the feed pipe from the carburettor float chamber union and plug the end of the pipe with a pencil (photo).
4 Slacken the hose clip and remove the breather hose from the carburettor body (photo).
5 Pull the distributor vacuum advance/retard hose union from the carburettor body (photo).
6 Slacken the accelerator cable to linkage securing nut (photo).
7 Press in the two accelerator cable retainer ears on the underside of the support bracket and pull the cable through the bracket (photo).
8 Slacken the nut securing the choke control cable to the choke lever and pull the complete cable through its location on the side of the carburettor (photo).
9 Slacken the top hose to thermostat housing securing clip and pull off the hose (photo).
10 Detach the Lucar terminal from the thermal transmitter located beneath the thermostat housing (photo).
11 Mark the spark plug HT leads to ensure correct refitting and detach the leads from the spark plugs (photo).
12 Slacken the clip securing the heater hose to the angled pipe on the left hand side of the cylinder head. Pull the hose from the pipe (photo).
13 Slacken the clip securing the vacuum servo unit hose to the union on the rear branch of the inlet manifold. Pull off the hose and tuck back on the bulkhead (photo).
14 Undo and remove the two rocker cover securing bolts together with the spacer, plain washer and seal (photo).
15 Lift away the rocker cover and its gasket (photo).
16 Undo and remove the two nuts, plain washers and bolts that secure the clamp around the exhaust downpipe to manifold joint (photo). Lift away the clamp halves.
17 Undo and remove the three nuts and spring washers securing the thermostat cover to the top of the cylinder head (photo). Lift the cover from the three studs and recover the gasket.
18 The thermostat may now be lifted out from its location in the cylinder head (photo).
19 Slacken the eight nuts securing the rocker shaft pedestals to the cylinder head in a progressive manner. Remove the nuts and spring washers (photo).
20 Recover the locking washer from Number 1 pedestal (photo).
21 Lift the rocker shaft assembly from the top of the cylinder head (photo).
22 Remove the push rods, keeping them in the relative order in which they were removed. The easiest way for this is to push them through a sheet of thin card in the correct sequence (photo).
23 Look for any shims located on the rocker shaft retaining studs and carefully lift from the studs (photo).
24 Slacken the remaining cylinder head nuts in a progressive manner in the order shown in Fig 1.6. Lift away the nuts and washers.
25 The cylinder head can now be removed by lifting upwards. If the head is jammed, try to rock it to break the seal. Under no circumstances try to prise it apart from the block with a screwdriver or cold chisel as damage may be done to the faces of the head and block. If the head will not free readily, turn the engine over using the starter motor as the compression in the cylinders will often break the cylinder head joint. If this fails to work, strike the head sharply with a plastic head or wooden hammer, or with a metal hammer onto a piece of wood on the side of the head. Under no circumstances hit the head directly with a metal hammer as this may cause the iron casting to fracture. Several sharp taps with a hammer at the same time pulling upwards should free the head. Lift the head off and place to one side (photo).
26 Recover the old cylinder head gasket (photo).

11.2 Battery earth terminal detachment

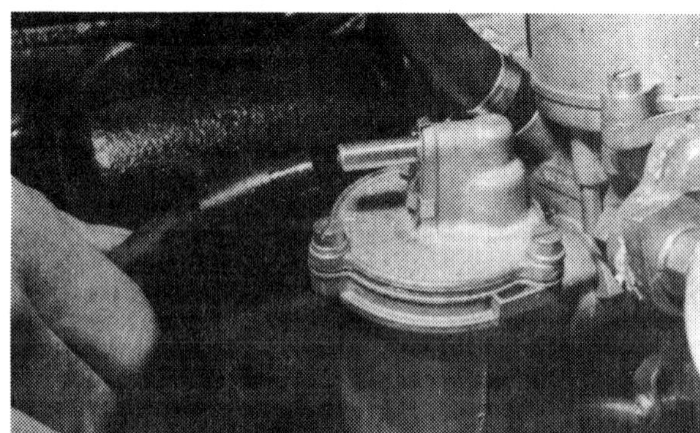

11.3 Fuel feed pipe detached from carburettor float chamber

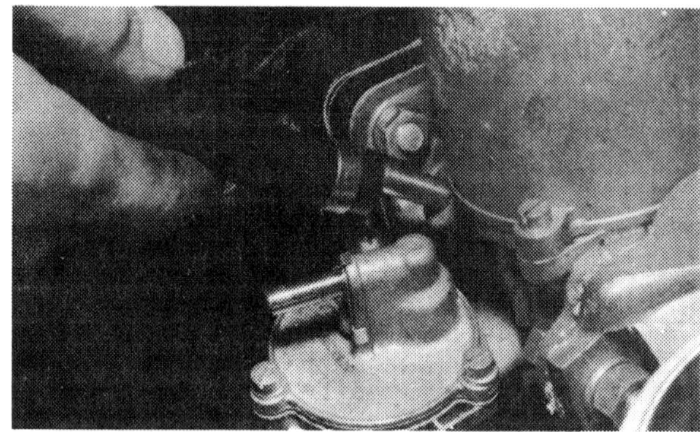

11.4 Breather hose detached from carburettor body

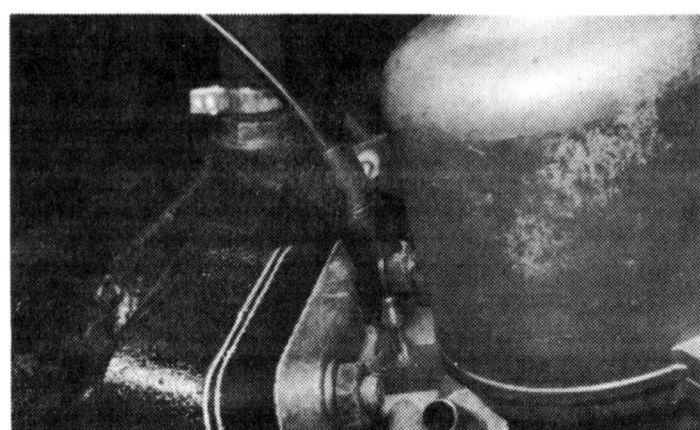

11.5 Vacuum hose detached from carburettor body

11.6 Accelerator linkage detachment

11.7 Detaching accelerator cable from support bracket

11.8 Choke control cable detached from linkage

11.9 Radiator top hose detachment from thermostat housing

11.10 Detaching cable from thermal transmitter

11.11 Detaching HT cables from spark plugs

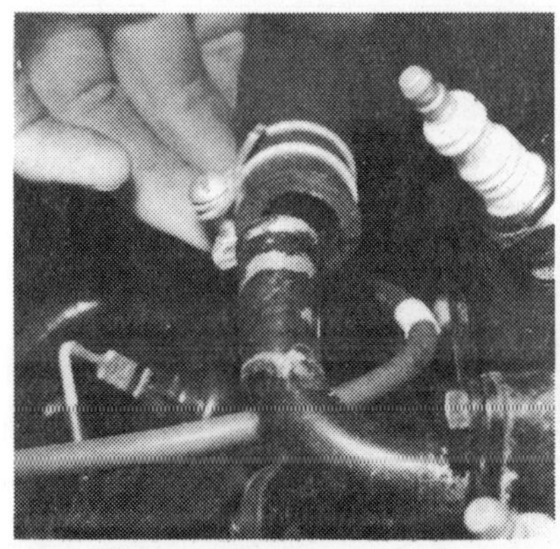

11.12 Removal of hose from pipe on side of cylinder head

11.13 Vacuum hose detachment from inlet manifold

11.14 Rocker cover securing bolt removal

11.15 Lifting away rocker cover

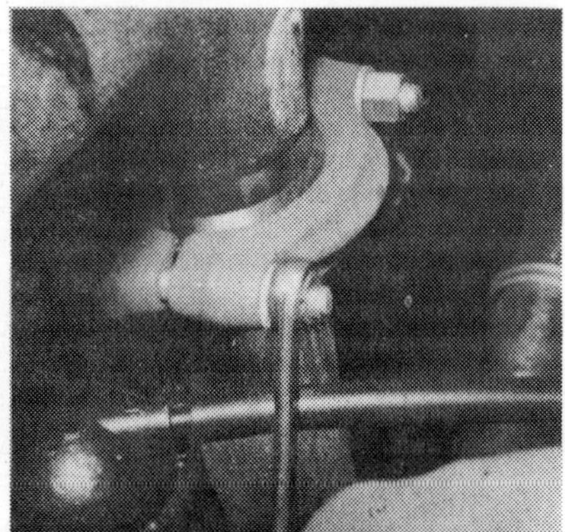

11.16 Removal of exhaust manifold to downpipe clamp

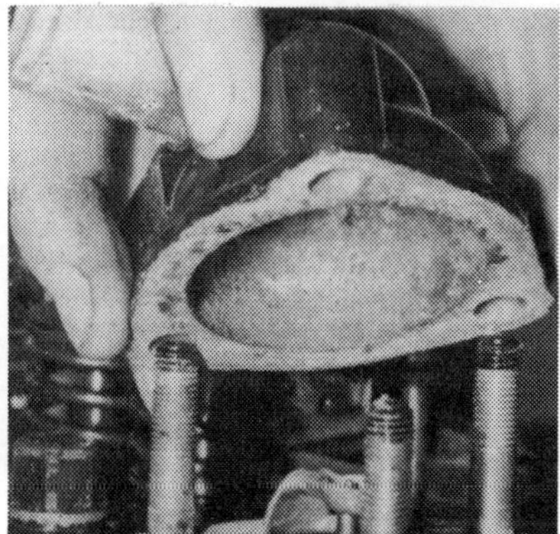

11.17A Lifting away thermostat cover

11.18 Thermostat removal from cylinder head

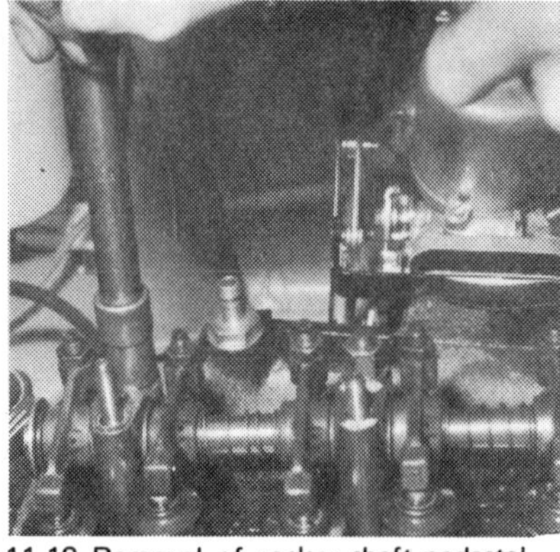
11.19 Removal of rocker shaft pedestal securing nut and spring washer

11.20 Lifting away special shaped washer

11.21 Lifting rocker shaft assembly from cylinder head

11.22 Removal of pushrods

11.23 Special shims located under rocker shaft pedestal studs

11.26 Lifting away cylinder head

11.27 Cylinder head gasket removal

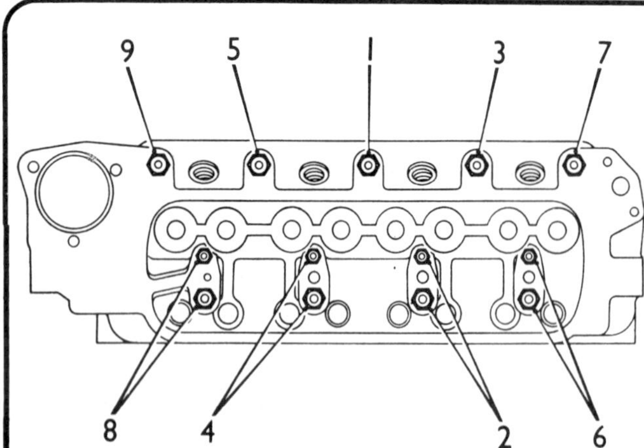

FIG 1.6 CYLINDER HEAD NUT SLACKENING SEQUENCE

12 Cylinder head removal - engine on bench

The sequence for removal of the cylinder head with the engine on the bench is basically identical to the latter operations for removal with the engine in the car. Refer to Section 11 and follow the instructions given in paragraphs 11, 13 to 27.

13 Valve removal

1 The valves are easily removed from the cylinder head by the following method; Compress each spring in turn with a universal valve spring compressor until the two halves of the collets can be removed. Release the compressor and lift away the spring top cup, the spring, oil seal, lower cup and the valve. (Fig 1.7).
2 If, when the valve spring compressor is screwed down, the valve spring top cup refuses to free and expose the split collet, do not continue to screw down on the compressor as there is a likelihood of damaging it.
3 Gently tap the top of the tool directly over the cup with a light hammer. This should free the cup. To avoid the compressor jumping off the valve retaining cup when it is tapped, hold the compressor firmly in position with one hand.
4 It is essential that the valves are kept in their correct sequence unless they are so badly worn that they are to be renewed. If they are going to be re-used place them in a sheet of card having eight holes numbered 1 to 8 corresponding with the relative positions the valves were in when fitted. Also keep the valve springs, cups etc., in this same correct order.

14 Valve guide - removal

Valve guide removal is a simple task but it is not recommended that you should do this because their replacement is too difficult to do accurately. It is far better to leave their removal and insertion to a BLMC garage (see also Section 42).

15 Rocker assembly - dismantling

1 To dismantle the rocker assembly, release the rocker shaft locating screw from Number 1 pedestal, remove the split pin, flat and spring washers from each end of the shaft and slide from the shaft the pedestals, rocker arms and rocker spacing springs. (Fig 1.8).
2 From the end of the shaft undo the plug which gives access to the inside of the rocker which can now be cleaned of sludge etc. Ensure the rocker arm lubricating holes are clear.

16 Timing cover, tensioner, gears and chain - removal

The timing cover, gears and chain can be removed with the engine in the car provided that the radiator and fan belt are removed first. The procedure for removing the timing cover, tensioner, gears and chain is otherwise the same irrespective of whether the engine is in the car or on the bench.
1 Bend back the locking tab of the crankshaft pulley locking washer under the crankshaft pulley retaining bolt.
2 Using a large socket undo and remove the bolt and lock washer.

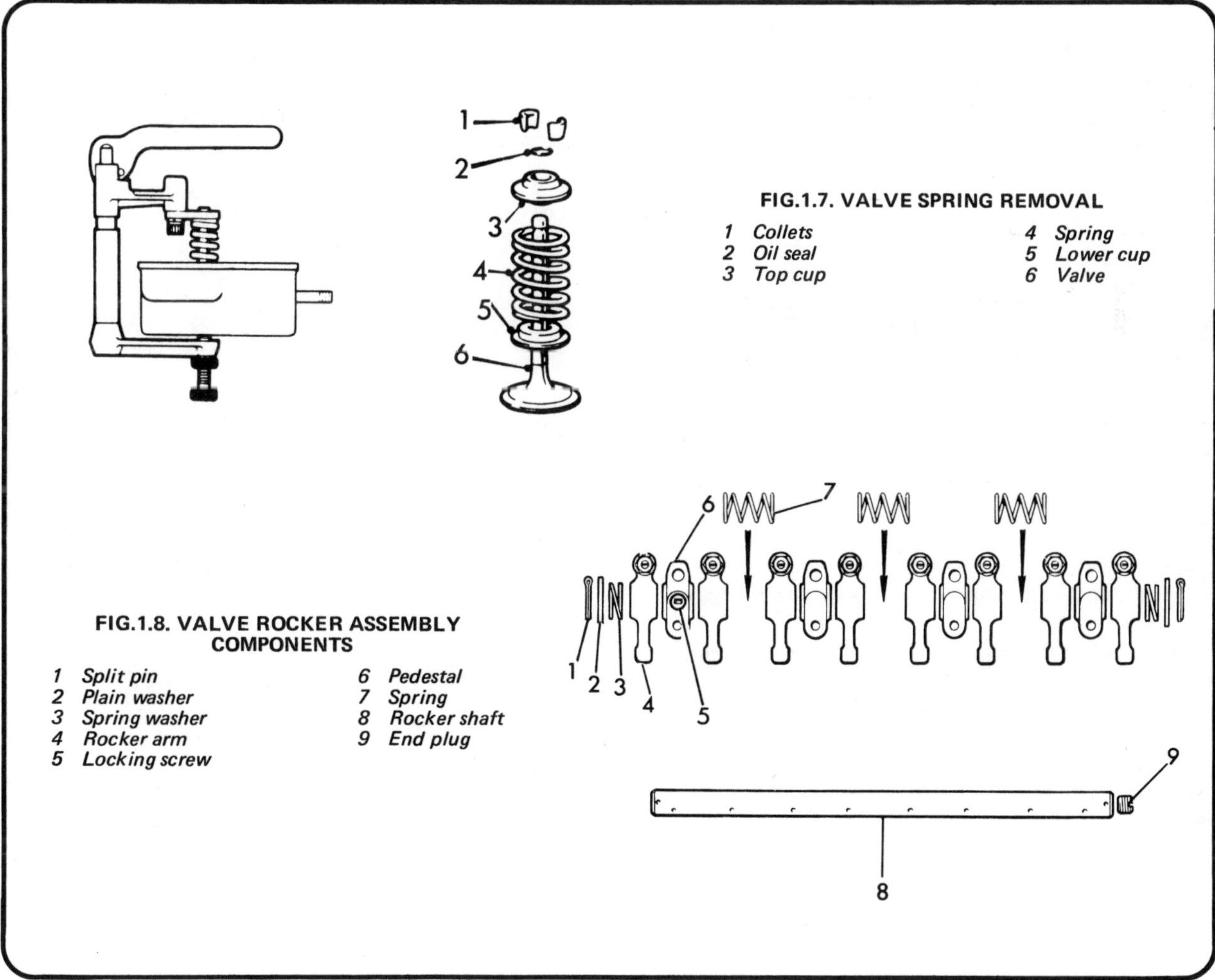

FIG.1.7. VALVE SPRING REMOVAL

1 Collets
2 Oil seal
3 Top cup
4 Spring
5 Lower cup
6 Valve

FIG.1.8. VALVE ROCKER ASSEMBLY COMPONENTS

1 Split pin
2 Plain washer
3 Spring washer
4 Rocker arm
5 Locking screw
6 Pedestal
7 Spring
8 Rocker shaft
9 End plug

3 Placing two large screwdrivers or tyre levers behind the crankshaft pulley wheel at 180° to each other carefully lever off the pulley. It is preferable to use a proper extractor if this is available but the large screwdrivers or tyre levers are quite suitable providing care is taken not to damage the pulley flange.
4 Remove the woodruff key from the crankshaft nose with a pair of pliers and note how the groove in the pulley is designed to fit over it. Place the woodruff key in a glass jar for it is a very small part and can easily become lost.
5 Unscrew the bolts holding the timing cover to the block. NOTE that three different sizes of bolt are used, and that each bolt makes use of a large flat washer as well as a spring washer.
6 Pull off the timing cover and its gasket.
7 With the timing cover off, take off the oil thrower noting which way round it is fitted.
8 Take the bottom plug from the chain tensioner, fit a 1/8 inch Allen key in the cylinder and turn the key clockwise until the slipper head is pulled right back and locked behind the limit head.
9 Bend back the locking tab on the washer under the camshaft retaining nut and unscrew the nut. Lift away the nut and lockwasher. Ease each timing gear forwards a little at a time by levering behind each gearwheel in turn with two large screwdrivers or tyre levers at 180° to each other. If the gear wheels are locked solid then it will be necessary to use a proper gearwheel and pulley extractor, and if one is available this should be used anyway in preference to levers. With both gearwheels safely off, remove the woodruff keys from the crankshaft and camshaft with a pair of pliers and place them in a jar for safe keeping. Note the number of very thin packing washers behind the crankshaft gearwheel and remove them very carefully.
10 To remove the tensioner knock back the tabs on the joint lockwasher and undo the two bolts which hold the tensioner and its backplate to the engine.

17 Camshaft - removal

The camshaft can be removed with the engine on the bench or in the car. If the camshaft is to be removed with the engine in the car, the radiator and fan belt must be removed after the cooling system has been drained. The timing cover, gears and chain, must be removed as described in Section 16. It is also necessary to remove the front grille, and the distributor drive shaft as described in Section 18. With the drive gear out of the way, proceed as follows:
1 Undo and remove the three bolts and spring washers which hold the camshaft locating plate to the block. The bolts are normally covered by the camshaft gearwheel.
2 Remove the plate. Recover the tappets if they are still in place and keep in the corect order as fitted in the engine.
3 The camshaft can now be withdrawn. It may be found necessary to release the engine mountings and lower the engine slightly. Take great care to remove the camshaft gently, and in particular ensure that the cam peaks do not damage the camshaft bearings as the shaft is drawn forwards.

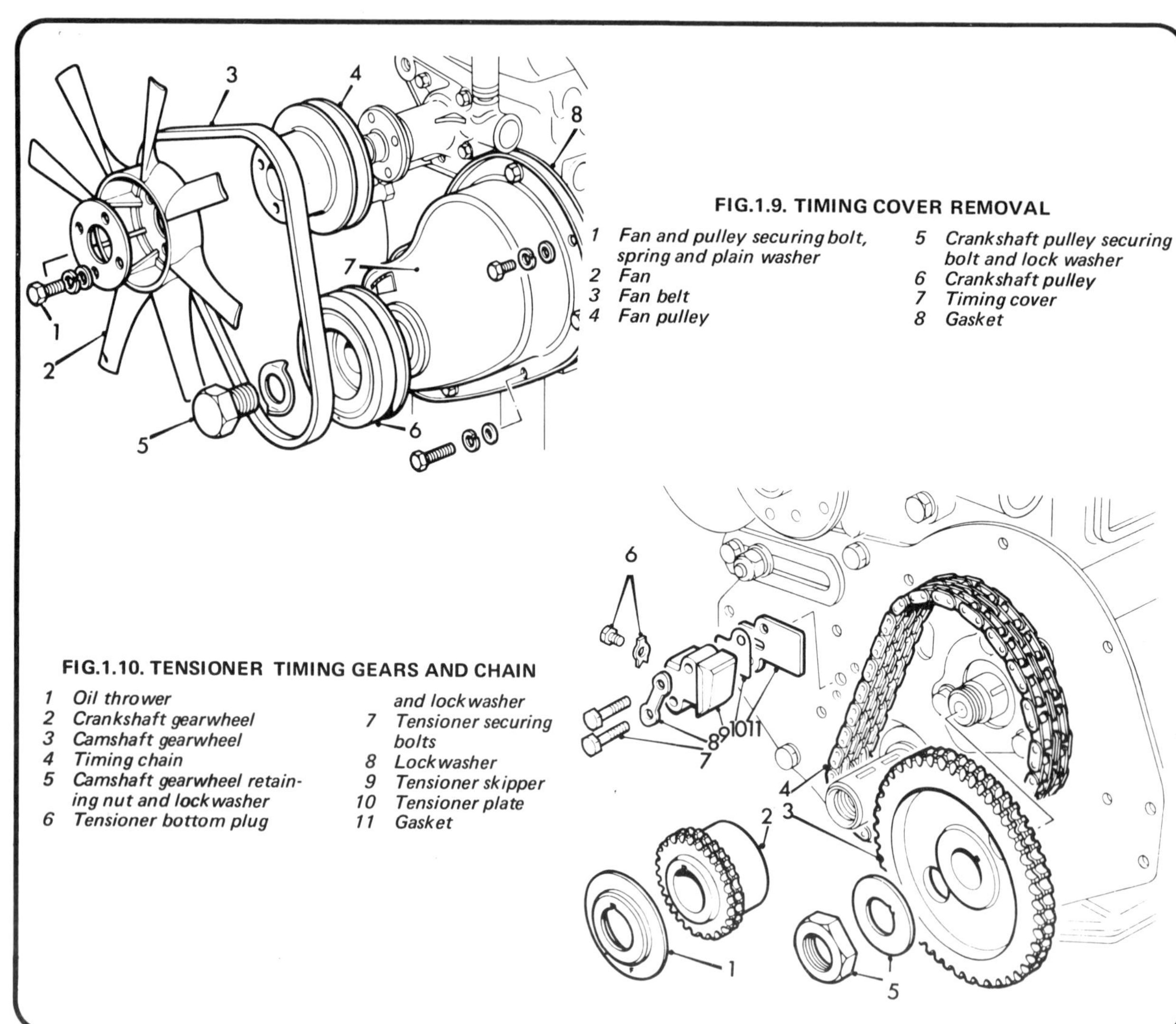

FIG.1.9. TIMING COVER REMOVAL

1 Fan and pulley securing bolt, spring and plain washer
2 Fan
3 Fan belt
4 Fan pulley
5 Crankshaft pulley securing bolt and lock washer
6 Crankshaft pulley
7 Timing cover
8 Gasket

FIG.1.10. TENSIONER TIMING GEARS AND CHAIN

1 Oil thrower
2 Crankshaft gearwheel
3 Camshaft gearwheel
4 Timing chain
5 Camshaft gearwheel retaining nut and lockwasher
6 Tensioner bottom plug
7 Tensioner securing bolts
8 Lockwasher
9 Tensioner skipper
10 Tensioner plate
11 Gasket

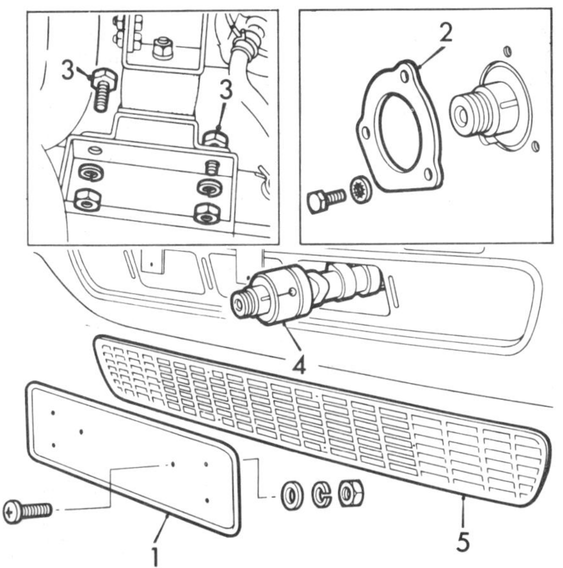

FIG.1.11. CAMSHAFT REMOVAL

1 Number plate
2 Camshaft locking plate
3 Engine mounting securing nut bolt and spring washer
4 Camshaft
5 Front lower grille

18 Distributor drive - removal

To remove the distributor drive with the sump still in position it is first necessary to remove one of the tappet cover retaining bolts. With the distributor and the distributor clamp plate already removed, this is achieved as follows:

1 Unscrew the single retaining bolt and spring washer to release the distributor housing.

2 Turn the crankshaft until No 1 piston is positioned at either 90° before or after the TDC position so that the pistons are halfway up the bores.

3 With the distributor housing removed, if the sump is still in position, screw into the end of the distributor drive shaft a 5/16 UNF bolt. A tappet cover bolt is ideal for this purpose. The drive shaft can then be lifted out, the shaft being turned slightly in the process to free the shaft skew gear from the camshaft skew gear.

4 If the sump has already been removed then it is a simple matter to push the driveshaft out from inside the crankcase.

19 Sump, piston, connecting rod and big end bearing - removal

The sump, pistons and connecting rods can be removed with the engine still in the car or with the engine on the bench. Proceed with the appropriate methods in either case for removing the cylinder head. The pistons and connecting rods are drawn up out of the top of the cylinder bores.

1 Undo and remove the two bolts, spring and plain washers securing the sump connecting plate to the gearbox bellhousing if the engine is still in the car.

2 Undo and remove the bolts and spring washers holding the sump in position. Lift away the sump and gasket (photo).

3 To gain access to all main bearings it is now necessary to remove the oil pump and strainer.

4 Undo and remove the three bolts and spring washers that secure the strainer to the oil pump cover. Lift away the strainer (photo).

5 Undo and remove the three nuts and spring washers that secure the oil pump body to the studs. Carefully withdraw the oil pump (photo). Note that on reassembly it will be necessary to reset the ignition timing.

6 Undo and remove the big end cap retaining nuts using a socket and remove the big end caps one at a time, taking care to keep them in the right order and the correct way round (photo). Ensure that the shell bearings are also kept with their correct connecting rods and caps unless they are to be renewed.

Normally the numbers 1 to 4 are stamped on adjacent sides of the big end caps and connecting rods, indicating which cap fits on which rod and which way round the cap fits. If no numbers or lines can be found then scratch mating marks across the joint from the rod to the cap with a sharp screwdriver; One line for connecting rod Number 1, two for connecting rod number 2 and so on. This will ensure there is no confusion later as it is most important that the caps go back in the position on the connecting rods from which they were removed.

7 If the big end caps are difficult to remove they may be gently tapped with a soft hammer.

8 To remove the shell bearings press the bearing opposite the groove in both connecting rod and the connecting rod cap, and the bearing shell will slide out easily.

9 Withdraw the pistons and connecting rods upwards and ensure they are kept in the correct order, for replacement in the same bore. Refit the connecting rod caps and bearings to the rods if the bearings do not require renewal to minimise the risk of getting the caps and rods muddled.

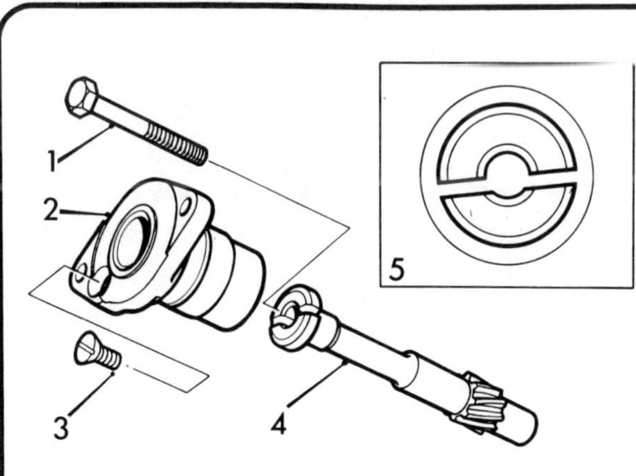

FIG.1.12. DISTRIBUTOR DRIVE

1 Distributor clamp securing bolt
2 Distributor housing
3 Screw - distributor housing to cylinder block
4 Distributor drive shaft
5 Inset: Correct position of drive shaft slot

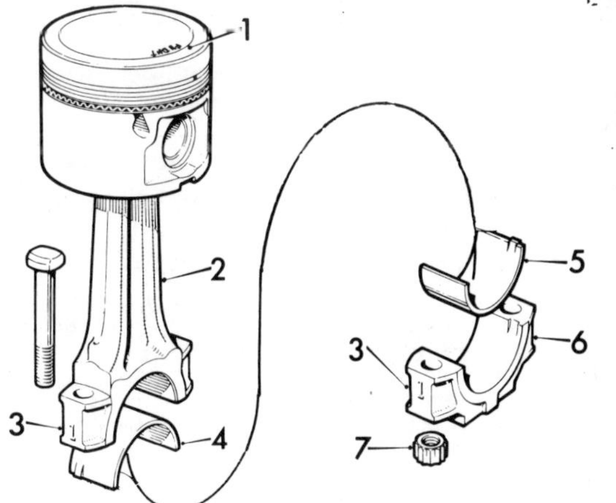

FIG.1.13. PISTON AND CONNECTING ROD ASSEMBLY WITH PRESS FIT GUDGEON PIN

1 Piston - note identification marks
2 Connecting rod
3 Identification mark
4 Upper shell bearing half
5 Lower shell bearing half
6 End cap
7 Multi sided nut

19.2 Removal of sump securing bolts

19.4 Oil pump strainer removal

19.5 Lifting away oil pump from mount ing studs

19.6 Big end cap retaining nut removal

20 Gudgeon pin - removal

A press type gudgeon pin is now used and requires a special BLMC tool No. 18 G1150 with adaptor 18 G1150C to remove and replace the pin. This tool is shown in Fig 1.14 and must be used in the following manner:

1 Securely hold the hexagonal body in a firm vice and screw back the large nut until it is flush with the end of the main centre screw. Well lubricate the screw and large nut as they have to withstand high loading. Now push the centre screw in until the nut just touches the thrust race.

2 Fit the adaptors number 18 G1150C onto the main centre screw with the piston ring cut a way positioned uppermost. Then slide the parallel sleeve with the groove end first onto the centre screw.

3 Fit the piston with the 'FRONT' or 'A' mark on towards the adaptor on the centre screw. This is important because the gudgeon pin bore is offset and irreparable damage will result in fitting the wrong way round. Next fit the remover/replacer bush on the centre screw with the flange end towards the gudgeon pin.

4 Screw the stop nut onto the main centre screw and adjust it until approximately 0.032 inch (0.8 mm) end play ('A' in Fig 1.14 exists, and lock the stop nut securely with the lock screws. Now check that the remover/replacer bush and parallel sleeve are positioned correctly in the bore on both sides of the piston. Also check that the curved face of the adaptor is clean and slide the piston onto the tool, so it fits into the curved face of the adaptor with the piston rings over the cut-a-way.

5 Screw the large nut up to the thrust race and holding the lock screw turn the large nut with a ring spanner or long socket until the piston pin is withdrawn from the piston.

6 Some earlier models were fitted with fully floating gudgeon pins and circlips. See Fig 1.15.

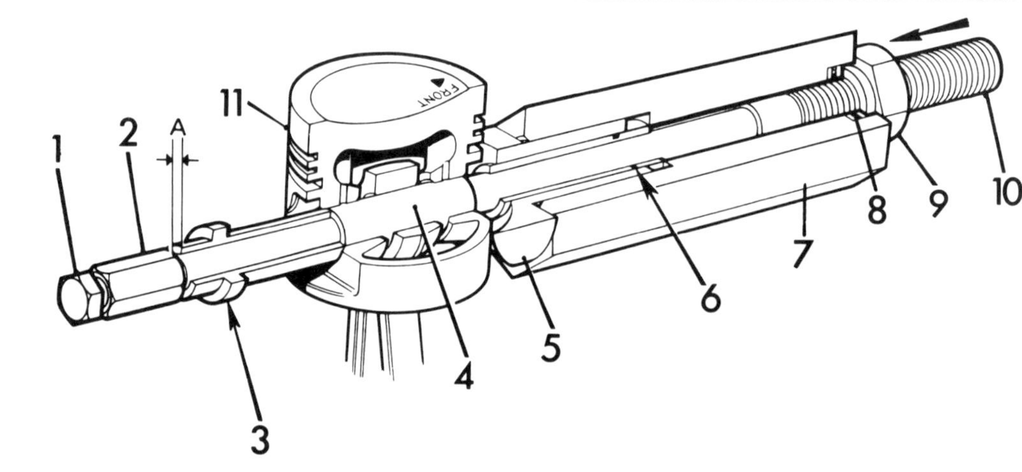

FIG.1.14. GUDGEON PIN REMOVAL USING BLMC TOOL 18G 1150 AND ADAPTORS 18G 1150C

1 Lock screw
2 Stop nut
3 Flange away from gudgeon pin remover/replacer bush
4 Gudgeon pin
5 Piston support adaptor
6 Groove in sleeve away from gudgeon pin
7 Service tool body
8 Thrust race
9 Large nut
10 Centre screw
11 Piston

21 Piston ring removal

1 To remove the piston rings, slide them carefully over the top of the piston, taking care not to scratch the aluminium alloy of the piston. Never slide them off the bottom of the piston skirt. It is very easy to break piston rings if they are pulled off roughly so this operation should be done with extreme caution. It is helpful to use an old 0.020 inch feeler gauge to facilitate their removal.
2 Lift one end of the piston ring to be removed out of its groove and insert the end of the feeler gauge under it.
3 Turn the feeler gauge slowly round the piston and as the ring comes out of its groove it rests on the land above. It can then be eased off the piston with the feeler gauge stopping it from slipping into any empty grooves if it is any but the top piston ring that is being removed.

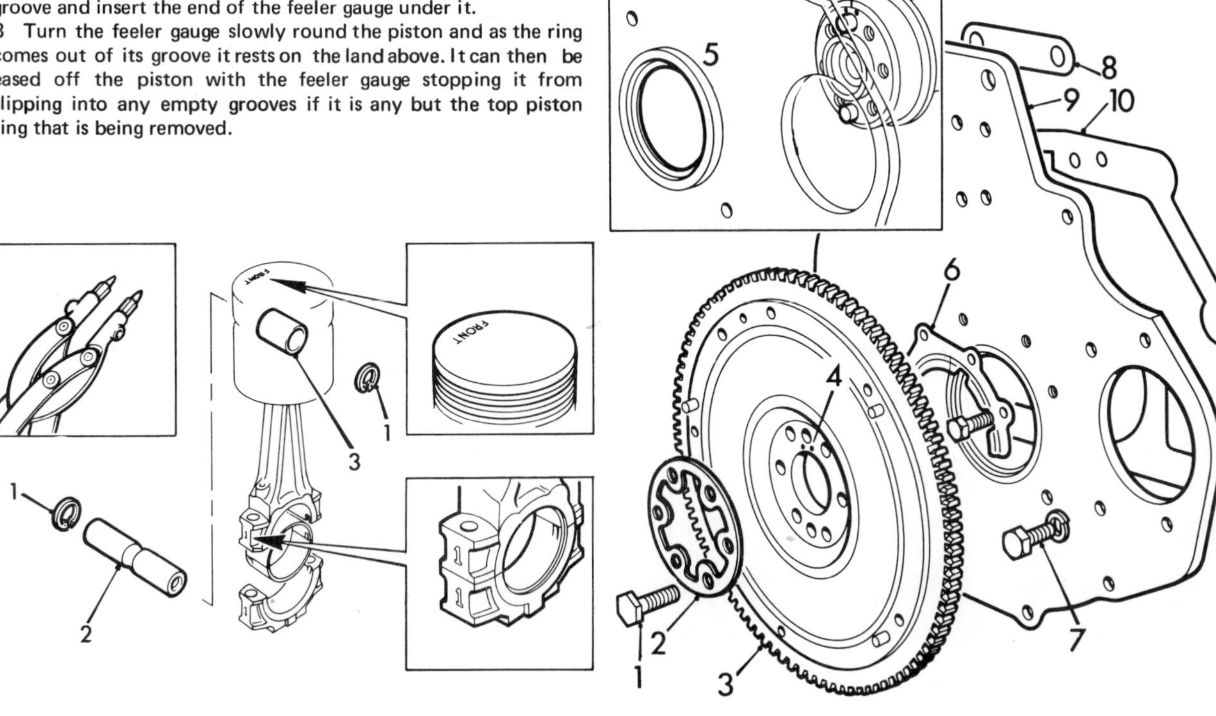

FIG.1.15. EARLIER TYPE FULLY FLOATING GUDGEON PIN

1 Circlip 2 Gudgeon pin 3 Little end bush

FIG.1.16. FLYWHEEL AND ENGINE BACKPLATE REMOVAL

1 Flywheel securing bolts
2 Shaped lock washer
3 Flywheel
4 Mating marks
5 Crankshaft rear oil seal
6 Oil sealer retainer
7 Backplate securing bolt and spring washer
8 Gasket - upper
9 Engine backplate
10 Gasket - lower

22 Flywheel and engine backplate - removal

Having removed the clutch (see Chapter 5) the flywheel and engine backplate can be removed. It is only possible for this complete operation to be carried out with the engine out of the car.
1 Bend back the lockwasher tabs and then undo and remove the six bolts securing the flywheel to the end of the crankshaft. Lift away the shaped lock washer and the flywheel.
2 Some difficulty may be experienced in removing the bolts by rotation of the crankshaft every time pressure is put on the spanner. The only answer is to lock the crankshaft in position whilst the bolts are removed with a wooden wedge placed between the crankshaft and the side of the block inside the crankcase.
3 The engine backplate is held in position by a number of bolts and spring washers of varying size. Release the bolts noting where the different size bolts fit and place them together to avoid their becoming lost. Lift away the backplate from the block complete with the paper gasket.

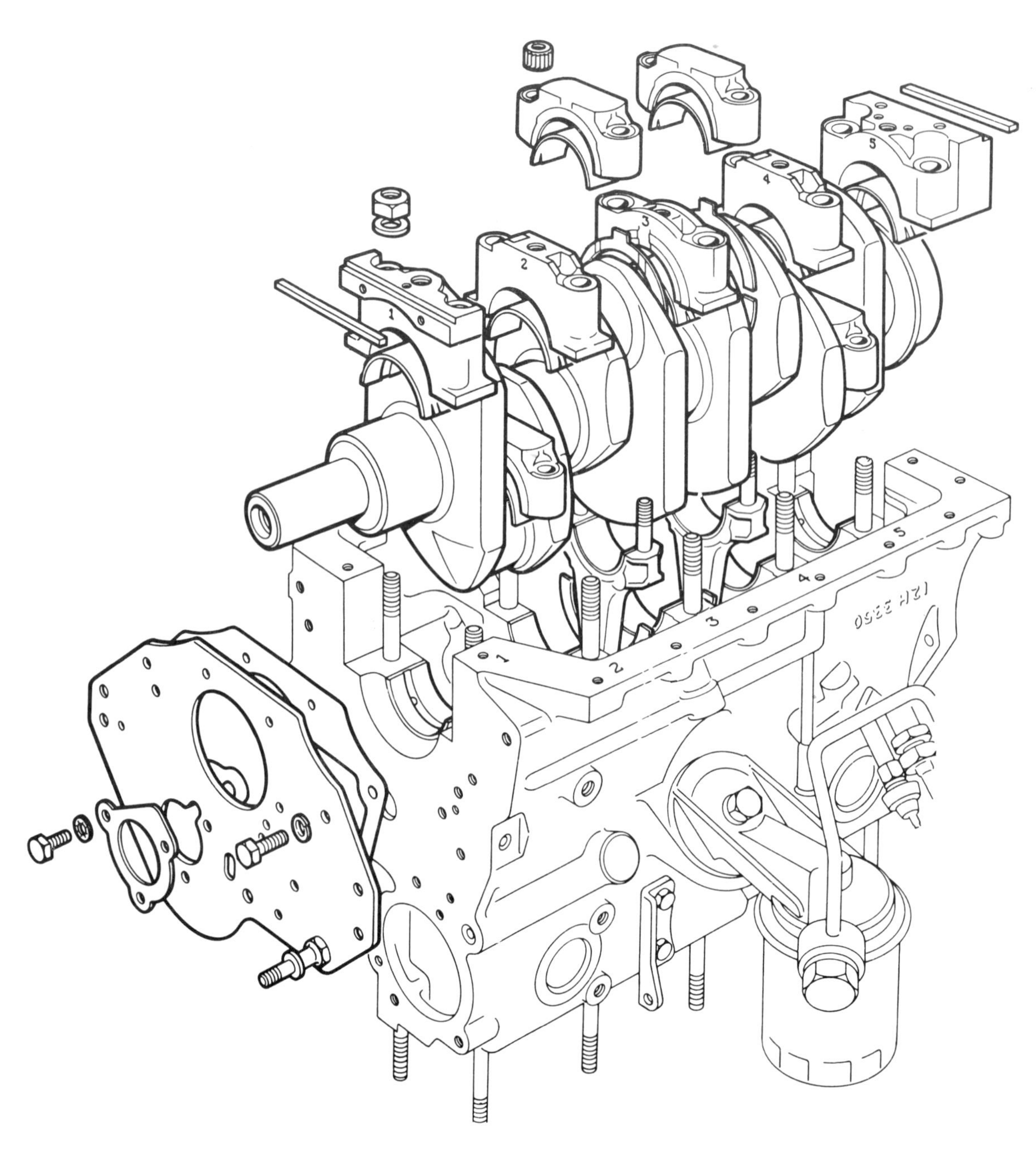

FIG.1.17. CRANKSHAFT AND MAIN BEARING REMOVAL

23 Crankshaft and main bearing - removal

Drain the engine oil, remove the timing gears and remove the sump, oil pump, big end bearings, flywheel and engine backplate as already described. Removal can only be attempted with the engine on the bench:

1 Undo and remove the ten nuts securing the main bearing caps to the cylinder block. Then undo and remove the two bolts and spring washers which hold the front main bearing cap against the engine front plate. It will be beneficial if the front plate is completely removed, so remove the remaining securing bolts and spring washers and lift away together with the paper gasket.

2 Make sure that the main bearing caps are numbered 1 to 5 on the front faces and also have the worn 'FRONT' towards the front.

3 Remove the main bearing caps and the bottom half of each bearing shell, taking care to keep the bearing shells in the right caps.

4 When removing the centre bearing cap, note the bottom semi-circular halves of the thrust washers, one half lying on either side of the main bearing. Lay them with the centre bearing along the corect side.

5 Slightly rotate the crankshaft to free the uper halves of the bearing shells and thrust washers which should now be lifted away and placed over the correct bearing cap.

6 Remove the crankshaft by lifting it away from the crankcase.

24 Lubrication system - description

A force feed system of lubrication is fitted with oil circulated around the engine from the sump below the cylinder block. The level of engine oil in the sump is indicated by the dipstick which is fitted on the right hand side of the engine. The optimum level is indicated by the maximum mark. The level of oil in the sump, ideally, should neither be above or below this line. Oil is replenished via the filler cap towards the front of the rocker cover.

The eccentric rotor type oil pump is bolted within the left hand side of the crankcase and is driven by a short shaft from the skew gear on the camshaft which also drives the distributor shaft.

The pump is of the non-draining variety to allow rapid pressure build up when starting from cold. Oil is drawn from the sump through a gauge screen in the oil strainer, this being shown in Fig 1.20 and is sucked up the pick up and drawn into the oil pump. From the oil pump it is forced under pressure along a gallery on the right hand side of the engine, and through drillings to the big end, main and camshaft bearings. A small hold in each connecting rod allows a jet of oil to lubricate the cylinder wall with each revolution.

From the camshaft front bearing, oil is fed through drilled passages in the cylinder block and head to the front rocker pedestal where it enters the hollow rocker shaft. Holes drilled in the shaft allow for the lubrication of the rocker arms and the valve stems and push rod ends. This oil is at a reduced pressure to the oil delivered to the crankshaft bearings. Oil from the front camshaft bearing lubricates the timing gears and the timing chain. Oil returns to the sump by various passages, the tappets being lubricated by oil returning via the push rod drillings in the block.

A full flow cartridge type filter is fitted and oil passes through this filter before it reaches the main oil gallery. The oil pump is passed directly from the oil pump to the filter.

25 Oil filter - removal and replacement

1 The external oil filter is of the disposable cartridge type and is located on the right hand side of the engine.

2 Before removing the cartridge place an absorbent cloth around the base to catch the oil released from the cartridge when it has been unscrewed.

3 To renew the oil filter unscrew the old cartridge from the filter head and discard it. Smear the seal on the new filter with a little oil and position it on the filter head. Screw it on and tighten with the hands only. Do not attempt to tighten with a spanner or strap wrench.

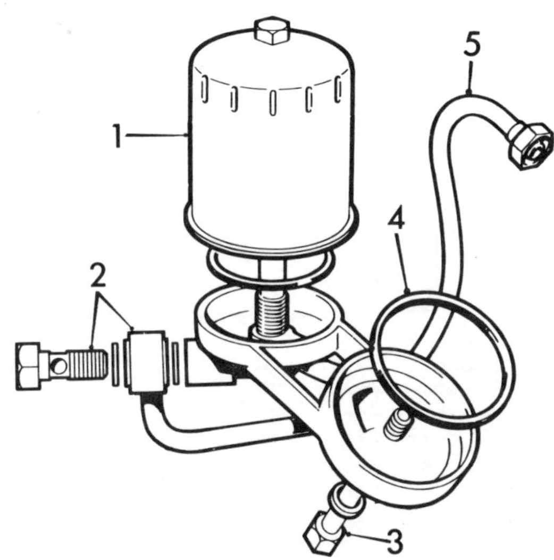

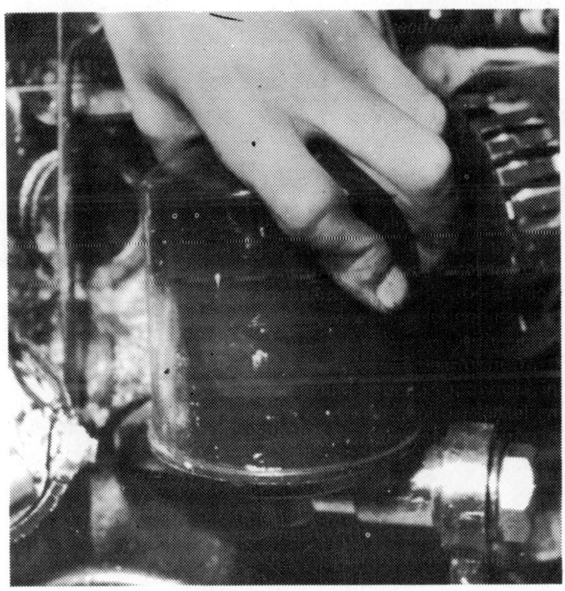

FIG.1.18. OIL FILTER ASSEMBLY

1 Filter cartridge
2 Supply pipe union to filter head
3 Filter head securing bolt
4 'O' ring
5 Supply pipe

26 Oil pressure relief valve - removal and replacement

To prevent excessive oil pressure - which might result when the engine oil is thick and cold - an oil pressure relief valve is built into the left hand side of the engine at the rear. The relief valve is identified externally by a large 9/16 inch domed hexagon nut.

1 To dismantle the valve unscrew the domed nut and remove it complete with sealing washer. The relief spring and valve can then be easily extracted.

2 In position the valve fits over the opposite end of the relief valve spring resting in the dome of the hexagon nut, and bears against a machined seating in the block. When the oil pressure exceeds 70 lb/sq in (4.92 kg cm2), the valve is forced off its seat and the oil by-passes it and returns via a drilling directly into the sump.

3 Check the tension of the spring by measuring its length. It is shorter than 3 in (76 mm) it should be replaced with a new spring.

4 Examint the valve for signs of pitting which, if evident, it should be carefully lapped using cutting paste. Remove all traces of paste when a good seating has been obtained.

5 Reassembly of the relief valve is the reverse sequence to removal.

27 Oil pump - removal and dismantling

1 With the sump removed undo and remove the three bolts and spring washers that secure the oil strainer to the pump housing. Lift away the oil strainer (Fig 1.20).

2 Undo and remove the nuts and spring washers from the three studs which hold the oil pump to the underside of the crankcase. Lift away the pump and its driveshaft. Recover the pump gasket.

3 Unscrew and remove the three bolts and spring washers that secure the pump cover to the pump body. Carefully pull the cover from the two dowels which hold it in its correct position on the housing (Fig 1.21).

4 Pull out from the pump body and outer rotor and the inner rotor together with pump shaft.

28 Timing chain tensioner - removal and dismantling

1 Remove the cover from the timing gears as described in Section 16 and lock the rubber tensioner in the fully retracted position by removing the bottom plug from the tensioner body and fitting a 1/8 inch Allen key in the cylinder. Turn the key clockwise until the slipper head is pulled right back and locked behind the limit head.

2 Knock back the tabs of the joint lockwasher and undo the two bolts which hold the tensioner and its backplate to the engine.

3 Pull the rubber slipper together with the spring and plunger from the tensioner body. Fit the Allen key to its socket in the cylinder, and holding the slipper and plunger firmly, turn the key clockwise to free the cylinder and spring from the plunger (Fig 1.22).

29 Engine - examination and renovation - general

With the engine stripped and all parts thoroughly cleaned, every component should be examined for wear. The following items should be checked and, where necessary, renewed or renovated as described later.

30 Crankshaft - examination and renovation

Examine the crankpin and main journal surfaces for signs of scoring or scratches and check the ovality of the crankpins at different positions with a micrometer. If more than 0.001 inch (0.0254 mm) out of round, the crankpins will have to be reground. It will also have to be reground if there are any scores or scratches present. Also check the journals in the same fashion. BMC 'B' series engine centre main bearing are prone to failure. This is not always immediately apparent, but slight vibration in an otherwise normally smooth engine and a very slight drop in oil pressure under normal conditions are clues. If the centre main bearing is suspected of failure it should be investigated immediately, by dropping the sump and removing the centre main bearing cap. Failure to do this will result in badly scored centre main journal. If it is necessary to regrind the crankshaft and fit new bearings, an engineering works will be able to decide how much metal to grind off and be able to supply the correct undersize shells to fit.

31 Big end and main bearings - examination and renovation

1 Big end bearing failure is usually accompanied by a noisy knocking from the crankcase and a slight drop in oil pressure. Main bearing failure is accompanied by vibration which can be quite severe as the engine speed rises and falls, and a drop in oil pressure.

2 Bearings which have not broken up, but are badly worn will give rise to low oil pressure and some vibration. Inspect the big ends, main bearings and thrust washers for signs of general wear, scoring, pitting and scratches. The bearings should be a matt grey in colour. With lead indium bearings, should a trace of copper in colour be noticed the bearings are badly worn, for the lead bearing has worn away to expose the indium underlay. Renew the bearings if they are in this condition or if there is any sign of scoring or pitting.

3 The undersizes available are designed to correspond with regrind sizes 0.010 in bearings are correct for a crankshaft reground 0.010 in undersize. The bearings are in fact slightly more than the stated undersize as running clearances have been allowed for during their manufacture.

4 Very long engine life can sometimes be achieved by changing big end bearings at 30,000 miles and main bearings at 50,000 miles, irrespective of bearing wear. Normally, crankshaft wear is infinitesimal and regular changes of bearings may ensure mileages of between 100,000 and 120,000 miles before crankshaft regrinding becomes necessary. Crankshafts normally have to be reground because of scoring due to bearing failure.

5 Once dismantled only refit new bearing shells. It is false economy to replace old bearings even if they have run for only an hour!

32 Cylinder bores - examination and renovation

1 The cylinder bores must be examined for taper, ovality, scoring and scratches. Start by carefully examining the top of the bores, if they are worn fractionally a very slight ridge will be found on the thrust side. This marks the top of the piston travel. You will have a good indication of the bore wear prior to dismantling the engine, or removing the cylinder head. Excessive oil consumption accompanied by blue smoke from the exhaust is a sure sign of worn cylinder bores and piston rings.

2 Measure the diameter of the bore just under the ridge with a micrometer and compare it with the diameter at the bottom of the bore, which is not subject to such wear. If the difference between the two measurements is more than 0.006 inch (0.1524mm) then it will be necessary to fit a 'ring set' or to have the cylinders rebored and fit oversize pistons and rings. If no micrometer is available remove the rings from one piston and place the piston in each bore in turn about ¾ inch (19mm) below the top of the bore. If an 0.010 inch (0.254mm) feeler gauge can be slid between the piston and the cylinder wall on the thrust side of the bore then remedial action must be taken. Oversize pistons are available in the following sizes:

+ 0.010 inch (0.254mm)	+ 0.030 inch (0.762mm)
+ 0.020 inch (0.508mm)	+ 0.040 inch (1.016mm)

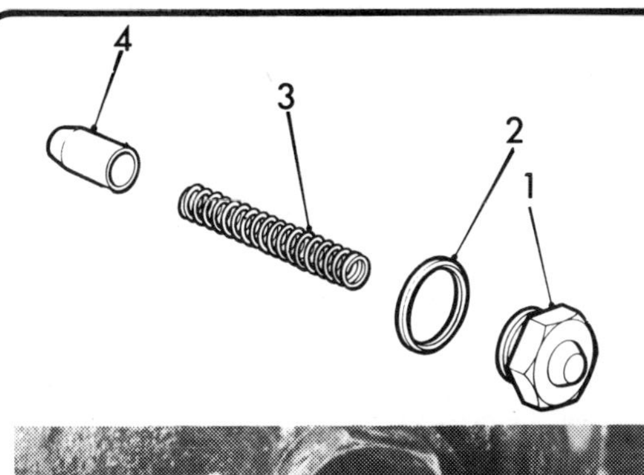

FIG.1.19. OIL PRESSURE RELIEF VALVE

1 *Domed nut*
2 *Sealing washer*
3 *Valve spring*
4 *Valve*

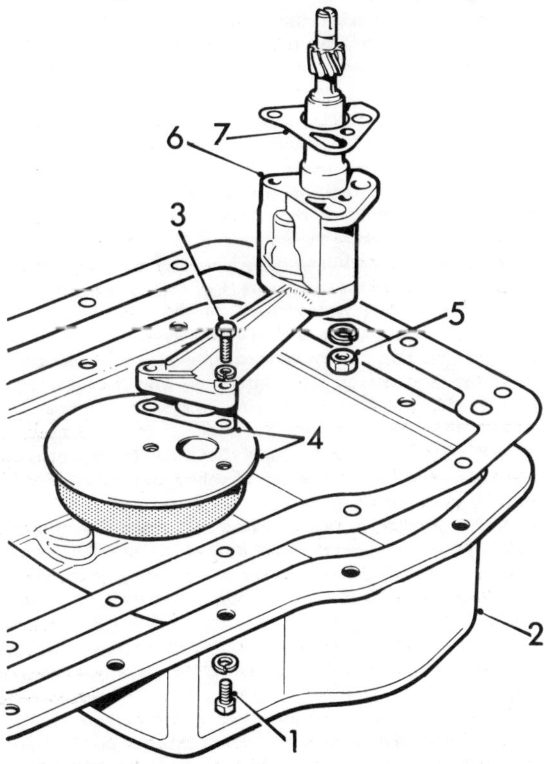

FIG.1.20. OIL PUMP REMOVAL

1 *Sump securing bolt and spring washer*
2 *Sump*
3 *Oil strainer securing bolt and spring washer*
4 *Oil strainer and gasket*
5 *Oll pump securing nut and spring washer*
6 *Oil pump*
7 *Gasket*

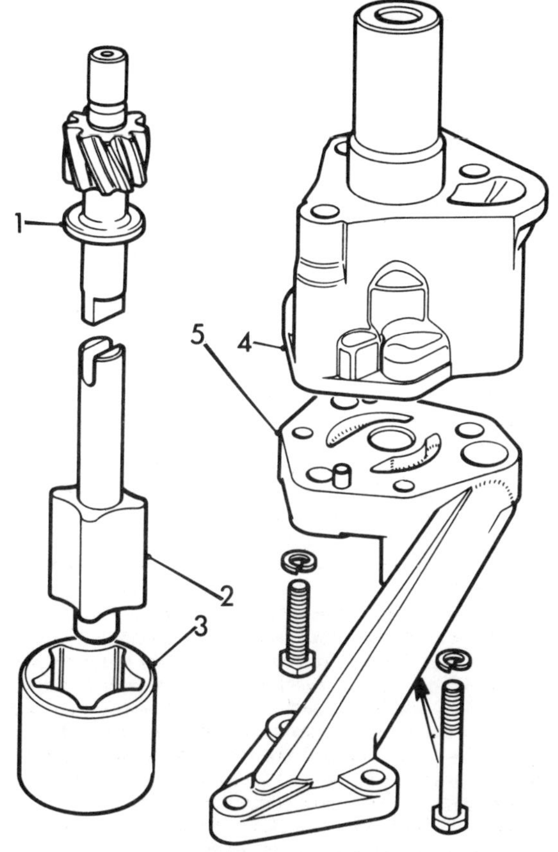

FIG.1.21. OIL PUMP COMPONENTS

1 *Pump shaft*
2 *Inner rotor*
3 *Outer rotor*
4 *Pump body*
5 *Pump cover*

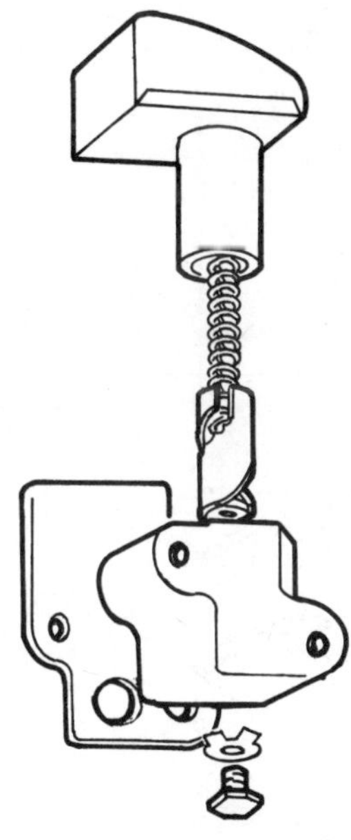

FIG.1.22. TIMING CHAIN TENSIONER COMPONENTS

3 These are accurately machined to just below these measurements so as to provide correct running clearances in bores bored out to the exact oversize dimensions.

4 If the bores are slightly worn buy not so badly worn as to justify reboring them, special oil control rings can be fitted to the existing pistons which will restore compression and stop the engine burning oil. Several different types are available and the manufacturers instructions concerning their fitting must be followed closely.

33 Pistons and piston rings - examination and renovation

1 If the old pistons are to be refitted carefully remove the piston rings and then thoroughly clean them. Take particular care to clean out the piston ring grooves. Do not scratch the aluminium in any way. If new rings are to be fitted to the old pistons, then the top ring should be stepped, so to clear the ridge left above the previous top ring. If a normal but oversize new ring is fitted it will hit the ridge and break, because the new ring will not have worn in the same way as the old.

2 Before fitting the rings on the pistons each should be inserted approximately 3 inches (76mm) down the cylinder bore and the gap measureed with a feeler gauge as shown in Fig.1.23. This should be between the limits given in the specifications at the beginning of this Chapter. It is essential that the gap is measured at the bottom of the ring travel, for if it is measured at the top of a worn bore and gives a perfect fit, it could easily seize at the bottom. If the ring gap is too small rub down the ends of the ring with a very fine file until the gap is correct when fitted. To keep the rings square in the bore for measurement, line each one up in turn with an old piston in the bore upside down, and use the piston to push the ring down about 3 inches (76mm). Remove the piston and measure the piston ring gap.

3 When fitting new pistons and rings to a rebored engine the ring gap can be measured at the top of the bore as the bore will now not taper. It is not necessary to measure the side clearance in the piston ring grooves with rings fitted, as the groove dimensions are accurately machined during manufacture. When fitting new oil control rings to the pistons it may be necessary to have the grooves widened by machining to accept the new under rings. In this instance the manufacturer will make this quite clear and will supply the address to which the pistons must be sent for machining.

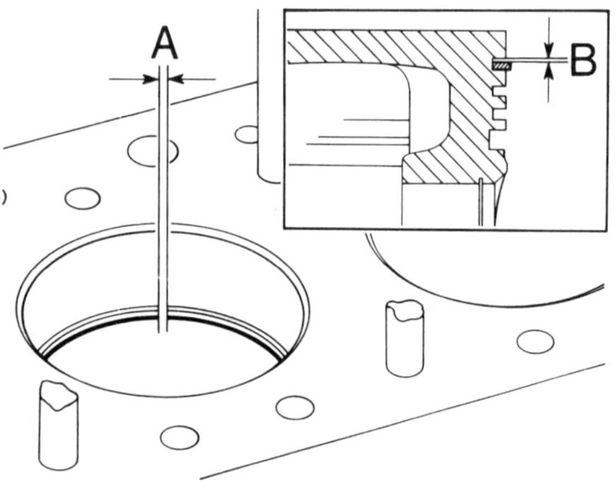

FIG.1.23. PISTON RING MEASUREMENT

4 When new pistons are fitted, take great care to it the exact size best suited to the particular bore of your engine. BLMC go one stage further than merely specifying one size piston for all standard bores. Because of very slight differences in cylinder machining during production it is necessary to select just the right piston for the bore. A range of different sizes are available either from the piston manufacturer or from the local BLMC stores.

5 Examination of the cylinder block face will show adjacent to each bore a small diamond shaped box with a number stamped in the metal. Careful examination of the piston crown will show a matching diamond and number. These are the standard piston sizes and will be the same for all bores. If the standard pistons are to be refitted or standard low compression pistons changed to standard high compression pistons, then it is essential that only pistons with the same number in the diamond are used. With larger pistons, the amount of oversize is stamped in an elipse on the piston crown.

6 On engines with tapered second and third compression rings, the top narrow side of the ring is marked with a 'T'. Always fit this side uppermost and carefully examine all rings for this mark before fitting.

34 Camshaft and camshaft bearings - examination and renovation

1 Carefully examine the camshaft bearings for wear. If the bearings are obviously worn or pitted or the metal underlay just showing through, then they must be renewed. This is an operation for your local BLMC garage or local engineering works as it demands the use of specialised equipment. The bearings are removed using a special drift after which the new bearings are pressed in, care being taken that the oil driving in the bearings line up with those in the block. With another special tool the bearings are then reamed in position.

2 The camshaft itself should show no sign of wear, but, if very slight scoring marks can be removed by gently rubbing down with very fine emery cloth or an oil stone. The greatest care must be taken to keep the cam profiles smooth.

35 Valves and seats - examination and renovation

1 Examine the heads of the valves for pitting or burning, especially the heads of the exhaust valves. The valve seatings should be examined at the same time. If the pitting on the valves is very slight the marks can be removed by grinding the seats and valves together with coarse, and then fine, valve grinding paste. Where bad pitting has occured to the valve seats it will be necessary to recut them and fit new valves. If the valve seats are so worn that they cannot be recut then it will be necessary to fit new valve seat inserts. These latter two jobs should be entrusted to a BLMC garage or engineering works. In practice it is very seldom that the seats are so badly worn that they require renewal. Normally it is the valve that is too badly worn, and you can easily purchase a new set of valves and match them to the seats by valve grinding.

2 Valve grinding is easily carried out. Place the cylinder head upside down on a bench with a block of wood at each end to give clearance for the valve stems. Alternatively place the head at 45o to a wall with the combustion chambers facing away from the wall.

3 Smear a trace of coarse carborundum paste on the seat face and apply a suction grinding tool to the valve head as shown in Fig.1.24. With a semi-rotary action, grind the valve head to its seat, lifting the valve occasionally to redistribute the grinding paste. When a dull matt even surface finish is produced on both the valve seat and the valve, then wipe off the paste and repeat the process with fine carborundum paste, lifting and turning the vlave to redistribute the paste as before. A light spring placed under the valve head will greatly ease this operation. When a smooth unbroken ring of light grey matt finish is produced, on both valve and valve seat faces, the grinding operation is complete.

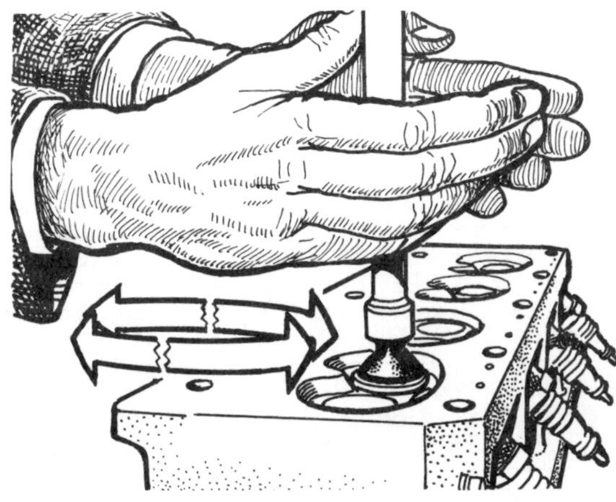

FIG.1.24. VALVE GRINDING USING HAND SUCTION TOOL. LIFT VALVE OFF SEAT OCCASIONALLY TO SPREAD GRINDING PASTE EVENLY OVER SEAT AND VALVE FACE

4 Scrape away all carbon from the valve head and the valve stem. Carefully clean away every trace of grinding compound, taking great care to leave none in the ports or in the valve guides. Clean the valves and valve seats with a paraffin soaked rag then wipe with clean rag. (If an air line is available blow clean).

36 Timing gear and chain - examination and renovation

1 Examine the teeth on both the crankshaft gear wheel and the camshaft gear wheel for wear. Each tooth forms an inverted 'V' with the gear wheel periphery and if worn, the side of each tooth under tension will be slightly concave in shape when compared with the other side of the tooth ie: one side of the inverted 'V' will be concave when compared with the other. If any sign of wear is present the gear wheels must be renewed.

2 Examine the links of the chain for side slackness and renew the chain if any slackness is noticeable when compared with a new chain. It is a sensible precaution to renew the chain every 30,000 miles (48,000 km) and at a lesser mileage if the engine is stripped down for a major overhaul. The actual rollers on a very badly worn chain may be slightly grooved.

37 Rocker and rocker shaft - examination and renovation

1 Remove the threaded plug with a screwdriver from the end of the rocker shaft and thoroughly clean out the shaft. As it acts as the oil passages for the valve gear, clean out these passages and make sure they are quite clear. Check the shaft for straightness by rolling it on a flat surface. It is most unlikely that it will deviate from normal, but, if it does, you must purchase a new shaft. The surface of the shaft should be free from any worn ridges caused by the rocker arms. If any wear is present, renew the rocker shaft. Wear is likely to have occured only if the rocker shaft oil holes have become blocked.

2 Check the rocker arms for wear of the rocker bushes, at the rocker arm face which bears on the valve stem, and of the adjusting ball ended screws. Wear in the rocker arm bush can be checked by gripping the rocker arm tip and holding the rockerarm in place on the shaft, noting if there is any lateral rocker arm shake. If any shake is present, and the arm is very loose on the shaft, remedial action must be taken. It is recommended that if a forged type of rocker arm is fitted it be taken to your local BLMC garage or engineering works to have the old bush drawn out and a new bush fitted. The correct placement of the bush shown in Fig.1.25.

If a pressed steel rocker arm is fitted, rebushing must not be undertaken but a new rocker arm obtained.

3 Check the tip of the rocker arm where it bears on the valve head, for cracking or serious wear on the case hardening. If none is present the rocker arm may be refitted, check the pushrods for straightness by rolling them on a flat surface. If bent they must be renewed.

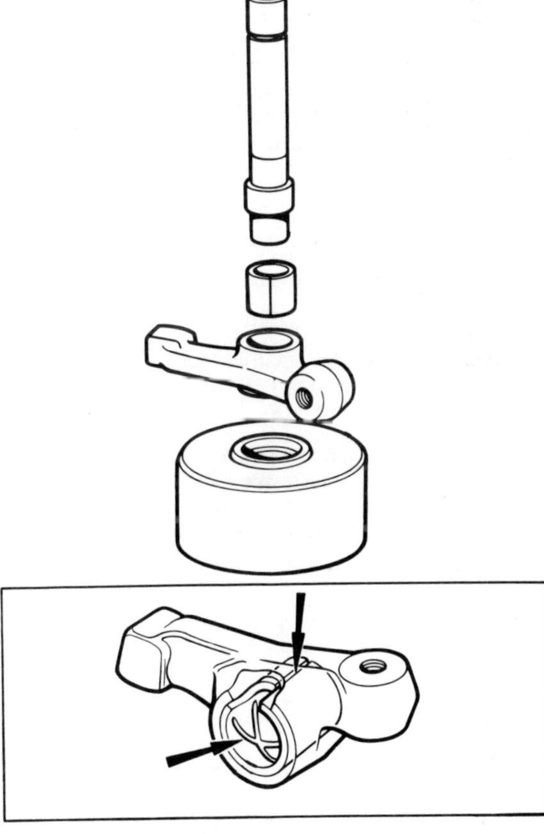

FIG.1.25. ROCKER BUSH REMOVAL AND CORRECT REPLACEMENT

38 Tappets - examination and renovation

Examine the bearing surface of the tappets which run on the camshaft. Any indentation in this surface or any cracks indicate serious wear and the tappets must be renewed. Thoroughly clean them out, removing all traces of sludge. It is most unlikely that the sides of the tappets will be worn, but if they are a loose fit in their bores and can be readily rocked, they should be discarded and new tappets fitted, It is unusual to find worn tappets, and any wear present is likely to occur through excessively high mileages.

39 Flywheel starter ring gear - examination and renovation

1 If the teeth on the flywheel starter ring gear are badly worn, or if some are missing, then it will be necessary to remove the ring. This is achieved by splitting the old ring using a cold chisel. Care must be taken not to damage the flywheel during this process.
2 To fit a new ring gear, it will be necessary to heat it gently and evenly with an oxy-acetyline flame until a temperature of approximately 350°C is reached. (This is indicated by a grey/brown surface colour). With the ring gear at this temperature, fit it to the flywheel with the front of the teeth facing the clutch fitting end of the flywheel. The ring gear should be either pressed or lightly tapped onto its register and left to cool naturally when the contraction of the metal on cooling will ensure that it is a secure and permanent fit. Great care must be taken not to overheat the ring gear, for if this happens the temperature of the ring gear will be lost.
3 An alternative method is to use a high temperature oven to heat the ring.
4 Because of the need of oxy-acetylene equipment or a special oven it is not practical for refitment to take place at home. Take the flywheel and new starter ring to an engineering works willing to do the job.

40 Oil pump - examination and renovation

1 Thoroughly clean all the component parts in petrol and then check the rotor end float and lobe clearances in the following manner:
2 Position the rotors in the pump and place the straight edge of a steel rule across the joint face of the pump. Measure the gap between the bottom of the straight edge and the top of the rotors with a feeler gauge as shown in Fig.1.26. If the measurement exceeds 0.005 inch (0.127mm) then check the lobe clearances as described in the following paragraph. If the lobe clearances are correct then remove the dowels from the joint face of the pump body and lap joint the inner face on a sheet of plate glass.
3 Measure the gaps between the peaks of the lobes and the peaks in the pump body with a feeler gauge, and if the gap exceeds 0.010 inch (0.254mm) then fit a replacement pump. This measurement is shown in Fig.1.26.

41 Cylinder head and bore - decarbonisation

1 This operation can be carried out with the engine either in or out of the car. With the cylinder head off, carefully remove with a wire brush and blunt, plastic scraper, all traces of carbon deposits from the combustion spaces and the ports. The valve stems and valve guides should also be freed from any carbon deposits. Wash the combustion spaces and posts down with petrol and scrape the cylinder head surface free of any foreign matter with the side of a steel rule or similar article. Take care not to scratch the surfaces.
2 Clean the pistons and top of the cylinder bores. If the pistons are still in the cylinder bores then it is essential that great care is taken to ensure that no carbon gets into the bores for this will scratch the cylinder walls or cause damage to the piston and rings. To stop it happening first turn the crankshaft so that two of the pistons are at TDC. Place a clean non-fluffy rag into the other two bores or seal them off with paper and masking tape. The waterways and pushrod holes should be covered with a small piece of masking tape to prevent particles of carbon entering the cooling system and damaging the water pump, or entering the lubrication system and causing damage to a bearing surface.
3 There are two schools of though as to how much carbon ought to be removed from the piston union. One is that a ring of carbon should be left around the edge of the piston and on the cylinder bore wall as an aid to keep oil consumption low. Although this is probably true for engines with worn bores, on fresh engines, however, the tendency is to remove all traces of carbon.
4 If all traces of carbon are to be removed, press a little grease into the gap between the cylinder walls and the two pistons which are to be worked upon. With a blunt scraper carefully scrape away all carbon from the piston crown, taking care not to scratch the aluminium. Also scrape away the carbon from the surrounding lip of the cylinder wall. When all carbon has been removed, scrape away the grease which will now be contaminated with carbon particles, taking care not to press any into the bores. To assist prevention of carbon build up the piston crown can be polished with a metal polish such as Brasso. Remove the rags or masking tape from the other two cylinders and turn the crankshaft so that the two pistons which were at the bottom are now at the top. Place non-fluffy rag into the other two bores or seal them off with paper and masking tape. Do not forget the water ways and oilways as well. Proceed as previously described.
5 If a ring of carbon is going to be left round the pistonthen this can be helped by inserting an old piston ring into the top of the bore to rest on the piston and ensure that carbon is not accidently removed. Check that there are no particles of carbon in the cylinder bores. Decarbonising is now complete.

42 Valve guides - examination and renovation

Examine the valve guides internally for wear. If the valves are a very loose fit in the guides and there is the slightest suspicion of lateral rocking, then new guides will have to be fitted, their correct location being shown in Fig.1.27. Try to compare them internally by visual inspection with a new guide as well.

43 Engine - reassembly -general

1 To ensure maximum life with minimum trouble from a rebuilt engine, not only must every part be correctly assembled but everything must be spotlessly clean, all the oilways must be clear, locking washers and spring washers must always be fitted where needed and all bearings and other working surfaces must be thoroughly lubricated during assembly. Before assembly begins renew any bolts or studs the threads of which are in any way damaged, and whenever possible use new spring washers.
2 Apart from your normal tools, a supply of non fluffy rag, an oil can filled with engine oil (an empty washing up liquid plastic bottle thoroughly cleaned and washed out, will do), a supply of new spring washers, a set of new gaskets and a torque wrench should be collected together

44 Crankshaft - replacement

Ensure that the crankcase is thoroughly clean and that all the oilways are clear. A thin twist drill is useful for cleaning them out. If possible blow them out with compressed air. Treat the crankshaft in the same fashion and then inject engine oil into the crankshaft oilways.

Commence work on rebuilding the engine by replacing the crankshaft and main bearings.

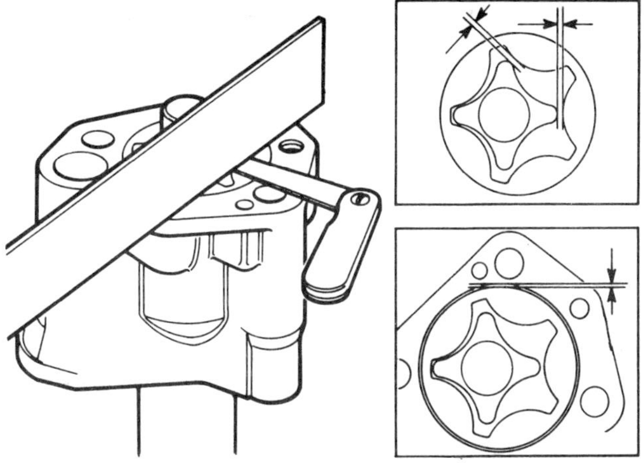

FIG.1.26. OIL PUMP WEAR CHECK

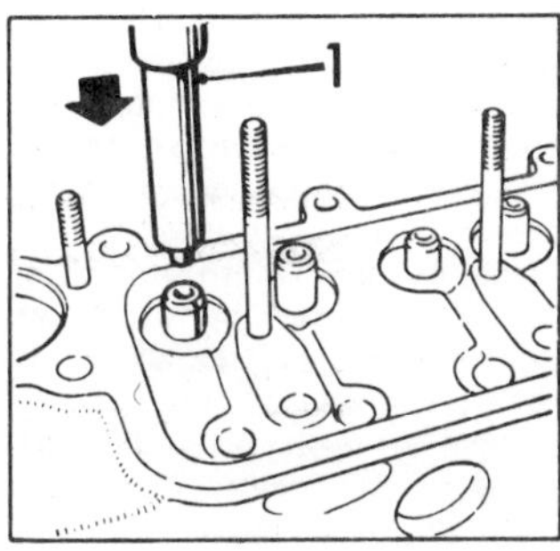

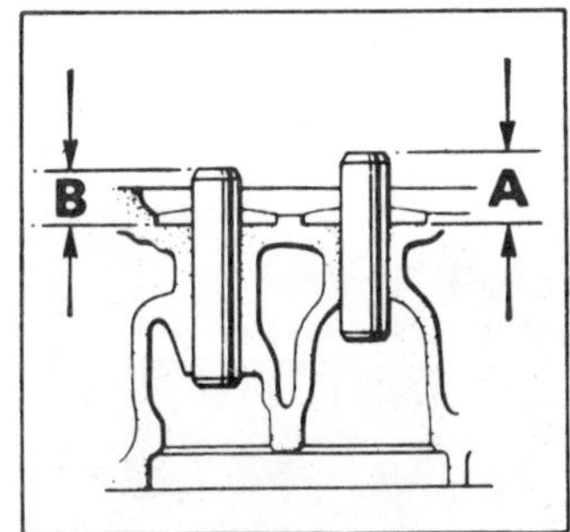

FIG.1.27. CORRECT FITTING DIMENSIONS OF VALVE GUIDE ABOVE MACHINED FACE OF VALVE SPRING SEAT

1 Shaped drift. A 0.75 in. (19.05mm) B 0.625 in. (15.87mm)

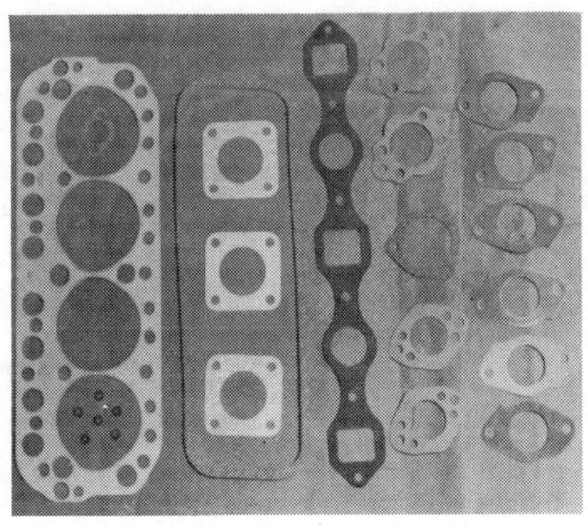

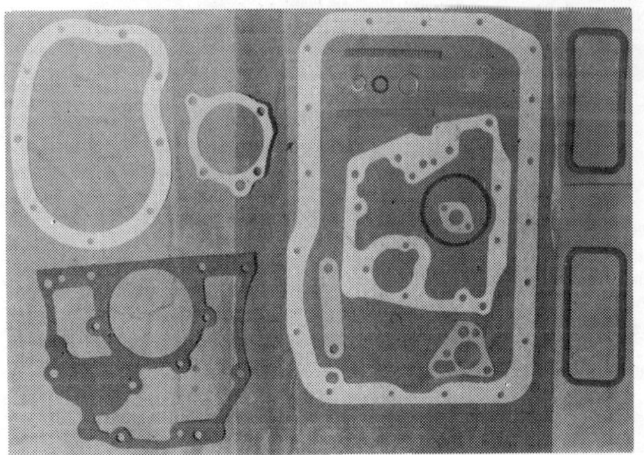

FIG.1.28. GASKET SETS

Left – cylinder head and manifolds *Right – sump and cylinder block*

1 Fit the five upper halves of the main bearing shells to their location in the crankcase, after wiping the location clean.
2 Note that on the back of each bearing is a tab which engages in locating grooves in either the crankcase or the main bearing cap housings (Fig.1.17).
3 If new bearings are being fitted, carefully clean away all traces of the protective grease with which they are coated.
4 With the five upper bearing shells securely in place, wipe the lower bearing cap housings and fit the five lower shell bearings to their caps ensuring that the right shell goes into the right cap if the old bearings are being refitted.
5 Wipe the recesses either side of the centre main bearing which locate the upper halves of the thrust washers.
6 Generously lubricate the crankshaft journals and the upper and lower main bearing shells and carefully lower the crankshaft into position. Make sure that it is the right way round.
7 Introduce the upper halves of the thrust washers (the halves without tabs) into their grooves either side of the centre main bearing, rotating the crankshaft in the direction towards the main bearing tab (so that the main bearing shells do not slide out). At the same time feed the thrust washers into the locations with their oil grooves outwards away from the bearing.
8 Fit the main bearing caps in position ensuring that they locate properly. The mating surfaces must be spotlessly clean or the caps will not seat correctly.
9 When replacing the centre main bearing cap ensure that the thrust washers, generously lubricated, are fitted with their oil grooves faing outwards and the locating tab of each washer is in the slot in the bearing cap

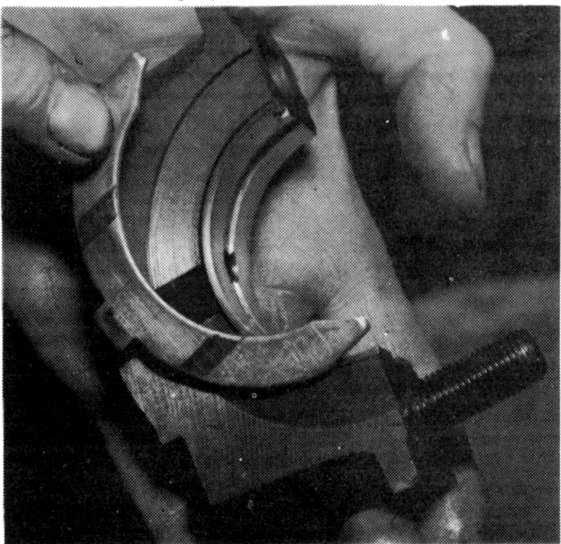

FIG.1.29. CRANKSHAFT THRUST WASHER FITMENT

10 Replace the main bearing cap nuts and screw them up finger tight.
11 Test the crankshaft for freedom of rotation. Should it be very stiff to turn or possess high spots a most careful inspection must be made, preferably by a skilled mechanic with a micrometer to trace the cause of the trouble. It is very seldom that any trouble of this nature will be experienced when fitted the crankshaft.
12 Tighten the main bearing nuts using a torque wrench set to 70 lb ft (9.7kg m) and recheck the crankshaft or freedom of rotation.
13 Using a screwdriver between one crankshaft web and main bearing cap lever the crankshaft forwards and check the end float using feeler gauges. This should be 0.002 - 0.003 inch (0.051 - 0.076mm). If excessive new thrust washers or slightly undersize ones must be fitted.
14 During removal of the crankshaft gear wheel it should have been noted that there were shims behind the gear wheel. Replace the shims and then the inner Woodruff key.

45 Piston and connecting rod - reassembly

If the same pistons are being used, then they must be mated to the same connecting rod with the same gudgeon pin. If new pistons are being fitted it does not matter which connecting rod are used with, but the gudgeon pins are not to be interchanged. See paragraph 8 for fully floating types. As the gudgeon pin is a press fit a special BLMC tool 18G 1150 with adaptors 18G 1150C is required to fit the gudgeon pin as shown in Fig.1.30 and should be used as follows:
1 Unscrew the large nut and withdraw the centre screw from the body a few inches. Well lubricate the screw thread and correctly locate the piston support adaptor.
2 Carefully slide the parallel sleeve with the groove end last onto the centre screw up as far as the shoulder. Lubricate the gudgeon pin and its bores in the connecting rod and piston with a graphited oil.
3 Fit the connecting rod and piston, side marked 'Front' or 'A' to the tool with the connecting rod entered on the sleeve up the the groove. Fit the gudgeon pin into the piston bore up to the connecting rod. Next fit the remover/replacer bush flange end towards the gudgeon pin.
4 Screw the stop nut onto the centre screw and adjust the nut to give a 0.032 inch (0.8mm) end play. 'B' as shown in Fig.1.30. Lock the nut securely with the lock screw. Ensure that the curved face of the adaptor is clean and slide the piston on the tool so that it fits into the curved face of the adaptor with the piston rings over the adaptor cut away.
5 Screw the large nut up the thrust race. Adjust the torque wrench to a setting of 16 lb ft (2.2kg m) if of the 'click' type which will represent the minimum load for an acceptable fit. Use the torque wrench previously set on the large nut, and a ring spanner on the lock screw. Pull the gudgeon pin into the piston until the flange of the remover/replacer bush is 0.032 inch (0.8mm) from the piston skirt. It is critically important that the flange is NOT allowed to contact the piston. Finally withdraw the BLMC service tool.
6 Should the torque wrench not 'click' or reach 16 lb ft (2.2kg m) throughout the pull, the fit of the gudgeon pin in the connecting rod is not within limits; the parts must be renewed.
7 Ensure that the piston pivots freely on the gudgeon pin and is free to slide sideways. Should stiffness exist wash the assembly in paraffin, lubricate the gudgeon pin with graphited oil and recheck. Again if stiffness exists dismantle the assembly and check for signs of ingrained dirt or damage.
8 On early type fully floating gudgeon pins make sure the little end bush in the connecting rod is lined up through the oilway orifice. Then heat the piston in boiling water and push the gudgeon pin through the piston, little end bush and out into the other side of the piston. Use circlip pliers to fit in the circlips at each end of the gudgeon pin. Be gentle at all times — use no force. See Fig.1.31.

46 Piston ring - replacement

1 Check that the piston ring grooves and oilways are thoroughly clean and blocked piston rings must always be fitted over the head of the piston and never from the bottom Fig.1.32.
2 Refitment is the exacting opposite procedure to removal, see Section 21.
3 Set all ring gaps 90° to each other.
4 An alternative method is to fit the rings by holding them slightly open with the thumbs and both your index fingers. This method requires a steady hand and great care for it is easy to open the ring too much and break it.
5 The special oil control ring requires a special fitting procedure. First fit the bottom rail of the oil control ring to the piston and position it below the bottom groove. Refit the oil control expander into the bottom groove and move the bottom oil control ring rail up into the bottom groove. Fit the top oil control rail into the bottom groove.
6 Inspect the ends of the expander are butting out overlapping as shown in the inset (A) in Fig.1.32.

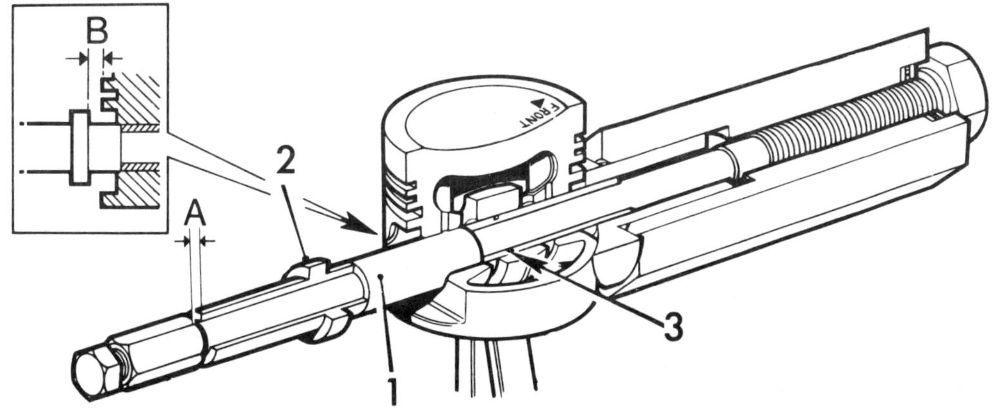

FIG.1.30. GUDGEON PIN REFITTING USING BLMC SERVICE TOOL 18G 1150 AND ADAPTORS 1150C

1 Gudgeon pin 2 Place flange towards gudgeon pin remover/replacer bush 3 Groove in sleeve towards gudgeon pin
A 0.032 in. (8 mm)
B 0.04 in. (1 mm)

FIG.1.31. GUDGEON PIN AND LITTLE END BUSH ASSEMBLY (FULLY FLOATING TYPE)

1 Gudgeon pin 2 Little end bush 3 Circlip

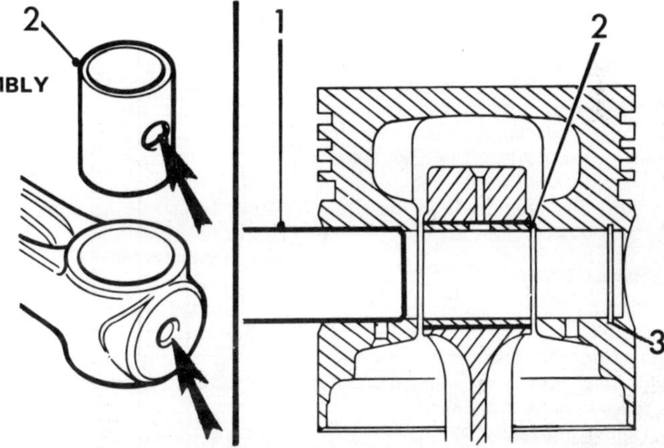

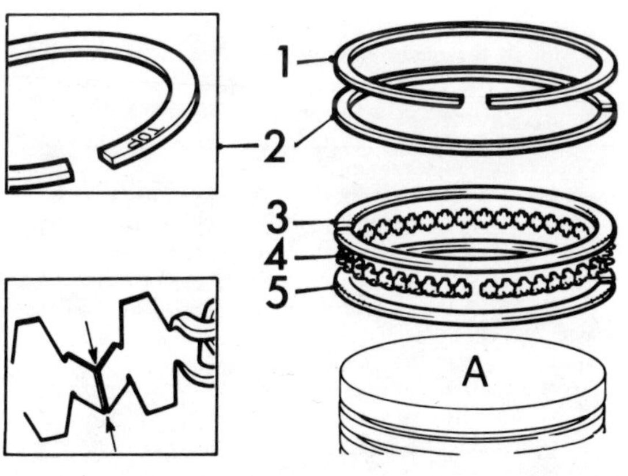

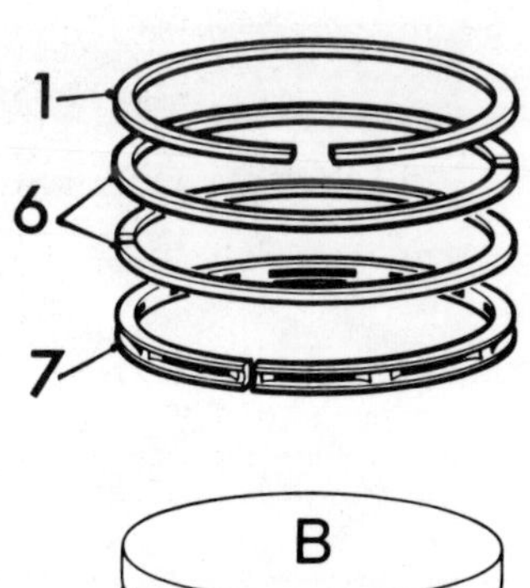

FIG.1.32. PISTON RING ASSEMBLIES

A Pressed fit gudgeon pin
B Fully floating gudgeon pin
1 Plain compression ring
2 Tapered compression ring
3 Top oil control ring rail
4 Oil control expander
5 Bottom oil control ring rail
6 Internal stepped compression ring
7 Plain oil control ring

47 Piston - replacement

Fit pistons complete with connecting rods, to the cylinder bores as follows:

1 Wipe the cylinder bores clean with clean non fluffy rag.

2 The pistons, complete with connecting rods, must be fitted to their bores from above. As each piston is inserted into the bore ensure that it is the correct piston/connecting rod assembly for that particular bore and that the front of the piston is towards the front of the bore assuming that the connecting rod is fitted correctly ie., towards the front of the engine. Lubricate the piston well with clean engine oil.

3 Check that the piston ring gaps are 90^{0} to each other.

4 The piston will slide into the bore only as far as the oil control ring and then it will be necessary to compress the piston rings into a clamp. The piston ring compressor should be fitted to the piston before it is inserted into the bore. If a proper piston ring clamp is not available then a suitable jubilee clip will do. Guide the piston into the bore until it reaches the ring compressor (Fig.1.33). Gently tap the piston into the cylinder bore with a wooden or plastic hammer.

48 Connecting rod to crankshaft - reassembly

1 Wipe the connecting rod half of the big end bearing location and the underside of the shell bearing clean, (as for the main bearing shells) and fit the shell bearing in position with its locating torque engaged with the corresponding groove in the connecting rod. Always fit new shells.

2 Generously lubricate the crankpin journals with engine oil and turn the crankshaft so that the crankpin is in the most advantageous position for the connecting rod to be drawn onto it.

3 Fit the bearing shell to the connecting rod cap in the same way as with the connecting rod itself.

4 Generously lubricate the shell bearing and offer up the connecting rod bearing cap to the connecting rod. Fit the connecting rod cap retaining nuts. It will be observed that these are special twelve sided nuts.

5 Tighten the retaining nuts to a torque wrench setting of 33 lb ft (4.6 kg m).

49 Camshaft - replacement

1 Fit the engine front plate with a new gasket between the cylinder block and plate and tighten the retaining bolts and spring washers.

2 Wipe the camshaft bearings and generously lubricate them with engine oil.

3 Temporarily refit the camshaft gear wheel and locating plate and secure with the retaining nut. Using feeler gauges check the end float which should not exceed 0.003 to 0.007 inch (0.07 - 0.18mm). If this maximum limit is exceeded obtain a new locating plate.

4 Remove the camshaft gear wheel retaining nut, gear wheel and locating plate.

5 Insert the camshaft into the crankcase gently, taking care not to damage the camshaft bearings with the sharp edges of the cams. Take care, the camshaft lobe edges are sharp.

50 Oil pump and drive shaft - replacement

Invert the cylinder block and insert the oil pump drive shaft and its thrust washer (if fitted), the latter being placed on the oil pump side of the gear teeth. Fit a new oil pump to crankcase gasket over the three studs followed by the oil pump. Ensure that the shaft dog correctly engages with the drive gear dog. Fit spring washers on the studs followed by the three nuts. Tighten to a torque wrench setting of 15 lb ft (1.9kg m).

51 Timing gears, chain tensioner, cover - replacement

1 Before reassembly begins check that the shim washers are in place on the crankshaft nose. If new gear wheels are being fitted it may be necessary to fit additional washers as detailed in paragraph 7. These washers ensure that the crankshaft gearwheel lines up correctly with the camshaft gearwheel (Fig.1.34).

2 Replace the woodruff keys in their respective slots in the crankshaft and camshaft and ensure that they are fully seated. If their edges are burred they must be cleaned with a fine file.

3 Lay the camshaft gearwheels on a clean surface so that the two timing dots are adjacent to each other. Slip the timing chain over them and pull the gearwheels back into mesh with the chain so that the timing dots, although further apart, are still adjacent to each other as shown in Fig.1.35.

FIG.1.33. PISTON FITMENT WITH CLAMP

FIG.1.34. SHIM WASHERS ON CRANKSHAFT

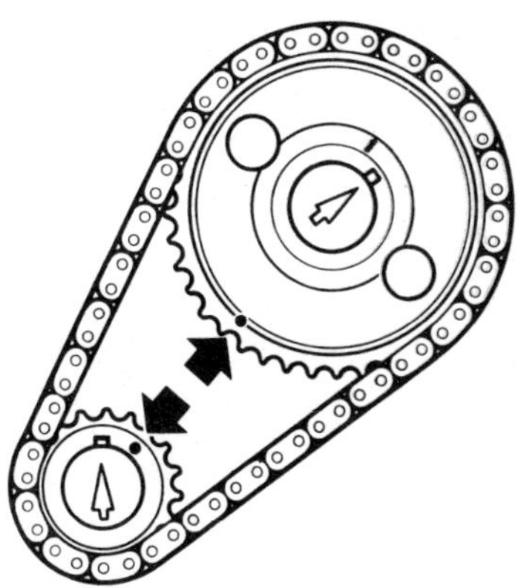

FIG.1.35. TIMING GEAR MARKS

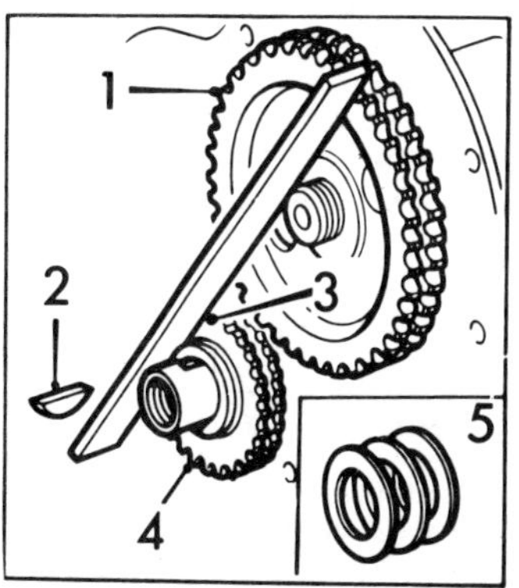

FIG.1.36. TIMING GEAR ALIGNMENT

1 Camshaft gear
2 Woodruff key
3 Straight edge
4 Crankshaft gear
5 Inset: Shims

4 Rotate the crankshaft so that the woodruff key is at top dead centre. The engine should be in the upright position.
5 Rotate the camshaft so that when viewed from the front the woodruff key is at one o'clock position.
6 Fit the timing chain and gearwheel assembly onto the camshaft and crankshaft keeping the timing marks adjacent. If the camshaft and crankshaft have been positioned accurately, it will be found that the keyways on the gearwheels will match the position of the keys, although it may be necessary to rotate the camshaft a fraction to ensure accurate lining up of the camshaft gear wheel.
7 Press the gearwheels into position on the crankshaft and camshaft as far as they will go. NOTE: If new gearwheels are being fitted they should be checked for alignment before being finally fitted to the engine. Place the gearwheels in position without the timing chain and place the straight edge of a steel rule from the side of the camshaft gear teeth to the crankshaft gearwheel and measure the gap between the steel rule and the gearwheel. Subtract 0.005 (0.127mm) from the feeler gauge reading and add the resultant thickness of crankshaft gear packing washers (Fig.1.36).
8 Next assemble the timing chain tensioner by inserting one end of the spring into the plunger and fit the other end of the spring into the cylinder.
9 Compress the spring until the cylinder enters the plunger bore and ensure the peg in the plunger engages the helical slot. Insert and turn the Allen key clockwise until the end of the cylinder is below the peg and the spring is held compressed.
10 Fit the backplate and secure the assembly to the cylinder block with the two bolts. Turn the tabs of the lockwasher shown in Fig.1.10.
11 With the timing chain in position, the tensioner can now be relaxed. Insert the Allen key and turn it clockwise so the sliper head moves forward under spring pressure against the chain. Do not under any circumstances turn the key anti-clockwise or force the slipper head into the chain. Replace the bottom plug and lock with a tab washer.
12 Replace the oil thrower so that the letter 'F' is on its front face ie., this face must be furthest from the engine.
13 Fit the locking washer to the camshaft gearwheel with its locating tab in the gearwheel keyway is shown.
14 Screw on the camshaft gearwheel retaining nut and tighten securely.
15 Bend up the locking tab of the locking washer to securely hold the camshaft retaining nut.
16 Generously oil the chain and gearwheels.
17 Ensure the interior of the timing cover and the timing cover flange is clean and generously lubricate the oil seal in the timing cover. Then with a new gasket in position, fit the timing cover to the block using the pulley to centralise the cover.
18 Screw in the timing cover retaining bolts with the flat washer next to the cover flange and under the spring washer. The ¼ inch bolts should be tightened with a torque spanner to 6 lb ft (0.83kg m) and the 5/16 inch bolts to 14 lb ft (1.94kg m).
19 Fit the crankshaft pulley to the nose of the crankshaft ensuring that the keyway engages with the woodruff key.
20 Fit the crankshaft retaining bolt locking washer in position and screw on the crankshaft pulley retaining nut. Tighten to a torque of 70 lb ft (9.69kg m) and bend over the locking washer.

52 Engine backplate - refitting

1 Wipe the rear face of the cylinder block and smear a little grease onto a new gasket. Carefully fit the gasket to the cylinder block.
2 Carefully refit the backplate, locating the dowel at the top of the cylinder block in the centre hole at the top of the backplate and the second dowel at the bottom left hand side of the cylinder block.
3 Refit the backplate to the cylinder block securing bolts and spring washers and tighten fully.

53 Sump refitting

1 After the sump has been thoroughly cleaned, scrape all traces of the old sump gasket from the sump flange, and fit new main bearing cap oil seals. Should the oil seal material stand out more than 1/16 inch (1.587mm) above the sump flange it must be cut back to this figure.
2 Thoroughly clean and scrape the crankshaft to sump flange. Apply grease to the crankcase to sump flange and carefully fit new gasket halves to the flange.
3 Carefully fit the sump to the underside of the crankcase.
4 Refit the sump retaining bolts, shaped washers and spring washers.
5 Tighten the sump bolts to a torque wrench setting of 6 lb ft (0.8kg m).

54 Oil pressure relief valve and switch - replacement

1 Assemble the valve components in the order of, valve, spring and domed nut with new washers.
2 Carefully insert the assembly into its location at the rear of the cylinder block. Tighten the domed nut fully.
3 Locate the oil pressure switch in its drilling in the side of the cylinder block just above the oil pressure relief valve and tighten firmly using an open ended spanner (photo).

55 Flywheel and clutch - refitting

1 Clean the mating faces of the crankshaft and flywheel and fit the flywheel to the dowel in the end of the crankshaft flange.
2 Replace the six flywheel securing bolts and circular washer and tighten these bolts to a torque wrench setting of 40 lb ft (5.5kg m). It will be necessary to lock the flywheel using a screwdriver through the sump bracket and the end engaged in the starter ring teeth.
3 Bend up the lockwasher tabs.
4 Refit the clutch disc and pressure plate assembly and lightly secure the position with the six bolts and spring washers (photo).
5 If a first motion shaft is available use this to line up the clutch disc with the crankshaft spigot bearing. As an alternative use a suitable piece of wood as a dowel (photo).
6 Firmly tighten the clutch securing bolts in a diagonal manner (photo). The flywheel may be locked using the screwdriver as described in paragraph 2.

56 Water and fuel pump - refitting

1 Make sure the mating faces of the water pump and cylinder block are free of old gasket or jointing compound.
2 Smear a little grease onto the water pump and place on a new gasket.
3 Fit the water pump to the cylinder block mating it to the dowels in the cylinder block face.
4 Refit and tighten the securing bolts and spring washers.
5 Clean the mating faces of the crankcase and fuel pump and fit a new set of gasket to the spacer. Slide the spacer and gaskets over the studs.
6 Refit the fuel pump and secure with the two nuts and spring washers.

57 Valve and spring - reassembly

To refit the valves and the valve springs to the cylinder head, proceed as follows:
1 Rest the cylinder head on its side, or if the manifold studs are fitted, with the gasket surface downwards.
2 Fit each valve and valve spring in turn, wiping down and lubricating each valve stem as it is inserted onto the same valve guide from which it was removed.
3 As each valve is inserted slip the oil control rubber ring into place just under the bottom of the cotter groove (use a new rubber ring if at all possible).
4 Move the cylinder head towards the edge of the work bench if it is facing downwards and slide it partially over the edge of the bench so as to fit the bottom half of the valve spring compressor to the valve head.
5 Slip the valve springs and cap over the valve stem.
6 With the base of the valve compressor on the valve head, compress the valve spring until the cotters can be sliped into place in the cotter grooves. Gently release the compressor,
7 Repeat this procedure until all eight valves and valve springs are fitted.

54.3 Oil pressure switch

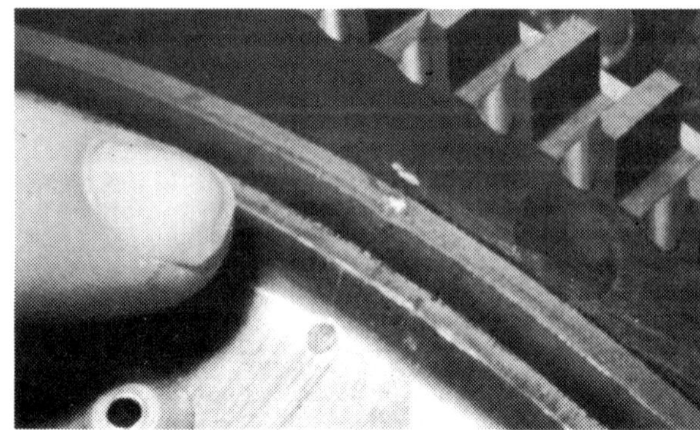
55.4 Clutch mating marks

55.5 Clutch disc centralisation

55.6 Tightening clutch securing bolts

58 Rocker shaft - reassembly

1 To reassemble the rocker shaft fit the split pin, flat washer, and spring washer at the rear end of the shaft and then slide on the rocker arms, rocker shaft pedestals, and spacing springs in the same order in which they were removed (Fig.1.8), and slip the locating plate into place. Finally, fit the front of the shaft the spring washer, plain washer and split pin, in that order.

59 Tappet and pushrod - replacement

Generously lubricate the tappets internally and externally and insert them in the bores from which they were removed through the tappet chest.

With the cylinder head in position fit the pushrods in the same order in which they were removed. Ensure that they locate properly in the stems of the tappets, and lubricate the pushrod ends before fitment. Refit the two tappet covers with new cork gaskets and tighten the bolts using a torque wrench set of 2 lb ft.

60 Cylinder head - replacement

1 After checking that both the cylinder block and cylinder head mating faces are perfectly clean, generously lubricate each cylinder with engine oil.

Always use a new cylinder head gasket. The old gasket will be compressed and incapable of giving a good seal.

2 Never smear grease on gasket cement either side of the gasket, for pressure leaks may blow through it.

3 The cylinder head gasket is marked FRONT and should be fitted in position according to the markings. The coper side will be upermost (photo).

4 Carefully lower the gasket into position ensuring that the stud threads do not damage the side of the holes through which they pass (photo).

5 The cylinder head may now be lowered over the studs until it rests on the cylinder head gasket (photo).

6 With the cylinder head in position fit the pushrods in the same order in which they were removed. Ensure that they locate properly in the stems of the tappets.

7 Refit the two tappet covers with new cork gaskets and tighten the two securing bolts and washers.

8 The rocker shaft assembly can now be lowered over its eight locating studs. Take care that the rocker arms are the right way round (photo). Lubricate the ball joints, and insert the rocker arm ball joints into the pushrod cups. NOTE: Failure to replace the ball joints in the cups can result in the ball joints seating on the edge of a pushrod or outside it when the head and rocker assembly is pulled down tight.

9 Fit the lock plate to the second pedestal.

10 Fit the four rocker pedestal nuts and washers, and then the four cylinder heads stud nuts and washers which also hold down the rocker pedestals. Pull the nuts down evenly, but without tightening them right up.

11 Fit the remaining nuts and washers to the cylinder head studs.

12 When all are in position tighten the rocker pedestal nuts to a torque wrench setting of 25 lb ft (3.4 kg m) and the cylinder head nuts to a torque wrench setting of 45 - 50 lb ft (6.2 - 6.9 kg m). The correct order is shown in Fig.1.6.

61 Rocker arm/valve - adjustment

1 The valve adjustments should be made with the engine cold. The importance of correct rocker/valve stem clearances cannot be overstressed as they vitally affect the performance.

2 If the clearances are set too wide, the efficiency of the engine is reduced as the valves open late and close earlier then was intended. If the clearances are set too close there is a danger that

60.3 Cylinder head gasket fitting position

60.4 Fitting new cylinder head gasket

60.5 Lowering cylinder head into position

60.12 Tightening cylinder head securing bolts

the stem and pushrods upon expansion when home will not allow the valves to close properly which will cause burning of the valve head and possible warping.

3 If the engine is in the car, to get at the rockers, it is merely necessary to remove the two holding down dome nuts from the cover, and then to lift the rocker cover and gasket away.

4 It is important that the clearance is set when the tappet of the valve being adjusted is on the heel of the cam (ie. opposite the peak). This can be done by carrying out the adjustments in the following order, which also avoids turning the crankshaft more than necessary.

Valve fully open	Check and adjust
Valve Number 8	Valve number 1
Valve Number 6	Valve number 3
Valve Number 4	Valve number 5
Valve Number 7	Valve number 2
Valve Number 1	Valve number 8
Valve Number 3	Valve number 6
Valve Number 5	Valve number 4
Valve Number 2	Valve number 7

5 The correct valve clearance is given in the Specifications at the beginning of this chapter. It is obtained by slackening the hexagonal locknut with a spanner while holding the ball pin against rotation with a screwdriver as shown in Fig.1.37. Then, still pressing down with the screwdriver, insert feeler gauge of the required thickness between the valve stem and head and the rocker arm and adjust the ball pin until the feeler gauge will just move in and out without nipping. Then still holding the ball pin in the correct position, tighten the locknut (photo).

6 An alternative method is to set the gaps with the engine running at idle speed. Although this method may be faster, more practice is needed and it is no more reliable.

7 Refit the rocker cover and gasket, and secure with the dome nuts and washers.

62 Distributor and distributor drive - replacement

It is important to set the distributor drive correctly otherwise the ignition timing will be totally incorrect. It is easy to set the distributor drive in apparently the right position, but in fact exactly 180° out, by omitting to select the correct cylinder which must not only be at TDC but must also be on its firing stroke with both valves closed. The distributor drive should therefore not be fitted until the cylinder head is in position and the valves can be observed. Alternatively, if the timing cover has not been replaced, the distributor drive can be replaced when the dots on the timing wheels are adjacent to each other.

1 The distributor drive shaft can only be fitted with the pistons half way up or down their bores. Turn the crankshaft so that the pistons are in this position (90° before or after TDC).

2 Screw a 5/16 inch UNF bolt about 3½ inches (90mm) long into the threaded hole in the top end of the shaft and fit the shaft to the engine.

3 Rotate the crankshaft so that No. 1 piston is at TDC and on its firing stroke (the dots in the timing gears will be adjacent to each other). When No 1 piston is at TDC the inlet valve on No 4 cylinder is just opening and the exhaust valve closing (photo).

4 With the pistons in the engine at TDC it will not be possible to remove the drive shaft, but it is possible to lift it sufficiently to bring it out of mesh with the drive gear on the camshaft. The drive shaft can then be turned to the correct timing position.

5 When the groove on the crankshaft pulley wheel is in line with the TDC pointer on the timing gear cover, then No 1 and No 4 piston are at TDC 'check that the No 4 cylinder valves are just rocking to ensure correct stroke for No1 cylinder.

6 Position the drive shaft so that the slot is just below the horizontal, and the larger of the two segments (one on each side of the slot) is at the top. As the gear on the shaft engages with the skew gear on the camshaft the drive gear will turn anti-clockwise until the top of the slot is adjacent to the 2 o'clock position. See Fig.1.12.

61.5A Adjustment of rocker arm/valve clearance

61.5B Checking clearance with feeler gauge

62.3 Timing marks on pulley and cover

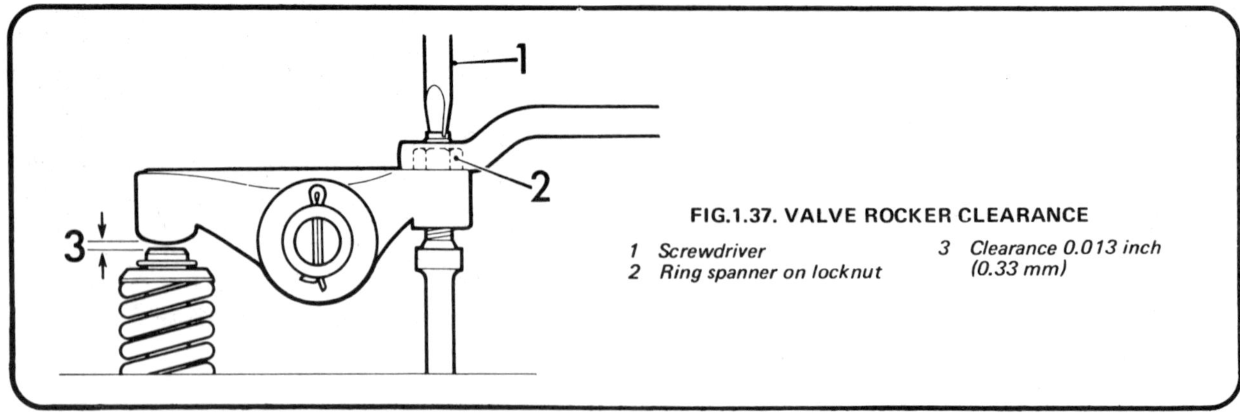

FIG.1.37. VALVE ROCKER CLEARANCE

1 Screwdriver
2 Ring spanner on locknut
3 Clearance 0.013 inch (0.33 mm)

7 Remove the bolt from the drive shaft.
8 Replace the distributor housing and lock it in position with the single bolt and spring washer. It is important that the correct bolt is used so that the head does not protrude above the face of the housing.
9 The distributor can now be replaced and the two securing bolts and spring washers which hold the distributor clamping plate to the distributor housing tightened. If the clamp bolt on the clamping plate was not previously loosened and the distributor body was not turned in the clamping plate, then the ignition timing will be as previously set. If the clamping bolt has been loosened, then it will be necessary to retime the ignition as described in Chapter 4.

63 Final assembly

1 Refit the rocker cover, using a new cork gasket and secure in position with the two domed nuts.
2 Fit the two tappet cover plates, using new gaskets and tighten the tappet chest bolts to a torque wrench setting of 2 lb ft (0.3kg m). Do not exceed this figure or the covers will distort and leak oil.
3 Fit a new manifold gasket over the studs taking care not to rip it as it passes over the stud threads.
4 Replace the manifold and secure in position with the six nuts, spring and large plain washers.
5 Insert the thermostat into its housing making sure the word 'FRONT' marked on the flange is towards the front of the engine.
6 Fit a new gasket taking care not to rip the gasket as it passes over the threads of the three studs. Then refit the thermostat housing cover and secure with the three nuts and spring washers.
7 If the dip stick guide tube was removed this should next be inserted into its drilling in the side of the crankcase.
8 Fit a new oil filter canister (see Section 25).
9 It should be noted that in all cases it is best to reassemble the engine as far as possible before refitting it to the car. This means that alternator, fan belt and other minor attachments should be replaced at this stage.

64 Engine replacement

Although the engine or engine and gearbox can be replaced by one man and a suitable hoist, it is easier if two are present. Generally replacement is the reverse sequence to removal. In addition however:
1 Ensure all the loose leads, cables etc., are tucked out of the way. It is easy to trap one and cause much additional work after the engine is replaced.
2 Refit the following:

a) Mounting nuts, bolts and washers.
b) Propeller shaft coupling.
c) Reconnect the clutch pipe to the slave cylinder and bleed the system (see Chapter 5).
d) Speedometer cable.
e) Gear change lever and surround.
f) Carpets.
g) Oil pressure switch cable.
h) Water temperature indicator sender unit cable.
i) Wire to coil, distributor and alternator.
j) Carburettor controls and air cleaner.
k) Exhaust manifold to down pipe.
l) Earth and starter motor cables.
m) Radiator and hoses.
n) Heater hoses.
o) Engine closed circuit breather hoses.
p) Vacuum advance and retard pipe.
q) Battery (if removed).
r) Fuel lines to carburettor(s) and pump.
s) Bonnet.

3 Finally check that the drain taps are closed and refill the cooling system with water and the engine with Castrol GTX.

65 Engine - initial start up after overhaul and major repair

Make sure that the battery is fully charged and that all lubricants, coolants and fuel are replenished.

If the fuel system has been dismantled, it will require several revolutions of the engine on the starter motor to pump petrol to the carburettor(s). An initial 'prime' of about 1/3 cupfull of petrol down the air intake(s) or the carburettor(s) will help the engine to fire quickly, thus relieving the load on the battery. Do not overdo this however, as flooding may result.

As soon as the engine fires and runs, keep it going at a fast tickover only (no faster) and bring it up to normal working temperatures.

As the engine warms up, there will be odd smells and some smoke from parts getting hot and burning off oil deposits. Look for water or oil which will be obvious if serious. Check also the clamp connection of the exhaust pipe to the manifold as these do not always 'find' their exact gas tight position until the warmth and vibration have acted on them, and it is almost certain that they will need tighening further. This should be done of course, with the engine

When the engine running temperature has been reached, adjust the idling speed as described in Chapter 3.

Stop the engine and wait a few minutes to see if any lubricant or coolant drips out.

Road test the car to check that the timing is correct and giving the necessary smoothness and power. Do not race the engine. If new bearings and/or pistons and rings have been fitted, it should be treated as a new engine and run in at reduced revolutions for 500 miles (800 km).

Symptom	Reason/s	Remedy
Engine will not turn over when starter switch is operated	Flat battery Bad battery connections Bad connections at solenoid switch and/or starter motor	Check that battery is fully charged and that all connections are clean and tight.
	Starter motor jammed	Rock car back and forth with a gear engaged. If ineffective remove starter (not automatic).
	Defective solenoid	Remove and check solenoid.
	Starter motor defective	Remove starter and overhaul.
Engine turns over normally but fails to fire and run	No spark at plugs	Check ignition system according to procedures given in Chapter 4.
	No fuel reaching engine	Check fuel system according to procedures given in Chapter 3.
	Too much fuel reaching the engine (flooding)	Check fuel system if necessary as described in Chapter 3.
Engine starts but runs unevenly and misfires	Ignition and/or fuel system faults	Check the ignition and fuel systems as though the engine had failed to start.
	Incorrect valve clearances	Check and reset clearances.
	Burnt out valves	Remove cylinder head and examine and overhaul as necessary.
Lack of power	Ignition and/or fuel system faults	Check the ignition and fuel systems for correct ignition timing and carburettor settings.
	Incorrect valve clearances	Check and reset the clearances.
	Burnt out valves	Remove cylinder head and examine and overhaul as necessary.
	Worn out piston or cylinder bores	Remove cylinder head and examine pistons and cylinder bores. Overhaul as necessary.
Excessive oil consumption	Oil leaks from crankshaft oil seal, rocker cover gasket, drain plug gasket, sump plug washer	Identify source of leak and repair as appropriate.
	Worn piston rings or cylinder bores resulting in oil being burnt by engine Smoky exhaust is an indication	Fit new rings or rebore cylinders and fit new pistons, depending on degree of wear.
	Worn valve guides and/or defective valve stem seals	Remove cylinder head and recondition valve guides and valves and seals as necessary.
Excessive mechanical noise from engine	Wrong valve to rocker clearances	Adjust valve clearances.
	Worn crankshaft bearings Worn cylinders (piston slap)	Inspect and overhaul where necessary.
Unusual vibration	Misfiring on one or more cylinders	Check ignition system.
	Loose mounting bolts	Check tightness of bolts and condition of flexible mountings.

NOTE: When investigating starting and uneven running faults do not be tempted into snap diagnosis. Start from the beginning of the check procedure and follow it through. It will take less time in the long run. Poor performance from an engine in terms of power and economy is not normally diagnosed quickly. In any event the ignition and fuel systems must be checked first before assuming any further investigation needs to be made.

Chapter 2 Cooling system

Contents

Specifications

Type	Pressurised system with expansion tank	
Thermostat type	Wax	
Thermostat settings: Standard	82º C (180º F)	
Hot climate	74º C (165º F)	
Cold climate	88º C (190º F)	
Blow off pressure of expansion tank cap	15 lb in^2 (1.05 kg cm^2)	
Fan belt tension	0.5 in (13mm) deflection on longest run.	
Water pump	Centrifugal type	
Bearing spindle diameter	0.6262 - 0.6267 in (15.901 - 15.918mm)	
Impeller bore	0.6244 - 0.6252 in (15.860 - 15.880mm)	
Pulley hub bore	0.6239 - 0.6247 in (15.847 - 15.867mm)	
Bearing assembly diameter	1.1813 - 1.1818 in (30.005 - 30.017mm)	
Body bore	1.1807 - 1.1811 in (29.99 - 30.00mm)	
Cooling system capacity (with heater)	9 pints (5.1 litres)	
TORQUE WRENCH SETTINGS	lb ft	kg m
Water pump retaining bolts	17	2.35
Water outlet elbow	8	1.11
Water pump pulley set screws	18	2.49
Thermal transmitter	16	2.21

1 General description

The engine cooling water is circulated by a thermo-syphon, water pump assisted system, and the coolant is pressurised. This is primarily to prevent premature boiling in adverse conditions and to allow the engine to operate at its most efficient running temperature; this being just under the boiling point of water. The overflow pipe from the radiator is connected to an expansion chamber which makes topping up virtually unnecessary. The coolant expands when hot, and instead of being forced down an overflow pipe and lost, it flows into the expansion chamber. As the engine cools the coolant contracts and because of the pressure differential flows back into the radiator.

The cap on the expansion chamber is set to a pressure of 15 lb ft (1.05 kg m) which increases the boiling point of the coolant to 230oF. If the water temperature exceeds this figure and the water boils, the pressure in the system faces the internal valve of the cap off its seat thus exposing the expansion tank overflow pipe down which the steam from the boiling water escapes and so relieves the pressure. It is therefore important to check that the expansion chamber cap is in good condition and that the spring behind the sealing washers has not weakened. Check that the rubber seal has not perished and its seating in the neck is clean to ensure a good seal. A special tool which enables a cap to be pressure tested is available at some garages.

The cooling system comprises the radiator, top and bottom hoses, heater hoses, the impeller water pump (mounted on the front of the engine it carries the fan blades and is driven by the fan belt) and, the thermostat.

The system functions as follows: Cold water from the radiator circulates up the lower radiator hose to the water pump where it is pushed round the water passages in the cylinder block, helping to keep the cylinder bores and pistons cool.

The water then travels up into the cylinder head and circulates round the combustion spaces and valve seats absorbing more heat. Then, when the engine is at its normal operating temperature, the water travels out of the cylinder head, past the now open thermostat into the upper radiator and so into the radiator. The water passes along the radiator from one side to the other where it is rapidly cooled by the rush of cold air through the horizontal radiator core. The water now cool reaches the bottom hose when the cycle is repeated.

When the engine is cold the thermostat (a valve which opens and closes according to water temperature) maintains the circulation of the same water in the engine by returning it via the by-pass hose to the cylinder block. Only when the correct minimum operating temperature has been reached, as shown in the specifications, does the thermostat begin to open allowing water to return to the radiator.

2 Cooling system - draining

With the car on level ground drain the system as follows:

1 With the cooling system cold unscrew and remove the radiator filler plug. DO NOT REMOVE THE PLUG WHILST THE ENGINE IS HOT.

2 If anti-freeze is being used in the cooling system it should be collected in a bowl located under the bottom hose. Do not carry out the instructions in paragraph 5.

3 Release the expansion tank pressure cap.

4 Undo and remove the cylinder block drain plug. This is located to the rear of the left hand side of the cylinder block.

5 Slacken the hose clip and carefully ease the bottom hose at its connection on the radiator.

6 When the coolant has finished running out of the cylinder block drain hole, probe the orifice with a short piece of wire to dislodge any particles of rust or sediment which may be causing a blockage preventing complete draining.

3 Cooling system - flushing

1 Generally even with proper use, the cooling system will gradually lose its efficiency as the radiator becomes choked with rust scale, deposits from water and other sediment. To clean the system out, remove the radiator filler plug, cylinder block plug and bottom hose and leave a hose running in the radiator filler plug hole for fifteen minutes.

2 Reconnect the bottom hose, refit the cylinder block plug and refill the cooling system as described in Section 4, adding a proprietary cleaning compound. Run the engine for fifteen minutes. All sediment and sludge should now have been loosened and may be removed by then draining the system and refilling again.

3 In very bad cases the radiator should be reverse flushed. This can be done with the radiator in position the cylinder block plug is left in position and hose placed in the bottom hose union of the radiator. Water under pressure is forced through the orifice and out of the filler plug hole.

4 The hose is then removed and placed in the filler plug hole and the radiator washed out in the usual manner.

4 Cooling system - filling

1 Fit the cylinder block drain plug and if the bottom hose has been removed it should be reconnected.

2 Fill the system slowly to ensure that no air locks develop. Check that the valve to the heater unit is open, otherwise an air lock may form in the heater. The best type of water to use in the cooling system is rain water.

3 Fill up the radiator to the level of the filler plug and top up the level of coolant in the expansion tank to the level indicated. Refit the radiator filler plug and expansion tank cap.

4 Start the engine and run at a fast idle speed for 30 seconds.

5 Stop the engine and top up the radiator through the filler plug and refit the plug.

6 Run the engine until it has reached its normal operating temperature. Stop the engine and allow to cool.

7 Top up the expansion tank to the level marked.

5 Radiator - removal and refitting

1 Drain the cooling system as described in Section 2.

2 Slacken the clip securing the expansion tank hose to the radiator. Carefully ease the hose from the union pipe on the radiator.

3 Slacken the clips securing the radiator top and bottom hoses to the radiator inlet pipes and carefully ease the two hoses from these pipes.

4 Undo and remove the screws with spring and plain washers securing the two top radiator mounting brackets to the front panel. Lift away these two brackets.

5 The radiator may now be lifted up from its lower mountings and away from the front of the car.

6 Refitting the radiator is the reverse sequence to removal. Refill the cooling system as described in Section 4. Carefully check to ensure that all hose joints are water tight.

6 Radiator - inspection and cleaning

1 With the radiator out of the car, any leaks can be soldered up or repaired with a compound such as Cataloy. Clean out the inside of the radiator by flushing as described in Section 3.

2 When the radiator is out of the car, it is advantageous to turn it upside down for reverse flushing. Clean the exterior of the radiator by hosing down the radiator matrix with a strong jet of water to clean away road dirt, dead flies etc.

3 Inspect the radiator hoses for cracks, internal and external perishing and damage caused by overtightening of the hose clips. Replace the hoses as necessary. Examine the radiator hose clips and renew them if they are rusted or distorted. The drain plugs and washers should be renewed if leaking.

7 Thermostat - removal, testing and replacement

To remove the thermostat, partially drain the cooling system (usually 4 pints, 2.27 litres is enough), loosen the upper radiator hose at the thermostat end and ease it off the elbow. Unscrew the three nuts and lift away the washers from the thermostat housing. Lift away the thermostat elbow from the studs followed by the paper joint and finally the thermostat itself.

Test the thermostat for correct functioning by suspending it together with a thermometer on a string in a container of cold water. Heat the water and note the temperature at which the thermostat begins to open. This should be 82oC (180oF) for a standard thermostat. It is advantageous in winter to fit a thermostat that does not open until 88oC (190oF). Discard the thermostat if it opens too early. Continue heating the water until the thermostat is fully open. Then let it cool down naturally. If the thermostat does not fully open in boiling water, or does not close down as the water cools, then it must be discarded and a new one fitted. If the thermostat is stuck open when cold this will be apparent when removing it from the housing.

Refitting the thermostat is the reverse procedure to removal. Always ensure that the cylinder head and thermostat housing elbow faces are clean and flat. If the thermostat elbow is badly corroded and eaten away, fit a new elbow. A new paper joint must always be used.

If a new winter thermostat is fitted, provided the summer one is functioning correctly it can be placed on one side and refitted in the spring. Thermostats should last for two to three years, at least, between renewal.

8 Water pump - removal and refitting

1 For safety reasons disconnect the battery.

2 Refer to Section 5 and remove the radiator.

3 Refer to Chapter 10 and remove the alternator.

4 Undo and remove the four bolts and spring washers securing the fan blades to the pulley hub. Lift away the circular metal plate, fan blades and pulley.

5 Slacken the clip securing the bottom hose to the water pump and carefully ease off the hose.

6 Undo and remove the four bolts and spring washers which hold the pump to the front of the cylinder block. Note these bolts are of different lengths and must be refitted in their original positions.

7 Lift away the pump and recover the paper gasket.

8 Refitting is the reverse sequence to removal but the following additional points should be noted:

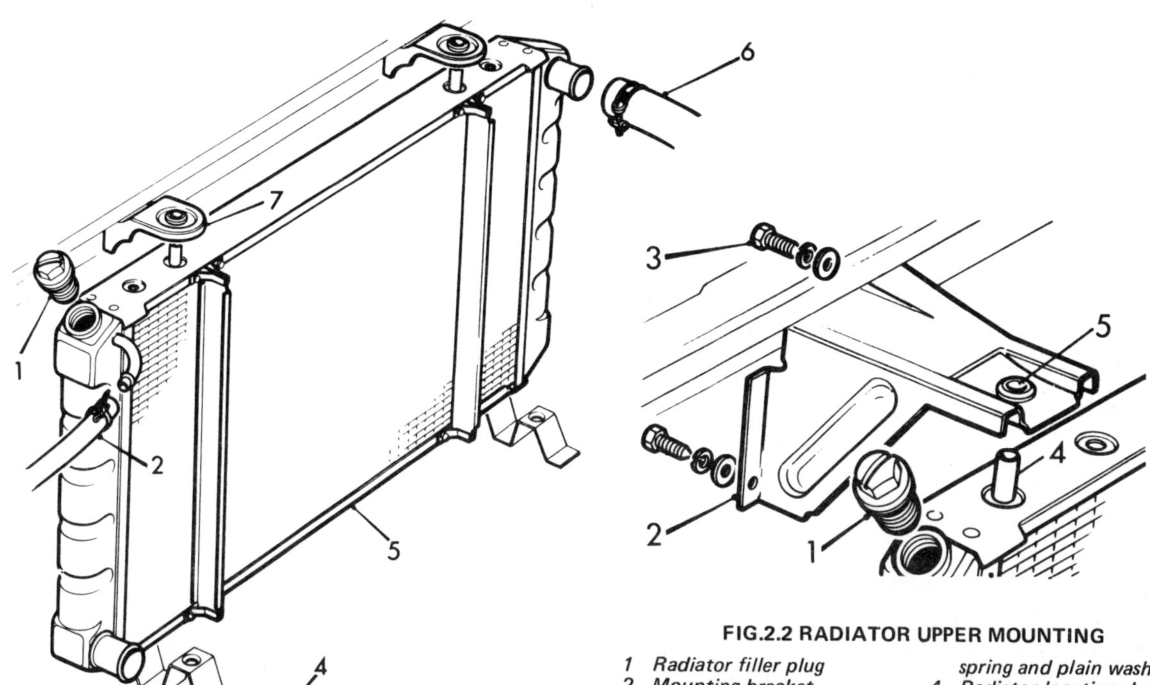

FIG.2.2 RADIATOR UPPER MOUNTING

1 Radiator filler plug
2 Mounting bracket
3 Bracket securing bolt, spring and plain washer
4 Radiator location dowel
5 Rubber grommet

FIG.2.1 RADIATOR ASSEMBLY

1 Filler plug
2 Hose to expansion tank
3 Lower mounting bracket (attached to body)
4 Bottom radiator hose
5 Radiator
6 Top radiator hose
7 Upper mounting bracket

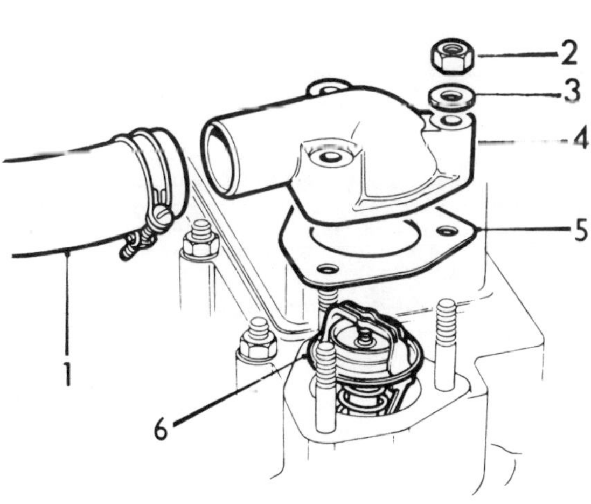

FIG.2.3 THERMOSTAT HOUSING

1 Radiator top hose
2 Nut
3 Plain washer
4 Thermostat housing
5 Gasket
6 Thermostat

FIG.2.4 WATER PUMP ATTACHMENTS

1 Fan securing bolts
2 Packing bolts
3 Fan
4 Pulley
5 Water pump retaining bolts
6 Radiator bottom hose
7 Inset. By pass hose

a) Clean the mating faces of the water pump body and cylinder block to ensure a good water-tight joint.
b) Always use a new paper gasket.
c) Adjust the fan belt tension as described in Section 11.

9 Water pump - dismantling and overhaul

If the water pump starts to leak, showing signs of excessive movement of the spindle, or is noisy during operation the pump can be dismantled and overhauled. Make sure that individual parts are available, perhaps a beyter alternative would be to fit a service exchange reconditioned pump.

1 Using a suitable universal puller or a press carefully press the bearing spindle out of the pulley hub.
2 Support the water pump body and carefully tap out the bearing assembly complete with impeller and seal.
3 Next press out the bearing spindle from the impeller and finally remove the water seal from the bearing spindle. Dismantling is now complete.
4 Thoroughly inspect all parts for wear or damage. Replace any faulty parts.
5 To reassemble first press the bearing assembly into the pump body until the dimensions are reached. (See Fig 2.6).
6 Support the bearing spindle and press the pulley hub onto the spindle until dimension B is reached. Again see Fig 2.6.
7 Fit the water seal into the pump body and suitably support the bearing spindle and press the impeller onto the spindle until there is a clearance of 0.20 - 0.30 inch (0.508 - 0.762 mm) between the impeller vanes and the body of the pump.
8 Should it be observed during reassembly that the interference fit of either the hub or impeller on the bearing spindle has been lost the hub and/or impeller must be renewed.

10 Fan belt - removal and replacement

If the fan belt is worn or has over stretched it should be renewed. The most usual reason for replacement is that the belt has broken in service. It is therefore recommended that a spare belt is always carried in the car. Replacement is a reversal of the removal procedure, but if replacement is due to breakage:

1 Loosen the alternator pivot and slotted link bolts and move the alternator towards the engine.
2 Carefully fit the belt over the crankshaft, water pump and alternator pulleys.
3 Adjust the belt as described in Section 11 and tighten the alternator mounting bolts, NOTE: after fitting a new belt it will require adjustment 250 miles (400 km) later.

11 Fan belt - adjustment

It is important to keep the fan belt correctly adjusted and should be checked every 6,000 miles (9,600 km) or 6 months. If the belt is loose it will slip, wear rapidly and cause the alternator and water pump to malfunction. If the belt is too tight the alternator and water pump bearings will wear rapidly and cause premature failure.

The fan belt tension is correct when there is 0.5 inch (13 mm) of lateral movement at the mid point position between the alternator pulley and the crankshaft pulley.

To adjust the fan belt, slacken the securing bolts and move the alternator in or out until the correct tension is obtained. It is easier if the alternator bolts are only slackened a little so it requires some effort to move the unit. In this way the tension of the belt can be arrived at more quickly than by making frequent adjustments. If difficulty is ecperienced in moving the unit away from the engine a tyre lever placed behind the unit and resting against the block gives a good control so that it can be held in position whilst the securing bolts are tightened. Be careful of the alternator cover - it is fragile.

12 Expansion tank

The radiator coolant expansion tank is mounted on the left hand inner wing panel and does not require any maintenance. It is important that the expansion tank pressure filler cap is not removed whilst the engine is hot.

Should it be found necessary to remove the expansion tank, disconnect the radiator to expansion tank hose connection at the radiator union having first slackened the clip. Remove the bracket screws and carefully lift away the tank and its hose.

Refitting is the reverse sequence to removal. Add either water or anti-freeze solution until it is up to the level mark.

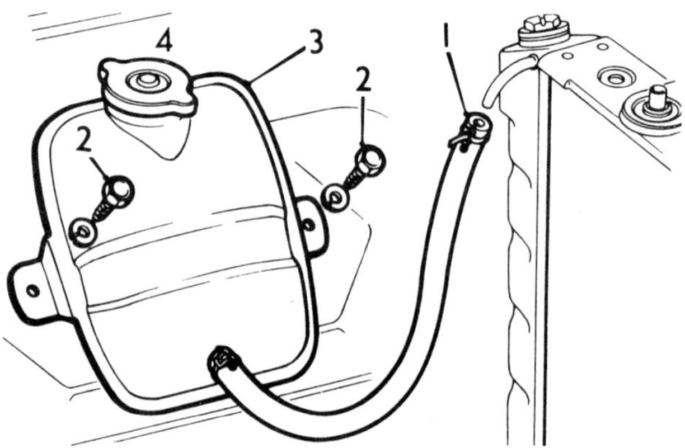

FIG.2.8 EXPANSION TANK ASSEMBLY

1 Hose to radiator
2 Mounting bolt and spring washer
3 Expansion tank
4 Pressure cap

13 Temperature gauge and thermal transmitter

The thermal transmitter is placed in the cylinder head just below the thermostat and is held in position by a special gland nut to ensure a water tight joint. It is connected to the gauge located on the instrument panel by a cable on the main ignition feed circuit and a special bi-metal voltage stabilizer.

If unsatisfactory gauge readings are being obtained the thermal transmitter may be tested by removing the cable connection on the transmitter and placing the metal cable end on a good earthing point, for example a paint free part of the cylinder head. Switch on the ignition and note movement of the gauge needle. If the needle moves to a hot sector a new thermal transmitter should be fitted. If the needle fails to move then a break in the wiring or a fault in the gauge (which is tested by substitution) will be the cause of the trouble.

To remove the thermal transmitter, partially drain the cooling system (usually 4 pints 2.27 litres is enough). Unscrew the transmitter gland nut from the side of the cylinder head. Withdraw the thermal transmitter. Refitting is the reverse procedure to removal.

For information on removing and refitting the gauge refer to Chapter 10.

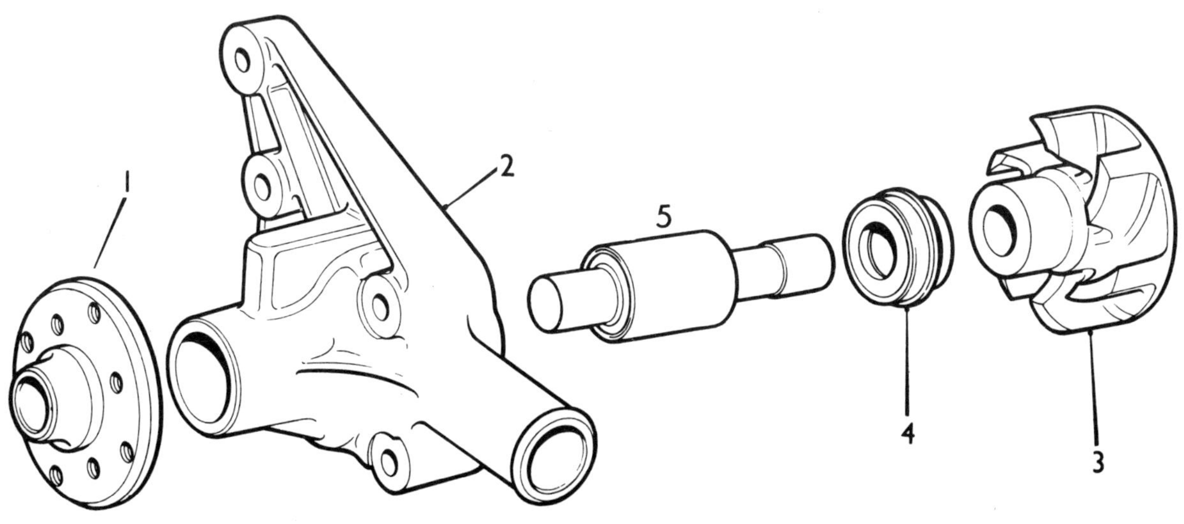

FIG.2.5 WATER PUMP COMPONENTS

1 Pulley hub *3 Impeller* *4 Seal* *5 Spindle and bearings*
2 Water pump body

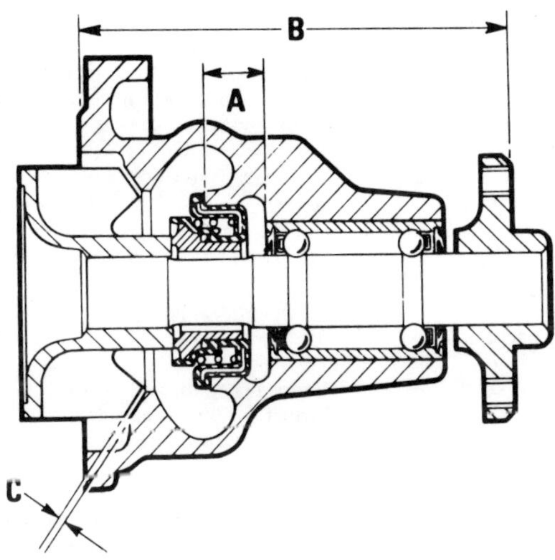

FIG.2.6 WATER PUMP REASSEMBLY DIMENSIONS

A 0.533 to 0.543 inch (13.54 to 13.79 mm)
B 3.712 to 3.732 inch (94.31 to 94.8 mm)
C 0.20 to 0.30 inch (0.508 to 0.762 mm)

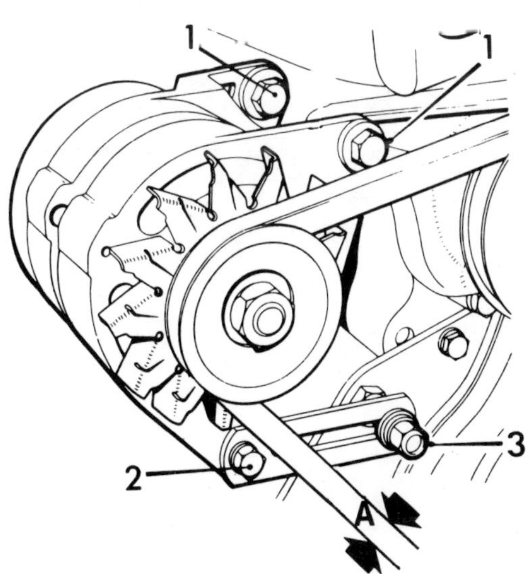

FIG.2.7 FAN BELT ADJUSTMENT

1 Upper mounting *3 Adjustment link securing nut*
2 Lower mounting *A 0.5 inch (13 mm)*

14 Anti-freeze mixture

1 Previous anticipated freezing conditions, it is essential that some anti-freeze, (Castrol anti-freeze) is added to the cooling system.
2 If Castrol anti-freeze is not available, any anti-freeze which conforms with specification BS 3151 and BS 3152 can be used. Never use an anti-freeze with an alcohol base as evaporation is too high.
3 Castrol Anti-freeze with an anti corrosion additive can be left in the cooling system for up to two years, but after six months it is advisable to have the specific gravity of the coolant checked at your local garage and thereafter, every three months.
4 Listed below are the amounts of anti-freeze which should be added to ensure adequate protection down to the temperature given.

Amount of anti-freeze	Protection to
331/3% mixture	
2½ pints (1.5 litres)	-19°C (-2°F)
50% mixture	
3¾ pints (2 litres)	-36°C (-33°F)

15 Fault Diagnosis

Cause	Trouble	Remedy
Heat generated in cylinder not being successfully diposed of by radiator	Insufficient water in cooling system	Top up radiator.
	Fan belt slipping (Accompanied by a shrieking noise on rapid engine acceleration)	Tighten fan belt to recommended tension or replace if worn.
	Radiator core blocked or radiator grill restricted	Reverse flush radiator, remove obstructions.
	Bottom water hose collapsed, impeding flow	Remove and fit new hose.
	Thermostat not opening properly	Remove and fit new thermostat.
	Ignition advance and retard incorrectly set (Accompanied by loss of pwer and perhaps, misfiring)	Check and reset igntion timing.
	Carburettor incorrectly adjusted (mixture too weak)	Tune carburettor.
	Exhaust system partially blocked	Check exhaust pipe for constrictive dents and blockages.
	Oil level in sump too low	Top up sump to full mark on dipstick.
	Blown cylinder head gasket (Water/steam being forced down the radiator overflow pipe under pressure)	Remove cylinder head, fit new gasket.
	Engine not yet run-in	Run-in slowly and carefully.
	Brakes binding	Check and adjust brakes if necessary.
Too much heat being dispersed by radiator	Thermostat jammed open	Remove and renew thermostat.
	Incorrect grade of thermostat fitted allowing premature opening of valve	Remove and replace with new thermostat which opens at a higher temperature.
	Thermostat missing	Check and fit correct thermostat.
Leaks in system	Loose clips on water hoses	Check and tighten clips if necessary.
	Top or bottom water hoses perished and leaking	Check and replace any faulty hoses.
	Radiator core leaking	Remove radiator and repair.
	Thermostat gasket leaking	Inspect and renew gasket.
	Pressure cap spring worn or seal ineffective	Renew pressure cap.
	Blown cylinder head gasket (Pressure in system forcing water/steam down overflow pipe)	Remove cylinder head and fit new gasket.
	Cylinder wall or head cracked	Dismantle engine, dispatch to engineering works for repair.

Chapter 3 Carburation

Contents

Specifications

Air cleaner

Type	Paper element

Carburettor 1.8

Make and type	Single SU HS6
Piston spring	Yellow
Jet size	0.10 in (2.54 mm)
Standard needle	BAQ

Carburettor 1.8 TC

Make and type	Twin SU HS4
Piston spring	Red
Jet size	0.090 in (2.29 mm)
Standard needle	AAS

Fuel pump

Make and type	SU mechanical AUF 707
Suction (minimum)	6 inches (152 mm) Hg.
Pressure (minimum)	3 lb.f/in^2 (0.21 kg.f.cm^2)F

Fuel tank

Type	Flat tank under rear floor vented by breather pipes
Capacity	11.5 gallons

Torque wrench setting	lb.ft.ft.	kg.f.m.
Manifold to cylinder head	15	2.07

1 General description

The fuel system comprises a fuel tank at the rear of the car, a mechanical fuel pump located on the left hand side of the crankcase and a single or twin horizontally mounted SU carburettor/s. A renewable paper element air cleaner is fitted which must be renewed at the recommended mileages. Operation of the individual components is described elsewhere in this chapter.

2 Fuel pump - general description

The mechanical operated fuel pump is located on the left hand side of the crankcase and is operated by a separate lobe on the camshaft.

As the camshaft rotates the rocker lever is actuated, one end of which is connected to the diaphragm operating rod. When the rocker arm is moved by the cam lobe the diaphragm, via a rocker

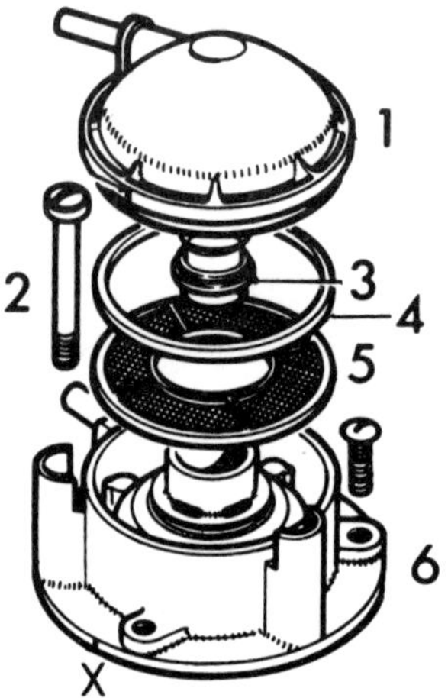

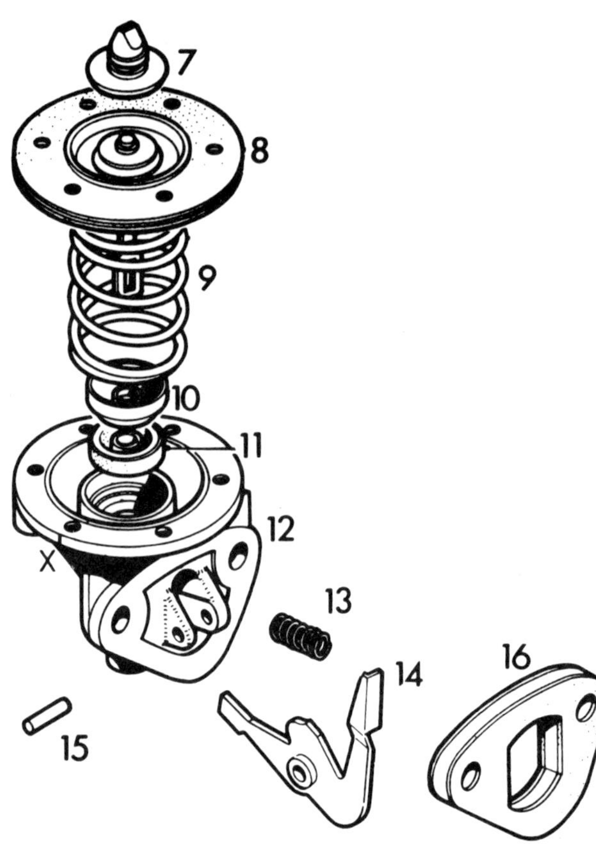

FIG 3.1 FUEL PUMP COMPONENT PARTS

1	*Cover*	*9*	*Spring*
2	*Cover retaining screws*	*10*	*Lower body seal cup*
3	*Cover insert*	*11*	*Lower body seal*
4	*Sealing ring*	*12*	*Lower body*
5	*Filter*	*13*	*Rocker lever spring*
6	*Upper body*	*14*	*Rocker lever*
7	*Combined inlet and outlet valve*	*15*	*Rocker pivot pin*
		16	*Insulator block*
8	*Diaphragm*	*'X'*	*Alignment marks*

arm, moves downwards causing fuel to be drawn in through the filter, past the inlet valve flap and into the diaphragm chamber. As the cam lobe moves round, the diaphragm moves upwards under the action of the spring, and fuel flows via the large outlet valve to the carburettor float chamber.

When the float chamber has the requisite amount of fuel in it, the needle valve in the top delivery line to hold the diaphragm down against the action of the diaphragm spring until the needle valve in the float chamber opens to admit more fuel.

3 Fuel pump - removal and replacement

1 Remove the fuel inlet and outlet connections from the fuel pump and plug ends of the pipes to stop loss of fuel or dirt ingress.

2 Unscrew and remove the two pump mounting flange nuts and washers. Carefully slide the pump off the two studs followed by the insulating block assembly and gasket.

3 Refitting is the reverse sequence to removal. Inspect the gaskets on either side of the insulating block and if damaged obtain and fit new ones.

4 Fuel pump - dismantling, inspection and reassembly

1 Thoroughly clean the outside of the pump in paraffin and dry. To ensure correct reassembly mark the cover and upper and lower body flanges (Fig.3.1).

2 Remove the three cover retaining screws, lift away the cover followed by the sealing ring and fuel filter (photo).

3 Remove the three remaining screws holding the upper body to the lower body. Separate the two halves taking care not to damage the diaphragm (photo).

4 As the combined inlet and outlet valve is a press fit into the body, very carefully remove the valve taking care not to damage the very fine edge of the inlet valve.

5 Lift away the insert from the outlet cover.

6 With the diaphragm and rocker held down against the action of the diaphragm spring, tap out the rocker lever pivot pin using a parallel pin punch. Lift at the rocker lever and spring (photo).

7 Lift out the diaphragm and spring having first well lubricated the lower seal to avoid damage as the spindle stirrup is drawn through. Unless the seal is damaged it should be left in position as a special extractor is required for removal.

8 Carefully wash the filter gauze in petrol and clean all traces of sediment from the upper body. Inspect the diaphragm for signs of distortion, cracking or perishing and fit a new one if suspect.

9 Inspect the fine edge and lips of the combined inlet and outlet valve and also check that it is a firm fit in the upper body. Finally inspect the outlet cover for signs of corrosion, pitting or distortion and obtain a new part if necessary.

10 To reassemble first check that there are no sharp edges on the diaphragm spindle and stirrup and well lubricate the oil seals. Insert the stirrup and spindle into the spring and then through the oil seal and position the stirrup ready for rocker lever engagement (photo).

11 Fit the combined inlet/outlet valve ensuring that the groove registers in the housing correctly. Check that the fine edge of the inlet valve contacts its seating correctly and evenly.

12 Match up the screw holes in the lower body and holes in the diaphragm and depress the rocker lever until the diaphragm lies flat, fit the upper body and hold in place by the three short screws, but do not tighten fully yet (photo).

13 Refit the filter, outlet cover insert, new sealing washer and outlet cover suitably positioned by aligning up the previously made marks. Replace the three long screws and then tighten all screws firmly in a diagonal pattern.

14 Insert the rocker lever and spring into the lower body and retaining in position using the rocker lever pivot pin.

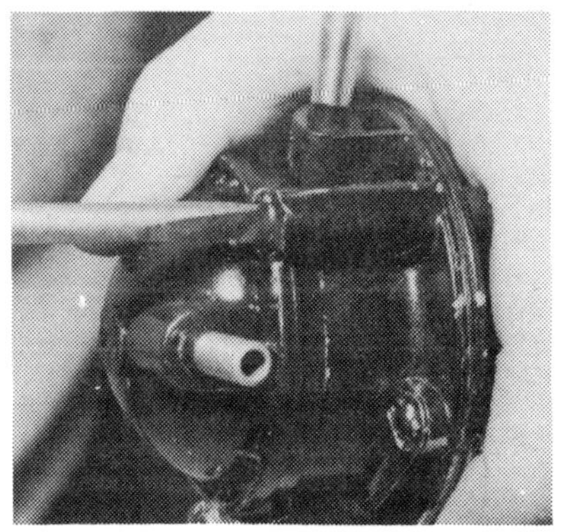
4.2A. Hold the pump firmly

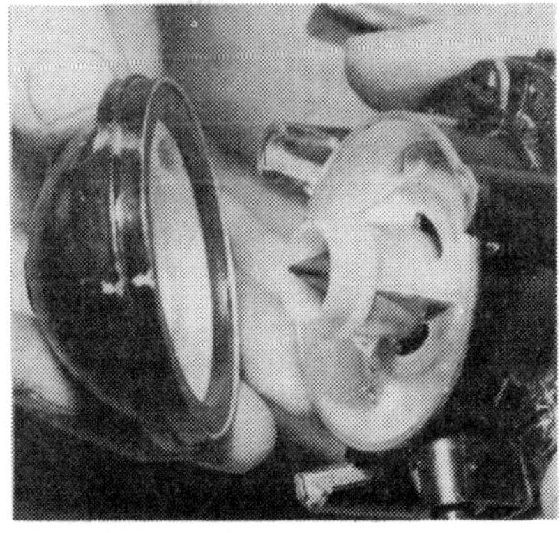
4.2B. Ease off the top cover

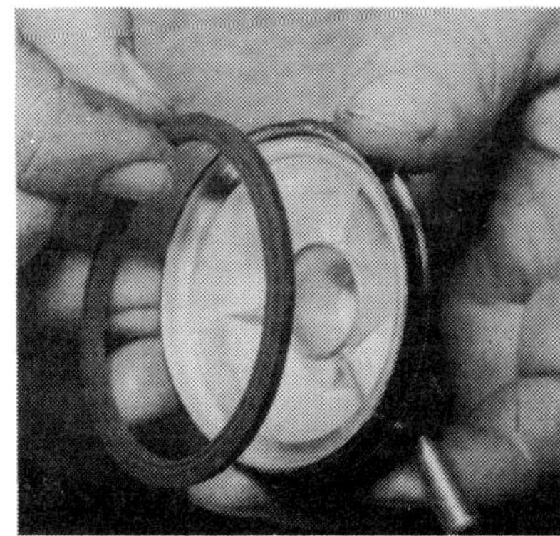
4.2C. Pick out the seal with your finger

4.3A. Undo evenly all round

4.3B. Pull the two halves apart

4.4. Be careful at this stage

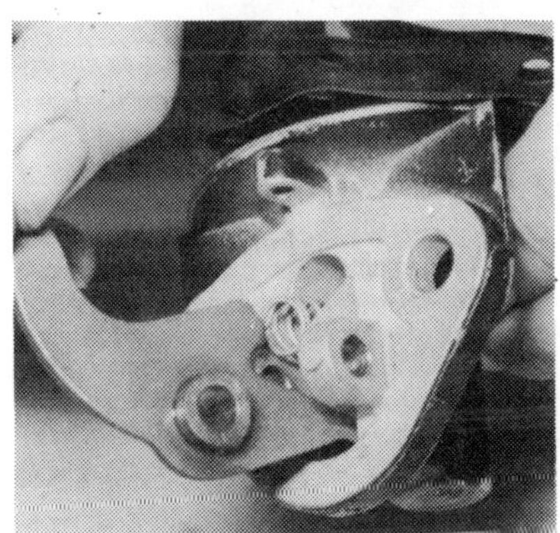
4.6A. Watch the little spring

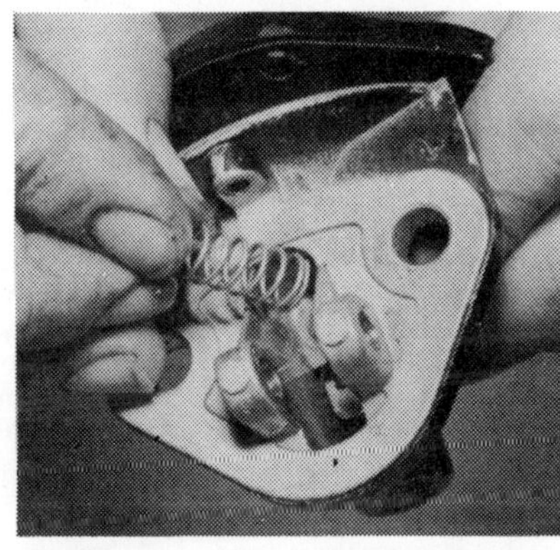
4.6B. Pull out the little spring now

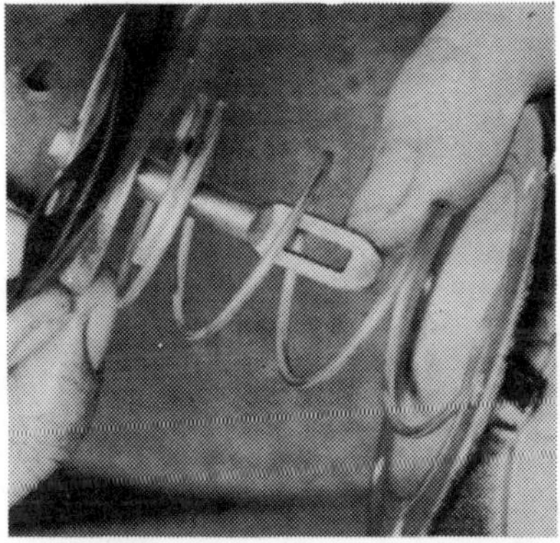
4.7A. Hold this spring whilst extracting the diaphragm

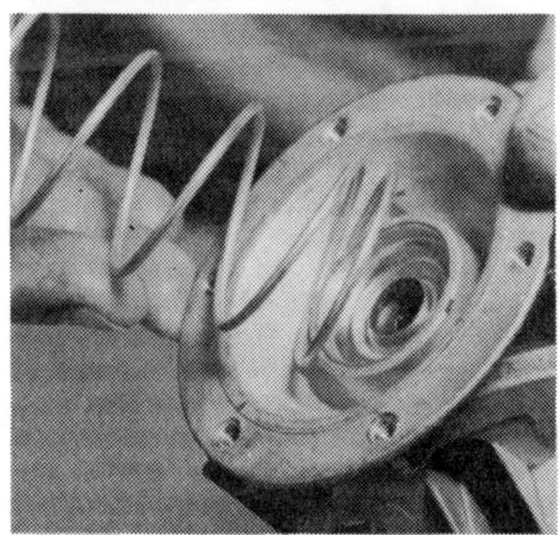
4.7B. Again be delicate with the spring

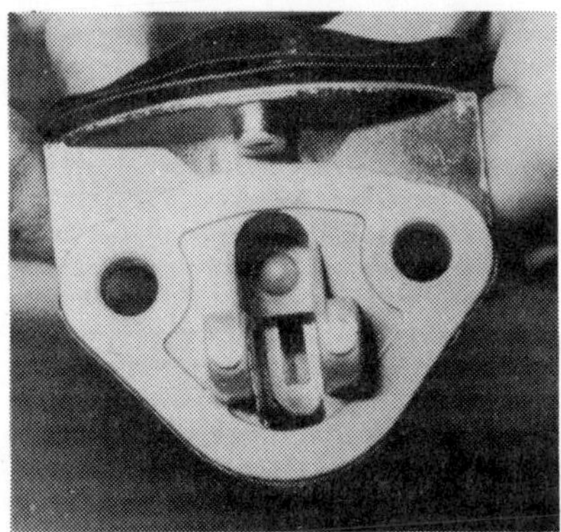
4.10. Press firmly but accurately with both hands

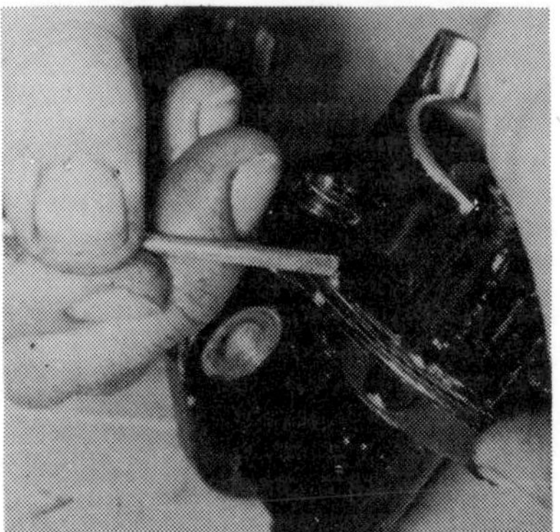
4.12. Line up the covers with the marks

5 Fuel pump - testing

If the pump is suspect or has been overhauled it may be dry tested by holding a finger over the inlet union and operating the rocker lever through three complete strokes. When the finger is released a suction noise should be heard. Next hold a finger over the outlet nozzle and press the rocker arm fully. The pressure generated should hold for a minimum of fifteen seconds.

6 Carburettor - description

1 The variable choke SU carburettor as shown in Fig.3.2 is relatively simple instrument, and is basically the same irrespective of its size and type. It differs from most other carburettors in that instead of having a number of various sized fixed jets for different conditions, only one variable jet is fitted to deal with all possible conditions.
2 Air passing rapidly through the carburettor draws petrol from the jet so forming the petrol/air mixture. The amount of petrol drawn from the jet depends on the position of the tapered carburettor needle, which moves up and down the jet orifice according to the engine load and throttle opening, thus effectively altering the size of jet so that exactly the right amount of fuel is metered for the prevailing conditions.
3 The position of the tapered needle in the jet is determined by engine vacuum. The shank of the needle is held at its top end in a piston which slides up and down the dashpot in response to the degree of manifold vacuum.
4 With the throttle fully open, the full effect of inlet manifold vacuum is felt by the piston which has an air bleed into the choke tube on the outside of the throttle. This causes the piston to rise fully, bringing the needle with it. With the accelerator partially closed, only slight inlet manifold vacuum is felt by the piston (although of course, on the engine side of the throttle the vacuum is greater), and the piston only rises a little, blocking most of the jet orifice with the metering needle.
5 To prevent the piston fluttering and giving a richer mixture when the accelerator pedal is suddenly depressed, an oil damper, and light spring are fitted inside the dashpot.
6 The only portion of the piston assembly to come into contact with the piston chamber or dashpot is the actual piston rod. All other parts of the piston assembly, including the lower choke portion, have sufficient clearance to prevent any direct metal to metal contact which is essential if the carburettor is to function correctly.
7 The correct level of the petrol in the carburettor is determined by the level of the float chamber. When the level is correct the float rises and, by means of a lever resting on top of it, closes the needle valve in the cover of the float chamber. This closes off the supply of fuel from the pump. When the level in the float chamber drops, as fuel is used in the carburettor, the float drops. As it does, the float needle is unseated so allowing more fuel to enter the float chamber and restore the correct level.

7 Carburettor (single) - removal and replacement

1 Unscrew the wing nut securing the air cleaner assembly and lift away the wing nut, fibre washer and air cleaner assembly.
2 Ease the fuel feed pipe from the union on the float chamber cover. Plug the end to prevent dirt ingress (Fig.3.3).
3 Slacken the clip and ease off the engine breather pipe from the union on the carburettor body.
4 Slacken the locknut and undo the nut locking accelerator cable to the control arm on the side of the carburettor body. Detach the accelerator cable.
5 Slacken the bolt securing the choke control cable to the operating linkage and detach the choke cable.
6 Undo and remove the four nuts and washers securing the carburettor body to the manifold studs. Lift away the

FIG 3.2 SU CARBURETTOR COMPONENT PARTS

1 Body
2 Piston lifting pin
3 Spring for pin
4 Sealing washer
5 Plain washer
6 Circlip
7 Piston chamber
8 Screw-piston chamber
9 Piston
10 Spring
11 Needle
12 Spring-needle
13 Support guide-needle
14 Locking screw-needle support guide
15 Piston chamber
16 Sealing washer-damper
17 Throttle adjustment screw
18 Spring for screw
19 Joint washers
20 Insulator block
21 Float-chamber and spacer
22 Joint washer-chamber
23 Float
24 Hinge pin-float
25 Lid-float chamber
26 Needle and seat
27 Baffle plate
28 Screw-float-chamber lid
29 Spring washer
30 Bolt-securing float-chamber
31 Spring washer
32 Plain washer
33 Throttle spindle
34 Throttle disc assembly
35 Screw-securing disc assembly
36 Washer-throttle spindle
37 Throttle return lever
38 Fast-idle screw
39 Spring
40 Lock washer-throttle spindle nut
41 Nut-throttle spindle
42 Jet assembly
43 Sleeve nut-jet flexible pipe
44 Washer
45 Gland
46 Ferrule
47 Jet bearing
48 Sealing washer
49 Jet locating nut
50 Spring
51 Jet adjustment nut
52 Pick-up lever
53 Link-pick-up lever
54 Screw-securing lever to jet
55 Pivot bolt
56 Pivot bolt tube-inner
57 Pivot bolt tube-outer
58 Distance washer
59 Cam lever
60 Washer
61 Spring-cam lever
62 Spring-pick-up lever
63 Throttle lever rod
64 Bush
65 Anchor tag
66 Lock washer-throttle lever rod
67 Progressive throttle linkage bracket
68 Throttle cable abutment bracket
69 Throttle return spring
70 Tension spring
71 Guide-suction chamber piston
72 Screw-securing guide

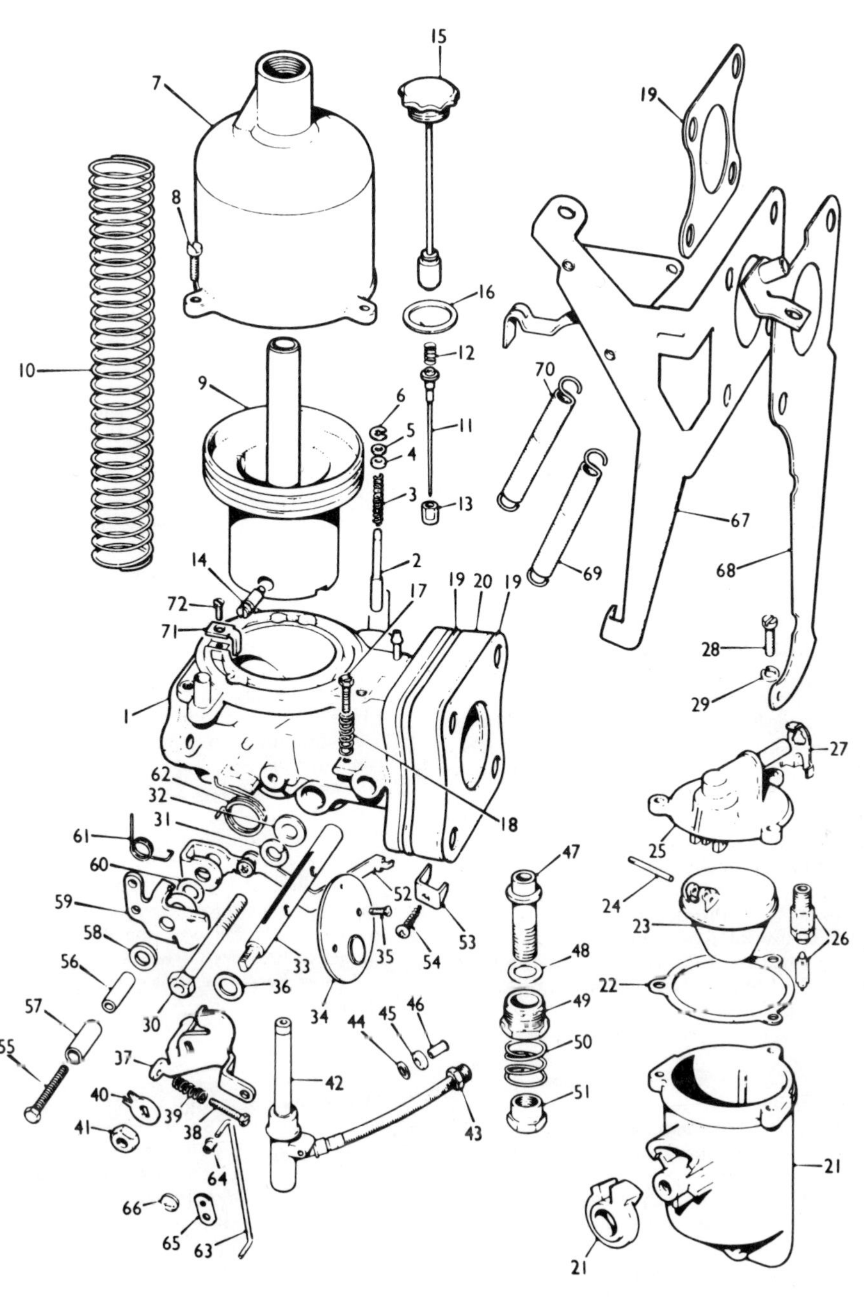
15
7
19
8
16
10
9
12
70
6
5
11
4
3
13
67
2
68
69
14
17
19
20
19
72
71
28
1
29
27
62
32
18
31
61
25
60
47
24
52
59
53
26
23
58
35
54
33
48
56
36
22
34
49
57
30
44
45
46
50
55
37
42
40
39
38
51
41
43
21
64
66
65
63
21

carburettor complete with abutment bracket and linkage.
7 Recover the insulator block and gaskets.
8 Refitting the carburettor is the reverse sequence to removal. Always fit new gaskets to the inlet manifold flange and one each side of the insulator block. Refer to Section 22, and adjust the choke control cable and to Section 21 for detail of the throttle cable adjustment.

8 Carburettor (twin) - removal and replacement

1 Undo and remove the four nuts and bolts that secure the air cleaner air manifolds to the carburettors. Lift away the air cleaner and air manifold assembly.
2 Ease the fuel feed pipe from the union on the front carburettor float chamber cover. Plug the end to prevent dirt ingress (Fig.3.4).
3 Detach the engine breather hose at the Y junction.
4 Detach the vacuum advance suction pipe for the carburettor body.
5 Slacken and then remove the nut and washer that secures the accelerator cable clamp.
6 Disconnect the choke control cable from the operating linkage.
7 Disconnect the three throttle return springs from the heat shield.
8 Undo and remove the four nuts and washers securing the carburettor body to the manifold studs. Lift away the carburettors.
9 Recover the insulator block and gaskets.
10 Refitting the carburettors is the reverse sequence to removal. Always fit new gaskets to manifold flanges and insulator blocks.
11 Refer to Section 22 and adjust the choke control cable and to Section 21 for details of the throttle cable adjustment.

9 Carburettor - dismantling and reassembly

1 Unscrew the piston damper and lift away from the chamber and piston assembly. Recover the fibre washer (Fig.3.2).
2 Using a screwdriver or small file, scratch identification marks on the suction chambers and carburettor body so that they may be fitted together again in their original position. Remove the three suction chamber retaining screws and lift the suction chamber from the carburettor body leaving the suction chamber in situ.
3 Lift the piston spring from the piston, noting which way round it is fitted, and remove the piston. Invert it and allow the oil in the damper bore to drain out. Place the piston in a safe place so that the needle will not be touched or the piston roll onto the floor. It is recommended that the piston be placed on the neck of a narrow jar with the needle inside, so acting as a stand.
4 Mark the position of the float chamber lid relative to the body, and unscrew the three screws holding the float chamber lid to the float chamber body. Remove the lid and withdraw the pin thereby releasing the float and float lever, using a spanner or socket remove the needle valve assembly.
5 Release the pick up lever return spring from its retaining lug.
6 Support the plastic moulded base of the jet and remove the screw retaining the jet pick up link and link bracket.
7 Carefully unscrew the flexible jet tube sleeve nut from the float chamber and lift away the jet assembly from the underside of the carburettor body. Note the gland, washer and ferrule at the end of the jet tube.
8 Undo and remove the jet adjustment nut and spring. Also unscrew the jet locknut and lift away together with the brass washer and jet bearing.
9 Unscrew and remove the lever pivot bolt and spacer. Detach the lever assembly and return springs noting the pivot bolt tubes, skid washer and the locations of the cam and pick up springs.
10 Close the throttle and lightly mark the relative position of the throttle disc and carburettor flange.
11 Unscrew the disc retaining screws, open the throttle and ease the disc from its slot in the throttle spindle.
12 Bend back the tabs of the lock washer securing the spindle nut. Undo and remove the nut and detach the lever arm, washer and throttle spindle.
13 Should it be necessary to remove the piston lifting pin, push it upwards and remove the securing clip. Lift away the pin and spring.
14 Reassembly is a straight reversal of the dismantling sequence.

10 Carburettor - examination and repair

The SU carburettor generally speaking is most reliable but even so it may develop one of several faults which may not be readily apparent unless a careful inspection is carried out. The common faults the carburettor is prone to are:
1 Piston sticking
2 Float needle sticking
3 Float chamber flooding
4 Water and dirt in the carburettor

In addition, the following parts are susceptible to wear after high mileages and as they vitally affect the economy of the engine they should be checked and renewed where necessary, every 24,000 miles (38,000 km).
a) The carburettor needle: If this has been incorrectly fitted at some time so that it is not centrally located in the jet orifice, then the metering needle will have a tiny ridge worn on it. If a ridge can be seen then the needle must be renewed. SU carburettor needles are made to very fine tolerances and should a ridge be apparent, no attempt should be made to rub the needle down with fine emery paper. If it is wished to clean the needle, it can be polished lightly with metal polish.
b) The carburettor jet: If the needle is worn it is likely that the rim of the jet will be damaged where the needle has been striking it. It should be renewed, otherwise fuel consumption will suffer. The jet can also be badly worn or ridged on the outside from where it has been sliding up and down between the jet bearing every time the choke has been pulled out. Removal and renewal is the only answer.
c) Check the edges of the throttle and choke tube for wear. Renew if worn.
d) The washers fitted to the base of the jet and under the float chamber lid may leak after a time and can cause a great deal of fuel wastage. It is wisest to renew them automatically when the carburettor is stripped down.
e) After high mileages the float chamber needle and seat are bound to be ridged. They are not an expensive item to replace and must be renewed as a set. They should never be renewed separately.

11 Carburettor - piston sticking

1 The hardened piston rod which slides in the centre guide tube in the middle of the dashpot is the only part of the piston assembly (which comprises the jet needle, suction disc and piston choke) which should make contact with the dashpot. The piston rim and choke periphery are machined to very fine tolerances so that they will not touch the dashpot or the choke tube walls.
2 After high mileage wear in the centre guide tube may allow the piston to touch the dashpot wall. This condition is known as sticking.
3 If piston sticking is suspected and it is wished to test for this condition, rotate the piston about the centre guide tube at the same time as sliding it up and down inside the dashpot wall then that portion of the wall must be polished with a metal polish until the clearance exists. In extreme cases fine emery cloth can be used.

Great care should be taken to remove only the minimum amount of metal to provide the clearance, as too large a gap will

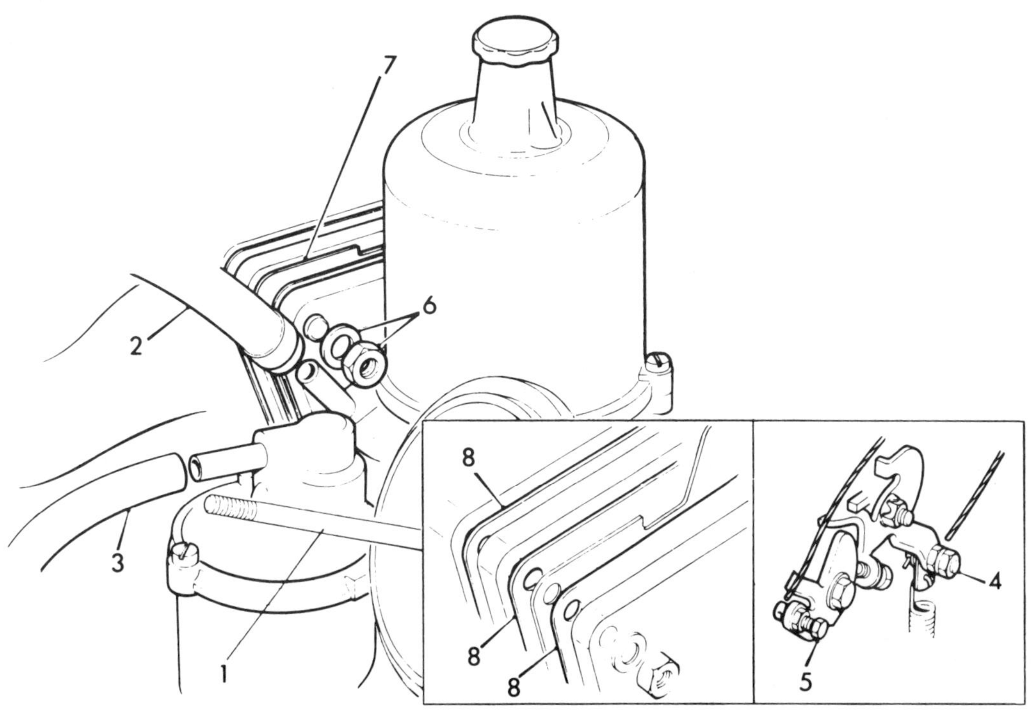

FIG 3.3 SU CARBURETTOR ATTACHMENTS - Single

1 Air cleaner attachment
2 Engine breather pipe
3 Fuel pipe from pump
4 Accelerator cable
5 Choke cable clamp bolt
6 Securing nut and plain washer
7 Abutment bracket and linkage
8 Joint washers

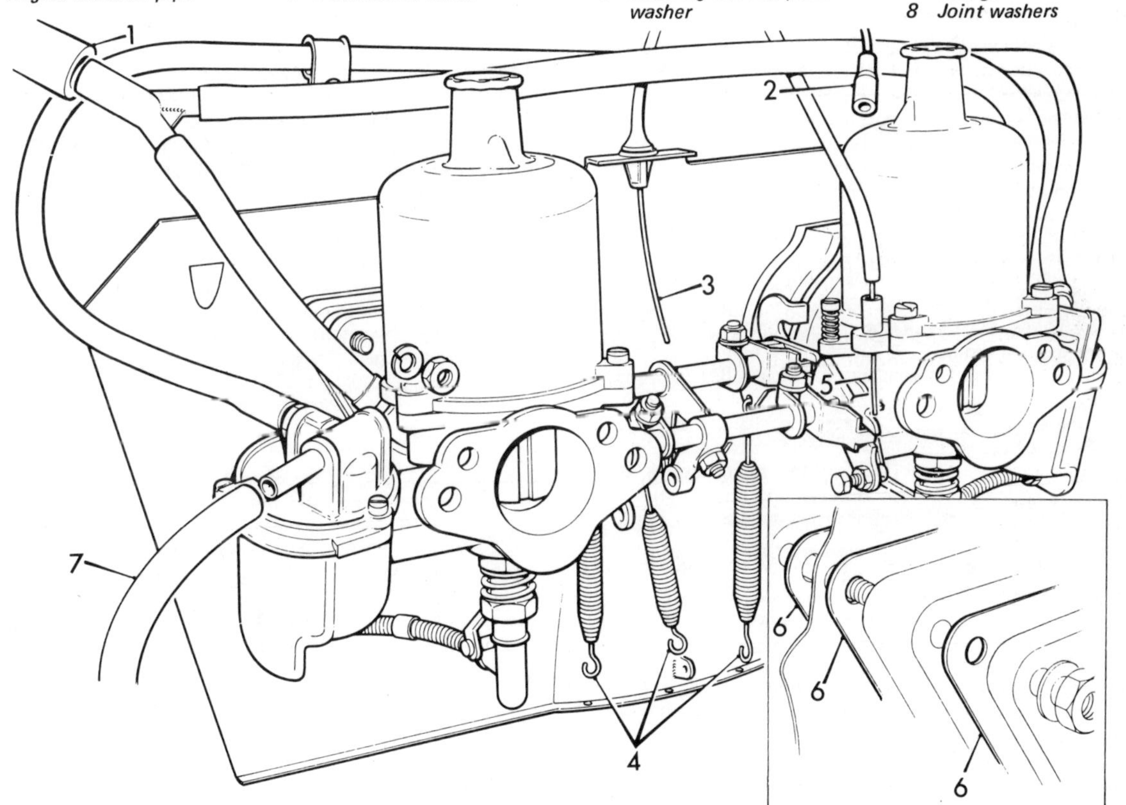

FIG 3.4 SU CARBURETTOR ATTACHMENTS - TWIN

1 Engine breather hose
2 Vacuum advance suction pipe
3 Accelerator cable
4 Throttle return springs
5 Choke control cable
6 Gaskets
7 Fuel feed pipe

cause air leakage and upset the function of the carburettor. Clean down the walls of the dashpot and the piston rim and ensure that there is no oil on them. A trace of oil may be judiciously aplied to the piston rod.
4 If the piston is sticking, under no circumstances try to clear it by trying to alter the tension of the light return spring.

12 Carburettor - float needle sticking

1 If the float needle sticks, the carburettor will soon run dry and the engine will stop, despite there being fuel in the tank.

The easiest way to check a suspected sticking float needle is to remove the inlet pipe at the carburettor and turn the engine over on the starter motor by pressing on the solenoid rubber button (manual gearbox) or operating the ignition/starter switch (automatic transmission). In the latter case remove the white lead on the ignition coil so that the engine does not start. If fuel spurts from the end of the pipe (direct it towards the ground, into a wad of cloth or into a jar) then the fault is almost certain to be a sticking float needle.
2 Remove the float chamber, dismantle the valve and clean the housing and float chamber out thoroughly.

13 Carburettor - float chamber flooding

If fuel emerges from the small breather hole in the cover of the float chamber this is known as flooding. It is caused by the float chamber needle not seating properly in its housing, normally this is because a piece of dirt of foreign matter is jammed between the needle and needle housing. Alternatively the float may have developed a leak or be maladjusted so that it is holding open the float chamber needle valve even though the chamber is full of petrol. Remove the float chamber cover, clean the needle assembly, check the setting of the float as described later in this chapter and shake the float to verify if any petrol has leaked into it.

14 Carburettor - water or dirt in carburettor

1 Because of the size of the jet orifice, water or dirt in the carburettor is normally cleaned. If dirt in the carburettor is suspected, lift the piston assembly and flood the float chamber. The normal level of the fuel should be about 1/16 inch (1.588mm) below the top of the jet, so that on flooding the carburettor the fuel should flow out of the jet hole.
2 If little or no petrol appears, start the engine (the jet is never completely blocked) and with the throttle butterfly fully open blank off the air intake. This will cause a partial vacuum in the choke tube and help suck out any foreign matter from the jet tube. Release the throttle as soon as the engine speed alters considerably. Repeat this procedure several times, stop the engine and then check the carburettor as described in the first paragraph of this section.
3 If this failed to do the trick then there is no alternative but to remove and blow out the jet.

15 Carburettor - jet centering

1 This operation is always necessary if the carburettor has been dismantled, but to check if this is necessary on a carburettor in service, first screw up the jet adjusting nut as far as it will go without forcing it, and lift the piston and then let it fall under its own weight. It should fall onto the bridge making a soft metallic click. Now repeat the above procedure but this time with the adjusting nut screwed right down. If the soft metallic click is not audible in either of the two tests proceed as follows;
2 Disconnect the jet link from the bottom of the jet, and the nylon flexible tube from the underside of the float chamber. Gently slide the jet and the nylon tube from the underside of the carburettor body. Next unscrew the jet adjusting nut and lift away the nut and the locking spring. Refit the adjusting nut without the locking spring and screw it up as far as possible without forcing. Replace the jet and tube but there is no need to reconnect the tube.
3 Slacken the jet locking nut so that it may be rotated with the fingers only. Unscrew the piston damper and lift away the damper. Gently press the piston down onto the bridge and tighten the locknut. Lift the piston using the lifting pin and check that it is able to fall freely under its own weight. Now lower the adjusting nut and check once again. If this time there is a difference in the two metallic clicks, repeat the centering procedure until the sound is the same for both tests.
4 Gently remove the jet and unscrew the adjusting nut. Refit the locking spring and jet adjusting nut. Top up the damper with oil, if necessary, and replace the damper. Connect the nylon flexible tube to the underside of the float chamber and finally reconnect the jet link.

16 Carburettor - float chamber fuel lever adjustment

1 It is essential that the fuel level in the float chamber is always correct otherwise excessive fuel consumption may occur. Carburettors fitted to later models have nqn adjustable floats.
2 With the carburettor fitted to the engine and the float chamber full of petrol remove the piston and dashpot assembly (early models only).
3 Check that the level of fuel in the jet is about 1/16 inch (1.588mm) below the top of the jet. If it is above or below this level it may be adjusted by removing the needle and seat from the underside of the float chamber lid and either add or remove washers so raising or lowering the relative position of the needle valve.

17 Carburettor - needle replacement

1 Should it be necessary to fit a new needle, first remove the piston and suction chamber assembly, marking the chamber for correct reassembly in its original position.
2 Slacken the needle clamping screw and withdraw the needle, guide and spring from the underside of the piston (Fig.3.5).
3 To refit the needle assembly fit the spring and guide to the needle and insert the assembly into the piston making sure that the guide is fitted flush with the face of the piston and the flat on the guide positioned adjacent to the needle guide locking screw. Screw in the guide locking screw.

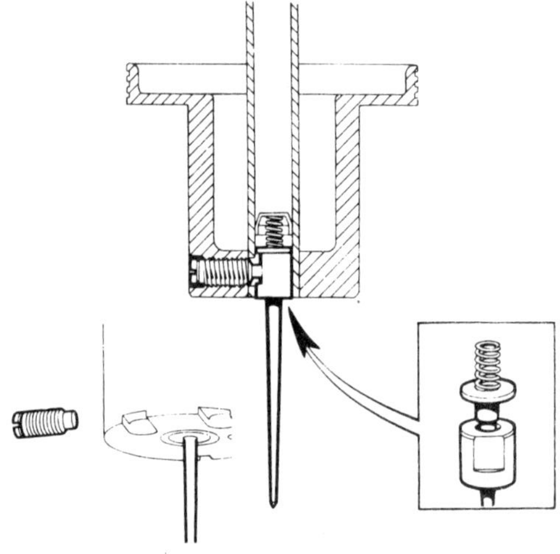

FIG 3.5 NEEDLE LOCATION IN PISTON

18 Carburettor (single) - adjustment and tuning

1 To adjust and tune a single SU carburettor proceed in the following manner. Check the colour of the exhaust at idling speed with the choke fully in. If the exhaust tends to be black and the tail pipe interior is also black, it is a fair indication that the mixture is too rich. If the exhaust is colourless and the deposit in the exhaust pipe is very light grey it is likely that the mixture is too weak. This condition may also be accompanied by intermittent misfiring, while too rich a mixture will be associated with 'hunting'. Ideally the exhaust should be colourless with a medium grey pipe deposit.

2 The exhaust pipe deposit should only be checked after a good run of at least 20 miles. Idling in city traffic and stop/start motoring is bound to produce excessive dark exhaust pipe deposits.

3 Once the engine has reached its normal operating temperature, detach the carburettor air cleaner.

4 Only two adjustments are provided on the SU carburettor. Idling speed is governed by the throttle adjusting screw and the mixture strength by the jet adjusting nut. The SU carburettor is correctly adjusted for the whole of its engine revolution range when the idling mixture strength is correct.

5 To adjust the mixture set the engine to run at about 1000 rpm by screwing in the throttle adjusting screw.

6 Check the mixture strength by lifting the piston of the carburettor approximately 1/32 inch (0.79mm) with the piston lifting pin so as to disturb the air flow as little as possible. If:

a) The speed of the engine increases appreciably the mixture is too rich.

b) The engine speed immediately decreases, the mixture is too weak.

c) The engine speed increases very slightly, the mixture is correct. To enrich the mixture rotate the adjusting nut which is at the bottom of the underside of the carburettor in a clockwise direction, ie, downwards. Only turn the adjusting nut a flat at a time and check the mixture strenth between each turn. It is likely that there will be a slight increase or decrese in rpm after the mixture adjustment has been made so the throttle idling screw should be turned so that the engine idles at 650 rpm.

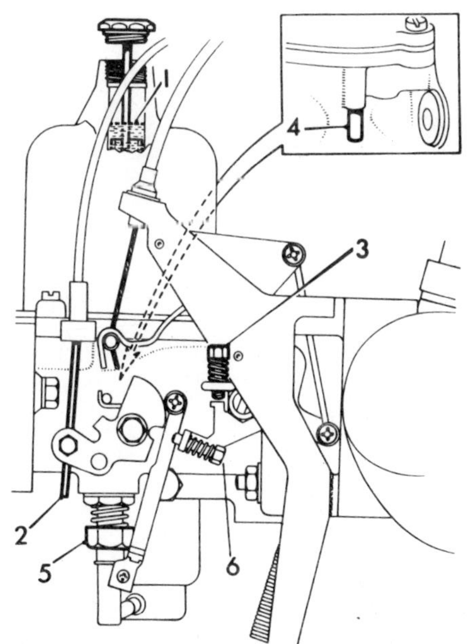

FIG 3.6 CARBURETTOR ADJUSTMENT POINTS

1 Oil dashpot
2 Throttle cable
3 Throttle adjustment screw
4 Piston lifting pin
5 Jet adjustment nut
6 Fast idle screw

19 Carburettor (twin) - adjusting and tuning

1 First ensure that the mixture is correct in each carburettor by disconnecting the linkage and adjusting each carburettor as described previously in this Chapter. With a twin SU carburettor installation, not only have the carburettors to be individually set to ensure correct mixture, but also the idling suction must be equal on both. It is best to use a vacuum synchronizing device such as that produced by Crypton. If this is not available, it is possible to obtain fairly accurate synchronization by listening to the hiss made by the air flow into the intake throat of each carburettor. A rubber tube held to the ear is useful for this adjustment.

2 The aim is to adjust the throttle butterfly disc so that an equal amount of air enters each carburettor, open the throttle discs together. Listen to the hiss from each carburettor intake and, if a difference in intensity is noticed between them, unscrew the throttle adjusting screw on the other carburettor until the hiss from both the carburettors is the same.

3 With the vacuum synchronizing device, all that is necessary is to place the instrument over the intake of each carburettor in turn and adjust the adjusting screws until the reading on the gauge is identical for both carburettors.

4 Tighten the levers on the interconnecting linkage to connect the two throttle discs of the two carburettors together, at the same time holding down the throttle adjusting screws against their idling stops. Synchronization of the two carburettors is now complete.

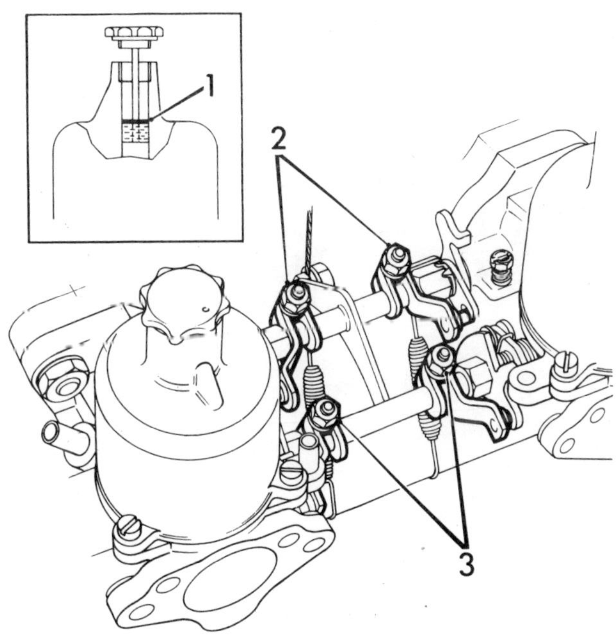

FIG 3.7 CARBURETTOR CONTROL ATTACHMENTS

1 Dashpot oil level
2 Throttle spindle inter-connection clamp
3 Jet control inter-connection clamp

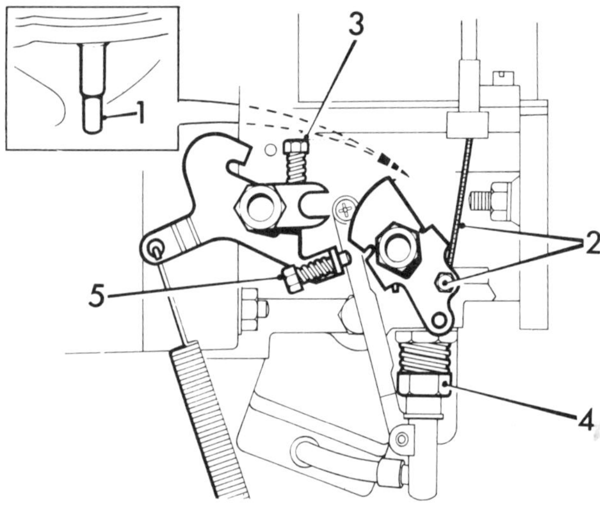

FIG 3.8 CARBURETTOR ADJUSTMENT POINTS

1 Piston lifting pin
2 Choke control cable attachment
3 Throttle adjusting screw
4 Jet adjustment nut
5 Fast idle screw

20 Carburettor (twin) - linkage adjustment

1 Set the throttle interconnection clamping levers so that the actuating pins rest on the lower arm of the forks (See Fig.3.9).
2 Insert a 0.020 inch (0.5mm) feeler gauge between the throttle shaft operating lever and the choke control interconnecting rod 'A'.
3 Tighten the throttle interconnection clamping lever bolts, ensuring that there is approximately 0.031 inch (0.79mm) end float on the interconnecting rod. Remove the feeler gauge.
4 An equal clearance of 0.012 inch (9.31mm) 'B' should now exist between each lever pin and the bottom of the fork on both carburettors.
5 Reposition the choke control interconnecting rod with approximately 0.031 inch (0.79mm) and clearance and tighten the clamp bolts.
6 Run the engine at 1000 to 1100 rpm and check the carburettor balance.
7 Reconnect the choke cable and pull out the control approximately 0.5 inch (13mm) until the linkage is just about to move the jet. Start the engine and adjust the fast idle screws to give an engine speed of 1000 to 1100 rpm when hot.

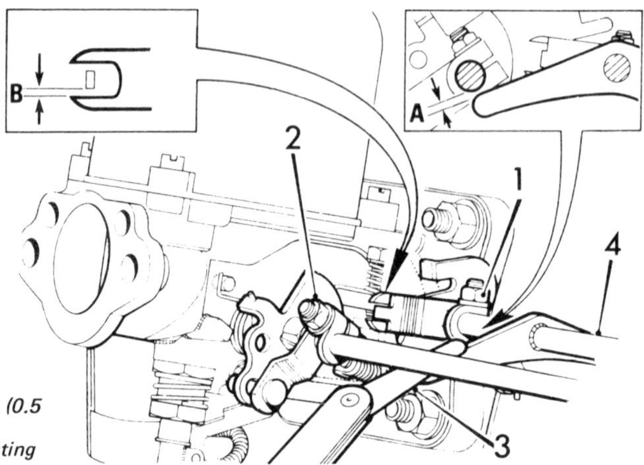

FIG 3.9 CARBURETTOR LINKAGE ADJUSTMENT

1 Throttle spindle clamp
2 Jet control clamp
3 Feeler gauge 0.020 in (0.5 mm)
4 Choke control connecting rod

21 Throttle cable - removal and refitting

1 Using two thin open ended spanners unscrew the cable trunnion screw (Fig.3.10).
2 Press in the plastic retainers located on the underside of the abutment bracket and carefully ease the cable through the bracket.
3 Detach the inner cable from the accelerator pedal and withdraw the cable into the engine compartment.
4 Refitting is the reverse sequence to removal but it is now necessary to adjust the effective length of the inner cable.
5 Pull down on the inner cable until all free movement of the throttle pedal is eliminated.
6 Hold the cable in this position and raise the cam operating lever until it just contacts the cam (Fig.3.11).
7 Move the trunnion up the cable until it contacts the operating lever, and tighten the trunnion screw.
8 Depress the throttle pedal and make sure that the cable has 1/16 inch (1.6mm) free movement before the cam operating lever begins to move.

22 Choke cable - removal and refitting

1 Using two thin open ended spanners slacken the cable trunnion screw (Fig.3.12).
2 Working behind the switch panel unscrew the large nut and shakeproof washer securing the control to the switch panel.
3 Carefully draw the cable through the body grommet and switch panel.
4 Refitting is the reverse sequence to removal but it is now necessary to adjust the effective length of the inner cable.
5 Set the position of the trunnion to give a free movement on the cable of 0.0625 inch (1.6mm) before the cam lever begins to move (Fig.3.13).
6 Pull out the control approximately 0.5 inch (13mm) until the linkage is just about to move the jet.
7 Start the engine and adjust the carburettor fast idle screw to five, an engine speed of 1000 to 1100 rpm.
8 Push the control knob fully in and check that there is a small gap between the end of the fast idle screw and the cam.

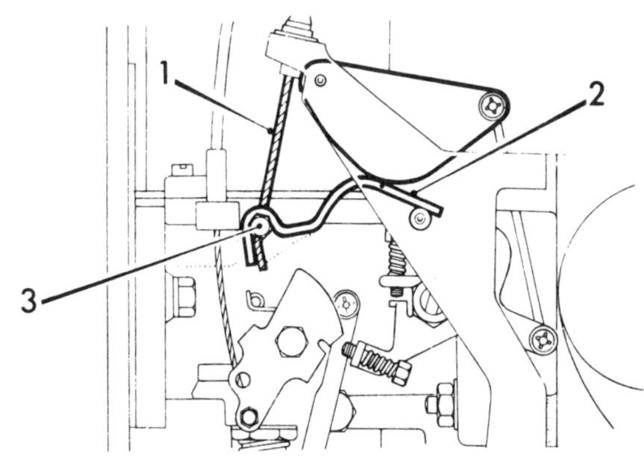

FIG 3.11 THROTTLE CABLE ADJUSTMENT

1 Inner cable
2 Cam operating lever
3 Trunnion

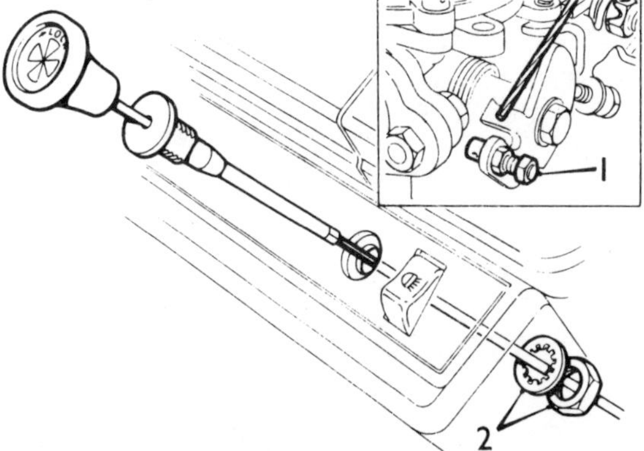

FIG 3.12 CHOKE CABLE REMOVAL

1 Trunnion screw
2 Cable securing nut and shakeproof washer

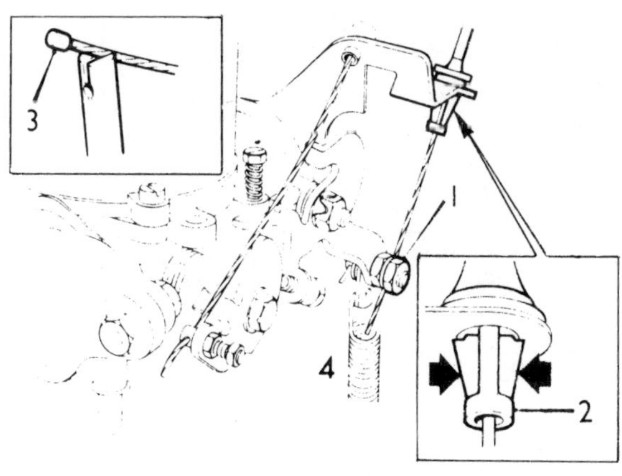

FIG 3.10 THROTTLE CABLE ATTACHMENT

1 Cable trunnion
2 Outer cable retainer
3 Inner cable connection to throttle pedal
4 Throttle return spring

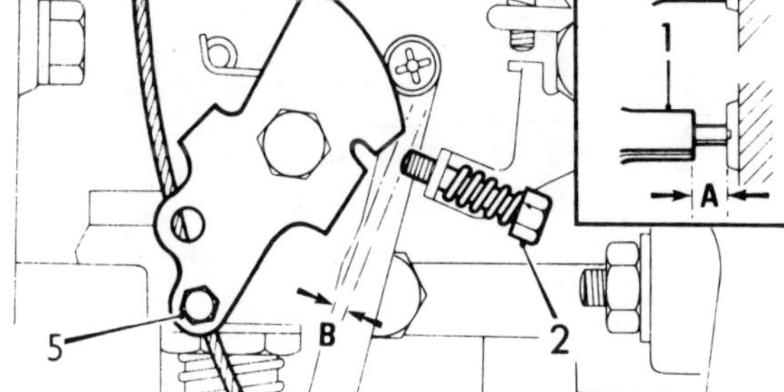

FIG 3.13 CHOKE CABLE ADJUSTMENT

1 Choke control knob (out)
2 Fast idle screw
3 Choke control knob (in)
A 0.5 inch (13 mm)
B 0.0625 inch (1.6mm)
5 Choke cable clamp bolt

23 Throttle pedal - removal and refitting

1 Refer to Fig.3.14 and detach the throttle cable from the end of the pedal.
2 Undo and remove the two nuts and spring washers securing the pedal bracket to the bulkhead panel. Lift the pedal assembly from the mounting studs.
3 Refitting the throttle pedal is the reverse sequence to removal.

24 Fuel tank - removal and refitting

1 For safety reasons, disconnect the battery.
2 Chock the front wheels, raise the rear of the car and support on axle stands located under the rear axle.
3 Unscrew the fuel tank drain plug and drain the contents of the fuel tank into a container of suitable capacity (Fig.3.15).
4 Detach the cable terminal from the fuel tank sender unit.
5 Using a pair of pliers open the clips securing the hoses and vent pipes and ease off the pipes.
6 Release the vent pipe adjacent to the filler cap.
7 Undo and remove the four bolts, spring and shaped washers securing the tank to the brackets welded to the underside of the body. Lift away the fuel tank.
8 Refitting the fuel tank is the reverse sequence to removal.

25 Fuel tank - cleaning

With time it is likely that sediment will collect in the bottom of the fuel tank condensation, resulting in rust and other impurities is sometimes found in the fuel tank of a car more than three or four years old.

With the tank removed it should be vigorously flushed out and then turned upside down and, if facilities are available, steam cleaned.

26 Fuel tank sender unit - removal and refitting

1 For safety reasons disconnect the battery.
2 Disconnect the fuel gauge sender unit cable.
3 Detach the main fuel pipe from the sender unit by squeezing the ears of the clip with a pair of pliers and pulling off the cable.
4 Using two crossed screwdrivers, remove the fuel gauge tank unit by turning through approximately 30° and lift away from the tank. Take great care not to bend the float wire.
5 If the sender unit is suspect, check the circuit, gauge and sender unit as described in Chapter 10.
6 Refitting is the reverse sequence to removal. Always fit a new sealing washer located between the fuel gauge tank unit and the tank itself.

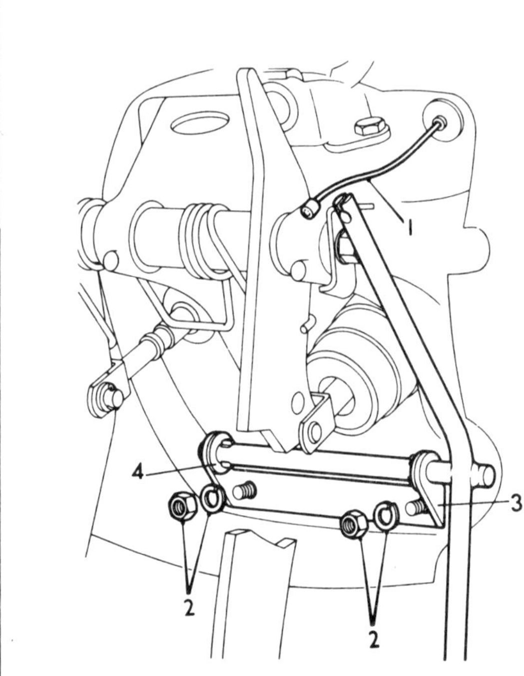

FIG 3.14 THROTTLE PEDAL FIXING

1 Throttle cable
2 Throttle pedal bracket securing nut and spring washer
3 Throttle pedal bracket
4 Clip

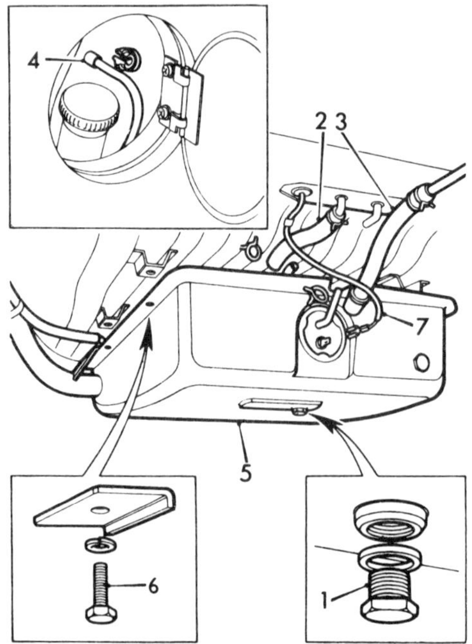

FIG 3.15 FUEL TANK ATTACHMENTS

1 Drain plug and washer
2 Vent pipe
3 Metal pipe to fuel pump
4 Vent pipe
5 Fuel tank
6 Securing bolt and spring washer
7 Sender unit electric cable

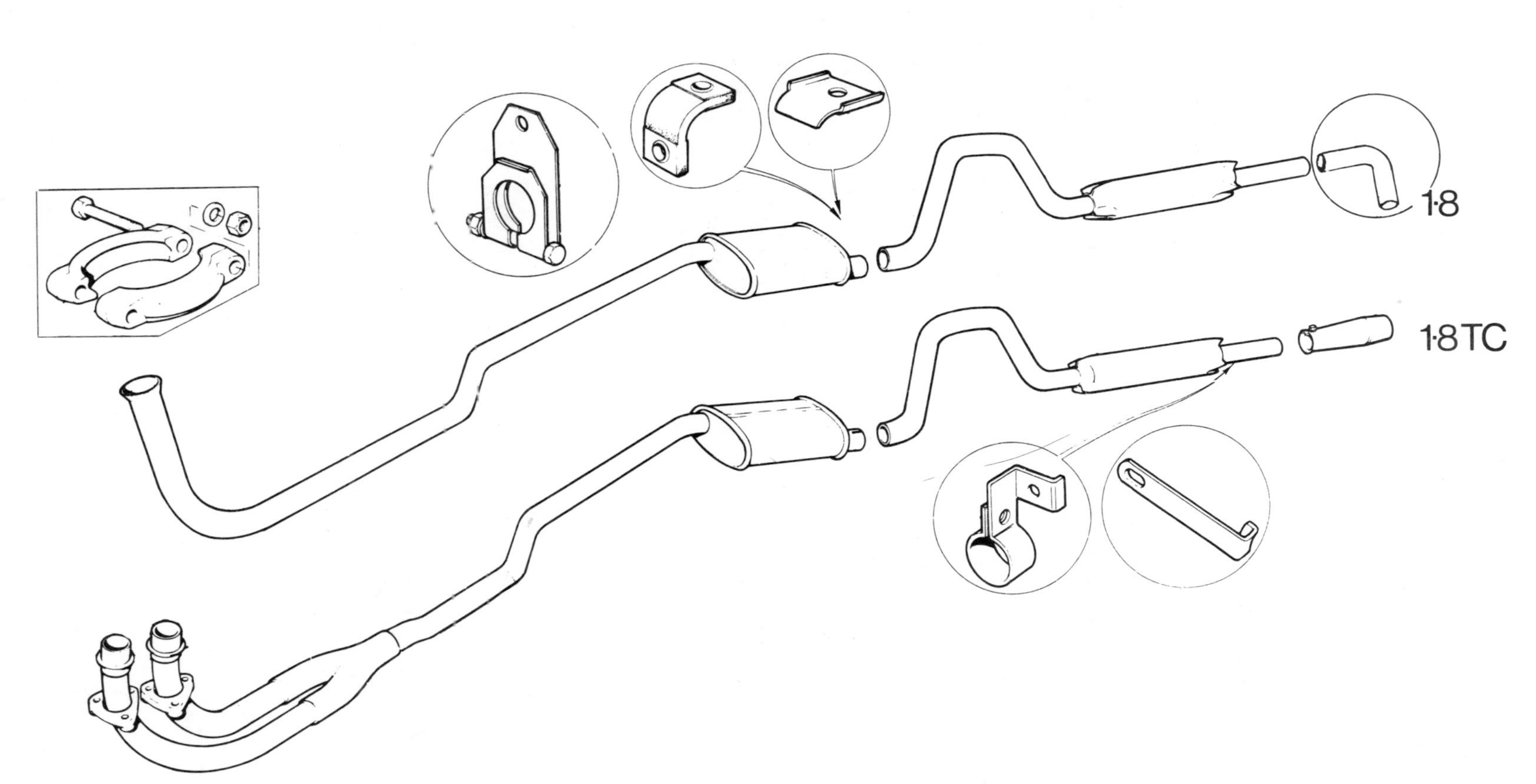

FIG 3.16. THE EXHAUST SYSTEMS SHOWING HANGER AND CLAMP POSITIONS

27 Fault diagnosis

Unsatisfactory engine performance and excessive fuel consumption are not necessarily the fault of the fuel system or carburettor. In fact they more commonly occur as a result of ignition faults. Before acting on the fuel system it is necessary to check the ignition system first. Even though a fault may lie in the fuel system it will be difficult to trace unless the ignition is correct.

The table below therefore, assumes that the ignition system is in order.

Symptom	Reason/s	Remedy
Smell of petrol when engine is stopped	Leaking fuel lines or unions	Repair or renew as necessary.
	Leaking fuel tank	Fill fuel tank to capacity and examine carefully at seams, unions and filler pipe connections. Repair as necessary.
Smell of petrol when engine is idling	Leaking fuel line unions between pump and carburettor	Check line and unions and tighten or repair.
	Overflow of fuel from float chamber due to wrong level setting or ineffective needle valve or punctured float	Check fuel level setting and condition of float and needle valve and renew if necessary.
Excessive fuel consumption for reasons not covered by leaks or float chamber faults	Worn needle	Renew needles.
	Sticking needle	Check correct movement of needle body.
Difficult starting, uneven running, lack of power, cutting out	One or more blockages	Dismantle and clean out float chamber and body.
	Float chamber fuel level too low or needle sticking	Dismantle and check fuel level and needle.
	Fuel pump not delivering sufficient fuel	Check pump delivery and clean or repair as required.
	Intake manifold gaskets leaking, or manifold fractured	Check tightness of mounting nuts and inspect manifold.
Fast idle; erratic	Air leak	Check manifold, brake servo, crankcase ventilator

Chapter 4 Ignition system

Contents

Specifications

Spark plugs	Champion N - 9Y
Size	14 mm
Gap	0.024 - 0.026 in (0.625 - 0.660 mm)
Firing order	1 3 4 2
Ignition coil	
1.8	Lucas 11C12 or Delco Remy 7992100 v
1.8TC	Lucas 16C6
Primary resistance at 20°C (68°F)	1.43 to 1.58 ohms
Consumption:	
Ignition on	4.5 to 5 amps at 13.5 volts
at 2000 rpm	1 amp
Distributor	Lucas 25 D 4
Serial No. 1.8 HC	41234
1.8 LC	41260
1.8 TC	41032
Direction of rotation	anti clockwise
Swell angle	60° ± 3°
Contact breaker gap	0.014 - 0.016 in (0.35 - 0.40 mm)
Condenser capacity	0.18 - 0.24 m.fd.
Static ignition timing	
1.8 SC	10° BTDC
1.8 TC	7° BTDC
Centrifugal advance	
1.8 HC	28° - 32° at 6000 rpm 26° - 30° at 4800 rpm 20° - 24° at 3600 rpm 10° - 14° at 2200 rpm 2 ° - 6 ° at 1200 rpm no advance below 300 rpm
1.8 LC	28° - 32° at 2500 rpm 20° - 24° at 1700 rpm 14° - 18° at 1200 rpm 2 ° - 6 ° at 600 rpm no advance below 600 rpm
1.8 TC	28° - 32° at 5400 rpm 24° - 28° at 4200 rpm 18° - 22° at 2300 rpm 12° - 16° at 1800 rpm 1 ° - 5 ° at 800 rpm No advance below 300 rpm
Vacuum advance:	
1.8 HC	
Starts	4 in (101.6 mm) HG
Finishes	12 in (304.8 mm) HG

1.8 LC	
Starts	6 in (152 mm) HG
Finishes	13 in (329.12 mm) HG
1.8 TC	
Starts	3 in (76.2 mm) HG
Finishes	8 in (203.2 mm) HG

TORQUE WRENCH SETTINGS	lb ft	kg m
Distributor clamp bolt	2.5	0.35
Distributor flange retaining screws	8 - 10	1.1 - 1.4
Spark plug	14	1.9

1 General description

In order that the engine may run correctly it is necessary for an electrical spark to ignite the fuel/air mixture in the combustion chamber at exactly the right moment in relation to engine speed and load. The ignition system is based on suplying low tension voltage from the battery to the ignition coil, where it is converted into high tension voltage. The high tension voltage is powerful enough to jump the spark plug gap in the cylinders many times a second under high compression pressure, providing that the ignition system is in good working order and that all adjustments are correct.

The ignition system comprises two individual circuits known as the low tension and high tension circuits.

The low tension circuit (sometimes known as the primary circuit) comprises the battery, lead to control bod, lead to the ignition switch, to the low tension or primary coil windings (terminal SW) and the lead from the low tension coil windings (terminal CB) to the contact breaker points and condenser in the distributor.

The high tension (secondary circuit) comprises the high tension or secondary coil windings, the heavily insulated ignition lead from the centre of the coil to the centre of the distributor cap, the rotor arm, the spark plug leads and the spark plugs.

The complete ignition system operation is as follows: Low tension voltage from the battery is changed within the ignition coil to high tension voltage by the opening and closing of the contact breaker points in the low tension circuit. High tension voltage is then fed via the carbon brush in the centre of the distributor cap to the rotor arm of the distributor. The rotor arm revolves inside the distributor cap and each time it comes into line with one of the four metal segments in the cap, these being connected to the spark plug leads, the opening and closing of the contact breaker points causes the high tension voltage to build up, jump the gap from the rotor arm to the appropriate metal segment and so, via the spark plug lead, to the spark plug where it finally jumps the gap between the two spark plug electrodes, one being connected to the earth system.

The ignition timing is advanced and retarded automatically to ensure the spark occurs at just the right instant for the particular load at the prevailing engine speed.

The ignition advance is controlled by a mechanical and vacuum operated system. The mechanical governor mechanism mechanism comprises two lead weights which move out under centrifugal force from the central distributor shaft as the engine speed rises. As they move outwards they rotate the cams relative to the distributor shaft, and so advance the spark. The weights are held in position by two springs, and it is the tension of the springs which is largely responsible for correct spark advancement.

When fitted the vacuum control comprises a diaphragm, one side of which is connected via a small bore tube to the carburettor, and the other side to the contact breaker plate. Depression in the induction manifold and carburettor, which varies with engine speed and throttle opening, causes the diaphragm to move, so moving the contact breaker plate and advancing or retarding the spark. A fine degree of control is achieved by a spring in the vacuum assembly.

2 Contact breaker points - adjustment

1 To adjust the contact breaker points so that the correct gap is obtained, first release the two clips securing the distributor cap to the distributor body, and lift away the cap. Clean the inside and outside the cap with a dry cloth. It is unlikely that the four segments will be badly burned or scored, but if they are the cap must be renewed. If only a small deposit is on the segments it may be scraped away using a small screwdriver.

2 Push in the carbon bush, located in the top of the cap, several times to ensure that it moves freely. The bush should protrude at least ¼ inch (6.35 mm).

3 Gently prise the contact breaker points open to examine the condition of their faces. If they are rough, pitted or dirty it will be necessary to remove them for resurfacing, or for replacement points to be fitted.

4 Presuming the points are satisfactory, or that they have been cleaned and replaced, measure the gap between the points by turning the engine over until the contact breaker arm is on the peak of one of the four cam lobes. A 0.014 - 0.016 in (0.36 - 0.40 mm) feeler gauge should now just fit between the points.

5 If the gap varies from this amount, slacken the contact plate securing screw and adjust the contact gap by inserting a screwdriver in the notched hole at the end of the plate, turning clockwise to decrease, and anti- clockwise to increase the gap. Tighten the securing screw and recheck the gap again.

6 Replace the rotor arm and distributor cap and clip the spring blade retainers into position.

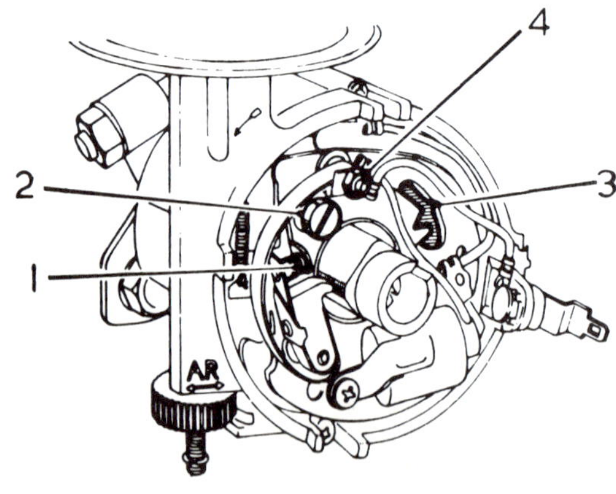

FIG.4.1. CONTACT BREAKER POINTS

1 Contact breaker points
2 Contact plate securing screw
3 Screwdriver slot
4 Moving contact spring and terminals securing nut

3 Contact breaker points - removal and replacement

1 If the contact breaker points are burned, pitted or badly worn, they must be removed and replaced.

2 To remove the points, unscrew the terminal nut and remove it together with the top insulating bush and both leads from the stud. Lift off tje contact breaker arm and remove the large fibre washer from the terminal pin.

3 The adjustable contact breaker plate is removed by unscrewing one holding down screw and removing it, complete with spring and flat washer.

4 Later type contact breaker points - Undo the nut securing the terminals to the contact breaker point assembly (Photo).

5 Lift the terminals from the threaded stud on the base plate assembly (photo).

6 Undo and remove the bolt and plain washer securing the contact breaker point assembly to the baseplate assembly (Photo).

7 Lift away the contact breaker point assembly (Photo).

8 To replace the points, first position the adjustable contact breaker plate, and secure it with its screw, spring and flat washer. Fit the fibre washer to the terminal pin and fir the contact breaker arm over it. Insert the flanged nylon bush with the condenser lead immediately under its head, and the low tension lead under that, over the terminal pin. Fit the steel washer and screw on the securing nut.

9 Later type contact breaker points. Place the contact breaker points assembly on the baseplate assembly and lightly secure with the bolt and plain washer.

10 Refit the terminal to the threaded stud and secure with the nut.

11 The points are now reassembled and the gap should be set as detailed in the previous section.

4 Condenser - removal, testing and replacement

1 The purpose of the condenser (capacitor) is to ensure that when the contact breaker points open there is no sparking across them which would waste voltage and cause wear.

2 The condenser is fitted in parallel with the contact breaker points. If it develops a short circuit, it will cause ignition failure, as the points will be prevented from interrupting the low tension circuit.

3 If the engine becomes very difficult to start, or begins to miss after several miles running, and the breaker points show signs of excessive burning, then the condition of the condenser must be suspect. A further test can be made by separating the points by hand with the ignition switched on. If this is accompanied by a flash it is indicative that the condenser has failed.

4 Without special test equipment, the only sure way to diagnose condenser trouble is to replace a suspected unit with a new one and note if there is any improvement. They are not expensive.

5 To remove the condenser from the distributor, remove the distributor cap and the rotor arm. Unscrew the contact breaker arm terminal nut, remove the nut, and flanged nylon bush. Undo and remove the condenser securing screw and lift away the condenser.

6 Replacement of the condenser is simply a reversal of the removal process. Take particular care that the condenser lead does not short circuit against any portion of the breaker plate.

5 Distributor - lubrication

1 It is important that the distributor cam is lubricated with petroleum jelly or grease at the specified mileages, and that the breaker arm, governor weights and cam spindle are lubricated with oil once every 6,000 miles (10,000 km).

2 Great care should be taken not to use too much lubricant, as any excess that might find its way onto the contact breaker points could cause burning and misfiring.

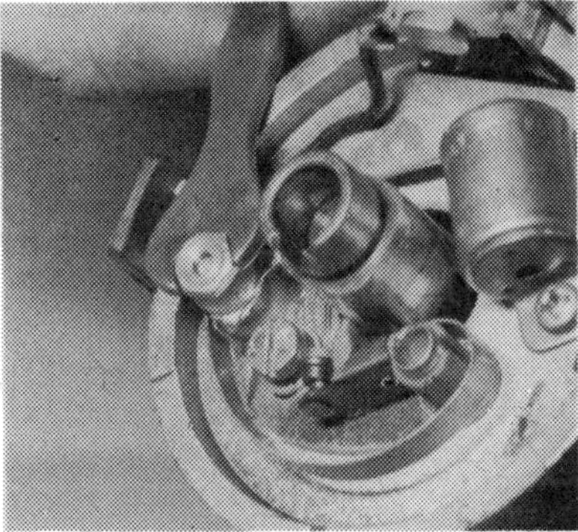

3.4 Try to use the correct 'distributor' spanner

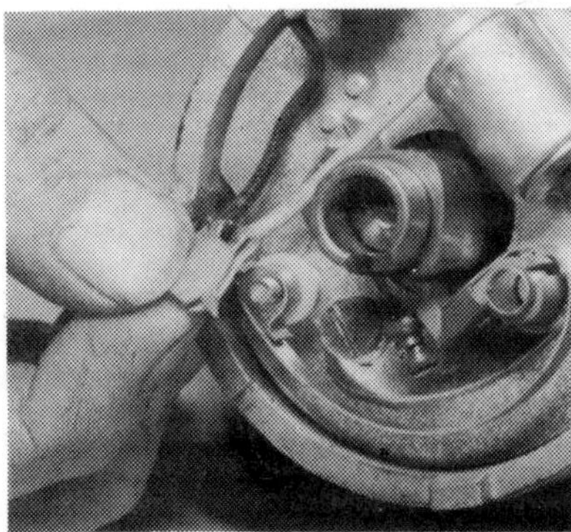

3.5 Release carefully

3.6 Use the right sized screwdriver - not too small

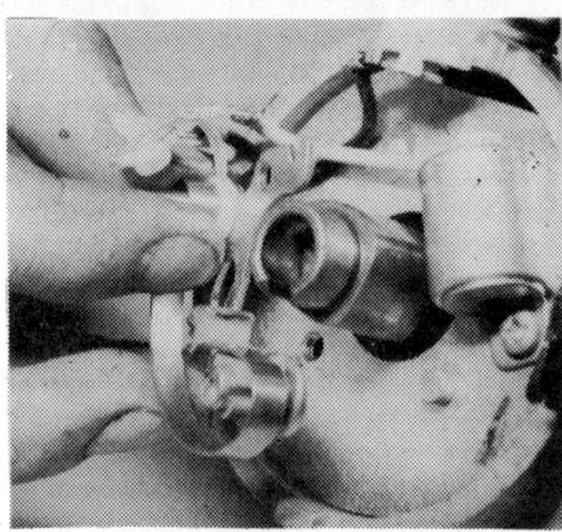

3.7 Use the thumb and two fingers

3 To gain access to the cam spindle, lift away the rotor arm. Drop no more than two drops of engine oil onto the screw head. This will run down the spindle when the engine is hot and lubricate the bearings. No more than ONE drop of oil should be applied to the pivot bush.

6 Distributor - removal and replacement

1 For safety reasons disconnect the battery.
2 Release the clips securing the distributor cap to the body and lift away the distributor cap.
3 Slowly turn the crankshaft until the groove in the crankshaft pulley lines up with the static ignition point on the timing indicator, and at the same time the rotor arm is pointing to the distributor cap segment which is connected to No 1 spark plug.
4 Disconnect the low tension lead from the terminal on the side of the distributor.
5 Detach the vacuum pipe from the distributor vacuum advance unit.
6 Undo and remove the two screws, spring and plain washers securing the distributor clamp plate to the cylinder block. The distributor may now be lifted up together with the clamp plate still attached.
7 If it is not wished to disturb the ignition timing, then under no circumstances should the clamp pinch bolt, which secures the distributor in its relative position in the clamp, be loosened. Providing the distributor is removed without the clamp being loosened from the distributor, and the engine is not turned, the ignition timing will not be lost.
8 Replacement is a reversal of the above sequence. If the engine has been turned, it will be necessary to retime the ignition. This will also be necessary if the clamp pinch bolt has been loosened. Tighten the flange retaining screws to a torque wrench setting of 8 - 10 lb ft (1.1 - 1.4 kg m).

7 Distributor - dismantling

1 With the distributor removed from the car and on the bench, if the distributor cap is still in position, ease back the clips and lift it away. Lift off the rotor arm. If it is very tight lever it off gently with a screwdriver (Photo).
2 Remove the contact breaker points as described in Section 3.
3 Remove the condenser securing screw from the contact plate by releasing its securing screw (Photo).
4 Release the vacuum unit flexible link from its mounting pin on the moving contact plate.
5 Unscrew and remove the two screws and washers which hold the contact breaker plate and base plate to the distributor body. Note the earth lead which is secured by one of the two screws. Remember to replace this lead on reassembly.
6 Lift away the contact breaker plate and base plate. Hold the contact breaker plate and turn the base plate in a clockwise direction to separate the two halves.
7 Note the position of the slot in the rotor arm drive in relation to the offset drive dog at the opposite end of the distributor. It is essential that this is reassembled correctly as otherwise the timing may be 180° out (photo).
8 Unscrew the cam spindle retaining screw which is located in the centre of the rotor arm drive shaft cam. Lift away the screw (photo).
9 Detach the two return springs from their posts, and separate the cam plate. Lift away the two control weights.
10 To remove the vacuum unit spring off the small circlip securing the advance adjustment knurled nut which should then be unscrewed. With the micrometer adjusting nut removed, release the spring and the micrometer adjusting nut lock spring clip. This is the clip that is responsible for the 'clicks' when the micrometer adjuster nut is turned and it is small and easily lost, as is the circlip, so put them in a safe place. Do not forget to replace the lock spring clip on reassembly.
11 It is necessary to remove the distributor drive shaft or spindle only if it is thought to be excessively worn. With a thin parallel pin punch drive out the retaining pin from the driving tongue collar on the bottom end of the distributor drive shaft. The shaft can then be removed. Recover the thrust washers.
12 The distributor is now ready for inspection.

8 Distributor - inspection and repair

1 Thoroughly wash all mechanical parts in petrol and wipe dry using a clean non-fluffy rag.
2 Check the contact breaker points as described in Section 3. Check the distributor cap for signs of tracking, indicated by a thin black line between the segments. Replace the cap if evident.
3 If the metal portion of the rotor arm is badly burned or loose, renew the arm. If slightly burnt, clean the arm with a fine file. Check that the carbon brush moves freely in the centre of the distributor cover.
4 Examine the fit of the contact breaker plate on the base plate and also check the breaker arm pivot for looseness, or wear, and obtain new as necessary.
5 Examine the centrifugal weights and pivot pins for wear, and renew the weights or cam assembly if a degree of wear is found.
6 Examine the shaft and fit of the cam assembly on the shaft. If the clearance is excesive compare the items with new units and renew either, or both, if they show excessive wear.
7 If the shaft is a loose fit in the distributor bush and can be seen to be worn, it will be necessary to fit a new shaft and bush. Renewal of the bush consists of drifting out the old bush and fitting a new one. NOTE: Before inserting a new bush it should be stod in engine oil for 24 hours or two hours in hot oil at 100°C (212°F).
8 If possible examine the length of the centrifugal weight springs and compare them with new springs. If they have stretched they should be renewed.

9 Distributor - reassembly

1 Reassembly is a straight forward reversal of the dismantling process. Note in addition:
2 Lubricate the centrifugal weights and other parts of the mechanical advance mechanism, the distributor shaft, and the portion of the shaft on which the cam bears with Castrol GTX oil during reassembly. Do not oil excessively but ensure that these parts are adequately lubricated.
3 On reassembling the cam driving pins with the centrifugal weights check that they are in the correct position so that when viewed from above, the rotor arm should be at the 6 o'clock position, and the small offset on the driving dog must be on the right.
4 Check the action of the weights in the fully advanced and fully retarded positions and ensure they are not binding.
5 Tighten the micrometer adjusting nut to the middle position of the timing scale.
6 Finally set the contact breaker points as described in Section 2.

10 Ignition - timing

1 If the clamp plate pinch bolt has been losened on the distributor and the static timing lost or if for any other reason it is wished to set the ignition timing proceed as follows:
2 Refer to Section 2 and check the contact breaker points. Reset as necessary.
3 Assemble the clamp plate to the distributor body but do not tighten the pinch bolt fully.
4 Slowly turn the crankshaft until the groove in the crankshaft pulley lines up with the static ignition point on the timing indicator and at the same time the distributor rotor is pointing to the distributor cap segment which is connected to No 1 spark plug if the distributor is fitted. No 1 cylinder should be at the top of the compression stroke and just about to commence the power stroke.

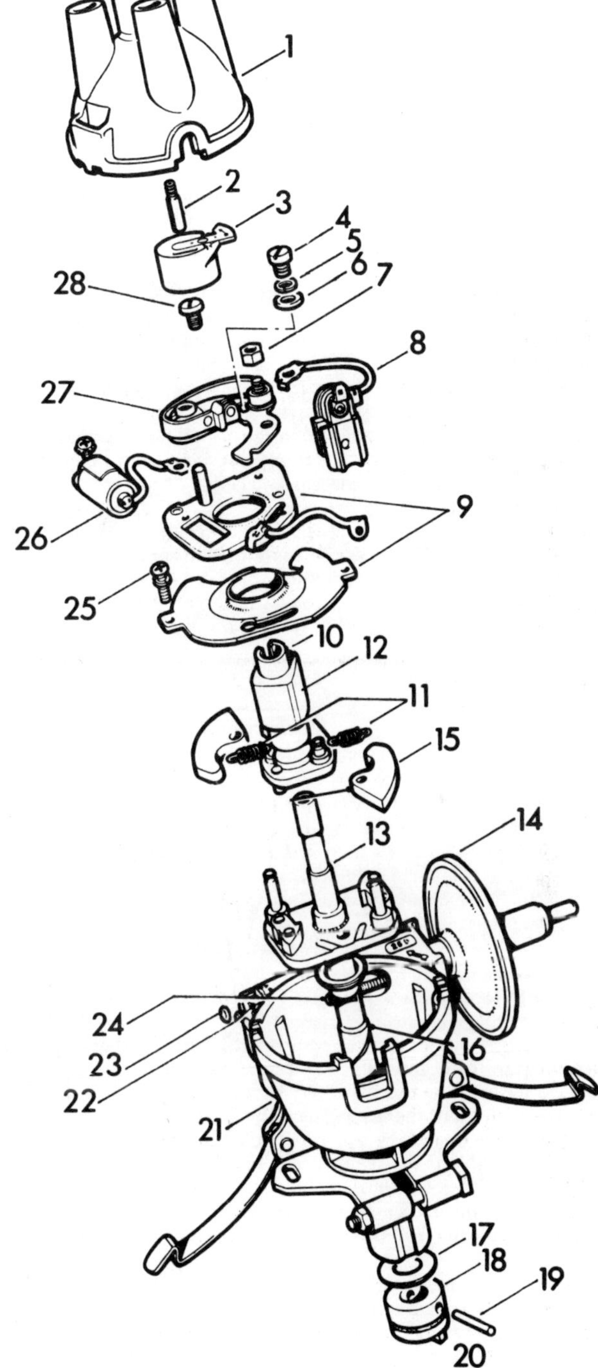

FIG.4.2. DISTRIBUTOR COMPONENT PARTS

1 Distributor cap
2 Carbon brush and spring
3 Rotor arm
4 Screw
5 Washer (spring)
6 Washer (plain)
7 Nut
8 Terminal block
9 Baseplate assembly
10 Note relative position of slot and offset dog (20)
11 Springs
12 Cam
13 Centre spindle (upper)
14 Vacuum unit
15 Centrifugal weight
16 Centre spindle (lower)
17 Thrust washer
18 Drive dog
19 Pin
20 Offset on dog (see also 10)
21 Body
22 Knurled unit flexible coupling
23 Circlip
24 Vacuum unit flexible coupling
25 Baseplate assembly securing bolt
26 Condenser
27 Contact breaker point assembly
28 Cam retaining screw

7.1 Be firm but not careless

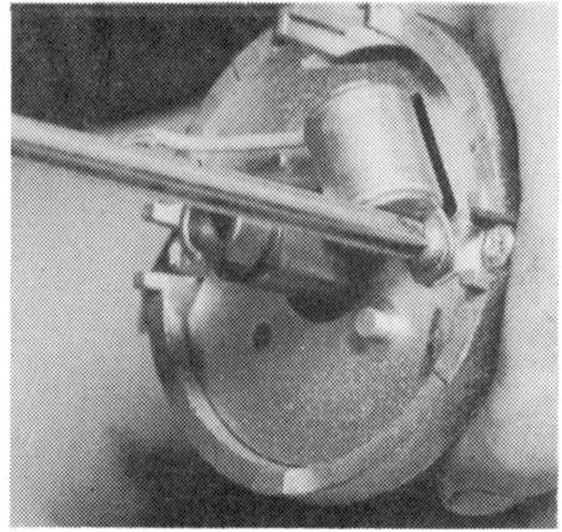
7.3 Use a Phillips screwdriver

7.6 Do not burr the screw

7.7 Cut out in rotor arm drive relative to offset drive dog

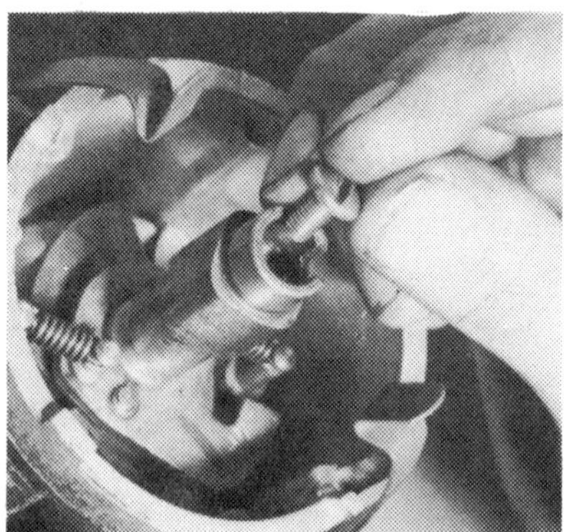
7.8 The screw can be held with a little grease to a screwdriver bit

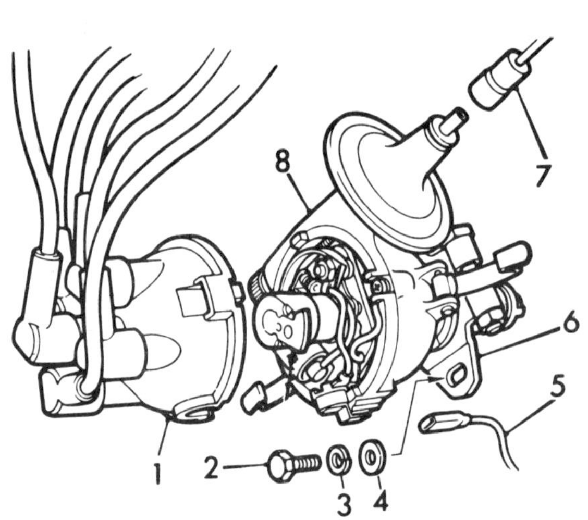

FIG.4.3. DISTRIBUTOR ATTACHMENT POINTS

1 *Distributor cap*
2 *Bolt*
3 *Spring washer*
4 *Plain washer*
5 *LH lead*
6 *Clamp*
7 *Vacuum pipe*
8 *Distributor body*

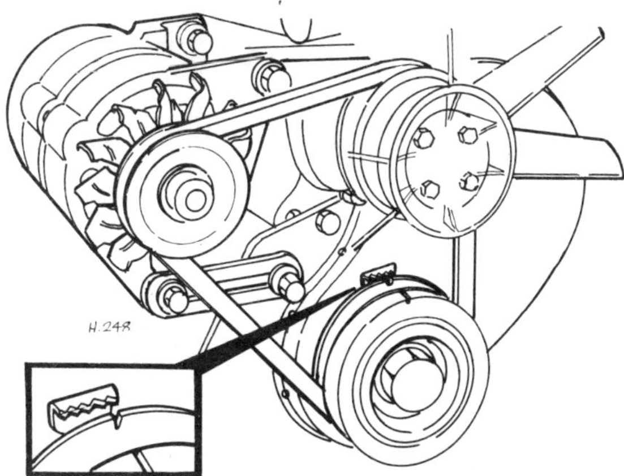

FIG 4.4 ALIGNMENT OF TIMING MARKS ON CRANKSHAFT PULLEY AND POINTER ON FRONT COVER

5 Fit the distributor with clamp plate and engage the driving dog into the distributor drive shaft. Provided the distributor drive shaft has not been disturbed or has been refitted correctly the rotor arm should now point to the segment in the distributor cap which leads to No 1 spark plug (the one nearest the fan).
6 Replace the two distributor clamp bolts, and with spring and plain washers, but do not tighten fully yet.
7 Slowly rotate the distributor body until the contact breaker points are just beginning to open. Tighten the clamp pinch bolt and the two securing bolts.
8 Replace the distributor cap and reconnect the spark plug leads. Do not forget the HT lead to the centre of the ignition coil.
9 If it was not found possible to align the rotor arm correctly, one of two things is wrong. Either the distributor drive shaft has been incorrectly refitted, in which case it must be removed and replaced as described in Chapter 1 or the distributor has been dismantled and the distributor cam spindle refitted 180o out. To rectify this, it will be necessary to partially dismantle the distributor, lift the cam spindle pin from the centrifugal weight holes and turn through 180o. Refit the pins into the weights and reassemble.
10 It should be noted that this adjustment is nominal and the final adjustment should be made under running conditions.
11 First start the engine and allow to warm up to normal running temperature, and then accelerate in top gear from 30 - 50 mph listening for heavy pinking of the engine. If this occurs, the ignition needs to be retarded slightly until the faintest trace of pinking can be heard under these operating conditions.
12 Since the ignition advance adjustment enables the firing point to be related correctly to the grade of fuel used, the fullest advantage of any change of fuel will only be obtained by re-adjustment of the ignition settings.
13 This is done by slight rotating the distributor or varying the setting of the index scale on the vacuum advance mechanism one or two divisions, checking to make sure that the best all round result is obtained.
14 Difficulty is sometimes experienced in determining exactly when the contact breaker points open. This can be ascertained most accurately by connecting a 12 volt bulb in parallel with the contact breaker points (one lead to earth and the other from the distributor low tension terminal). Switch on the ignition, and turn the advance and retard adjuster or the distributor body as applicable until the bulb lights up, indicating that the points have just opened.

11 Spark plugs and leads

1 The correct functioning of the spark plugs is vital for the proper running and efficient operation of the engine.
2 At intervals of 6,000 miles (10,000 km) the plugs should be removed, examined, cleaned, and if worn excessively, renewed. The condition of the spark plug can also tell much about the general condition of the engine.
3 If the insulator nose of the spark plug is clean and white, with no deposits, this is indicative of a weak mixture, or too hot a plug (a hot plug transfers heat away from the electrode slowly - a cold plug transfers heat away quickly).
4 If the insulator nose is covered with hard black looking deposits, then this is indicative that the mixture is too rich. Should the plug be black and oily then it is likely that the engine is fairly worn, as well as the mixture being to rich.
5 If the insulator nose is covered with light tan to greyish brown deposits, then the mixture is correct, and it is likely that the engine is in good condition.
6 If there are any traces of long brown tapering stains on the outside of the white portion of the plug, then the plug will have to be renewed, as this shows that there is a faulty joint between the plug body and the insulator, and compression is being allowed to leak away.
7 Plugs should be cleaned by a sand blasting machine, which will free them from carbon more than by cleaning by hand. The machine will also test the condition of the plugs under compression. Any plug that fails to spark at the recommended pressure should be renewed.
8 The spark plug gap is of considerable importance, as, if it is too large or too small the size of the spark and its efficiency will be seriously impaired. The spark plug gap should be set to 0.025 inch (0.6425 mm).
9 To set it, measure the gap with a feeler gauge, and then bend open, or close, the outer plug electrode until the correct gap is achieved. The centre electrode should never be bent as this may crack the insulation and cause plug failure, if nothing worse.
10 When replacing the plugs, remember to use new washers and replace the leads from the distributor cap in the correct firing order which is 1, 3, 4, 2. No. 1 cylinder being the one nearest the fan.
11 The plug leads require no maintenance other than being kept clean and wiped over regularly. At intervals of 6,000 miles (10,000 km), however, pull each lead off the plug in turn and remove them from the distributor cap. Water can seep down these joints giving rise to a white corrosive deposit which must be carefully removed from the end of each cable.

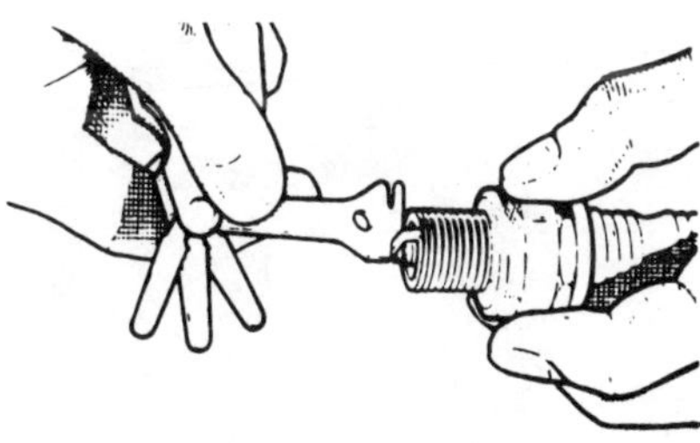

FIG 4.5 CORRECT METHOD OF RESETTING SPARK PLUG GAP

FIG 4.6 SPARK PLUG ELECTRODE CONDITIONS

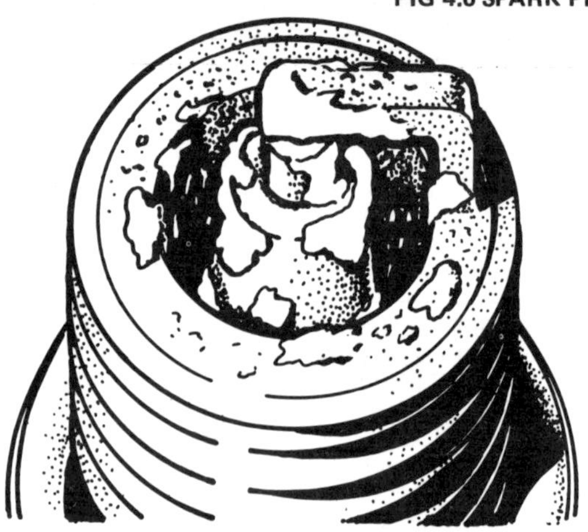

White deposits and damaged porcelain insulation indicating overheating

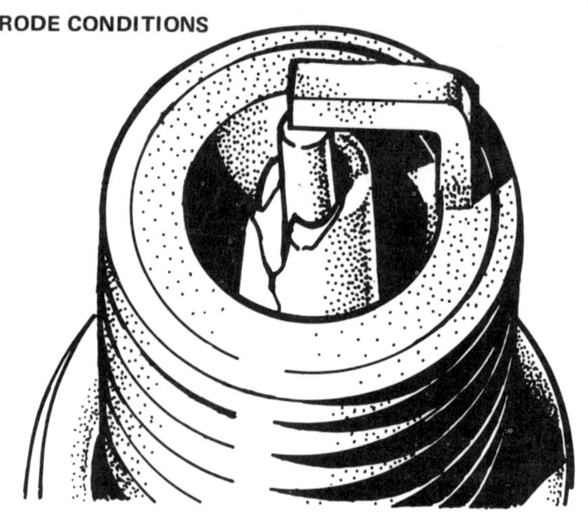

Broken porcelain insulation due to bent central electrode

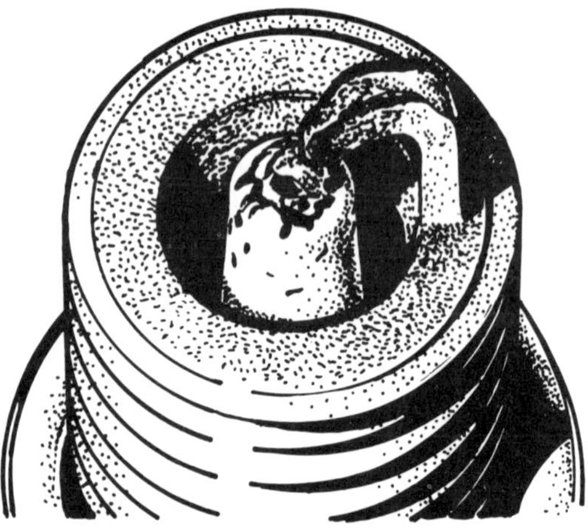

Electrodes burnt away due to wrong heat value or chronic pre-ignition (pinking)

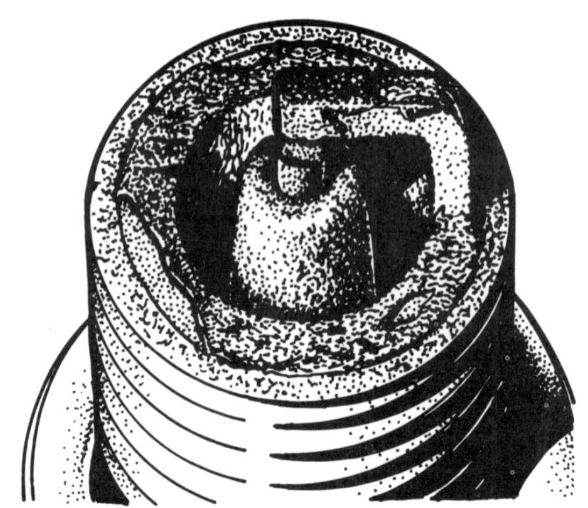

Excessive black deposits caused by over-rich mixture or wrong heat value

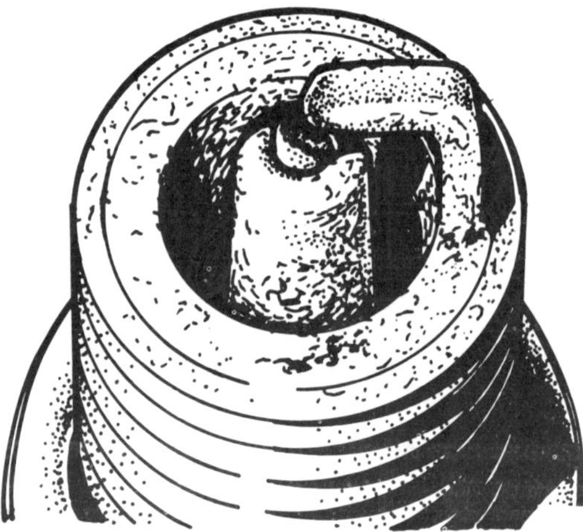

Mild white deposits and electrode burnt indicating too weak a fuel mixture

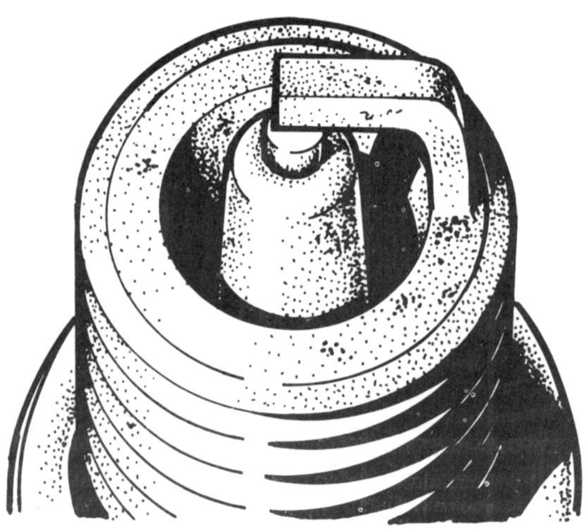

Plug in sound condition with light greyish brown deposits

12 Ignition system - fault symptoms

There are two general symptoms of ignition faults. Either the engine will not fire, or the engine is difficult to start and misfires. Igf the engine will not fire, or the engine is difficult to start and misfires. If it is a regular misfire, i.e. the engine is only running on two or three cylinders, the fault is alsmost sure to be in the high tension, circuit. If the misfiring is intermittent, the fault could be in either the high or low tension circuits. If the engine stops suddenly, or will not start at all, it is likely that the fault is in the low tension circuit. Loss of power and overheating, apart from faulty carburettor settings, are normally due to faults in the distributor, or incorect ignition timing.

13 Fault diagnosis - engine fails to start

1 If the engine fails to start and it was running normally when it was last used,first check that there is fuel in the petrol tank. If the engine turns over normally on the starter motor and the battery is evidently well charged, then the fault may be in either the high or low tension circuits. First check th e HT circuit. NOTE - If the battery is known to be fully charged, the ignition comes on, and the starter motor fails to turn the engine, CHECK THE TIGHTNESS OF THE LEADS ON THE BATTERY TERMINALS and also the secureness of the earth lead to the CONNECTION TO THE BODY. It is quite common for the leads to have worked loose, even if they look and feel secure. If one of the battery terminal posts gets very hot when trying to operate the starter motor this is a sure indication of a faulty connection to that terminal.

2 One of the commonest reasons for bad starting is wet or damp spark plug leads and distributor. Remove the distributor cap. If the condensation is visible, internally dry the cap with a rag and also wipe over the leads. Replace the cap.

3 If the engine still fails to start, check that current is reaching the plugs by disconnecting each plug lead in turn at the spark plug ends and holding the end of the cable about 3/16 inch (4.726 mm) away from the cylinder block. Spin the engine on the starter motor by passing the rubber button on the starter motor solenoid switch (under the bonnet) for manual gearbox models. For automatic transmission models a second person should operate the ignition/starter switch.

4 Sparking between the end of the cable and the block should be fairly strong with a regular blue spark (hold the lead with rubber to avoid electric shocks). If current is reaching the spark plugs, then remove them and clean and regap them to 0.024 - 0.026 inch (0.625 - 0.660 mm). The engine should now start.

5 Spin the engine as before, when a rapid succession of blue sparks between the end of the lead and the block indicate that the coil is in order, and that either the distributor cap is cracked, the carbon brush is stuck or worn, the rotor arm is faulty, or the contact points are burnt, pitted or dirty. If the parts are in bad shape, clean and reset them as described in Section 3.

6 If there are no sparks from the end of the lead from the coil, then check the connections of the lead to the coil and distributor cap, and if they are in order, check out the low tension circuit starting with the battery.

7 Switch on the ignition and turn the crankshaft so that the contact breaker points have fully opened. Then, with either a 20 bolt boltmeter or bulb and length of wire, check that current from the battery is reaching the starter solenoid switch. No reading indicates that there is a fault in the cable to the switch or in the connections at the switch or at the battery terminals. Alternatively, the battery earth lead may not be properly earthed to the body.

8 If in order, check that current is reaching terminal A (the one with the brown lead) in the control box, by connecting the voltmeter between A and earth point. If there is no reading, this indicates a faulty cable or loose connection between the solenoid switch and the A terminal. Remedy and the car will start.

9 Check with the voltmeter between the control box terminal A and earth. No reading means a fault in the control box. Fit a new control box and start the car.

10 If in order, then check that current is reaching the ignition switch by connecting the voltmeter to the ignition switch input terminal (the one connected to the brown cable) and earth. No reading indicates a break in the wire or a faulty connection at the switch or A1 terminals.

11 If the correct reading (approx 12 volts) is obtained check the output terminal on the ignition switch (the one with the white cable) no reading means that the ignition switch is broken. Replace with a new unit and start the car.

12 If current is reaching the ignition switch output terminal, then check the A3 terminal on the fuse unit with the voltmeter. No reading indicates a break in the wire or loose connections between the ignition and the A3 terminal. Even if the A3 - A4 fuse is broken, current should still be reaching the coil as it does not pass through the fuse. Remedy and the car should now start.

13 Check the switch terminal on the coil (it is marked + and the lead from the switch is connected to it). No reading indicates loose connections or a broken wire from the A3 terminal on the fuse unit. If this proves to be at fault, remedy and re-start the car.

14 Check the contact breaker terminal on the coil (it is marked - and the lead to the distributor is connected to it). If no reading is recorded on the voltmeter then the coil is broken and must be replaced. The car should start when a new coil has been fitted.

15 If a reading is obtained at the - terminal then check the wire from the coil for loose connections etc. The final check on the low tension circuit is across the contact breaker points. No reading indicates a broken condenser, which when replaced will enable the car to finally start.

14 Fault diagnosis - engine misfires

1 If the engine misfires regularly, run it at a fast idling speed, and short out each of the spark plugs in turn by placing an insulated screwdriver across the plug terminal to the cylinder block.

2 No difference in engine running will be noticed when the plug in the defective cylinder is short circuited. Short circuiting the working plugs will accentuate the misfire.

3 Remove the plug lead from the end of the defective plug and hold it about 3/16 in (4.76 mm) away from the block. Restart the engine. If sparking is fairly strong and regular the fault must lie in the spark plug.

4 The plug may be loose, the insulation may be cracked or the electrodes may have burnt away giving too wide a gap for the spark to jump across. Worse still, the earth electrode may have broken off. Either renew the plug, or clean it, reset the gap and then test it.

5 If there is no spark at the end of the plug lead, or if it is weak and intermittent, check the ignition lead from the distributor to the plug. If the insulation is cracked or damaged, renew the lead. Check the connections at the distributor cap.

6 If there is still no spark, examine the distributor cap carefully for signs of tracking. This can be recognised by a very thin black line running between two or more segments, or between a segment and some other part of the distributor. These lines are paths which now conduct electricity across the cap thus letting it run to earth. The only answer is to fit a new distributor cap.

7 Apart from the ignition timing being incorrect, other causes of misfiring have already been dealt with under the section dealing with failure of the engine to start.

8 If the ignition timing is too far retarded, it should be noted that the engine will tend to overheat, and there will be quite a noticeable drop in power. If the engine is overheating and power is done, and the ignition is correct, then the carburettor should be checked, as it is likely that this is where the fault lies. See Chapter 3 for details.

Chapter 5 Clutch and actuating mechanism

Contents

Specifications

Type	Borg and Beck or Laycock, diaphragm spring
Drive plate diameter	8 inch (203mm)
Number of damper springs	6
Damper spring colour	3 dark green/light green, 1 dark green/lavender, 1 dark green/white, 1 dark green/orange
Facing materials (identification colour)	H26 Wound yarn green/red WR7 Wound yarn white RYZ Wound yarn blue DSW8 Wound asbestos red
Master cylinder bore	0.625 in (15.8750mm)
Slave cylinder bore	0.875 in (22.2mm)

1 General description

The Marina 1.8 models are fitted with an 8 inch diameter diaphragm spring clutch operated hydraulically by a master and slave cylinder.

The clutch comprises a steel cover which is bolted and dowelled to the rear face of the flywheel and contains the pressure plate and clutch disc or driven plate.

The pressure plate, diaphragm spring, and release plate are all attached to the clutch assembly cover.

The clutch disc is free to slide along the splined first motor shaft and is held in position between the flywheel and pressure place by the pressure of the diaphragm spring.

Friction lining material is riveted to the clutch disc which has a spring cushioned hub to absorb transmission shocks and to help ensure a smooth take off.

The clutch is actuated hydraulically. The pendant clutch pedal is connected to the clutch master cylinder and hydraulic fluid reservoir by a short pushrod. The master cylinder and hydraulic reservoir are mounted on the engine side of the bulkhead in front of the driver.

Depressing the clutch pedal moves the piston in the master cylinder forwards so forcing hydraulic fluid through the clutch hydraulic pipe to the slave cylinder.

The piston in the slave cylinder moves forward on the entry of the fluid and actuates the clutch release arm by means of a short push rod. The opposite end of the release arm is forked and is located behind the release bearing.

As this pivoted clutch release arm moves backwards it bears against the release bearing pushing it forwards to bear against the release plate, so moving the centre of the diaphragm spring inwards. The spring is sandwiched between two annular rings which act as fulcrum points. As the centre of the spring is pushed out, so moving the pressure plate backwards and disengaging the pressure plate from the clutch disc.

When the clutch pedal is released, the diaphragm spring forces the pressure plate into contact with the high friction linings on the clutch disc and at the same time pushes the clutch disc a fraction of an inch forwards on its splines so engaging the clutch disc with the flywheel. The clutch disc is now firmly sandwiched between the pressure plate and the flywheel so the drive is taken up.

As the friction linings on the clutch disc wear the pressure plate automatically moves closer to the disc to compensate. There is therefore no need to periodically adjust the clutch.

2 Clutch system - bleeding

1 Gather together a clean jam jar, a length of rubber tubing which fits tightly over the bleed nipple on the slave cylinder, a tin of hydraulic brake fluid and someone to help.

2 Check that the master cylinder is full. If it is not, fill it and cover the bottom two inches of the jar with hydraulic fluid.

3 Remove the rubber dust cap from the bleed nipple (if fitted) on the slave cylinder, and with a suitable spanner open the bleed nipple approximately three quarters of a turn.

4 Place one end of the tube securely over the nipple and insert the other end in the jam jar so that the tube orifice is below the level of the fluid.
5 The assistant should now depress the pedal and hold it down at the end of its stroke. Close the bleed screw and allow the pedal to return to its normal position.
6 Continue this series of operations until clear hydraulic fluid without any traces of air bubbles emerge from the end of the tubing. Make sure that the reservoir is checked frequently to ensure that the hydraulic fluid does not drop too far thus letting air into the system.
7 When no more air bubbles appear, tighten the bleed nipple on the downstroke.
8 Replace the rubber dust cap (if fitted) over the bleed nipple. Allow the hydraulic fluid in the jar to stand for at least 24 hours before reusing it to allow all the minute air bubbles to escape.

3 Clutch pedal - removal and replacement

1 Refer to Chapter 12 and remove the parcel shelf.
2 Straighten the ears and extract the split pin that retains the master cylinder operating rod yoke to pedal clevis pin. Lift away the plain washer and withdraw the clevis pin.
3 Straighten the ears and extract the split pin from the clutch pedal end of the pedal pivot shaft. Lift away the plain washer.
4 Carefully release the pedal return spring from the pedal and slide the pedal from the end of the shaft.
5 Inspect the pedal bush for signs of wear which if evident, either the old bush should be drifted out and a new one fitted, or a new pedal assembly obtained.
6 Refitting is the reverse sequence to removal. Lubricate the pedal bush and shaft and also the spring coils to prevent squeaking.

4 Clutch - removal and refitting

1 Remove the gearbox as described in Chapter 6, Section 2.
2 With a scriber or file mark the relative position of the clutch cover and flywheel to ensure corect refitting if the original parts are to be used.
3 Remove the clutch assembly by unscrewing the six bolts holding the cover to the rear face of the flywheel. Unscrew the bolts diagonally half a turn at a time to prevent distortion of the cover flange, also to prevent an accident caused by the cover flange binding on the dowels and suddenly flying off.
4 With the bolts and spring washers removed, lift the clutch assembly off the locating dowels. The driven plate or clutch disc will fall out at this stage, as it is not attached to either the clutch cover assembly or the flywheel. Carefully make a note of which way round it is fitted.
5 It is important that no oil or grease gets on the clutch disc friction linings, or the presure plate and flywheel faces. It is advisable to handle the parts with clean hands and to wipe down the pressure plate and flywheel faces with a clean dry rag before inspection or refitting commences.
6 To refit the clutch place the clutch disc against the flywheel with the clutch spring housing facing outwards away from the flywheel. On no account should the clutch disc be replaced the wrong way round as it will be found quite impossible to operate the clutch with the friction disc incorrectly fitted.
7 Replace the clutch cover assembly loosely on the dowels. Replace the six bolts and spring washers and tighten them finger tight so that the clutch disc is gripped but can still be moved.
8 The clutch disc must now be centralised so that when the engine and gearbox are mated, the gearbox input shaft splines will pass through the splines in the centre of the hub.
9 Centralisation can be carried out quite easily by inserting a round bar or long screwdriver through the hole in the centre of the clutch, so that the end of the bar rests in the small hole in the end of the crankshaft containing the input shaft bearing bush. Moving the bar sideways or up and down will move the clutch disc in whichever direction is necessary to achieve centralisation.
10 Centralisation is easily judged by removing the bar and viewing the driven plate hub in relation to the hole in the centre of the diaphragm spring. When the hub opens exactly in the centre of the release bearing hole all is correct. Alternatively, if an old input shaft can be borrowed this will eliminate all the guesswork as it will fit the bush and centre of the clutch hub exactly, obviating the need for visual alignment.
11 Tighten the clutch bolt firmly in a diagonal sequence to ensure that the cover plate is pulled down evenly, and without distortion of the flange.
12 Mate the engine and gearbox, bleed the slave cylinder if the pipe was disconnected and check the clutch for correct operation.

5 Clutch inspection

1 In the normal cause of events clutch dismantling and reassembly is the term used for simply fitting a new clutch pressure plate and friction disc. Under no circumstances should the diaphragm spring clutch unit be dismantled. If a fault develops in the pressure plate asembly an exchange replacement unit must be fitted.
2 If a new clutch disc is being fitted it is false economy not to renew the release bearing at the same time. This will preclude having to replace it at a later date when wear on the clutch linings is very small.
3 Examine the clutch disc friction linings for wear or loose rivets and the disc for rim distortion, cracks and worn splines.
4 It is always best to renew the clutch driven plate as an assembly to preclude further trouble, but, if it is wished to merely renew the linings, the rivets should be drilled out, and not knocked out with a centre punch. The manufacturers do not advise that the linings only are renewed and personal experience dictates that it is far more satisfactory to renew the driven plate complete than to try to economise by fitting only new friction linings.
5 Check the machined faces of the flywheel and the pressure plate. If either is badly grooved it should be machined until smooth, or replaced with a new item. If the pressure plate is cracked or split it must be renewed.
6 Examine the hub splines for wear and also make sure that the centre hub is not loose.

6 Clutch flexible hose - removal and replacement

1 Wipe the slave cylinder end of the translucent hose to prevent dirt ingress. Obtain a clean and dry glass jam jar and have it ready to catch the hydraulic fluid during the next operation.
2 Carefully detach the hose from the metal pipe at the slave cylinder end and place in the jam jar. Allow all the hydraulic fluid to drain out.
3 Detach the hose from the metal pipe at the master cylinder end.
4 Undo and remove the self tapping screw securing the pipe bracket to the bulkhead. Do not refit the original pipe.
5 To fit the new pipe dip the ends in brake fluid to act as a lubricant and push the ends onto the metal pipe.
6 It will be necessary to bleed the clutch hydraulic system as described in Section 2 of this Chapter.

7 Clutch master cylinder - removal and refitting

1 Drain the fluid from the clutch master reservoir by attaching a rubber tube to the slave cylinder bled nipple. Undo the nipple by approximately three quarters of a turn and then pump the fluid out into a suitable container by means of operating the clutch pedal. Note that the pedal must be held in against the floor at the completion of each stroke and the bleed nipple

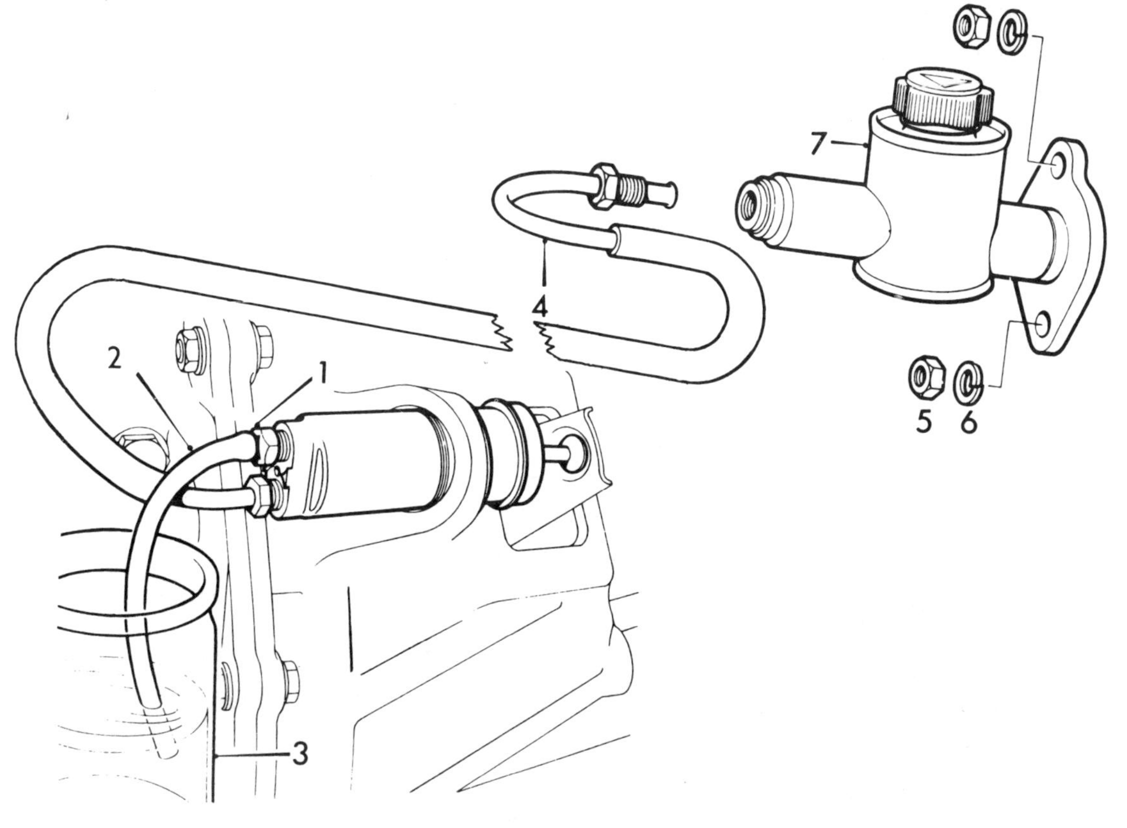

FIG.5.1. CLUTCH BLEEDING

1 Bleed nipple
2 Bleed tube
3 Glass jar
4 Flexible pipe
5 Nut
6 Washer
7 Master cylinder

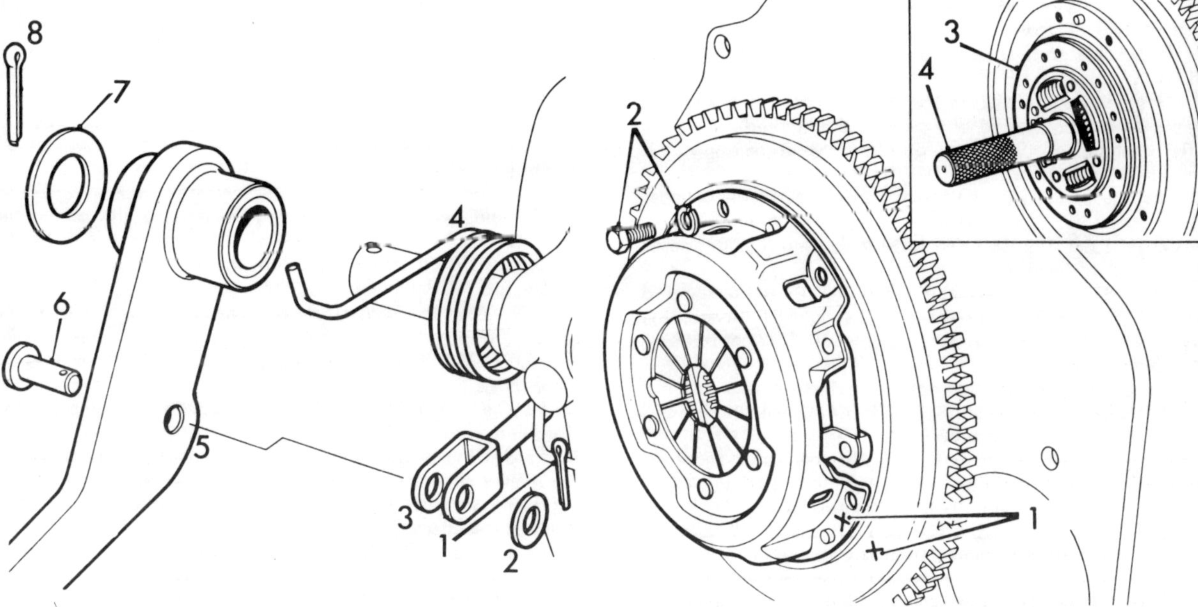

FIG.5.2. CLUTCH PEDAL MOUNTING

1 Split pin
2 Plain washer
3 Pushrod
4 Spring
5 Clutch pedal
6 Clevis pin
7 Plain washer
8 Split pin

FIG.5.3. CLUTCH MOUNTED ON FLYWHEEL

1 Alignment marks
2 Securing bolt and spring washer
3 Clutch drive plate
4 Mandrel

tightened before the pedal is allowed to return. When the pedal has returned to its normal position loosen the bleed nipple and repeat the process, until the clutch master cylinder is empty.
2 Place a rag under the master cylinder to catch any hydraulic fluid that may be spilt. Unscrew the union nut from the end of the metal pipe where it enters the clutch master cylinder and gently pull the pipe clear.
3 Straighten the ears and extract the split pin from the operating fork clevis pin on the pedal.
4 Unscrew and remove the two nuts and spring washers securing the master cylinder and lift away. Take care not to allow any hydraulic fluid to come into contact with the paintwork as it acts as a solvent.
5 Refitting the master cylinder is the reverse sequence to removal. Bleed the system as described in Section 2 of this Chapter.

8 Clutch master cylinder - dismantling, examination and reassembly

1 Ease back the rubber dust cover from the push rod end.
2 Using a pair of circlip pliers release the circlip retaining the push rod assembly. Lift away the push rod complete with rubber boot and plain washer.
3 By shaking hard, the piston with its seal, dished washer, second seal, and spring retainer may be removed from the cylinder bore.
4 Lift away the long spring noting which way round it is fitted.
5 If the prove stubborn carefully use a foot pump air jet on the hydraulic pipe connection and this should move the internal parts, but do take care as they will fly out. We recommend placing a pad over the push rod end to catch the parts.
6 Carefully ease the secondary cup seal from the piston noting which way round it is fitted.
7 Thoroughly clean the parts in brake fluid or methylated spirits. After drying the items inspect the seals for signs of distortion, swelling, splitting or hardening although it is recommended new rubber parts are always fitted after dismantling as a matter of course.
8 Inspect the bore and piston for signs of deep scoring marks which, if evident, means a new cylinder should be fitted. Make sure the by pass ports are clear by poking gently with a piece of thin wire.
9 As the parts are refitted to the cylinder bore make sure that they are thoroughly wetted with clean hydraulic fluid.
10 Refit the secondary cup seal onto the pistom making sure it is the correct way round.
11 Insert the spring with its retainer into the master cylinder bore.
12 Next refit the main cup seal with its flat end facing towards the open end of the bore.
13 Replace the wavy washer and carefully insert the piston into the bore. The small end of the piston should be towards the wavy washer. Make sure that the lip of the seal does not roll over as it enters the bore.
14 Smear a little rubber grease onto the ball end of the push rod and refit the push rod assembly. Slide down the plain washer and secure in position with the circlip.
15 Pack the rubber dust cover with rubber grease and place over the end of the master cylinder.

9 Clutch slave cylinder - removal and replacement

1 Wipe the top of the master cylinder reservoir and unscrew the cap. Place a piece of polythene sheet over the top of the reservoir and replace the cap. This will stop hydraulic fluid syphoning out during subsequent operations.
2 Wipe the area around the hydraulic pipe on the slave cylinder and disconnect the metal pipe from the slave cylinder.
3 Turn the slave cylinder until the flat on the shoulder faces the clutch housing.
4 Using a piece of metal bar or a large screwdriver carefully draw the clutch release lever rearwards until it is possible to lift out the slave cylinder. It will be found helpful to push the operating rod into the slave cylinder so assisting in lifting out the slave cylinder.
5 Refitting the slave cylinder is the reverse sequence to removal. It is very important that the bleed nipple is uppermost as it will be impossible to bleed all air from the system.
6 Bleed the clutch hydraulic system as described in Section 2.

10 Clutch slave cylinder - dismantling, examination and reassembly

1 Clean the outside of the slave cylinder before dismantling.
2 Pull off the rubber dust cover and by shaking hard, the piston, seal, filler and spring should come out of the cylinder bore.
3 If they prove stubborn carefully use a foot pump air jet on the hydraulic hose connection and this should remove the internal parts, but do take care as they will fly out. We recommend placing a pad over the dust cover end to catch the parts.
4 Wash all internal parts with either brake fluid or methylated spirits and dry using a non fluffy rag.
5 Inspect the bore and piston for signs of deep scoring which, if evident, means a new cylinder should be fitted.
6 Carefully examine the rubber components for signs of swelling, distortion, splitting, hardening or other wear although it is recommended new rubber parts are always fitted after dismantling.
7 All parts should be reassembled wetted with clean hydraulic fluid.
8 Refit the spring, large end first into the cylinder bore.
9 Replace the cup filler into the bore.
10 Fit a new cup seal and replace the piston making sure that both are fitted the correct way round.
11 Apply a little rubber grease to both ends of the push rod and also pack the dust cover.
12 Fit the dust cover over the end of the slave cylinder engaging the lips over the groove in the body.
13 Fit the push rod to the slave cylinder by pushing through the hole in the dust cover.

11 Clutch release bearing assembly - removal and overhaul and refitting

1 To gain access it is necessary to remove the gearbox as described in Chapter 6.
2 Detach the operating lever from the release bearing and slide off the bearing assembly.
3 If the bearing is worn or shows signs of overheating it may be removed using a large bench vice or a press and suitable packing.
4 When refitting a new bearing always apply the load to the inner race.
5 Fit the release bearing onto the gearbox first motion shaft front end cover.
6 Engage the pivots of the operating lever into the groove in the release bearing and at the same time engage the lever retaining spring clip with the fulcrum pin in the gearbox housing.
7 Press the operating lever filler into position.
8 Replacement of the gearbox is now the reverse sequence to removal.

12 Fault diagnosis and remedy

There are four main faults in which the clutch and release mechanism are prone. They may occur by themselves, or in conjunction with any of the other faults. They are clutch squeal, slip, spin and judder.

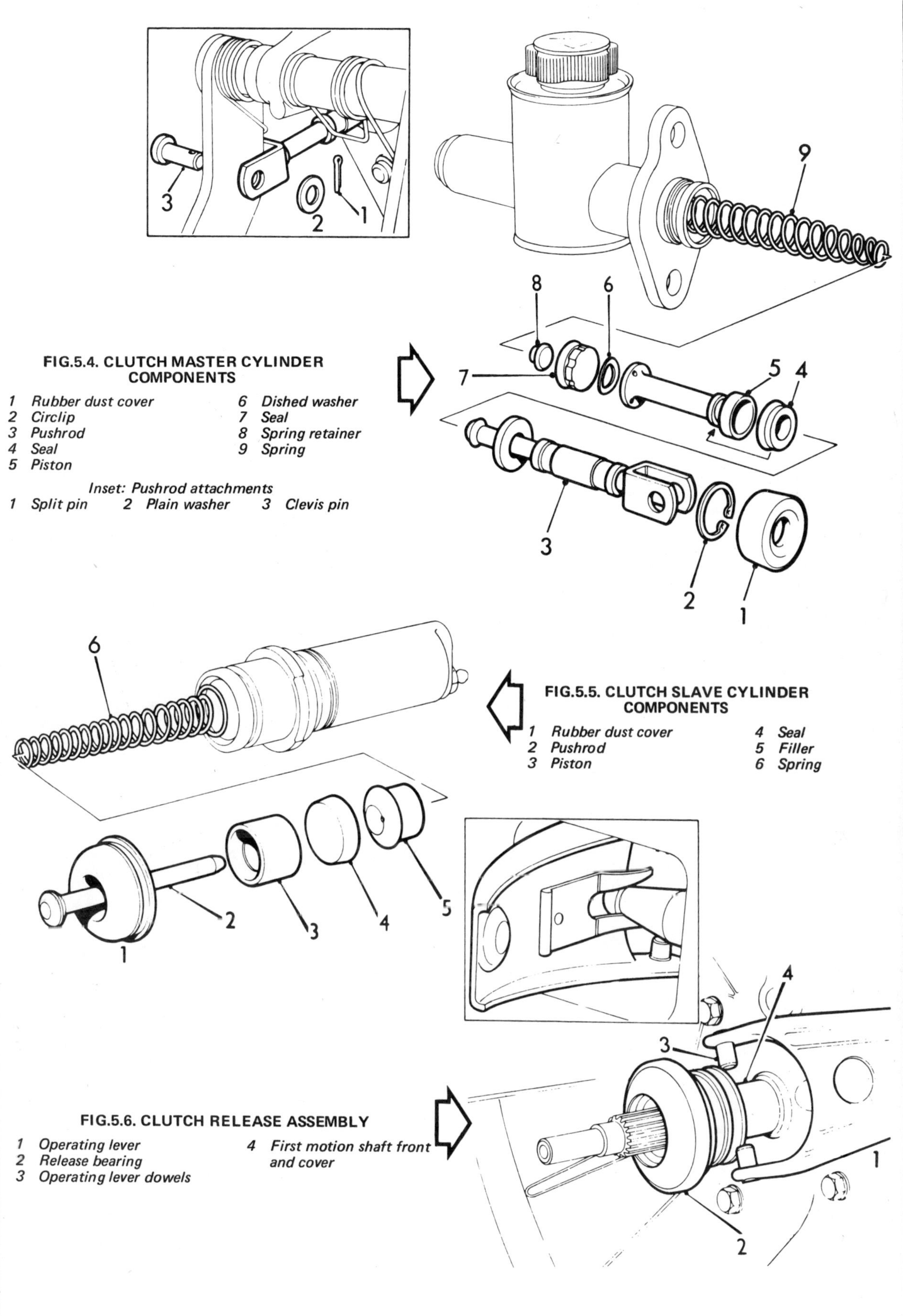

FIG.5.4. CLUTCH MASTER CYLINDER COMPONENTS

1	*Rubber dust cover*	6	*Dished washer*
2	*Circlip*	7	*Seal*
3	*Pushrod*	8	*Spring retainer*
4	*Seal*	9	*Spring*
5	*Piston*		

Inset: Pushrod attachments

1 Split pin   2 Plain washer   3 Clevis pin

FIG.5.5. CLUTCH SLAVE CYLINDER COMPONENTS

1	*Rubber dust cover*	4	*Seal*
2	*Pushrod*	5	*Filler*
3	*Piston*	6	*Spring*

FIG.5.6. CLUTCH RELEASE ASSEMBLY

1	*Operating lever*	4	*First motion shaft front and cover*
2	*Release bearing*		
3	*Operating lever dowels*		

13 Clutch squeal

1 If on taking up the drive or when changing gear, the clutch squeals, this is indicative of a badly worn clutch release bearing.
2 As well as regular wear due to normal use, wear of the clutch release bearing is much accentuated if the clutch is ridden or held down for long periods in gear, with the engine running. To minimise wear of this component the car should always be taken out of gear at traffic lights and for similar hold ups.
3 The clutch release bearing is not an expensive item, but difficult to get at.

14 Clutch slip

1 Clutch slip is a self evident condition which occurs when the clutch friction plate is badly worn, oil or grease have got onto the flywheel or pressure plate faces, or the pressure plate itself is faulty.
2 The reason for clutch slip is that due to one of the faults above, there is either insufficient pressure from the pressure plate, or insufficient friction from the friction plate to ensure solid drive.
3 If small amounts of oil get onto the clutch, they will be burnt off under the heat of the clutch engagement, and in the process, gradually darken the linings. Excessive oil on the clutch will burn off leaving a carbon deposit which can cause quite bad slip, or fierceness, spin and judder.
4 If clutch slip is suspected, and confirmation of this condition is required, there are several tests which can be made.
5 With the engine in second or third gear and pulling lightly sudden depression of the accelerator pedal may cause the engine to increase its speed without any increase in road speed. Easing off on the accelerator will then give a definite drop in engine speed without the car slowing.
6 In extreme cases of clutch slip the engine will race under normal acceleration conditions.
7 If slip is due to oil or grease on the linings a temporary cure can sometimes be effected by squirting carbon tetrachloride into the clutch. The permanent cure is, of course, to renew the clutch driven plate and trace and rectify the oil leak.

15 Clutch spin

1 Clutch spin is a condition which occurs when there is a leak in the clutch hydraulic actuating mechanism, there is an obstruction in the clutch either in the first motion shaft or in the operating lever itself, or the oil may have partially burnt off the clutch lining and have left a resinous deposit which is causing the clutch disc to stick to the pressure plate or flywheel.
2 The reason for clutch spin is that due to any, or a combination of, the faults just listed, the clutch pressure plate is nor completely freeing from the centre plate even with the clutch pedal fully depressed.
3 If clutch spin is suspected, the condition can be confirmed by extreme difficulty in engaging first gear from rest, difficulty in changing gear, and very sudden take up of the clutch drive at the fully depressed end of the clutch pedal travel as the clutch is released.
4 Check the clutch master cylinder and slave cylinder and the connecting hydraulic pipe for leaks. Fluid in one of the rubber dust covers fitted over the end of either the master or slave cylinder is a sure sign of a leaking piston seal.
5 If these points are checked and found to be in order then the fault lies internally in the clutch, and it will be necessary to remove the clutch for examination.

16 Clutch judder

1 Clutch judder is a self evident condition which occurs when the gearbox or engine mountings are loose or too flexible. When there is oil in the face on the clutch friction plate: or when the clutch pressure plate has been incorectly adjusted.
2 The reason for clutch judder is that due to one of the faults just listed, the clutch pressure plate is not freeing smoothly from the friction disc, and is snatching.
3 Clutch judder normally occurs when the clutch pedal is released in first or reverse gears, and the whole car shudders as it moves backwards or forwards.

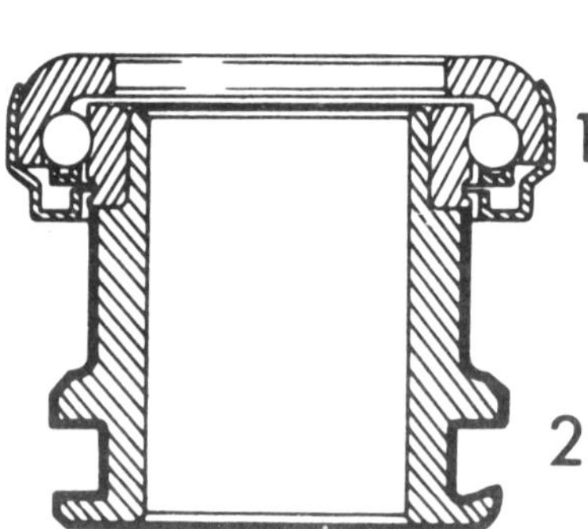

FIG.5.7. CROSS SECTION THROUGH CLUTCH RELEASE BEARING

1 Bearing assembly *2 Bearing carrier*

Chapter 6 Gearbox and automatic transmission

Contents

Specifications

Manual gearbox	4 forward speeds, 1 reverse. Synchromesh fitted to all forward speeds
Gearbox ratios:	
Fourth (top)	1.000 : 1
Third	1.307 : 1
Second	1.926 : 1
First	3.111 : 1
Reverse	3.422 : 1
Overall ratios:	
Fourth (top)	3.636 : 1
Third	4.751 : 1
Second	7.003 : 1
First	11.313 : 1
Reverse	12.444 : 1
Road speed per 1000 rpm in top gear	18.1 mph (29.2 kph)
2nd and 3rd gear endfloat on bushes	0.002 – 0.006 in (0.050 – 0.152 mm)
Endfloat of bushes on shaft	0.004 – 0.006 in (0.101 – 0.152 mm)
Washer sizes available:	
Colour code Plain	0.152 – 0.154 in (3.860 – 3.911 mm)
Green	0.156 – 0.158 in (3.962 – 4.013 mm)
Blue	0.161 – 0.163 in (4.089 – 4.140 mm)
Orange	0.165 – 0.167 in (4.191 – 4.241 mm)
Laygear needle roller retaining rings:	
Fitted depth - inner	0.840 – 0.850 in (21.336 – 21.590 mm)
outer	0.010 – 0.015 in (0.254 – 0.381 mm)
Centre bearing to circlip endfloat	0.000 – 0.002 in (0.000 – 0.050 mm)
Washer sizes available:	
Colour code - Plain	0.199 – 0.121 in (3.022 – 3.073 mm)
Green	0.122 – 0.124 in (3.123 – 3.173 mm)
Blue	0.125 – 0.127 in (3.198 – 3.248 mm)
Orange	0.128 – 0.130 in (3.273 – 3.323 mm)
Reverse idler gear bush - fitted depth	Flush to 0.010 in (0.254 mm) below gear face
Automatic transmission	Borg Warner model 35
Shift speeds ('D' selected with accelerator in kickdown position)	
Upshift	
1 – 2	36 – 43 mph (58 – 69 kph)
2 – 3	61 – 67 mph (98 – 108 kph)
Downshift	
3 – 2	56 – 63 mph (90 – 101 kph)
2 – 1 or 3 – 1	29 – 38 mph (47 – 61 kph)

Ratios:		
First	2.39 : 1	
Second	1.45 : 1	
Third	1 : 1	
Reverse	2.09 : 1	
Capacities		
Manual gearbox	1½ pints (0.85 litres)	
Automatic transmission		
Oil pan only	5 pints (3 litres)	
With torque converter	9.5 pints (5.4 litres)	
With torque converter and oil cooler	11 pints (6.2 litres)	
Torque wrench settings		
Manual gearbox	lb.f.ft.	kg.f.m.
Flywheel housing retaining bolts	28 – 30	3.9 – 4.1
Rear extension to gearbox bolts	18 – 20	2.4 – 2.7
Drive flange nuts	90 – 100	12.4 – 13.8
Automatic transmission		
Drive flange nut	55 – 60	7.6 – 8.3
Drive plate to crankshaft	50	6.9
Converts to drive plate bolts	25 – 30	3.4 – 4.1
Oil pan to gearbox bolts	9 – 12	1.2 – 1.6
Drain plug	8 – 10	1.1 – 1.4
Starter inhibitor switch locknut	4 – 6	0.5 – 0.8

1 General description

The manual gearbox fitted contains four forward and one reverse gear. Synchromesh is fitted to all four forward gears.

The gear change lever is mounted on the extension housing and operates the selector mechanism in the gearbox by a long shaft. When the gear change lever is moved sideways the shaft is rotated so that the pins in the gearbox end of the shaft locate in the appropriate selector fork. Forward or rearward movement of the gear change lever moves the selector fork which in turn moves the synchromesh unit outer sleeve until the gear is firmly engaged. When reverse gear is selected, a pin on the selector shaft engages with a lever and this in turn moves the reverse idler gear into mesh with the laygear reverse gear and mainshaft. The direction of rotation of the mainshaft is thereby reverse.

The gearbox input shaft is splined and it is onto these splines that the clutch driven plate is located. The gearbox end of the input shaft is in constant mesh with the laygear cluster, and the gears formed on the laygear are in constant mesh with the gears on the mainshaft with the exception of the reverse gear. The gears on the mainshaft are able to rotate freely which means that when the neutral position is selected the mainshaft does not rotate.

When the gear change lever moves the synchromesh unit outer sleeve via the selector fork, the synchromesh cup first moves and friction caused by the conical surfaces meeting takes up initial rotational movement until the mainshaft and gear are both rotating at the same speed. This condition achieved, the sleeve is able to slide over the dog teeth of the selected gear and thereby giving a firm drive. The synchromesh unit inner hub is splined to the mainshaft and because the outer sleeve is splined to the inner hub engine torque is passed to the mainshaft and propeller shaft.

2 Gearbox - removal and replacement

1 The gearbox can be removed in unit with the engine as described in Chapter 1. An alternative method is to separate the gearbox bellhousing from the engine end plate, lower the gearbox and remove from under the car, leaving the engine in position. Use this method if only clutch and/or gearbox repairs are to be made.

2 Disconnect the battery, raise the car and put on axle stands if a ramp is not available. The higher the car is off the ground the easier it will be to work underneath.

3 Undo the gearbox drain plug and drain the oil into a clean container. When all oil has drained out replace the drain plug.

4 Undo and remove the two nuts and plain washers that secure the exhaust manifold to downpipe clamp.

5 Refer to Chapter 3 and remove the carburettor(s).

6 Wipe the top of the clutch master cylinder and unscrew the cap. Place a piece of thin polythene sheet over the filler neck and refit the cap. This is to stop clutch hydraulic fluid syphoning out during subsequent operations.

7 Undo the union nut that secures the clutch hydraulic pipe to the end of the slave cylinder. Unscrew the hydraulic pipe clip securing screw and tie back the hydraulic pipe.

8 Unscrew and remove the self tapping screws securing each carpet finisher to the door sill. Lift away the finisher and carpeting so exposing the gear change lever rubber moulding retaining plate.

9 Undo and remove the self tapping screws securing the gear change lever rubber moulding retaining plate to the floor panel. Lift away the plate. Then slide the rubber moulding and foam sleeve up the gear change lever. Note that sealer is used under the rubber moulding flange.

10 Turn the gear change lever retaining cup in an anti clockwise direction so releasing the bayonet fixing. Ease the gear change lever up, at the same time being prepared to depress the plunger and spring in the fulcrum ball. Recover the plunger and spring from the fulcrum ball.

11 With a scriber or file mark the gearbox and propeller shaft drive flanges to ensure correct refitting. Then undo and remove the four locknuts and bolts that secure the gearbox and propeller shaft drive flange. Using string or wire tie the propeller shaft to the torsion bar.

12 Undo and remove the bolt and spring washer that secures the speedometer drive cable retaining clip on the side of the gearbox extension. Lift away the clip and carefully withdraw the speedometer cable.

13 Make a note of the electric cable connections to the starter motor, detach the cables and undo and remove the two bolts and spring washers securing the starter motor. Carefully lift away the starter motor.

14 On single carburettor models slacken the clip screw and then undo and remove the nut, spring washer and bolt from the exhaust steady bracket.

15 Using a hoist or jack support the weight of the engine and gearbox. If a jack is being used place it under the rear of the sump with a piece of wood between jack and sump.

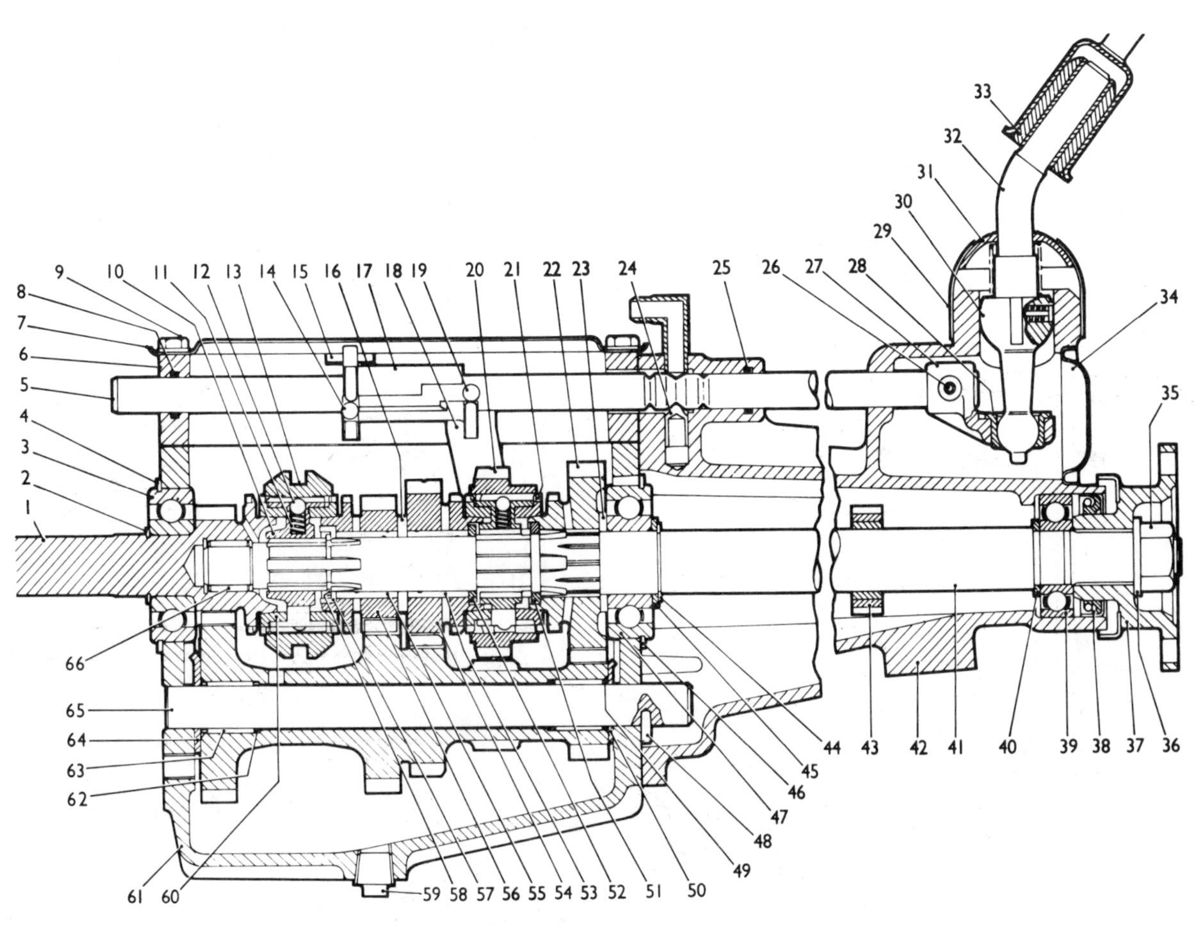

FIG 6.1 THE MANUAL GEARBOX - CROSS SECTION

1 Input shaft (1st motion shaft
2 Circlip
3 Front ball bearing
4 Snap ring
5 Gear selector shaft
6 Gearbox top extension
7 Top cover
8 Selector shaft 'O' ring
9 Top cover bolt
10 3rd/4th speed synchro hub
11 Spring
12 Ball bearing
13 3rd/4th speed operating sleeve
14 Selector shaft pin
15 Interlock spool plate
16 Selective washer
17 Interlock spool
18 Reverse operating lever
19 Selector shaft roll pin
20 Mainshaft reverse gear
21 Synchromesh cup
22 1st speed gear
23 Thrust washer
24 Detent plunger
25 Selector shaft 'O' ring
26 Yoke pin
27 Gear lever yoke
28 Seat
29 Dust cover
30 Lower gear - change lever
31 Dust cover seal
32 Upper gear change lever
33 Bush
34 End cover
35 Self locking nut
36 Flange washer
37 Flange and stoneguard
38 Seal
39 End ball bearing
40 Thrust washer
41 Mainshaft
42 Gearbox rear extension
43 Speedometer drive gear
44 Circlip
45 Selective washer
46 Snap-ring
47 Centre ball bearing
48 Layshift dowel
49 Bearing outer retaining ring
50 Rear thrust washer
51 Split collar
52 Thrust washer
53 Gear bush
54 3rd speed gear
55 Gear bush
56 2nd speed gear
57 Thrust washer
58 Circlip
59 Drain plug
60 Synchromesh cup
61 Gearbox casing
62 Bearing inner retaining ring
63 Needle rollers
64 Front thrust washer
65 Layshift
66 Needle roller bearing

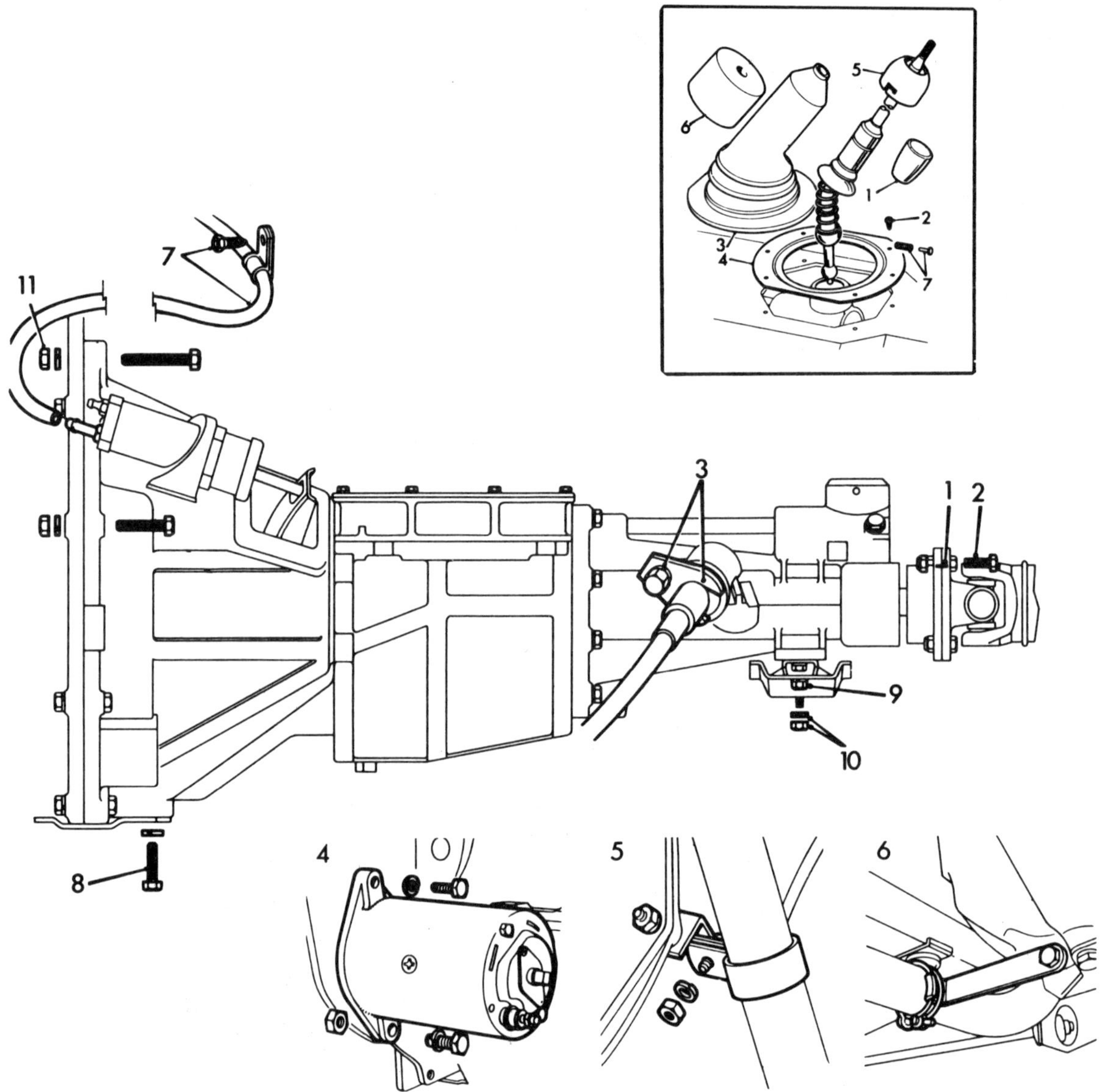

FIG 6.2 GEARBOX REMOVAL. SUMMARY OF ITEMS TO BE DISCONNECTED

1 Drive and propeller shaft flange marks
2 Flange securing bolt and locknut
3 Speedometer cable
4 Starter motor
5 Exhaust pipe bracket at engine backplate
6 Exhaust pipe underbody bracket
7 Clutch hydraulic pipe bracket
8 Sump plate
9 Rear mounting to body
10 Rear mounting to gearbox
11 Bellhousing securing nuts and bolts

INSET: Gear change lever assembly

1 Knob
2 Screw
3 Rubber moulding
4 Moulding retaining plate
5 Cup
6 Foam sleeve
7 Plunger and spring

16 Undo and remove the two bolts, plain and spring washers that secure the sump connecting plate to the underside of the gearbox bellhousing.

17 Undo and remove the two bolts, flat and spring washers that secure the gearbox rear cross member to the underside of the body frame.

18 Undo and remove the nut and spring washer that secures the rear cross member to the rear mounting.

19 Undo and remove the seven bolts and spring washers securing the flywheel housing to the mounting plate.

20 Disconnect the power unit braided earthing strap.

21 Make sure the weight of the gearbox is not allowed to be taken solely on the first motion shaft as it bends easily.

22 Lower the rear of the engine until there is sufficient clearance between the top of the bellhousing and underside of the body and carefully draw the gearbox rearwards. Lift away the gearbox from the underside of the car.

23 Refitting the gearbox is the reverse sequence to removal. Do not forget to refill the gearbox if the oil has been previously drained. It will be necessary to bleed the clutch hydraulic system as described in Chapter 5.

3 Gearbox - dismantling

1 Before commencing work, clean the exterior of the gearbox thoroughly using a solvent such as paraffin or 'Gunk'. After the solvent has been applied and allowed to stand for a time, a vigorous jet of water will wash off the solvent together with all oil and dirt. Finally wipe down the exterior of the unit with a dry non fluffy rag.
2 NOTE: All numbers in brackets refer to Fig.6.3 unless stated otherwise.
3 Detach the operating lever from the release bearing and slide off the bearing assembly.
4 Undo and remove the five bolts securing the clutch bell-housing to the gearbox casing. Note that the lowermost bolt has a plain copper washer whereas the remaining bolts have spring washers.

5 Lift away the bellhousing. Recover the paper gasket from the front of the gearbox casing.
6 Withdraw the oil seal carrier from the bellhousing and ease off the rubber 'O' ring. If there were signs of oil leaks from the front of the gearbox into the clutch bellhousing the oil seal should be removed using a screwdriver and a new one obtained. Note that the lip faces outwards as shown in Fig.6.1.
7 Undo and remove the nine bolts and spring washers securing the top cover to the main casing. Lift away the cover and paper gasket. The main casing has been modified on later cars – the top extension and main casing are now one casting. If the gearbox is of the earlier type comprising two parts temperarily replace two of the bolts to hold the two parts together.
8 Note which way up the interlock spool is fitted and lift it from the top of the main casing.
9 Undo and remove the one bolt and spring washer securing the reverse lift plate (26) to the rear extension. Lift away the lift plate.
10 Using a screwdriver carefully remove the rear extension end cover (13).
11 With a mole wrench hold the drive flange (81) and using a socket wrench undo and remove the locking nut (83) and plain washer (82).
12 Tap the drive flange (81) from the end of the mainshaft (78).
13 Lift out the speedometer drive pinion and housing assembly (21-24) from the rear extension.
14 Make a special note of the location of the selector shaft pegs and interlock spool (37) so that there will be no mistakes on reassembly.
15 Using a suitable diameter parallel pin punch carefully remove the roll pin (38) from the bellhousing end of the selector shaft (39).
16 Undo and remove the eight bolts and spring washers securing the rear extension (12) to the gearbox casing (92).
17 Draw the rear extension rearwards whilst at the same time feeding the interlock spool (37) from the selector shaft (39).
18 With the rear extension (12) and selector shaft (39) away from the gearbox casing lift out the interlock spool (37).
19 Recover the paper gasket (8) from the rear face of the gearbox casing (92).
20 If oil was leaking from the end of the rear extension or the bearing (80) requires renewal, the oil seal must be removed and discarded. It must never be refitted but always renewed. Ease it out with a screwdriver noting which way round the lip is fitted.
21 To remove the bearing obtain a long metal drift and tap it out working from inside the rear extension. Note which way round the bearing is fitted as indicated by the lettering.
22 Slide the washer from over the end of the mainshaft.
23 Make a special note of the location of the speedometer drive gear (71) on the mainshaft, if necessary by taking a measurement.
24 Using a tapered but blunt drift drive the speedometer drive gear frm the mainshaft. Beware because it is very tight and it can break.
25 Using a suitable diameter drift tap out the selector fork shaft (43) towards the front of the gearbox casing.
26 Note the location of the two forward gear selector forks (41, 42) and lift these from the synchromesh sleeve (48, 62).
27 Using a suitable diameter drift tap out the layshaft (90) working from the front of the gearbox casing. This is because there is a layshaft restraining pin (91) at the rear to stop it rotating.
28 Invert the gearbox and this will allow the laygear cluster (86) to drop into the bottom of the casing.
29 Using a small drift placed on the bearing outer track tap out the gearbox input shaft (76). If necessary recover the caged needle roller bearing (77), from the end of the mainshaft.
30 The mainshaft may now be drifted rearwards slightly sufficiently to move the bearing and locating circlip (67). Using a screwdriver between the circlip (68) and casing ease the bearing out of its bore and from its locating shoulder on the mainshaft. Lift away the bearing from the end of the mainshaft.
31 The complete mainshaft may now be lifted away through the top of the gearbox main casing.
32 Unscrew the dowl bolt (30) that locks the reverse idler shaft (31) to the gearbox casing. Lift away the bolt and spring washer.
33 Using a small drift tap the reverse idler shaft rearwards noting the hole in the shaft into which the dowel bolt locates.
34 Note which way round the reverse idler is fitted and lift it from the casing.
35 Lift out the laygear cluster noting which way round it is fitted.
36 Recover the two thrust washers noting that the tags locate in grooves in the gearbox casing.

4 Gearbox - examination

1 The gearbox has been stripped, presumably, because of wear or malfunction, possibly excessive noise, ineffective synchromesh or failure to stay in a selected gear. The cause of most gearbox ailments is failure of the ball bearings on the input or mainshaft and wear on the synchro rings, both the core surfaces and dogs. The nose of the mainshaft which runs in the needle roller bearing in the input shaft is also subject to wear. This can prove very expensive as the mainshaft would need replacement and this represents about 20% of the total cost of a new gearbox.
2 Examine the teeth of all gears for signs of uneven or excessive wear and, of course, chipping. If a gear on the mainshaft requires replacement check that the corresponding laygear is not equally damaged. If it is the whole laygear may need replacing also.
3 All gears should be a good running fit on the shaft with no signs of rocking. The hubs should not be a sloppy fit on the splines.
4 Selector forks should be examined for signs of wear or ridging on the faces which are in contact with the operating sleeve.
5 Check for wear on the selector rod and interlock spool.
6 The ball bearings may not be obviously worn but if one has gone to the trouble of dismantling the gearbox it would be short sighted not to renew them. The same applies to the four synchronizer rings although for these the mainshaft has to be completely dismantled for the new ones to be fitted.
7 The input shaft bearing retainer is fitted with an oil seal and this should be removed if these are any signs that oil has leaked past it into the clutch housing or, of course, if it is obviously damaged. The rear extension has an oil seal at the rear as well as a ball bearing race. If either have worn or oil has leaked past the seal the parts should be renewed.
8 Before finally deciding to dismantle the mainshaft and replace parts it is advisable to make enquiries regarding the availability of parts and their cost. It may still be worth considering exchange gearbox even at this stage. You should reassemble it before exchange.

5 Input shaft - dismantling and reassembly

1 Place the input shaft in a vice, splined end upwards, and with a pair of circlip pliers, remove the circlip which retains the ball bearing in place. Lift away the spacer.
2 With the bearing resting on the top of open jaws of the vice and splined end upwards, tap the shaft through the bearing with a soft faced hammer. Note that the offset circlip groove in the outer track of the bearing is towards the front of the input shaft.
3 Lift away the oil flinger.
4 Remove the oil caged needle roller bearing from the centre of the rear of the input shaft if it is still in place.
5 Remove the circlip from the old bearing outer track and transfer it to the new bearing.
6 Replace the oil flinger and with the aid of a block of wood and vice tap the bearing into place. Make sure it is the right way round.
7 Finally refit the spacer and bearing retaining circlip.

6 Mainshaft - dismantling and reassembly

1 The component parts of the mainshaft are shown in Fig.6.4.
2 Lift the 3rd and 4th gear synchromesh hub and operating sleeve assembly from the end of the mainshaft.
3 Remove the 3rd gear synchromesh cup.
4 Using a small screwdriver ease the 3rd gear retaining circlip from its groove in the mainshaft. Lift away the circlip.
5 Lift away the 3rd gear thrust washer.
6 Slide the 3rd gear and bush from the mainshaft followed by the thrust washer. Note this is a selective thrust washer.
7 Slide the 2nd gear and bush from the mainshaft followed by the grooved washer. Note which way round it is fitted.
8 Detach the 2nd gear synchromesh cup from inside the 2nd and 1st gear synchromesh hub and lift away.
9 Slide the 2nd and 1st gear synchromesh hub and reverse gear sleeve assembly from the mainshaft. Recover the 1st gear synchromesh cup.
10 Using a small electricians screwdriver lift out the two split collars from their groove in the mainshaft.
11 Slide the 1st gear mainshaft washer from the mainshaft and follow this with the 1st gear and its bush.
12 The mainshaft is now completely dismantled.

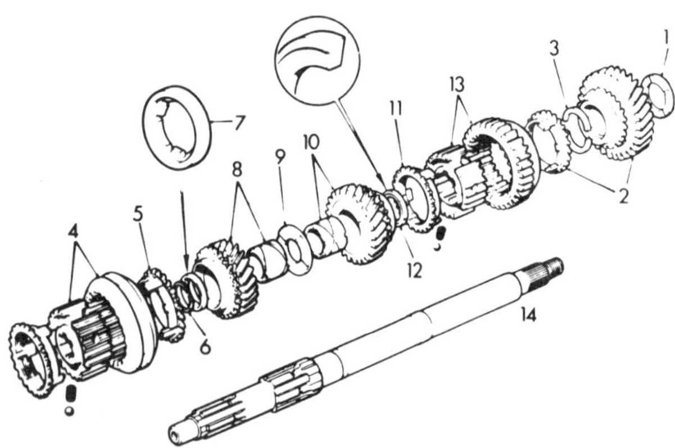

FIG 6.4 MAINSHAFT ASSEMBLY

1 Thrust washer
2 1st speed gear and synchro cup
3 Split collar
4 3rd and 4th speed synchro unit
5 Synchro cup
6 Mainshaft circlip
7 3rd speed gear thrust washer
8 3rd speed gear and bush
9 Selective washer
10 2nd speed gear and bush
11 Synchromesh cup
12 Thrust washer
13 1st/2nd speed synchro
14 Mainshaft

FIG 6.3 GEARBOX COMPONENTS

1 Oil filler level plug
2 'O' ring
3 'O' ring
4 Gearbox top extension
5 Joint gasket
6 Top cover
7 Top cover bolt
8 Joint gasket
9 Plug
10 Detent plunger
11 Detent spring
12 Rear extension
13 End cover
14 Dust cover
15 Knob
16 Upper gear-change lever
17 Dust cover washer
18 Lower gear-change lever
19 Seat
20 Gear lever yoke
21 Speedometer pinion
22 'O' ring
23 Housing
24 Seal
25 Retaining clip
26 Reverse lift plate
27 Oil seal
28 Reverse light switch set screw
29 Magnet
30 Reverse idler spindle locating screw
31 Reverse idler spindle
32 Reverse idler gear bush
33 Reverse idler gear
34 Reverse idler distance piece
35 Reverse operating lever pin
36 Reverse operating lever
37 Interlock spool
38 Selector shaft roll pin
39 Gear selector shaft
40 Interlock spool plate
41 3rd/4th speed selector fork
42 1st/2nd speed selector fork
43 Selector fork shaft
44 Synchromesh cup
45 Ball bearing
46 Spring
47 3rd/4th speed synchro hub
48 3rd/4th speed operating sleeve
49 Synchromesh cup
50 Mainshaft circlip
51 3rd speed gear thrust washer
52 3rd speed gear
53 Gear bush
54 Selector washer
55 Gear bush
56 2nd speed gear
57 Thrust washer
58 Synchromesh cup
59 Ball bearing
60 Spring
61 1st/2nd speed operating sleeve
62 Mainshaft reverse gear
63 Synchromesh cup
64 Split collar
65 1st speed gear
66 Thrust washer
67 Mainshaft centre bearing
68 Snap-ring
69 Selective washer
70 Circlip
71 Speedometer wheel
72 Circlip
73 Snap-ring
74 Ball bearing
75 Oil flinger
76 1st motion shaft (input shaft)
77 Needle roller bearing
78 Mainshaft
79 Washer
80 Ball bearing
81 Drive flange
82 Washer
83 Self locking nut
84 Front thrust washer
85 Bearing outer retaining ring
86 Laygear gear cluster
87 Bearing inner retaining ring
88 Needle rollers
89 Rear thrust washers
90 Layshaft
91 Layshaft dowel
92 Gearbox casing

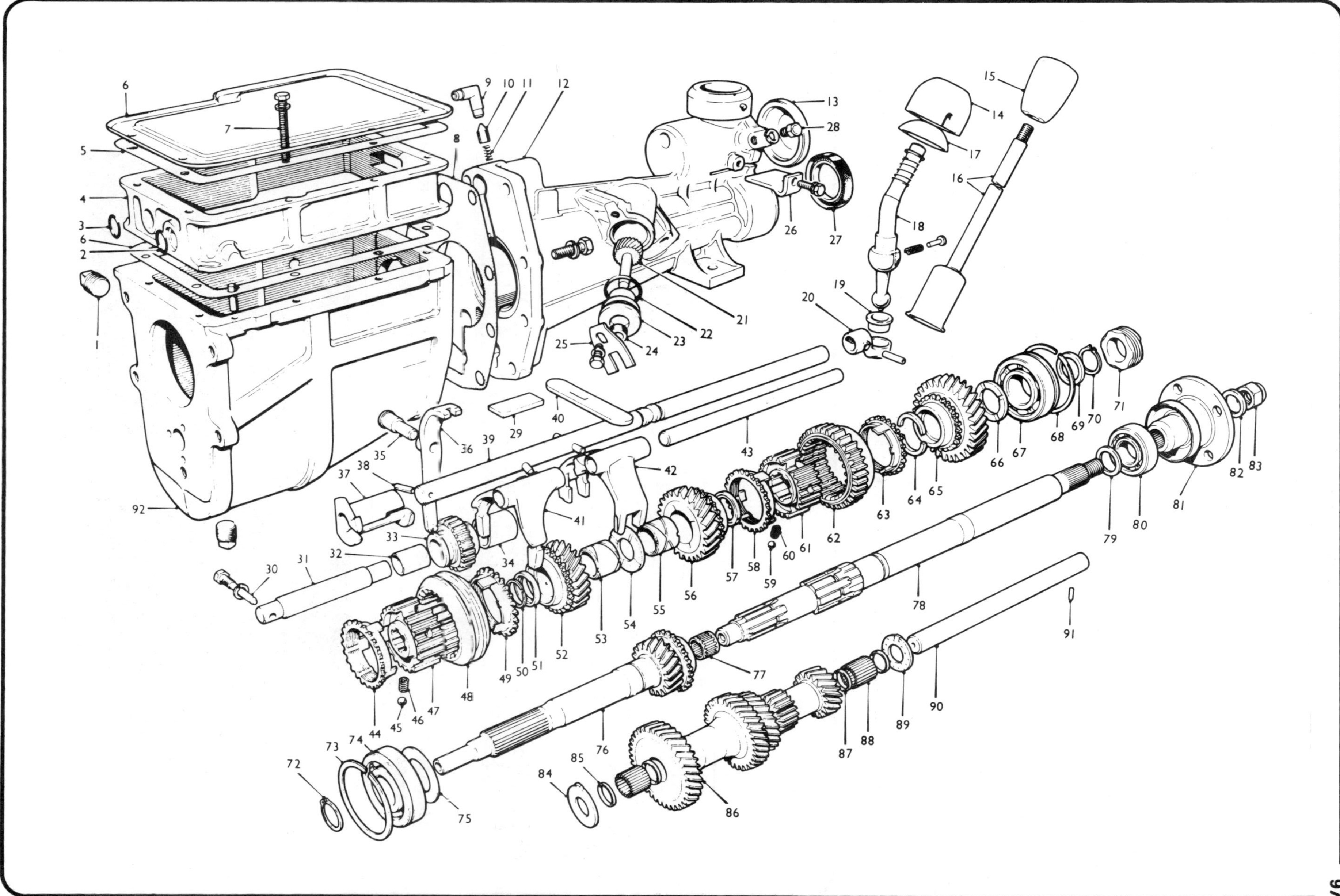
1
2
3
4
5
6
6
7
8
9
10
11
12
13
14
15
16
17
18
19
20
21
22
23
24
25
26
27
28
29
30
31
32
33
34
35
36
37
38
39
40
41
42
43
44
45
46
47
48
49
50
51
52
53
54
55
56
57
58
59
60
61
62
63
64
65
66
67
68
69
70
71
72
73
74
75
76
77
78
79
80
81
82
83
84
85
86
87
88
89
90
91
92

13 Before reassembling refer to Fig.6.5 and measure the end float of the 2nd and 3rd gears on their respective bushes. The end float should be within the limits quoted in the specifications. Obtain a new bush if necessary to achieve the correct end float.

14 Temporarily refit the 2nd gear washer, oil grooved face away from the mainshaft shoulder, to the mainshaft. Assemble to the mainshaft the 3rd gear bush, selective washer 2nd gear bush, 3rd gear thrust washer with its oil grooved face to the bush, and fit the 3rd gear mainshaft circlip. Measure the end float of the bushes on the mainshaft which should be within the limits quoted in the specifications. Obtain a new selective washer to obtain the correct end float. Remove the parts from the mainshaft.

15 To reassemble first slide the bush into the 1st gear hub (photo).
16 Insert the washer into the coned end of the 1st gear (photo).
17 Slide the 1st gear onto the mainshaft followed by the larger washer (photo).
18 Fit the two halves of the split collar into the groove in the mainshaft and push the 1st gear hard up against the collar (photo).
19 Fit the synchromesh cup onto the cone of the 1st gear (photo).
20 Slide the 1st and 2nd gear synchromesh hub and reverse gear sleeve on the mainshaft and engage it witthe synchromesh cup (photo).
21 Fit the 2nd gear synchromesh cup to the synchromesh hub (photo).
22 Fit the 2nd gear washer onto the end of the mainshaft splines so that the oil grooved face is towards the front of the mainshaft (photo).
23 Slide the 2nd gear bush onto the mainshaft (photo).
24 Fit the 2nd gear onto the bush on the mainshaft and engage the taper with the internal taper of the synchromesh cup (photo).
25 Fit the 2nd and 3rd gear selective washer (photo).
26 Slide the 3rd gear bush onto the mainshaft (photo).
27 Fit the 3rd gear onto the bush on the mainshaft, the cone facing the front of the mainshaft (photo).
28 Slide the 3rd gear thrust washer onto the mainshaft splines (photo).
29 Ease the 3rd gear retaining circlip into its groove in the mainshaft. Make quite sure it is fully seated (photo).
30 Fit the 3rd gear synchromesh cup onto the cone of the 3rd gear (photo).
31 Finally slide the 3rd and 4th gear synchromesh hub and operating sleeve assembly and engage it with the synchrmesh cup (photo).

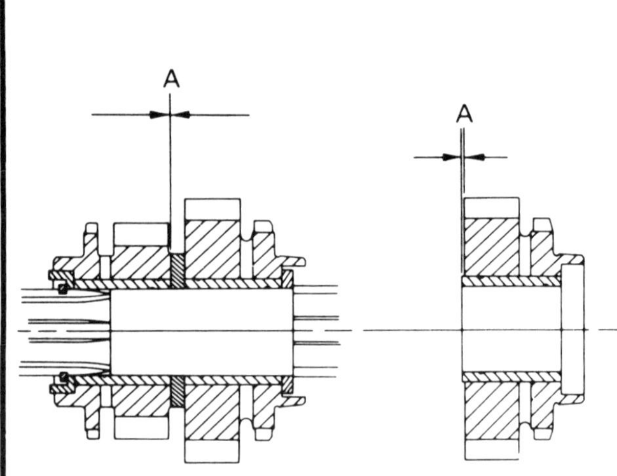

FIG 6.5 MAINSHAFT GEAR END FLOAT

A = 0.002 to 0.006 inch (0.050 to 0.152 mm)

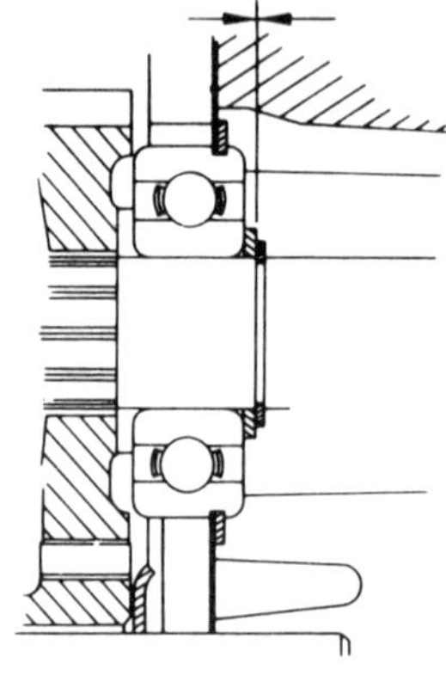

FIG 6.6 SELECTIVE WASHER THICKNESS 'A'

6.15 Sliding bush into 1st gear hub

6.16 Fitting washer into coned end of 1st gear

6.17 Fitting 1st gear and large washer onto mainshaft

6.18 Inserting split collar into groove

6.19 Synchromesh cone for 1st gear

6.20 Fitting synchromesh hub and reverse gear sleeve

6.21 2nd gear synchromesh cup placement on synchromesh hub

6.22 The oil grooves face must face towards front of mainshaft

6.23 Sliding 2nd gear bush onto mainshaft

6.24 Fitting 2nd gear onto bush

6.25 2nd and 3rd gear selective washer

6.26 Sliding 3rd gear bush onto mainshaft

6.27 Fitting 3rd gear onto bush

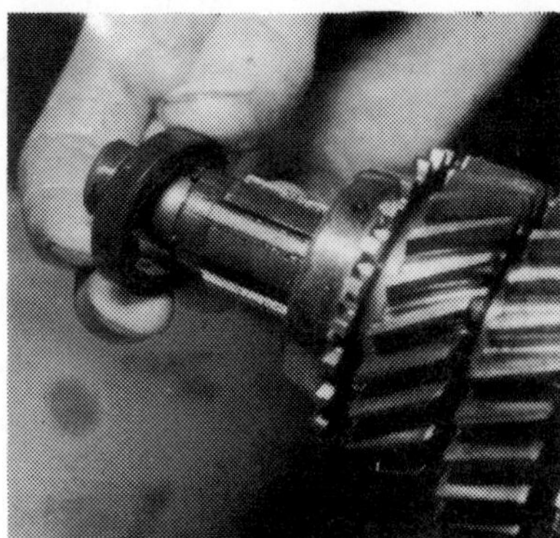

6.28 Sliding 3rd gear thrust washer onto mainshaft

6.29 The circlip must be correctly located in its groove

6.30 Fitting 3rd gear synchromesh cup onto synchromesh hub

6.31 Sliding 3rd and 4th gear synchromesh hub assembly onto mainshaft

7 Gearbox - reassembly

1 Place the magnet in the base of the gearbox. On later produced gearboxes the magnet is cast into the gearbox casing (photo).

2 Position the laygear needle bearing roller bearing inner retainers into the laygear bore. Apply Castrol LM Grease to the ends of the laygear and replace the needle rollers. Retain in position with the outer retainers (photo).

3 Make up a piece of tube the same diameter as the layshaft and the length of the laygear plug thrust washers and slide the tube into the laygear. This will retain the needle rollers in position. Apply grease to the thrust washers and fit to the ends of the laygear. The tags must ace outwards (photo).

4 Carefully lower the laygear into the bottom of the gearbox casing (photo).

5 Fit the reverse gear operating lever to the operating lever pivot. Hold the reverse idler in its approximate fitted position and slide in the idler shaft, drilled end first (photo).

6 Carefully line up the drilled hole in the idler shaft and gearbox casing and replace the dowel bolt and spring washer (photo).

7 The assembled mainshaft may now be fitted into the gearbox casing (photo).

8 Ease the mainshaft bearing up the mainshaft, circlip offset on the outer track towards the rear (photo).

9 Place a metal lever in the position shown in this photo so supporting the mainshaft spigot (photo).

10 Using a suitable diameter tube carefully drift the mainshaft bearing into position in the rear casing (photo).

11 Fit the 3rd gear synchromesh cup onto the end of the input shaft.

12 Lubricate the needle roller bearing and fit into the end of the input shaft.

13 Fit the input shaft to the front of the gearbox casing, taking care to engage the synchromesh cup with the synchromesh hub (photo).

14 Tap the input bearing until the circlip is hard up against the front gearbox casing. Check that the mainshaft bearing outer track circlip is hard up against the rear casing. Refit the washer and circlip.

15 Invert the gearbox. Fit the pin into the drilled hole in the layshaft and carefully insert the layshaft from the rear of the main casing. This will push out the previously inserted tube. The pin must be to the rear of the main casing (photo).

FIG 6.7 LAYGEAR BEARING ASSEMBLIES

1 Bearing outer retaining ring
2 Needle rollers
3 Bearing inner retaining ring
4 Laygear

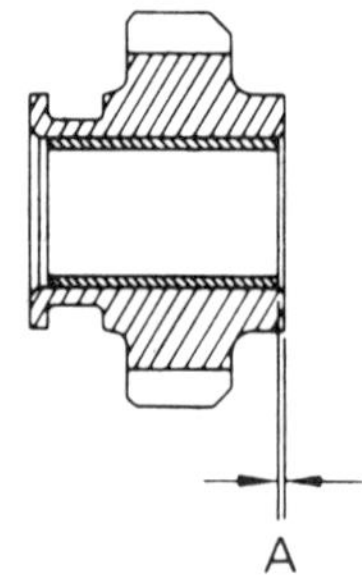

FIG 6.8 CORRECT REVERSE IDLER BUSH LOCATION

A = 0.0000 to 0.010 in (0.0000 to 0.254 mm)

7.1 Location of magnet

7.2 Inserting needle bearing rollers

7.3 Thrust washer with tag facing outwards

7.4 Lowering laygear into gearbox casing

7.5 Sliding idler shaft into position

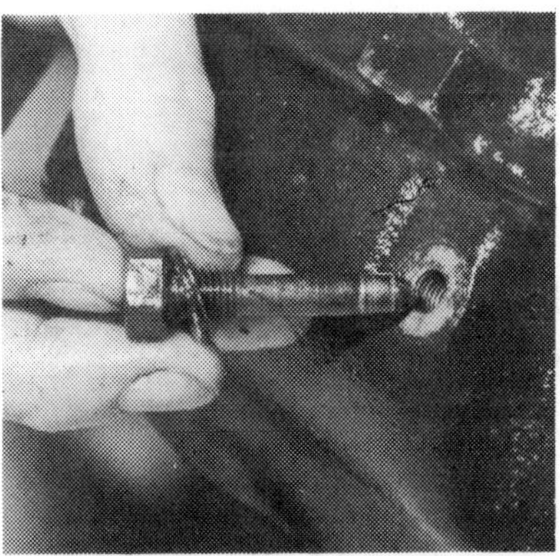

7.6 Special dowel bolt with shaped end

7.7 Fitting mainshaft into gearbox casing

7.8 Sliding bearing up mainshaft

7.9 Supporting mainshaft spigot

7.10 Drifting bearing into position

7.12 Inserting the needle roller bearing into input shaft

7.13 Fitting input shaft

16 Line up the layshaft pin with the groove in the rear face and push the layshaft fully home (photo).
17 Fit the 3rd and 4th gear selector fork to the synchromesh sleeve (photo).
18 Fit the 1st and 2nd gear selector fork to the synchromesh sleeve (photo).
19 Slide the selector fork shaft from the front through the two selector forks and into the rear of the main casing (photo).
20 Fit a new gasket to the rear face of the main casing and retain in position with a little grease (photo).
21 Place the speedometer drive gear onto the mainshaft and using a tube drive the gear into its previously noted position (photo).
22 Slide the washer up the mainshaft to the speedometer drive gear (photo).
23 Place the rear extension bearing into its bore, letters facing outwards (photo).
24 Tap the bearing into position using a suitable diameter socket (photo).
25 Fit a new rear extension oil seal and tap into position with the previously used socket. The lip must face inwards (photo).
26 Slide the interlock spool onto the selector shaft making sure it is the correct way round as shown. This is to give an idea of the final fitted position. Remove the interlock spool again (photo).
27 Place the interlock spool on the selector forks with the flanges correctly engaged (photo).
28 Offer up the gearbox rear extension to the rear of the main casing, at the same time feeding the selector shaft through the interlock spool. It will be necessary to rotate the selector shaft to obtain correct engagement (photo).
29 Secure the rear extension with the eight bolts and spring washers (photo).
30 Refit the spring pin into the end of the selector shaft ensuring the ends are equidistant from the shaft (photo).

31 This photo shows the interlock spool and selector shaft correctly aligned with the pegs engaged (photo).

32 Insert the speedometer driven gear and housing into the rear extension (photo).
33 Fit the drive flange onto the mainshaft splines (photo).
34 Hold the drive flange and tighten the retaining nut and washer fully (photo).
35 Replace the reverse lift plate and secure with the bolt and spring washer (photo).
36 Refit the rear extension end cover and tap into position with the end of the lip flush with the end of the casing (photo).

37 Replace the interlock spool plate in the same position as was noted before removal (photo).
38 Fit a new gasket to the top of the gearbox casing and replace the top cover (photo).
39 Secure the top cover with the nine bolt and spring washers which should be progressively tightened in a diagonal manner (photo).
40 Fit a new O ring to the input shaft retainer and refit the retainer (photo).
41 Fit a new gearbox casing front face gasket and retain in position with a little grease (photo).
42 Move the gearbox to the end of the bench and offer up the clutch bellhousing (photo).
43 Replace the five bolts securing the bellhousing to the main casing. Note four bolts have spring washers and the fifth (lowermost) has a copper washer (photo).
44 Slide the clutch release bearing assembly onto its guide at the same time engaging the release lever (photo).
45 If the gearbox was removed in unit with the engine it may now be reattached. Secure in position with the retaining nuts, bolts and spring washers (photo).
46 Refill the gearbox with 1½ pints (0.85 litres) Castrol Hypoy B (photo).

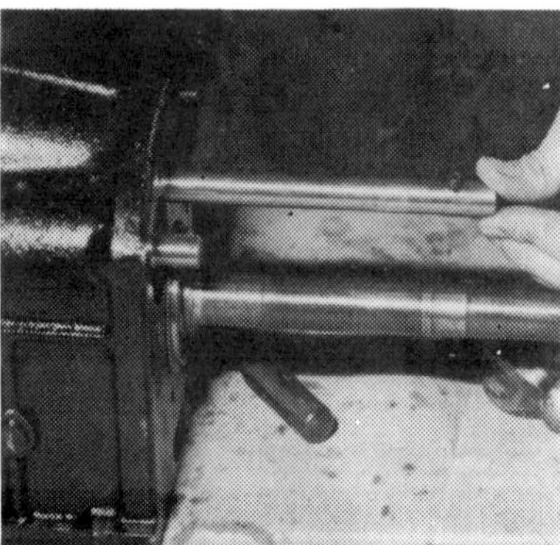
7.15 The pin must be to the rear of the gearbox casing

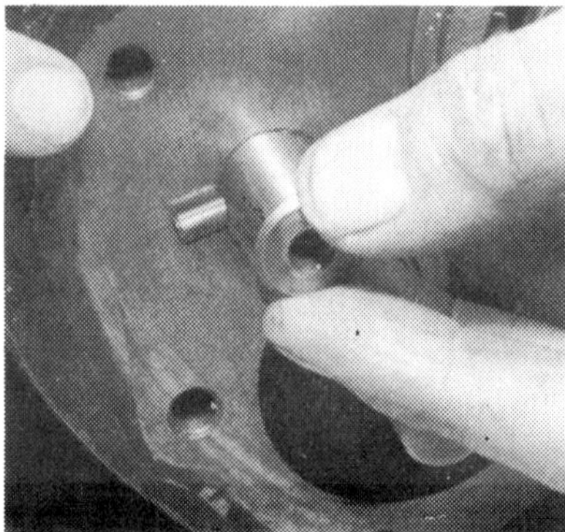
7.16 Lining up pin with groove

7.17 Fitting 3rd and 4th gear selector fork to synchromesh sleeve

7.18 Fitting 1st and 2nd gear selector fork to synchromesh sleeve

7.19 Inserting selector fork shaft through selector forks

7.20 Fitting new gasket to gearbox casing rear face

7.21 Drift speedometer drive gear up to previously made mark

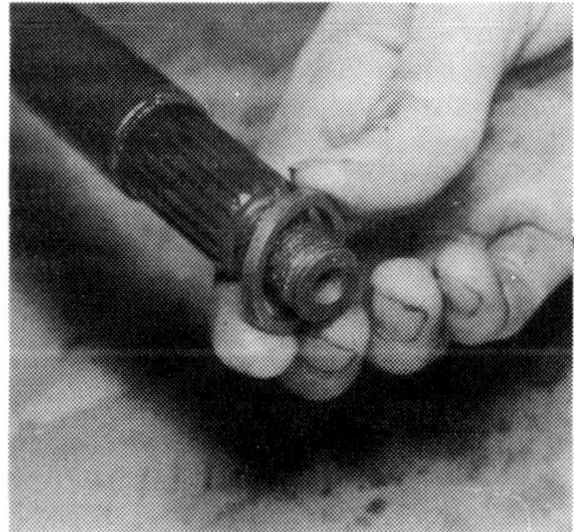

7.22 Slide washer up mainshaft to speedometer drive gear

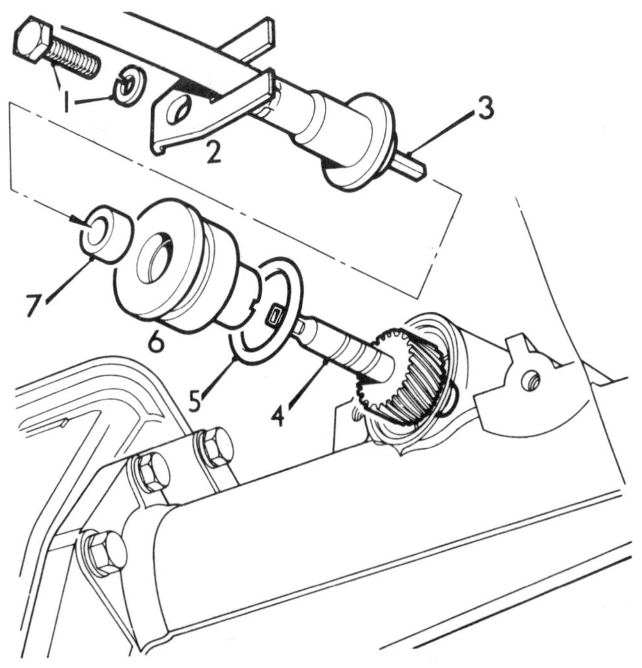

FIG 6.9 SPEEDOMETER DRIVE ASSEMBLY

1 Bolt and spring washer
2 Retaining clip
3 Inner cable
4 Speedometer pinion
5 'O' ring
6 Housing
7 Seal

7.23 The bearing code letters must face outwards

7.24 Using socket and hammer to tap bearing into position

7.25 Fitting rear extension oil seal with lip facing inwards

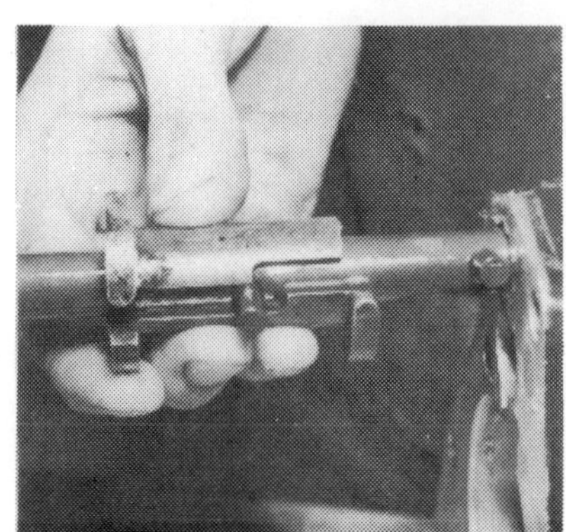

7.26 Trial fitting of interlock spool

7.27 Fitting interlock spool to selector forks

7.28 Rotate the selector shaft to obtain correct engagement

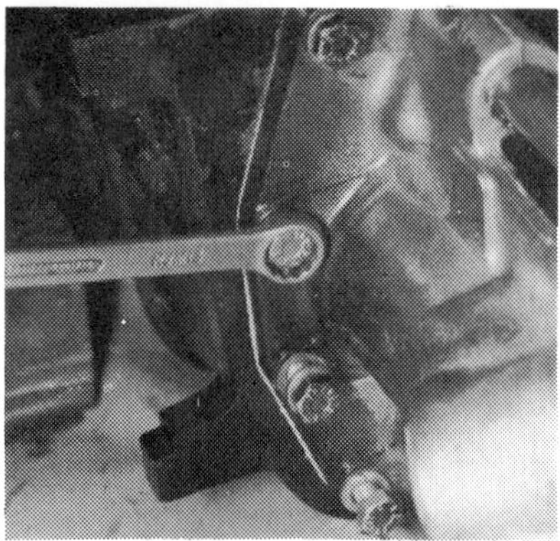
7.29 Tightening rear extension securing bolts in a progressive manner

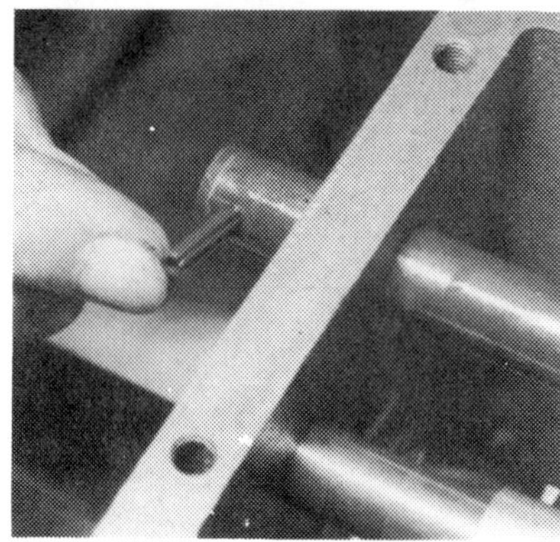
7.30 Refitting spring pin to end of selector shaft

7.31 Interlock spool and selector shaft aligned with pegs engaged

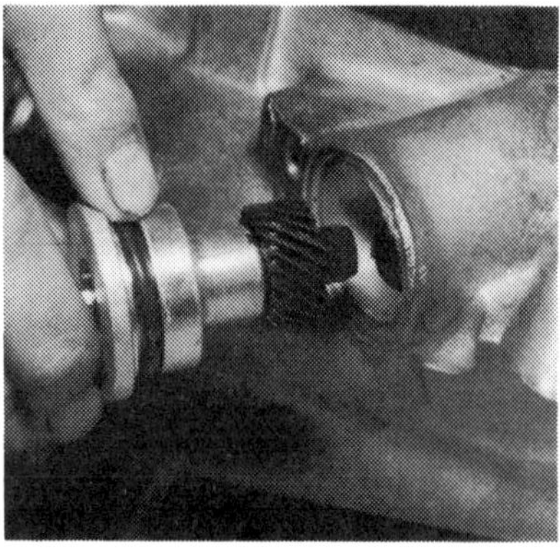
7.32 Insert speedometer driven gear assembly into rear extension

7.33 Offering up the flange to mainshaft

7.34 Tightening flange retaining nut

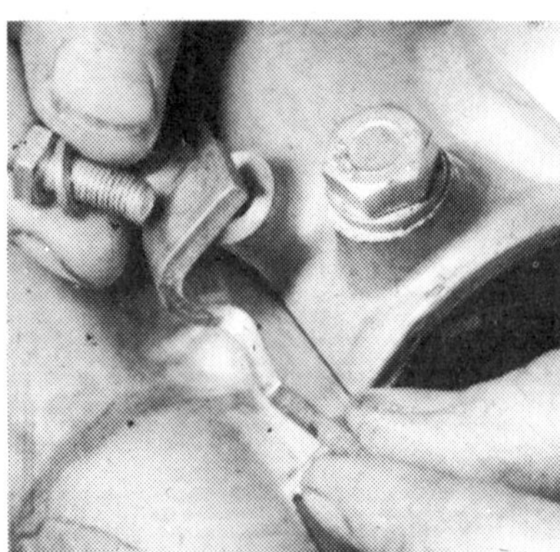
7.35 Refitting reverse lift plate

7.36 The lip must be flush with end of casing

7.37 Refitting interlock spool plate

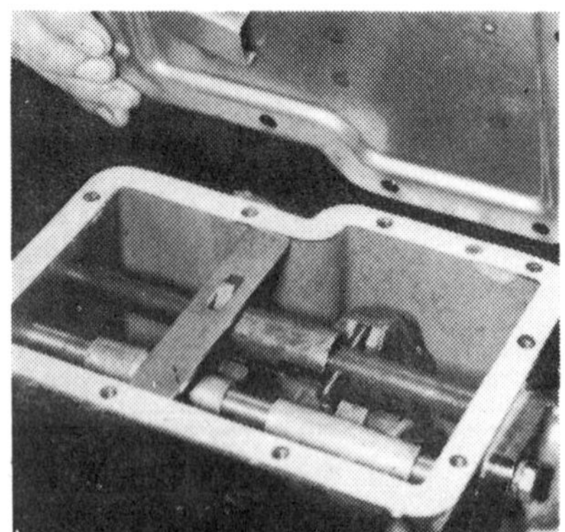
7.38 Positioning top cover on new gasket

7.39 Securing top cover to gearbox casing

7.40 Fitting new 'O' ring to input shaft retainer

7.41 Fit a new gasket to gearbox casing front face

7.42 Positioning clutch bellhousing

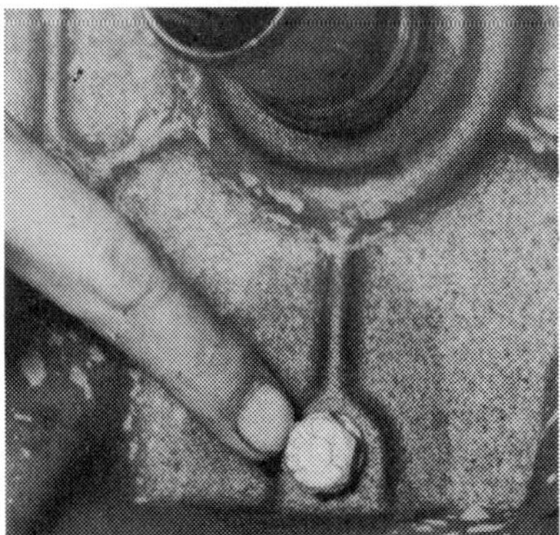
7.43 This bolt requires a copper washer

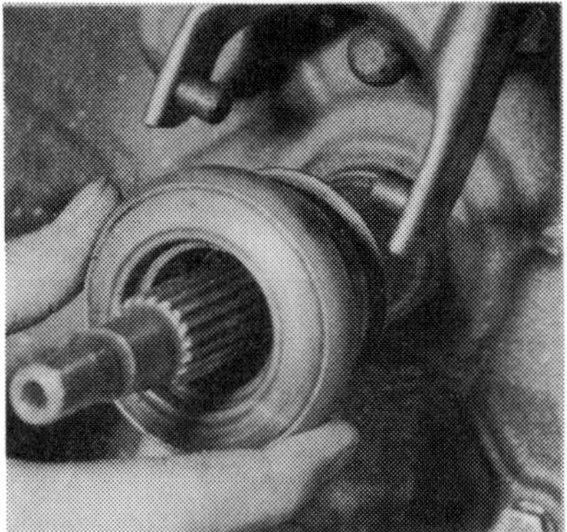
7.44 Sliding clutch release bearing assembly onto its guide

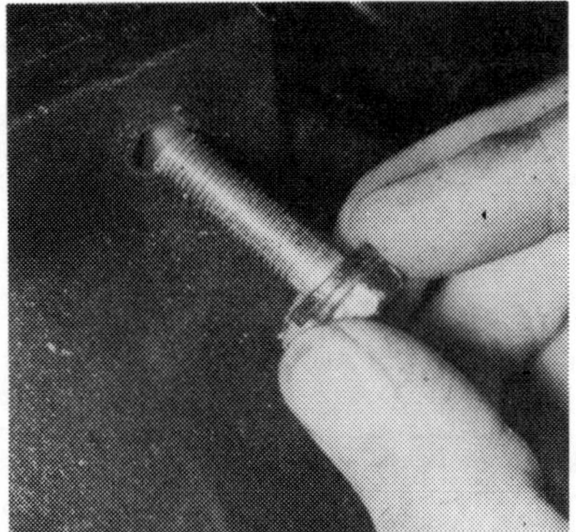
7.45 Clutch bellhousing upper flange bolts replacement

7.46. Use a funnel if possible - flexitops will work

8 Manual gearbox - fault diagnosis

Symptom	Reason/s	Remedy
WEAK OR INEFFECTIVE SYNCHROMESH		
General wear	Synchronising cones worn, split or damaged	Dismantle and overhaul gearbox. Fit new gear wheels and synchronising cones
	Synchromesh dogs worn, or damaged	Dismantle and overhaul gearbox. Fit new synchromesh unit.
JUMPS OUT OF GEAR		
General wear or damage	Broken gearchange fork rod spring	Dismantle and replace spring.
	Gearbox coupling dogs badly worn	Dismantle gearbox. Fit new coupling dogs.
	Selector fork rod groove badly worn	Fit new selector fork rod.
EXCESSIVE NOISE		
Lack of maintenance	Incorrect grade of oil in gearbox or oil level too low	Drain, refill, or top up gearbox with correct grade of oil.
	Bush or needle roller bearings worn or damaged	Dismantle and overhaul gearbox. Renew bearings.
	Gearteeth excessively worn or damaged	Dismantle and overhaul gearbox. Renew gear wheels.
	Laygear thrust washers worn allowing excessive end play	Dismantle and overhaul gearbox. Renew thrust washers.
EXCESSIVE DIFFICULTY IN ENGAGING GEAR		
Clutch not fully disengaging	Clutch pedal adjustment incorrect	Adjust clutch pedal correctly.

9. Automatic transmission - general description

Borg-Warner automatic transmission is fitted.

The automatic transmission system comprises two main components: a three-element hydrokinetic torque converter coupling capable of torque multiplication at an infinitely variable ratio between 2:1 and 1:1 and a torque speed responsive and hydraulically operated epicyclic gearbox comprising a planetary gear set providing three forward ratios and reverse ratio.

Due to the complexity of the automatic transmission unit, if performance is not up to standard, or overhaul is necessary, it is imperative that this is undertaken by BLMC main agents who will have special equipment for accurate fault diagnosis and rectification.

The content of the following sections is therefore solely general and servicing information.

10. Automatic transmission - fluid level

It is important that the transmission fluid is manufactured to the correct specification, use Castrol TQF. The capacity of the unit is approximately 9½ pints (5.4 litres) - with oil cooler 11 pints (6.2 litres), when dry, but for a drain and refill, which is not actually necessary except during repairs, the capacity will be approximately 5 pints (3 litres) as the converter cannot be completely drained. The location of the dipstick is shown in Fig. 6.12. Full information on checking the oil level will be found in the Routine maintenance section at the beginning of this manual.

11. Automatic transmission - removal and replacement

1 Any suspected faults must be referred to the main agent before unit removal as with this tupe of transmission its fault must be confirmed using special equipment before it is removed from the car.
2 As the automatic transmission is relatively heavy it is best if the car is raised from the ground on ramps but it is possible to remove the unit if the car is placed on high axle stands.
3 Disconnect the battery.
4 Disconnect the downshift cable from the throttle linkage at the side of the carburettor.
5 Remove the dipstick from its guide tube.
6 Detach the exhaust downpipe from the manifold. Release the support clip from the support bracket.
7 Undo the bolt securing the engine earth cable to the torque converter.
8 Place a clean container of 8 pints (4.55 litres) capacity under the sump drain plug, remove the drain plug and allow to drain Replace the drain plug.
9 Release the spire nut securing the manual selector rod to the gearbox lever. Draw the selector rod from the lever.
10 Make a note of the electric cable connections to the starter inhibitor and reverse lamp switch. Detach the cable terminals.
11 Undo the dipstick filler tube union nut whilst the adaptor is held to stop if moving.
12 If an oil cooler is fitted wipe the area around the two union nuts and undo the nuts. Plug the ends to stop dirt ingress.
13 With a scriber or file mark the propeller shaft and gearbox flanges so that they may be refitted in their original positions.
14 Undo and remove the four locknuts and bolts that secure the two flanges together.
15 Lift the front end of the propeller shaft away from the rear of the gearbox and tie to the torsion bar with spring or wire.
16 Undo and remove the speedometer cable clamp bolt and spring washer on the gearbox extension. Lift away the clamp and withdraw the inner cable.
17 Using a hoist take the weight of the complete power unit or alternatively a hydraulic jack to take the weight under the torque converter housing.
18 Undo and remove the two bolts, spring and plain washers that secure the rear mounting cross member to the underside of the body.
19 Carefully lower the gearbox so as to give access to the top,
20 Using a second jack support the weight of the gearbox.
21 Undo and remove the six bolts and spring washers that secure the gearbox to the torque converter housing.
22 Very carefully draw the gearbox rearwards until it is clear of the torque converter and then lift away from the underside of the car. It is very important that the weight of the gearbox is not allowed to hang on the input shaft.
23 Refitting is the reverse sequence to removal but in addition:
24 Carefully align the converter and front pump driving dogs and slots in the horizontal plane.
25 Carefully align and then locate the input shaft and drive dogs.
26 Tighten the six gearbox securing bolts to a torque wrench setting of 8 to 13 lb ft (1.1 to 1.8 kg cm).
27 Refill the gearbox with Castrol TQF and check the fluid level as described in Section 9.

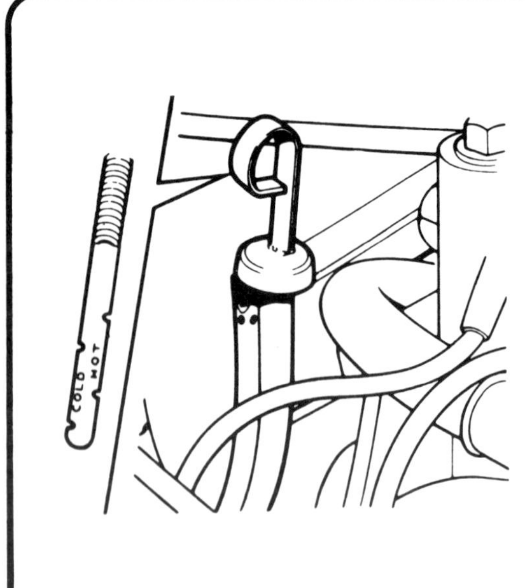

FIG.6.12. LOCATION OF AUTOMATIC TRANSMISSION DIPSTICK AND FILLER TUBE

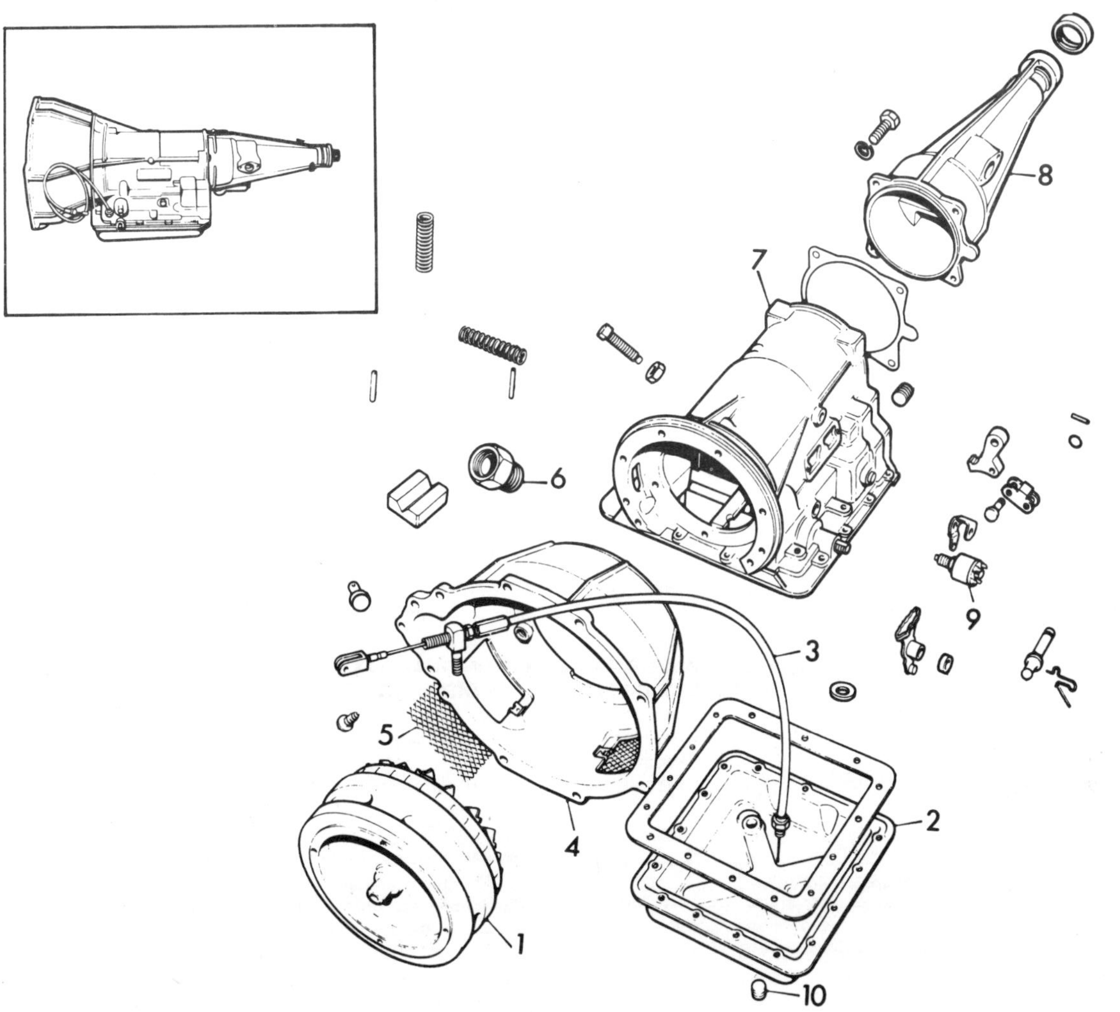

FIG.6.10. MAIN COMPONENTS OF EXTERNAL CASING WITH TORQUE CONVERTER
Inset: Borg Warner model 35 (assembled)

1 Torque converter
2 Oil pan
3 Downshift cable
4 Converter housing
5 Stone guard
6 Dipstick tube adaptor
7 Case assembly
8 Rear extension housing
9 Inhibitor switch
10 Sump drain plug

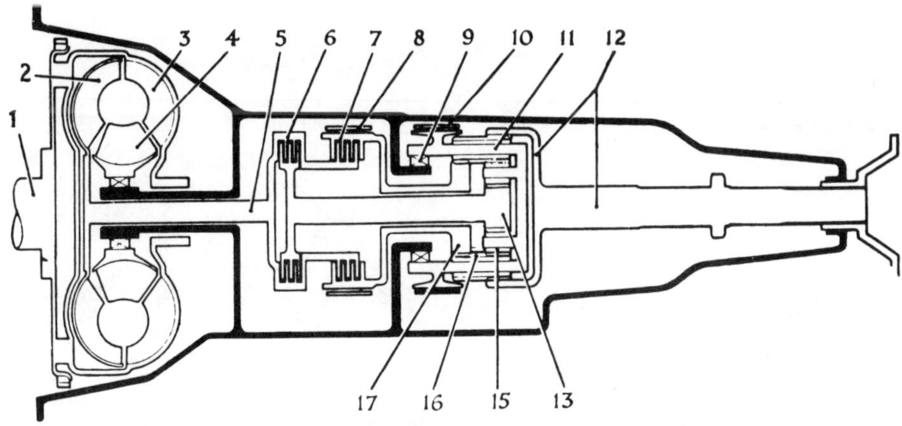

FIG.6.11. MAIN MECHANICAL COMPONENTS IN SECTION

1 Engine crankshaft
2 Turbine
3 Impeller
4 Stator
5 Input shaft
6 Front clutch
7 Rear clutch
8 Front brake band
9 Unidirectional clutch
10 Rear brake band
11 Plant pinion carrier
12 Ring gear and output shaft
13 Forward sun gear and shaft
14 Parking pawl teeth
15 Short planet pinion
16 Long planet pinion
17 Reverse sun gear

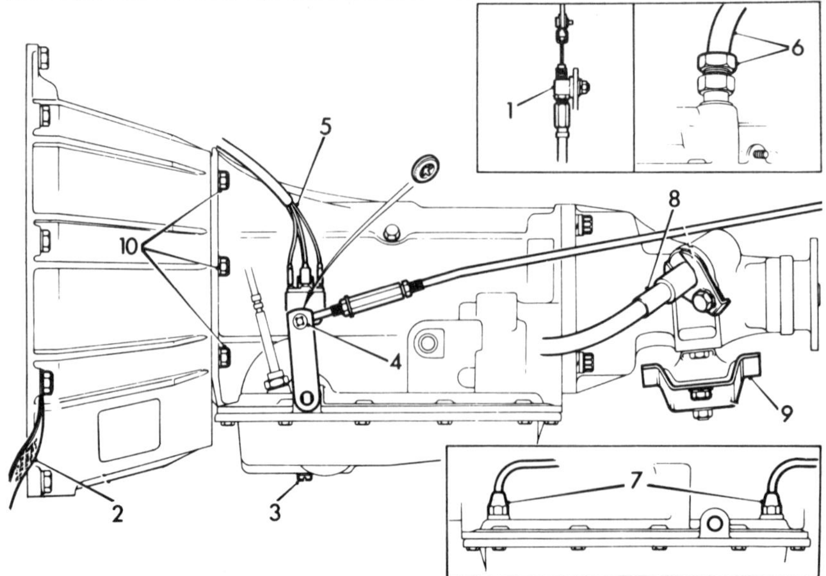

FIG.6.13. AUTOMATIC TRANSMISSION GEARBOX REMOVAL. SUMMARY OF ITEMS TO BE DISCONNECTED

1 Downshift cable
2 Earth cable
3 Drain plug
4 Manual selector rod
5 Starter inhibitor and reverse light switch
6 Dipstick tube
7 Oil cooler pipes
8 Speedometer cable
9 Rear mounting
10 Bolts and spring washers

12. Torque converter - removal and replacement

1 Refer to Section 1 and remove the gearbox.
2 Undo and remove the starter motor electric cable terminal secuirng nut and washers. Detach the cable. Pre engaged starter motor, detach the cable terminals from the solenoid.
8 Undo and remove the two starter motor securing nut and spring washer and bolt and spring washer. Lift away the starter motor.
4 Undo and remove the two bolts and spring washers securing the engine sump connecting plate to the torque converter housing.
5 Support the weight of the engine and then undo and remove the bolts and spring washers that secure the torque converter housing to the gearbox mounting plate.
6 Lower the rear of the engine until it is possible to lift away the torque converter housing.
7 With a scriber mark the relative positions of the drive plate and torque converter if these are to be refitted. This will ensure they are replaced in their original positions.
8 Working through the aperture in the mounting plate, turn the converter, unlock the tab washers and then progressively slacken the four bolts.
9 Support the torque converter and completely remove the bolts and lock washers. Lift away the torque converter. Be prepared to mop up oil that will issue from the torque converter as it cannot be drained completely.
10 Refitting the torque converter is the reverse sequence to removal but in addition:
11 Position the torque converter onto the drive plate aligning up the previously made marks if original parts are being refitted. Refit the four bolts with new tab washers and tighten in a progressive manner to a final torque wrench setting of 25 to 30 lb ft (3.4 to 4.1 Kg fm). Bend over the lock tabs.
12 Check that the dowel is in position and then place the converter housing in position on the mounting plate aligning the dowel hole. Refit the bolts and spring washers and tighten in a progressive manner to a torque wrench setting of 8 to 13 lb ft. (1.1 to 1.8 Kg fm).

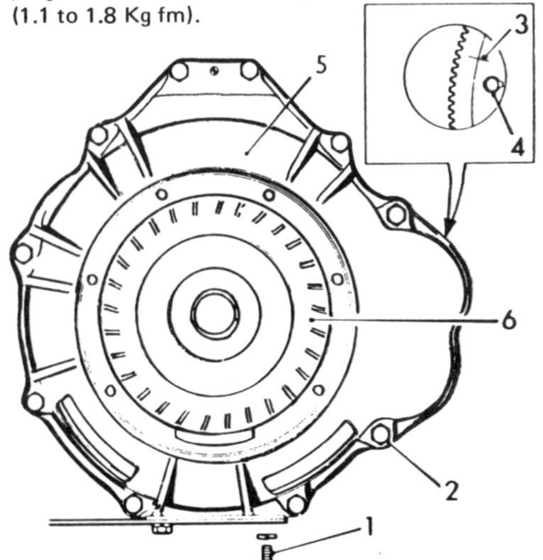

FIG.6.14. TORQUE CONVERTER REMOVAL

1 Sump connecting plate securing bolt
2 Housing retaining bolts
3 Alignment marks
4 Securing plate
5 Housing
6 Torque converter

13. Starter inhibitor/reverse light switch - check and adjustment

1 Firmly chock all wheels and apply the handbrake.
2 Make a note of the electrical cable connections to the switch and then detach the terminals. Starter terminals (narrow) white/ red. Reverse terminals (wide) green/green and brown.
3 Connect a test lamp and battery across the starter terminals (Fig.6.15) - these are the narrow ones - and select positions P R N D 2 1 in order. The test light should only come on in the P and N positions.
3 Connect the test lamp and battery across the reverse light terminals - these are the wide ones - and select ' 1 2 D N R P' in order. The test light should only come on in the R position.
4 If adjustment is necessary leave the test light connected to the reverse terminals. If the light is out slacken the switch locknut using a cranked spanner. Do not grip the switch body.
5 Unscrew the switch slowly until the test light comes on. Screw the switch in until the light just goes out and mark the relative positions of the switch and case.
6 Connect the test light to the starter terminals and the light should be off. Slowly screw in the switch until the test light comes on (approximately three quarters of a turn) and mark the position of the switch relative to the previous made mark on the case. Remove the test light.
7 Turn the switch until it is mid way between the two marks and retighten the locknut.
8 Reconnect the cables to the switch.
9 Check that the starter motor only operates in the P and N position of the selector and that the reverse light only comes on in the R position.
10 If the switch is to be renewed always apply a little liquid sealer to the threads of the new switch to stop any possibility of oil leaks from this point.

14. Downshift cable - adjustment

Before the cable is adjusted it is necessary to confirm that it is the cable that is malajusted and not some other fault. Generally if difficulty is experienced in obtaining 2:1 downshift in the 'kick-down' position at just below 31 mph it is an indication that the outer cable is too short. If there is a bumpy or delayed shift at low throttle opening it is an indication the outer cable is too long.

During production of the car the adjustment is set by a crimped stop on the carburettor end of the inner cable and it is unusual for this setting to change except at high mileages when the inner cable can stretch. To adjust proceed as follows:–
1 Apply the handbrake firmly and chock the front wheels.
2 Run the engine until it reaches normal operating temperature. Adjust the engine idle speed to approximately 700–750 rpm with the selector in the 'D' position.
3 Stop the engine and with an open spanner slacken the locknut (4), Fig.6.16, and adjust the outer cable control to the stop (2), should the stop have been moved or be loose it will be necessary to remove the transmission sump pan.
4 Reset the engine idle to normal speed with the selector in the 'N' position. Stop the engine.
5 Wipe the area around the drain plug and sump. Place a clean container of at least 8 pints capacity under the pan drain plug. Undo the plug and allow the oil to drain into the container.
6 Undo and remove the fifteen sump pan retaining bolts and spring washers. Take care not to damage the joint between the transmission casing and sump pan.
7 Refer to Fig.6.16 and check that the position of the downshift cam is in the idling position as shown in the illustration.
8 Adjust the length of the outer cable so as to remove all the slack from the inner cable.
9 Again refer to Fig.6.16 and check the position of the downshift cam with the throttle pedal in the 'kickdown' position as shown in the illustration.
10 Refit the sump pan joint, sump pan and retaining bolts with spring washers. Tighten the bolts in a diagonal pattern.
11 Refill the transmission with correct grade transmission fluid.

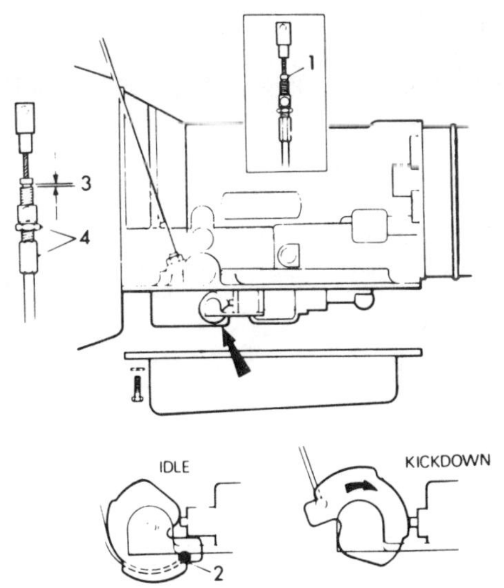

FIG 6.16 DOWNSHIFT CABLE ADJUSTMENT

1 Nipple *3 Clearance*
2 Cable located in cam *4 Adjuster/locknut*

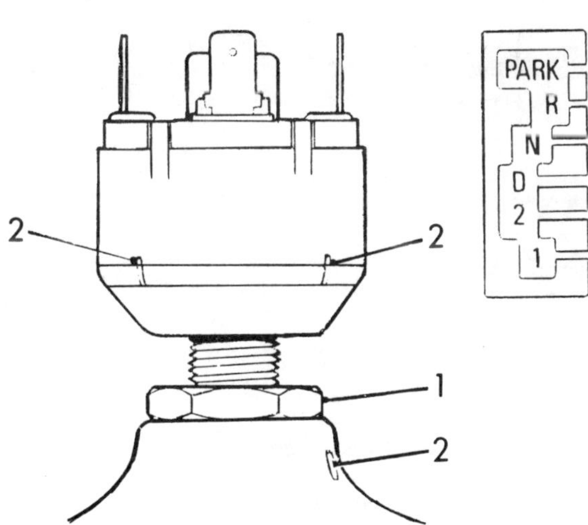

FIG 6.15 STARTER INHIBITOR/REVERSE LIGHT SWITCH

1 Locknut *2 Pencil mark*

15. Selector linkage - adjustment

1 Apply the handbrake firmly.
2 Move the selector handle to the 'N' position and adjust its position slightly to ensure that it is under the control of the control valve detent.
3 Move the selector handle to the 'P' position and release the handbrake. Rock the car to and fro and the pawl should hold the vehicle. If either of the two above conditions do not exist the selector rod must be reset.
4 Refer to Fig.6.17 and disconnect the selector rod from the manual lever.
5 Move the manual lever fully forwards as far as it will go and then move it back by three detents (clicks) to the neutral position.
6 Hold the selector in the 'N' position and the end of the selector rod should enter the hole in the manual lever.
7 If necessary adjust the length of the selector rod with the turnbuckle until the selector rod end will enter the hole.
8 Reconnect the selector rod and lighten the turnbuckle locknuts.
9 Carefully move the selector handle into all positions to make sure that the control valve detent is not over-ridden.

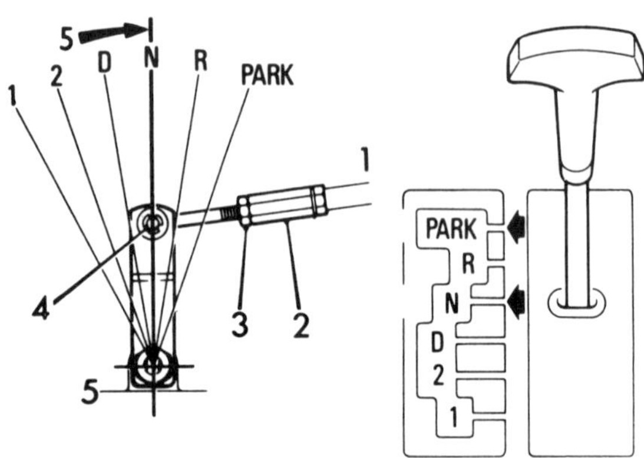

FIG.6.17. SELECTOR LINKAGE ADJUSTMENT

1 Selector rod
2 Turnbuckle
3 Locknut
4 Spire nut
5 Manual lever

16. Automatic transmission - fault diagnosis

Stall test procedure

The function of a stall test is to determine that the torque converter and gearbox are operating satisfactorily.
1 Check the condition of the engine. An engine which is not developing full power will affect the stall test readings.
2 Allow the engine and transmission to reach correct working temperatures.
3 Connect a tachometer to the vehicle.
4 Check the wheels and apply the handbrake and footbrake.
5 Select L or R and depress the throttle to the 'kickdown' position. Note the reading on the tachometer which should be 1800 rpm. If the reading is below 1000 rpm suspect the converter for stator slip. If the reading is down to 1200 rpm the engine is not developing full power. If the reading is in excess of 2000 rpm, suspect the gearbox for brake band or clutch slip.

NOTE: Do not carry out a stall test for a longer period than 10 seconds, otherwise the transmission will overheat.

Converter diagnosis

Inability to start on steep gradients, combined with poor acceleration from rest and low stall speed (1000 rpm), indicates that the converter stator uni-directional clutch is slipping. This condition permits the stator to rotate in an opposite direction to the impeller and turbine, and torque multiplication cannot occur.

Poor acceleration in third gear above 30 mph and reduced maximum speed, indicates that the stator uni-directional clutch has seized. The stator will not rotate with the turbine and impeller and the 'fluid flywheel' phase cannot occur. This condition will also be indicated by excessive overheating of the transmission although the stall speed will be correct.

Road test procedure

Road testing procedure is given with a diagnosis and rectification plan. It is not expected that the dig owner will be able to undertake much rectification work should it be necessary but it will enable him to understand the working a little better.

Selector position		D	D,2	D,2	1	R
	Ratio	3	2	1	1	
Applied	Front clutch	*	*	*	*	
	Rear clutch	*				*
	One-way clutch			*		
	Front band		*			
	Rear band				*	*
Driven	Forward sun	*	*	*	*	
	Reverse sun	*				*
Held	Planet carrier			*	*	*
	Reverse sun		*			

ROAD TEST	FAULT DIAGNOSIS	RECTIFICATION See the chart overleaf
1. Check that the starter will operate only with the selector lever in 'P' and 'N' and that the reverse lights (when fitted) operate only in 'R'	Starter will not operate in 'P' or 'N'	19
	Starter operates in all selector positions	20
2. Apply the hand and foot brakes and with the engine idling select 'N–D', 'N–2', 'N–I' and 'N–R'. Gearbox engagement should be felt in each position	Excessive bump on engagement of 'D', '2', 'I' or 'R'	4, 3
3. Check the stall speed in 'I' and 'R'.	High stall speed:	
	a With slip and squawk in 'L'	1, 2, 3, 13a, c, f, 11
	b With slip and squawk in 'R'	1, 2, 3, 13a, c, f, e, 12
Do not stall for more than 10 seconds	Low stall speed: more than 600 rpm below normal	21
	Low stall speed: less than 600 rpm below normal	23
4. Transmission at normal temperature, select 'D'; Release the brakes and accelerate with minimum throttle. Check for 1–2 and 2–3 shifts. Confirm that third gear has been obtained by selecting '2' when a 3–2 shift should be felt	No drive in 'D' '2' or 'I'	1, 2, 3, 13a, 11, 16
	No drive in 'D', drive in 'I'	1, 2, 3, 16
	No drive in 'D', '2', 'I' or 'R'	1, 2, 3, 13a, 11, 16, 17
	Delayed or no 1–2 shift	3, 14, 13a, 5, 6
	Slip on 1–2 shift	2, 3, 5, 6, 7, 13c, f
	Delayed or no 2–3 shift (if normal drive in 'R', omit 12)	3, 14, 13,g, h, c, d, 5, 6, 12
NOTE: A feature of this transmission is that a slight increase in throttle depression between 15 and 30 mph (25 and 48 kmph) may produce a 3–2 down-shift (part throttle down-shift)	Slip or engine run-up on 2–3 shift	2, 3, 5, 13a, c, 12
	Bumpy gear-shifts	3
	Drag in 'D' and '2'	8
	Drag or binding on 2–3 shift	5, 6
5. From a standing start, accelerate using 'kick-down'. Check for 1–2 and 2–3 shifts	Slip and squawk or judder on full throttle take-off in 'D'	1, 2, 3, 13a, c, 11
	Loss of performance and overheating in third gear	21
	Other possible faults are as given in test No. 4	Continue as in test 4
6. a. At 40 mph (65 kmph) in top gear release the accelerator and select '2'. Check for 3–2 shift and engine braking. Check for 2–1 roll out	No 3–2 down-shift or engine braking	1, 5, 6, 7, 12
b. At 15 mph (25 kmph) in second gear release the accelerator and select 'I'. Check for 2–1 shift	No 2–1 down-shift and engine braking	8, 9, 10
7. a. At 40 mph (65 kmph) in top gear, depress the accelerator to kick-down, when the gearbox should down-shift to second gear	Transmission will not down-shift	3, 13f, g, 14
b. At 20 mph (30 kmph) in second gear, depress the accelerator to kick-down when the gearbox should down-shift to first gear	Transmission will not down-shift	3, 13f, g, 14
8. a. Stop, engage 'I' and accelerate to 20 mph (30 kmph). Check for clutch slip or break-away noise (squawk) and that no up-shift occurs	Slip, squawk or judder on take-off in 'L'	1, 2, 3, 13, 11
	Transmission up-shifts	1
b. Stop, engage 'R' and reverse the vehicle using full throttle if possible. Check for clutch or break-away noise (squawk)	Slip, squawk or judder on take-off in 'R'	1, 2, 3, 13b, c, e, f, g,12
	As above, with engine braking available in 'I'	1, 2, 3
	Slip but no judder on take-off in 'R'. No engine braking available in 'I'	1, 2, 3, 8, 9, 10
	Drag in 'R'	5
	No drive in 'R', no engine braking in 'I'	1, 2, 3, 8, 13e,f,g, 9, 10, 12
	As above, with engine braking in 'I'	1, 2, 3, 13e, 12
9. Stop the vehicle facing downhill, apply the brakes and select 'P'. Release the brakes and check that the pawl holds. Re-apply the brakes before disengaging 'P' Repeat facing uphill	Parking pawl inoperative	1, 15
	Miscellaneous:	
	Screech or whine increasing with engine speed	17
	Grinding or grating noise from gearbox	18
	Knocking noise from torque converter area	22
	At high speeds in 'D' transmission downshifts to second ratio and immediately upshifts back to third ratio	12

RECTIFICATION CHART

1. Recheck fluid level
2 Check manual linkage adjustment
3 Check adjustment of down-shift valve cable
4 Reduce engine idle speed
5 Check adjustment of front band
6 Check front servo seals and fit of tubes
7 Check front band for wear
8 Check adjustment of rear band
9 Check rear servo seal and fit of tubes
10 Check rear band for wear
11 Examine front clutch, check ball valve and seals, also forward sun gear shaft sealing rings. Verify that cup plug in driven shaft is not leaking or dislodged.
12 Examine rear clutch, check ball valve and seals. Verify that rear clutch spring seat inner lip is not proud. Check fit of tubes.
13 Strip valve bodies and clean, checking:
   a. Primary regulator valve sticking
   b Secondary regulator valve sticking
   c Throttle valve sticking
   d Modulator valve sticking
   e Servo orifice control valve sticking
   f 1 to 2 shift valve sticking
   g 2 to 3 shift valve sticking
   h 2 to 3 shift valve plunder sticking
14 Strip governor valve and clean
15 Examine parking pawl, gear, and internal linkage
16 Examine one-way clutch
17 Strip and examine pump and drive tangs
18 Strip and examine gear train
19 Adjust starter inhibitor switch inwards
20 Adjust starter inhibitor switch outwards
21 Replace torque converter
22 Examine torque converter drive plate for cracks or fracture
23 Check engine performance

Chapter 7 Propeller shaft

Contents

Specifications

Split in two halves (front and rear), tubular with centre bearing

Diameter : Front	3 in (76.2 mm)
Rear	2 in (50.8 mm)
Universal joints	Hardy Spicer with roller bearings

TORQUE WRENCH SETTING	lb ft	kg m
Centre bearing mounting bolts	22	3.0
Flange retaining bolt nuts	28	3.8

1 General description

Drive is transmitted from the gearbox to the rear axle by means of a finely balanced Hardy Spicer tubular propeller shaft split into two halves and supported at the centre of a rubber mounted bearing.

Fitted to the front, centre and rear of the propeller shaft assembly are universal joints which allow for vertical movement of the rear axle and slight movement of the complete power unit on its rubber mountings. Each universal joint comprises a four legged centre spider, four needle roller bearings and two yokes.

Fore and aft movement of the rear axle is absorbed by a sliding spline at the rear of the propeller shaft assembly. This is splined and mates with a sleeve and yoke assembly. When assembled a dust cap, steel washer, and cork washer seal the end of the sleeve and sliding joint.

The yoke flange of the front universal joint is fitted to the gearbox mainshaft flange with four bolts, spring washers and nuts, and the yoke flange on the rear universal joint is secured to the pinion flange on the rear axle in the same way.

2 Propeller shaft - front - removal and replacement

1 Jack up the rear of the car and support on firmly based axle stands. Alternatively position the rear of the car on a ramp. Chock the front wheels.
2 The propeller shaft is carefully balanced to fine limits and it is important that it is replaced in exactly the same position prior to its removal. Scratch marks on the gearbox, differential pinion and propeller shaft drive flanges for correct re-alignment when refitting.
3 Support the weight of the front propeller shaft. Undo and remove the four gearbox end flange nuts and bolts.
4 Support the weight of the rear propeller shaft. Undo and remove the four axle end flange nuts and bolts.
5 Undo and remove the two bolts, spring and plain washers that retain the centre bearing mounting to the body brackets.
6 Lift away the propeller shaft assembly from the underside of the car.
7 To separate the two halves of the propeller shaft assembly, first bend back the locking washer tab and undo and remove the retaining bolt. Lift away the 'C' washer and tab washer.
8 Draw the front propeller shaft away from the rear propeller shaft universal joint splines.
9 Reconnection and refitting the two propeller shaft halves is the reverse sequence to removal but the following additional points should be noted.
a) Ensure that the mating marks scratched on the propeller shaft, gearbox and differential pinion flanges are lined up.
b) Tighten the centre bearing mounting bolts to a torque wrench setting of 22 lb ft (3.0 kg m).
c) Tighten the front and rear flange retaining nuts to a torque wrench setting of 28 lb ft (3.8 kg m).

3 Propeller shaft - rear - removal and replacement

The sequence for removing the rear propeller shaft is the same as for removing the front propeller shaft in that the complete assembly must be removed first and then the two halves parted. See Section 2.

4 Universal joints - inspection and repair

1 Wear in the needle roller bearings is characterised by vibration in the transmission, 'clonks' on taking up the drive, and in extreme cases of lack of lubrication, metallic squeaking, and ultimately grating and shrieking sounds as the bearings break up.
2 It is easy to check if the needle roller bearings are worn with the propeller shaft in position, by trying to turn the shaft with one hand, and the other hand holding the rear axle flange when the rear universal is being checked, and the front half coupling when the front universal joint is being checked. Any movement

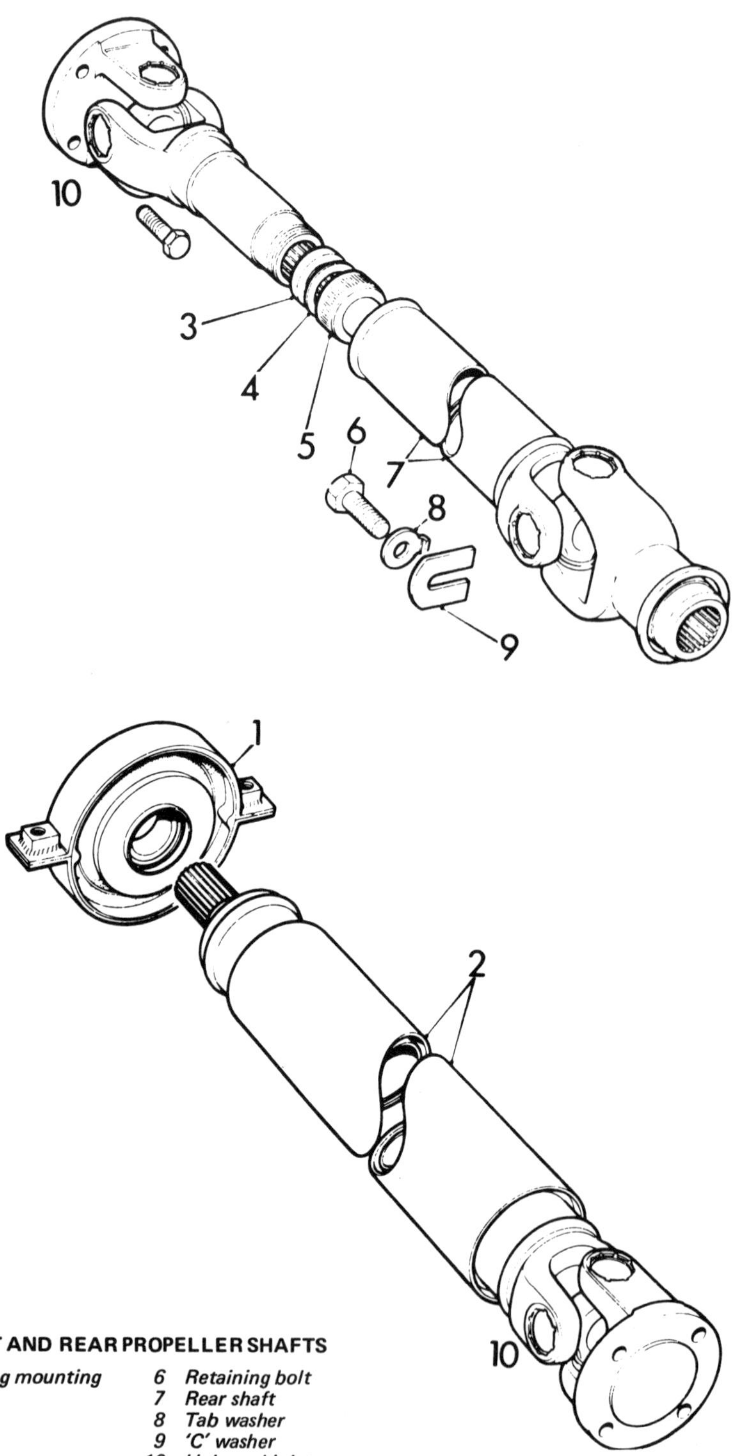

FIG.7.1. FRONT AND REAR PROPELLER SHAFTS

1	*Centre bearing mounting*	6	*Retaining bolt*
2	*Front shaft*	7	*Rear shaft*
3	*Seal*	8	*Tab washer*
4	*Seal retainer*	9	*'C' washer*
5	*Screw cap*	10	*Universal joints*

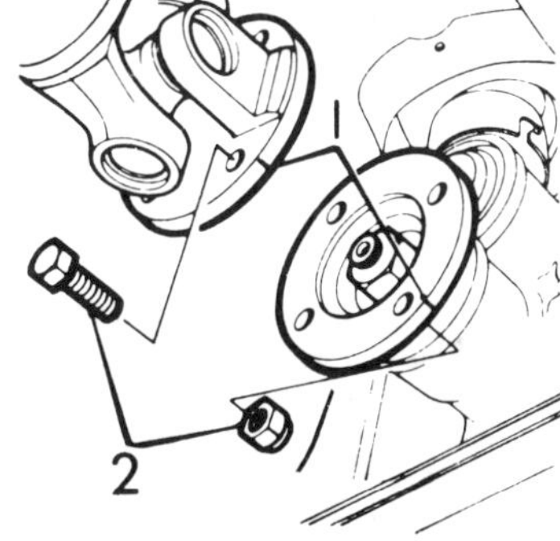

FIG.7.2. PROPELLER SHAFT ATTACHMENTS

1 Front/rear propeller shaft and gearbox/rear axle flanges
2 Securing bolt and self locknut

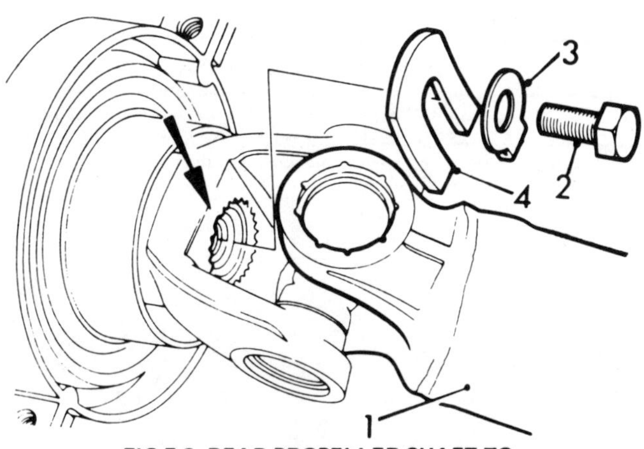

FIG.7.3. REAR PROPELLER SHAFT TO CENTRE BEARING ATTACHMENT

1 Rear propeller shaft
2 Bolt
3 Lockwasher
4 'C' washer

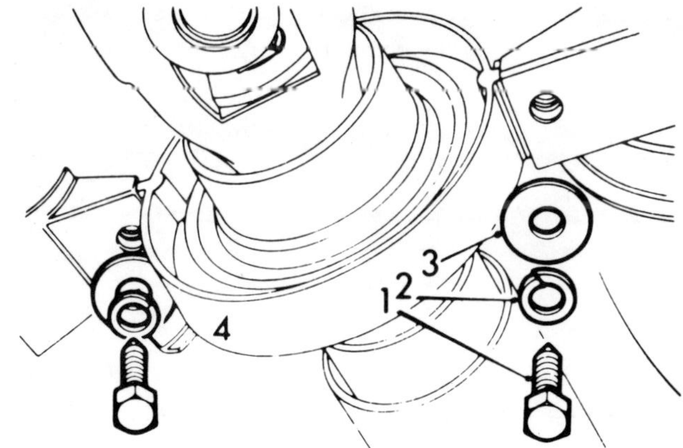

FIG.7.4. CENTRE BEARING ATTACHMENT

1 Bolt
2 Spring washer
3 Plain washer
4 Centre bearing assembly

between the propeller shaft and the front, centre or rear half couplings is indicative of considerable wear. If worn, the old bearings and spider will have to be discarded and a repair kit, comprising new universal joint spiders, bearings, oil seals, and retainers purchased. Make sure this kit is available to you before dismantling. Check also by trying to lift the shaft and noticing any movement in the splines.

3 Test the propeller shaft for wear, and if worn it will be necessary to purchase a new rear half coupling, or if the yokes are badly worn, an exchange half propeller shaft. It is not possible to fit oversize bearings and journals to the trunnion bearing holes.

5 Universal joints - renewal

This is not a diy task as the bearing cups are staked in position. Unless this staking is done absolutely correctly on reassembly of the yokes, there is a danger of the universal joint breaking-up — this could be very dangerous to a car moving at speed.

If the universal joints require renewal, fit an exchange reconditioned propeller shaft or have the job done professionally.

6 Centre bearing - removal and replacement

1 Refer to Section 2 and remove the propeller shaft assembly. Separate the two halves.

2 Using a universal puller and suitable thrust block (a suitable size bolt will do) draw the centre bearing from the end of the front propeller shaft.

3 To fit a new bearing simply drift it into position using a piece of suitable diameter metal tube.

4 Reconnect and refit the propeller shaft assembly, this being the reverse sequence to removal.

7 Sliding joint - dismantling, overhaul and reassembly

1 Refer to Section 2 and remove the propeller shaft assembly.

2 Unscrew the dust cap from the sleeve and then slide the sleeve from the shaft. Take off the steel washer and the cork washer.

3 With the sleeve separated from the shaft assembly the splines can be inspected. If worn it will be necessary to purchase a new sleeve assembly.

4 To reassemble, fit the dust cap, steel washer, and a new cork gasket over the splined part of the propeller shaft.

5 Grease the splines and then line up the arrow on the sleeve assembly with the arrow on the splined portion of the propeller shaft, and push the sleeve over the splines. Fit the washers to the sleeve and screw up the dust cap.

Chapter 8 Rear axle

Contents

Specifications

Type	Hypoid - semi floating
Ratio	3.636:1 (11/40)
Distance of bearing from threaded end of axle shaft	2.84 in (69.94mm)
Differential bearing shims	0.003 in (0.076mm)
	0.005 in (0.127mm)
	0.010 in (0.254mm)
	0.020 in (0.508mm)
Differential case - maximum stretch	0.008 in (0.20 mm)
Differential pinion gears thrust washer range	8 in 0.002 in (0.05mm) increments
Thrust washer range	0.027 in (0.685mm) - 0.043 in (1.092mm)
Crown wheel runout (max)	0.003 in (0.076mm)
Crown wheel optimum setting	0.005 in (0.127mm)
Pinion bearing pre-load	15 to 18 lb ft (0.17 - 0.21 kg m)
Pinion head washer sizes:	
Standard	0.077 in (1.956mm)
Alternative	0.075 in (1.905mm) - 0.096 in (2.438mm) in a range of 21 increments
Pinion bearing shims	0.003 in (0.76mm)
	0.005 in (0.127mm)
	0.010 in (0.254mm)
	0.030 in (0.762mm)
Lubricant capacity	1.25 pints (0.71 litres)

TORQUE WRENCH SETTINGS	lb ft	kg m
Backplate securing nuts	18	2.5
Axle shaft nut	85	11.7
Differential case to axle retaining nuts	20	2.7
Pinion bearing pre-load	15 - 18	0.17 - 0.21
Drive flange nut	90	12.4
Axle to spring 'U' bolt nuts	14	1.9
Propeller shaft flange retaining nuts	28	3.8

1 General description

The rear axle is of the semi floating type and is held in place by semi-elliptic springs. These springs provide the necessary lateral and longitudinal location of the axle. The rear axle incorporates a hypoid crownwheel and pinion, and a two pinion differential. All repairs can be carried out to the component parts of the rear axle without removing the axle casing from the car.

The crownwheel and pinion together with the differential gears are mounted on the differential unit which is bolted to the front face of the banjo type axle casing.

Adjustments are provided for the crownwheel and pinion backlash, pinion depth of mesh, pinion shaft bearing pre-load, and backlash between the differential gears. All these adjustments may be made by varying the thickness of the various shims and thrust washers.

The axle or half shafts are easily withdrawn and are splined at their inner ends to it into the splines in the differential wheels. The inner wheel bearing races are mounted on the outer ends of the axle casing and are secured by nuts and lock washers. The rear bearing outer races are located in the hubs.

2 Rear axle - removal and replacement

1 Check the front wheel, jack up the rear of the car and place on firmly based axle stands located under the body and forward of the rear axle.
2 With a scriber or file mark the pinion and propeller shaft drive flange so that they may be refitted in their original positions.

3 Undo and remove the four nuts and bolts that secure the rear propeller shaft flange to the pinion flange. Lower the propeller shaft.
4 Remove the wheel trims, undo and remove the wheel nuts and lift away the road wheels.
5 Wipe the top of the brake master cylinder reservoir, unscrew the cap and place a piece of thin polythene sheet over the top of the reservoir. Refit the cap. This will prevent hydraulic fluid syphoning out during subsequent operations.
6 Wipe the area around the union nut on the brake feed pipe at the axle bracket. Unscrew the union nut.
7 Undo and remove the locknut and washer from the flexible hose.
8 Detach the flexible hose from its support bracket.
9 Extract the split pins locking the brake lever clevis pins. Lift away the plain washers and withdraw the clevis pins.
10 Undo and remove the nut and spring washer that secures the compensating lever pin to the axle case suport bracket. Lift away the compensating lever assembly.
11 Undo and remove the bolt and spring washer that secures the hand brake cable clip to the axle casing.
12 Using axle stands or other suitable means support the weight of the rear axle.
13 Undo and remove the eight 'U' bolt locknuts.
14 Detach the shock absorber mounting brackets and move back to one side. If necessary tie back with string or wire.
15 Detach the lower mounting plates and rubber pads.
16 Lift away the 'U' bolts and rubber bump stops.
17 The rear axle may now be lifted over the rear springs, and drawn away from one side of the car. Make a special note of the location of the spring packing wedge, upper locating plates and rubber pad.
18 Refitting the rear axle is the reverse sequence to removeal. The following additional points should be noted:
a) Make sure that the spring packing wedges are refitted in their original positions.
b) Inspect the rubber mounting pads and if they show signs of deterioration fit new ones.
c) Tighte the 'U' bolt nuts to a torque wrench setting of 14 lb ft (1.9 kg m).
d) It will be necessary to bleed the brake bydraulic system. See Chapter 9.

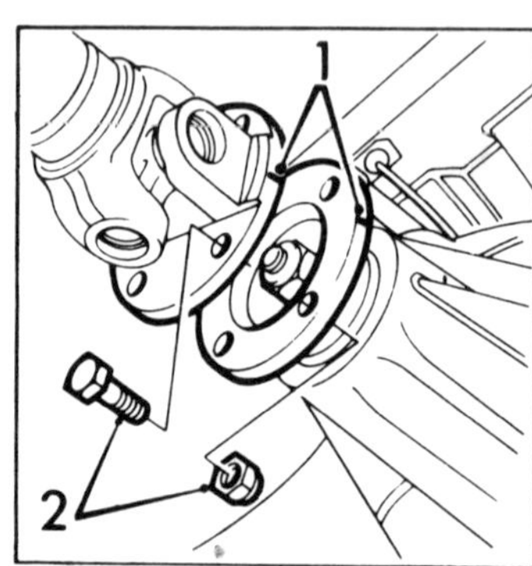

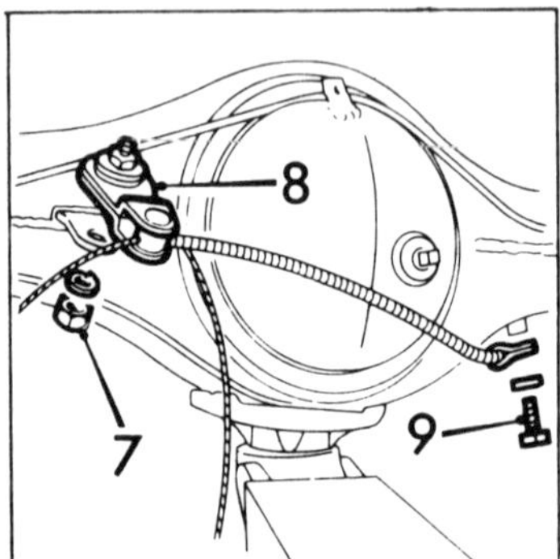

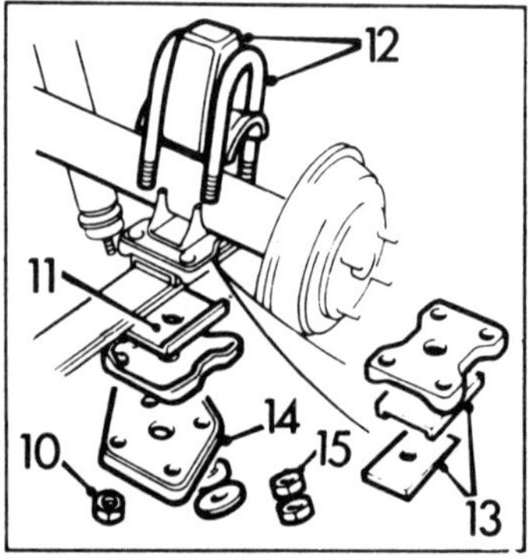

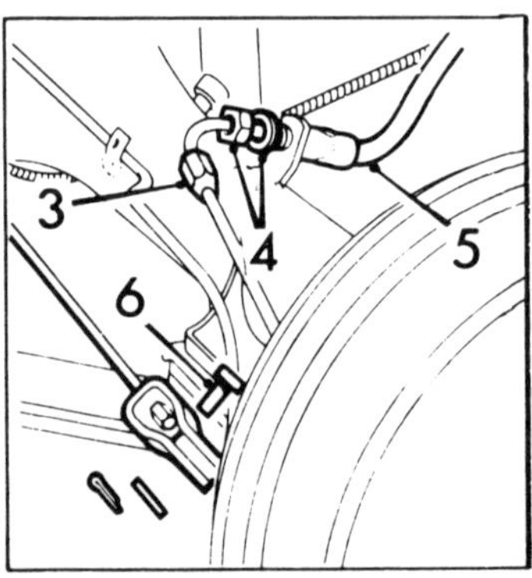

FIG.8.2. REAR AXLE ATTACHMENT POINTS FOR AXLE REMOVAL

1 Propeller shaft and pinion drive flange mating marks
2 Bolt and self locking nut
3 Brake hydraulic pipe union nut
4 Brake hydraulic flexible hose locknut and washer
5 Brake hydraulic flexible hose
6 Handbrake cable clevis pin, plain washer and split pin
7 Compensating lever nut and spring washer
8 Compensator
9 Cable mounting bracket bolt and spring washer
10 'U' bolt locknuts
11 Rubber pad
12 'U' bolts and rubber bump stops
13 Spring packing wedge upper locating plate rubber pad
14 Shock absorber mounting plate
15 Shock absorber retaining nut and locknut

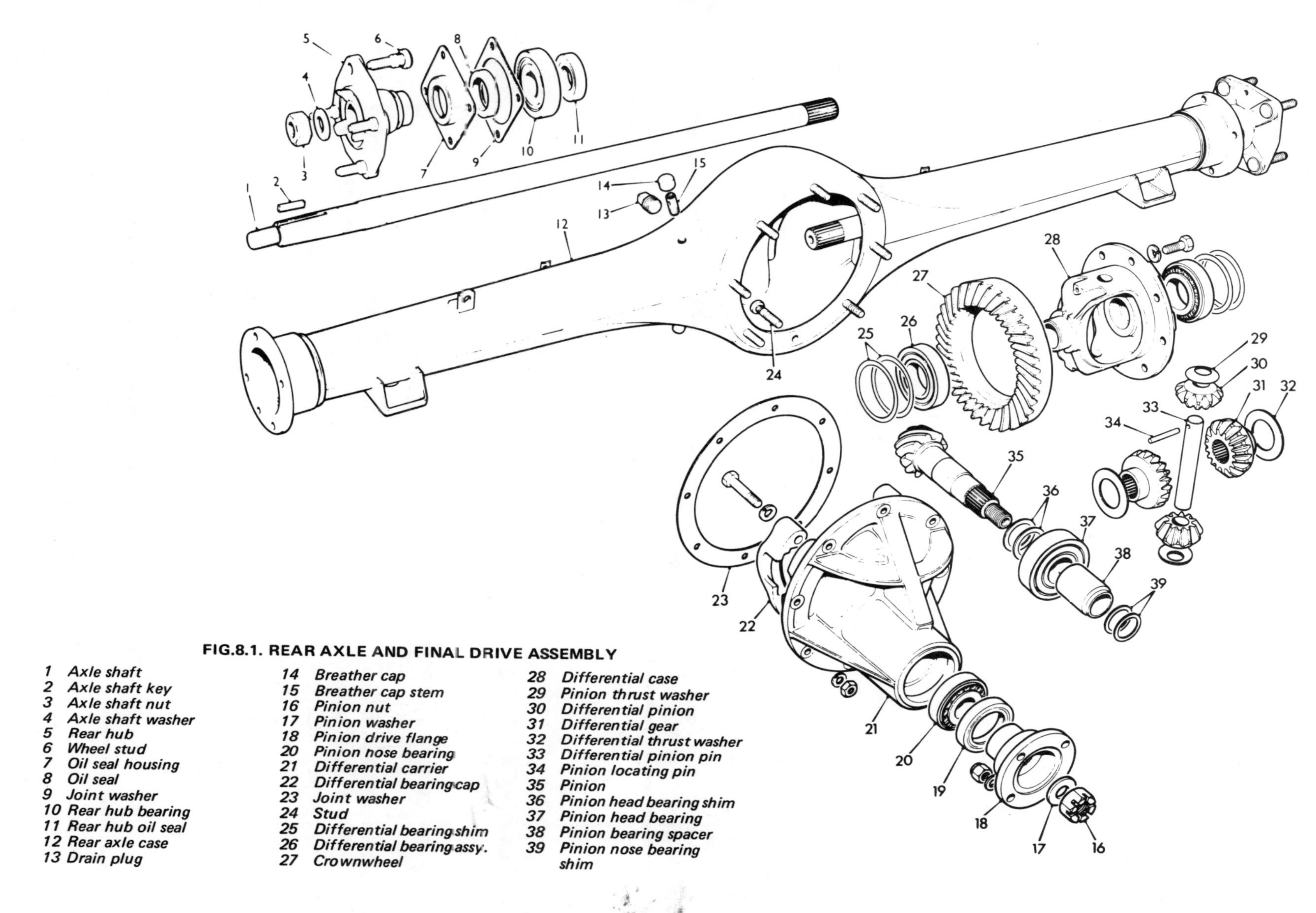

FIG.8.1. REAR AXLE AND FINAL DRIVE ASSEMBLY

1 *Axle shaft*
2 *Axle shaft key*
3 *Axle shaft nut*
4 *Axle shaft washer*
5 *Rear hub*
6 *Wheel stud*
7 *Oil seal housing*
8 *Oil seal*
9 *Joint washer*
10 *Rear hub bearing*
11 *Rear hub oil seal*
12 *Rear axle case*
13 *Drain plug*
14 *Breather cap*
15 *Breather cap stem*
16 *Pinion nut*
17 *Pinion washer*
18 *Pinion drive flange*
20 *Pinion nose bearing*
21 *Differential carrier*
22 *Differential bearing cap*
23 *Joint washer*
24 *Stud*
25 *Differential bearing shim*
26 *Differential bearing assy.*
27 *Crownwheel*
28 *Differential case*
29 *Pinion thrust washer*
30 *Differential pinion*
31 *Differential gear*
32 *Differential thrust washer*
33 *Differential pinion pin*
34 *Pinion locating pin*
35 *Pinion*
36 *Pinion head bearing shim*
37 *Pinion head bearing*
38 *Pinion bearing spacer*
39 *Pinion nose bearing shim*

3 Axle shaft, bearing and oil seal - removal and replacement

1 Chock the front wheels, jack up the rear of the car and place on firmly based axle stands. Remove the rear wheel.
2 Undo and remove the axle shaft nut and plain washer.
3 Undo and remove the two screws that secure the brake drum to the hub flange. Lift away the brake drum.
4 Should it be tight to remove, back off the brake adjusters and using a soft faced hammer tap outwards on the circumference of the brake drum.
5 Using a universal puller and suitable thrust block over the end of the axle shaft draw off the rear hub from the axle shaft.
6 Extract the split pin from the handbrake lever clevis pin at the rear of the brake backplate. Lift away the plain washer and withdraw the clevis pin so separating the handbrake cable yoke from the handbrake lever.
7 Wipe the top of the brake master cylinder reservoir, unscrew the cap and place a piece of thin polythene sheet over the top of the reservoir. Refit the cap. This will prevent hydraulic fluid syphoning out during subsequent operations.
8 Wipe the area of the brake pipe union/s at the rear of the wheel cylinder and unscrew the union/s from the wheel cylinder.
9 Undo and remove the four nuts, spring washers and bolts that secure the brake backplate to the axle casing.
10 Make a note of the fitted position of the dry lip relative to the brake slave cylinder and remove the oil catcher.
11 The brake backplate assembly may now be lifted away.
12 Remove the rear hub of leading it should be renewed. To remove the old seal careully ease it out using a screwdriver. Once removed an oil seal must never be refitted.
13 Place a clean container under the end of the axle banjo to catch any oil that will issue from the end.
14 Using a screwdriver a pair of pliers remove the axle shaft key and put in a safe place where it will not be lost.
15 Using either an impact slide hammer or, if not available, mole grips on the end of the axle shaft (with the nut refitted), draw the axle shaft from the casing.
16 The inner oil seal may be removed by using a piece of metal bar shaped in the form of a hook. Pull on the seal and draw it from inside the axle casing.
17 If required the bearing may be removed from the axle shaft by placing the bearing on the top of the jaws of the vice and driving the axle shaft through using a soft faced hammer on the end of the axle shaft nut.
18 Refitting the oil seal, bearing and axle shaft is the reverse sequence to removal but the following additional points should be noted:
a) Pack the bearing with a lithium based grease. Lubricate the new oil seal with a little Castrol GTX.
b) When refitting the oil seal the clip must face inwards.
c) Using a suitable diameter tube drift the bearing onto the axle shaft until the distance of the bearing to the threaded end of the axle shaft is 2.84 inches (69.94 mm).
d) Always use a new rear hub joint washer.
e) The backplate securing nuts should be tightened to a torque wrench setting of 18 lb ft (2.5 kg m).
f) To ensure positive locking of the axle shaft nut always apply a little Loctite CV to the axle shaft thread.
g) Tighten the axle shaft nut to a torque wrench setting of 85 lb ft (11.7 kg m).
h) Top up the rear axle oil level.
i) Bleed the brake hydraulic system as described in Chapter 9.

4 Pinion oil seal - removal and replacement

1 Chock the front wheels, jack up the rear of the car and support on firmly based axle stands.
2 With a scriber or file mark the propeller shaft and pinion flanges so that they may be refitted correctly in their original positions.

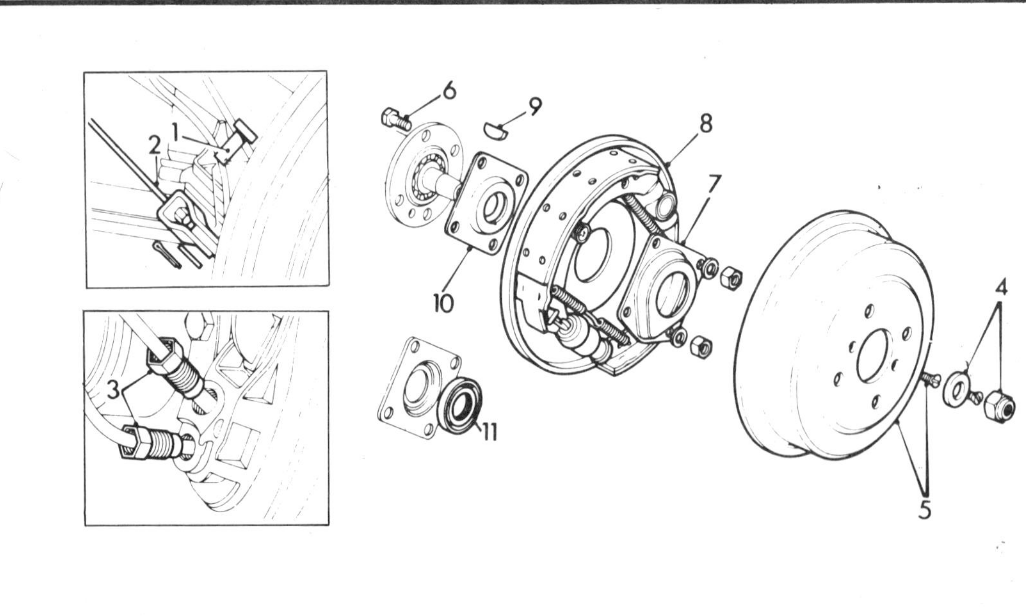

FIG.8.3. HUB AND AXLE SHAFT REMOVAL

1 Clevis pin, plain washer and split pin
2 Handbrake cable
3 Brake hydraulic pipe
4 Axle shaft nut and plain washer
5 Brake drum and retaining screw
6 Brake backplate securing screw
7 Oil catcher
8 Brake backplate assembly
9 Woodruff key
10 Oil seal housing
11 Oil seal

3 Undo and remove the four nuts, bolts and spring washers that secure the pinion flange to the propeller shaft flange. Lower the propeller shaft to the floor.
4 Apply the handbrake really firmly. Using a pair of pliers extract the flange nut locking split pin.
5 With a socket wrench unto the flange nut. Lift away the nut and plain washer.(See Fig.8.1).
6 Place a container under the pinion end of the rear axle to catch any oil that seeps out.
7 Using a universal puller and suitable thrust block draw the pinion flange from the pinion
8 The old oil seal may now be prised out using a screwdriver or thin piece of metal bar with a small hook on one end.
9 Refitting the new oil seal is the reverse sequence to removal, but the following additional points should be noted:
a) Soak the new oil seal in Castrol GTX for 1 hour prior to fitting.
b) Fit the new seal with the lip facing inwards using a tubular drift.
c) Tighten the driving flange nut to a torque wrench setting of 90 lb ft (12 kg m). Lock with a new split pin.
d) Top up the rear axle oil level as necessary.

5 Differential assembly - removal and replacement

1 If it is wished to overhaul the differential carrier assembly or to exchange it for a Factory reconditioned unit first remove the axle shaft as described in Section 2.
2 Makr the propeller shaft and pinion flanges to ensure their replacement in the same relative positon.
3 Undo and remove the four nuts and bolts from the flanges. Separate the two parts and lower the propeller shaft to the ground.
4 Place a container under the differential unit assembly to catch oil that will drain out during subsequent operations.
5 Undo and remove the eight nuts and spring washers that secure the differential unit assembly to the axle casing.
6 Draw the assembly forwards from over the studs on the axle casing. Lift away from under the car. Recover the paper joint washer.
7 Refitting the differential assembly is the reverse sequence to removal. The following additional points should be noted:
a) Always use a new joint washer and make sure the mating faces are clean.
b) Tighten the differential retaining nuts to a torque wrench setting of 20 lb ft (2.7 kg m).
c) Refill the axle with 1.2 pints (0.71 litres) of Castrol Hypoy B.

6 Differential unit - dismantling, inspection, reassembly and adjustment

Make sure before attempting to dismantle the differential that it is both necessary and economic. A special tool is needed and whilst not difficult some critical measurements have to be taken. It may well be cheaper to exchange the final drive assembly as a complete unit at the outset.
1 Obtain a special tool called an axle stretcher before commencing to dismantle the unit. It has a BLMC part number of 18C131C with adaptor plates 18G131E.
2 Hold the differential unit vertically in a vice and then using a scriber or dot punch mark the bearing caps and adjacent side of the differential carrier so that the bearing caps are refitted to their original positions.
3 Undo and remove the four bolts and spring washers securing the end caps.
4 Assemble the axle housing stretcher adaptor plates on the differential unit casing. Next fit the stretcher to the adaptor plates.

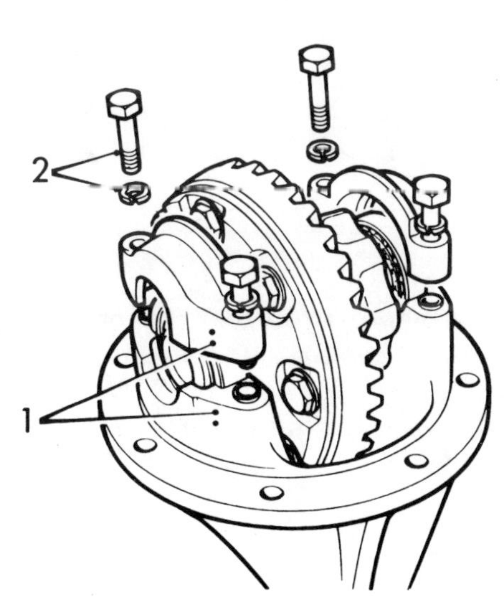

FIG.8.4. DIFFERENTIAL BEARING CAP REMOVAL

1 Bearing cap identification marks *2 Bearing cap securing bolt and spring washer*

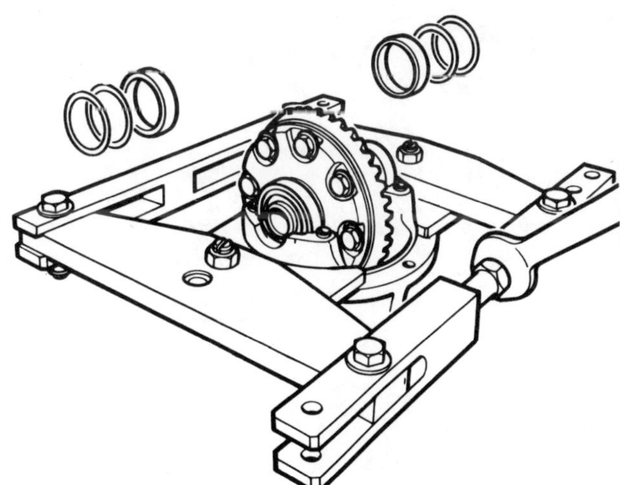

FIG.8.5. USE OF SPECIAL TOOL TO STRETCH AXLE CASING

5 The differential unit case should now be stretcher by tightening the nut three or four flats until the differential carrier can be levered out and the bearing shims and caps removed. IMPORTANT: To avoid damage to the case do not attempt to spread any more than is necessary. To assist each flat on the nut is numbered to give a check on the amount turned. The maximum stretch is 0.008 inch (0.20 mm). When removing the differential carrier do not lever against the spreader.
7 Mark the relative positions of the crownwheel and differential carrier to ensure correct refitting.
8 Undo and remove the eight bolts and spring washers securing the crownwheel to the differential carrier.
9 Separate the crownwheel from the differential carreir. If a little tight, tap with a soft faced hammer.
10 Using a parallel pin punch carefully drive out the differential pinion pin locking peg.
11 With a suitable diameter soft metal drift remove the differential pinion pin.
12 Rotate the differential gear wheels until the differential pinions are opposite the openings in the differential gear case, remove the differential pinions and their selective thrust washers. Keep the pinions and respective thrust washers together.
13 Remove the differential gear wheels and their thrust washers.
14 Transfer the differential unit casing from its position in the vice and hold the drive flange firmly in the jaws.
15 Extract the drive flange nut split pin and using a socket undo and remove the drive flange nut and washer.
16 Using a universal puller and suitable thrust block remove the drive flange from the pinion.
17 The pinion may next be removed. To do this carefully drive out using a hard wood block and hammer.
18 Remove the pinion bearing shims and spacer.
19 If the pinion bearings are to be renewed the inner bearings should be drawn off the pinion using a universal puller with long legs.
20 Lift the pinion head washer away from behind the pinion head.
21 Using a tapered soft metal drift carefully drift out the pinion outer bearing cup, bearing and oil seal. Also remove the pinion inner bearing cup.
22 Dismantling is now complete. Thoroughly wash all parts in petrol or paraffin and wipe dry using a clean non fluffy rag.
23 Lightly lubricate the bearings and reassemble. Test for signs of roughness by rotating the inner and outer tracks. Check the rollers for signs of pitting, wear or excessive looseness in their cage. Inspect the thrust washers for signs of excessive wear. Check for signs of wear on the differetial pinion shaft and pinion gears. Any parts that show signs of wear should be renewed.
24 The crownwheel and pinion must only be replaced as a matched pair. The pair number is etched on the outer face of the crownwheel and the forward face of the pinion.
25 If it is found that only one of the differential bearings is worn, both differential bearings must be renewed. Likewise if one piston bearing is worn, both pinion bearings must be renewed.
26 To reassemble first fit the differential bearing cones to the gear carrier using a piece of tube of suitable diameter.
27 Place the thrust washers behind the two differential gears and then fit them to their bores in the gear carrier. Make sure these gears rotate easily.
28 Place the two pinion gears in mesh with the two differential gears, leaving out the thrust washers and rotate the gear cluster until the pinion pin hole in the carrier is lined up with the pinions. Insert the pinion pin.
29 Press each pinion in turn firmly into mesh with the differential gears. Measure the required thrust washer thickness using feeler gauges so that no backlash exists.
30 Remove the pinion gears, keeping them in their respecitive positions and select a thrust washer whose thickness is the same as that determined by the feeler gauges. Eight thrust washers are available in 0.002 inch (0.05mm) increments from 0.027 inch to 0.041 inch (0.685 - 1.03mm).
31 Lubricate the thrust washers, pinions and pinion pin and reassemble into the differential carrier. Check that there is no

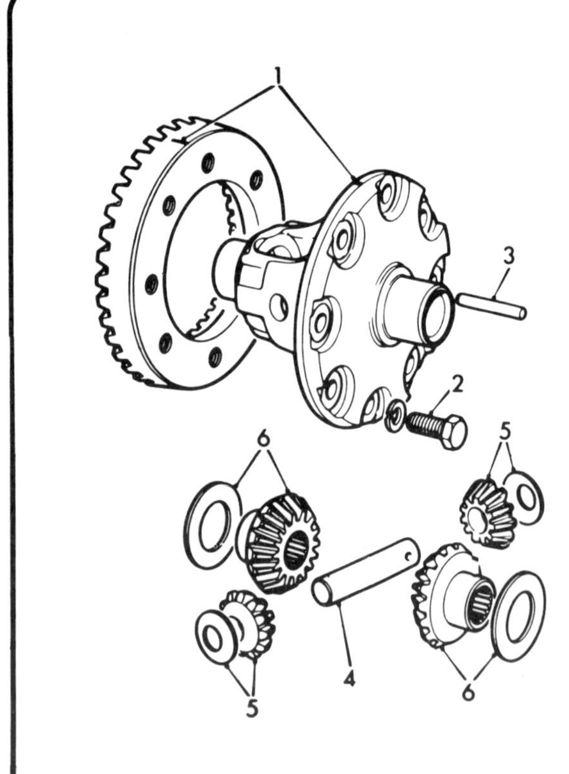

FIG.8.6. DIFFERENTIAL UNIT COMPONENTS

1 *Crownwheel and differential carrier mating marks*
2 *Crownwheel securing bolt and spring washer*
3 *Locking peg*
4 *Differential pinion pin*
5 *Differential pinion thrust washer*
6 *Differential gearwheel and thrust washer*

backlash. When this condition exists the gears will be stiff to rotate by hand.

32 Lock the pinion using the locking peg. Secure the peg by peening the metal of the differential carrier.

33 Carefully clean the crownwheel and gear carrier mating faces and fit the crownwheel. Any burrs can be removed with a fine oilstone. If the original parts are being used line up the previously made marks.

34 Secure the crownwheel with the eight bolts and spring washers which should be tightened in a diagonal and progressive manner.

35 Fit the carrier bearing cups to the bearings and place the assembly in the case. Leave out the shims at this stage.

36 Replace the bearing caps in their original positions and tighten the retaining bolts. Using either a dial indicator gauge or feeler gauges check the run out of the crownwheel and carrier. This must not exceed 0.003 inch (0.076mm).

37 If a reading in excess is obtained check for dirt on the crownwheel or carrier mating faces or under the bearing cups.

38 Remove the bearing cups again.

39 If the pinion bearing cups were removed for the fitting of new bearings, these should next be replaced. For this use a tube of suitable diameter and carefully drift them into position. Make sure they are fitted the correct way round with the tapers facing outwards.

40 Fit the spacer behind the pinion head and using a tube of suitable diameter refit the inner bearing again using a piece of metal tube of similar diameter.

41 Lubricate the bearing and fit the pinion to the casing. Slide on the bearing spacer, shamfered end towards the drive flange followed by the shims that were previously removed.

42 Lubricate the outer bearing and then fit to the end of the pinion.

43 Fit the drive flange and nut. Tighten the nut to a torque wrench setting of 90 lb ft (12.4 kg m). Rotate the pinion several times before the nut is fully tightened so that the bearings settle to their running positions.

44 If available use a pull scale and determine the bearing preload by wrapping string round the pinion flange and looking the other end onto the pull scale. The reading should be between 15 - 18 lb ft (0.17 - 0.21 kg m). Should the reading be in excess of this amount the shim thickness should be increased and conversely if the reading is two low decrease the shim thickness.

45 Remove the pinion nut, pinion and outer bearing and fit the required thickness shim to the pinion. Four shims are available in sizes from 0.003 - 0.030 inch (0.076 - 0.76mm). For assistance 0.001 inch (0.254mm) thickness shim equals aproximately 4 lb ft (0.04 kg m) pre-load.

46 Soak a new oil seal in Castrol GTX for 1 hour and then fit to the differential case. Replace the drive flange, washer and nut and tighten the nut to a torque wrench setting of 90 lb ft (12.4 kg m).

47 Lock the nut using a new split pin.

48 Place the bearing cups on the differential bearings and fit the differential carrier into the case. Replace the shims in their original positions.

49 Refit the bearing caps in their original positions and tighten the bearing cap bolts with spring washers in a progressive and diagonal manner.

50 Remove the axle spreader.

51 Using a dial indicatorgauge or feeler gauges and determine the total backlash which should be between 0.004 - 0.006 inch (0.10 - 0.15mm).

52 Should adjustment be necessary remove the shims behind the differential bearings once the caps have been removed and fit differential thickness shims. It should be noted that a movement of 0.002 inch (0.05mm) shim thickness from one differential bearing to the other will vary the backlash by approximately 0.002 inch (0.05mm).

53 Smear a little 'engineers blue' onto the crownwheel teeth and rotate the pinion in a forward and reverse direction several times.

54 The correct tooth marking on the crownwheel is shown in illustration 1, of Fig.8.6. If the position is different as shown in illustration 2 - 5 inclusive the arrows in the crownwheel and pinion diagrams to the right of the illustrations indicate the course of action to be taken.

55 When the correct tooth marking and backlash is correct the final drive unit may now be refitted.

See over for Fig.8.8. – correct tooth marking

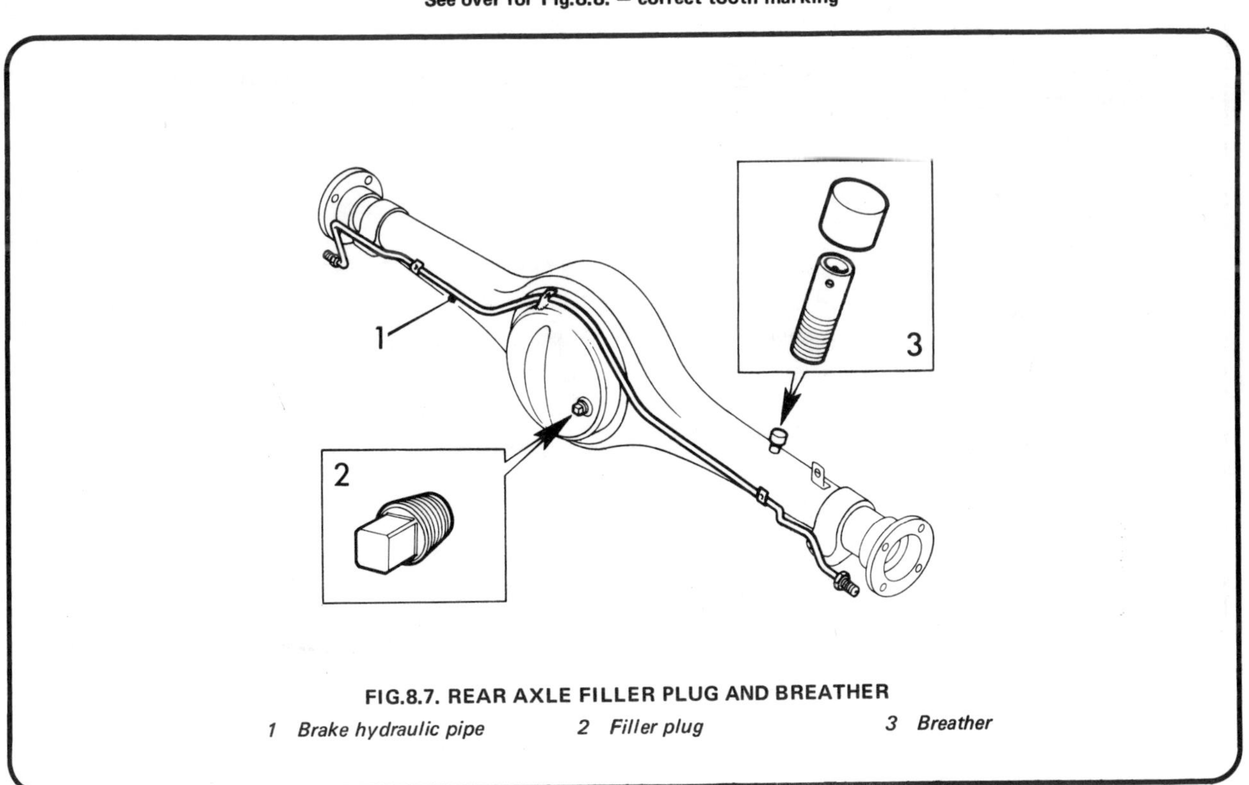

FIG.8.7. REAR AXLE FILLER PLUG AND BREATHER

1 *Brake hydraulic pipe* 2 *Filler plug* 3 *Breather*

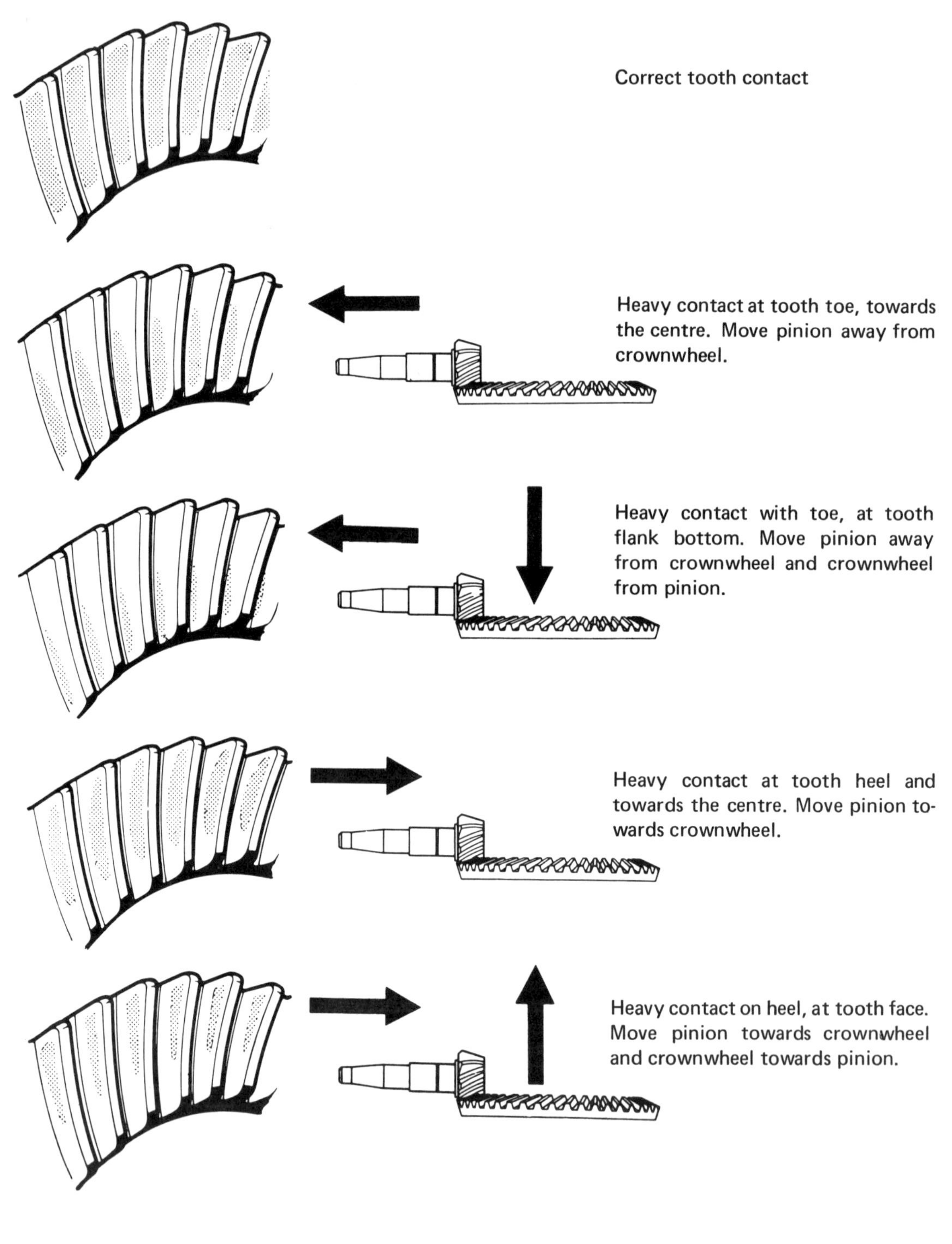

FIG.8.8. TOOTH MARKING FOR THE CROWNWHEEL

Chapter 9 Braking system

Contents

Specifications

Front - disc	
Disc diameter	9.785 in (248.5 mm)
Disc run-out	0.006 in (0.152 mm)
Total pad area	17.4 in^2 (286.77 cm^2)
Total swept area	182.8 in^1 (2671 cm^2)
Pad lining material (non servo)	DON 227
(with servo)	F 2430
Minimum pad thickness	1/16 in (1.6 mm)
Rear - drum	
Drum diameter	8 in (203.2 mm)
Lining dimensions	8 x 1.5 x 0.1875 in (203.2 x 38.1 x 4.76 mm)
Total swept area	76 in^2 (490.2 cm^2)
Lining material	DON 202
Wheel cylinder diameter	0.625 in' (15.87 mm)
Master cylinder diameter (non servo)	0.70 in (17.78 mm)
(with servo)	0.75 in (19.05 mm)
Servo unit	Girling Supervac

Torque wrench settings

	lb. f. ft.	Kg. f. m.
Bleed screw	4 – 6	0.5 – 0.8
Master cylinder retaining nuts	155 – 195	1.7 – 2.1
Caliper retaining bolts	50	6.9
Wheel cylinder retaining bolts	4 – 5	0.55 – 0.7
Backplate securing nuts and bolts	35 – 42	4.8 – 5.8
Brake disc securing bolts	38 – 45	5.25 – 6.22

1 General description

Disc brakes are fitted to the front and drum brakes to the rear of Marina 1.8. They are operated by hydraulic pressure created in the master cylinder when the brake pedal is depressed. This pressure is transferred to the respective wheel or caliper cylinders by a system of metal and flexible pipes and hoses.

The metal pipe to the rear brakes is connected to a flexible hose located on the right hand rear suspension. A short metal pipe connects the hose to the bottom union connection, on the rear right hand wheel cylinder. The upper part of the right hand wheel cylinder is connected to the lower part of the left hand wheel cylinder by a metal pipe which is attached to the rear axle casing.

The drum brakes are of the internally expanding type whereby the shoes and linings are moved outwards into contact with the rotating brake drum. One wheel cylinder is fitted.

The handbrake operates on the rear brakes only using a system of links and cables.

The front disc brakes are of the conventional fixed caliper design. Each half of the caliper contains a piston which operates in a bore, both being interconnected so that under hydraulic pressure their pistons move towards each other. By this action they clamp the rotating disc between two friction pads to slow rotational movement of the disc. Special seals are fitted between the piston and bore and these seals are able to stretch slightly when the piston moves, to apply the brake. When the hydraulic pressure is released the seals return to their natural shape and draw the pistons back slightly so giving a running clearance between the pads and disc. As the pads wear the piston is able to slide through the seal allowing wear to be taken up.

The front disc and the rear drum brakes are self adjusting.

A brake servo unit is fitted as standard on the 1.8 TC and as an optional extra to other 1.8 models. It is fitted between the brake pedal and master cylinder to add pressure on the master cylinder pushrod when the brake pedal is being depressed. This therefore reduces driver foot effort.

2 Bleeding the hydraulic system

Whenever the brake hydraulic system has been overhauled, a part renewed, or the level in the reservoir becomes too low, air will have entered the system, necessitating its bleeding. During the operation, the level of hydraulic fluid in the reservoir should not be allowed to fall below half full, otherwise air will be drawn in again.

1 Obtain a clean and dry glass jar, plastic tubing fifteen inches long and of suitable diameter to fit tightly over the bleed screw, and a supply of Castrol Girling Brake Fluid.

2 Check that on each rear brake backplate the wheel cylinder is free to slide within its locating slot. Ensure that all connections are tight and all bleed screws closed. Chock the wheels and release the handbrake.

3 Fill the master cylinder reservoir and the bottom inch of the jar with hydraulic fluid. Take extreme care that no fluid is allowed to come into contact with the paintwork as it acts as a solvent and it will damage the finish.

4 Remove the rubber dust cap (if fitted) from the end of the bleed screw on the front disc brake caliper which is furthest away from the master cylinder. Insert the other end of the bleed tube in the jar containing 1 inch of hydraulic fluid.

5 Use a suitable open ended spanner and unscrew the bleed screw about half a turn.

6 An assistant should now pump the brake pedal by first depressing it one full stroke followed by three short but rapid strokes and allowing the pedal to return of its own accord. Check the fluid level in the reservoir. Carefully watch the flow of fluid into the glass jar and, when air bubbles cease to emerge with the fluid, during the next down stroke, tighten the bleed screw. Remove the plastic bleed tube and tighten the bleed screw, preferably to a torque wrench setting of 4 - 6 ft ft (0.5 - 0.8 kg m). Replace the rubber dust cap.

7 Repeat operation in paragraphs 4 - 6 for the second front brake.

8 The rear brakes should be bled in the same manner as the front, except that each brake pedal stroke should be slow with a pause of three or four seconds between each stroke.

9 Sometimes it may be found that the bleeding operation for one or more cylinders is taking a considerable time. The cause is probably due to air being drawn past the bleed screw threads when the screw is lose. To counteract this condition, it is recommended that at the end of each downward stroke the bleed screw be tightened to stop air being drawn past the threads.

10 If after the bleed operation has been completed, the brake pedal operation still feels spongy, this is an indication that there is still air in the system, or that the master cylinder is faulty.

11 Check and top up the reservoir fluid level with fresh hydraulic fluid. Never reuse old brake fluid.

3 Front disc brake caliper pad - removal and refitting

1 Chock the rear wheels, apply the handbrake, jack up the front of the car and support on firmly based axle stands. Remove the road wheel.

2 Extract the two pad retaining pin spring clips and withdraw the two retaining pins (Fig.9.1).

3 Lift away the brake pads and anti squeak shims noting which way round the shims are fitted.

4 Inspect the thickness of the lining material and, if it is less than 1/16 inch (1.6mm) the pads must be renewed. If one of the pads is slightly more worn than the other, it is permissible to change these round.

5 If new pads are being fitted always use those manufactured to the recommended specifications given at the beginning of this Chapter.

6 To refit the pads, it is first necessary to extract a little brake fluid from the system. To do this, fit a plastic bleed tube to the bleed screw and immerse the free end in 1 inch of hydraulic fluid in a jar. Slacken off the bleed screw one complete turn and press

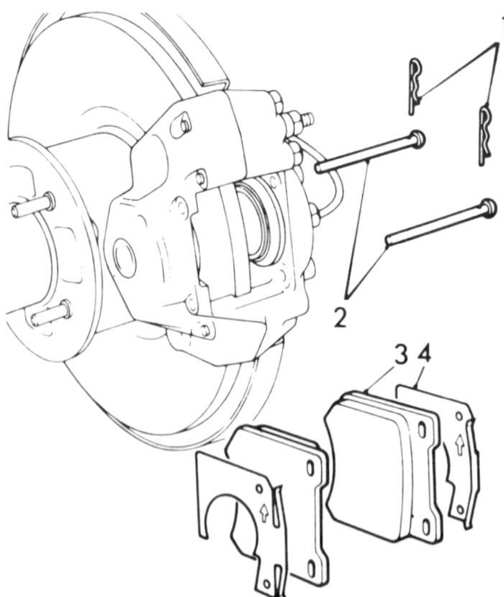

FIG.9.1. FRONT DISC BRAKE PAD REMOVAL

1 Spring clip | *2 Retaining pin* | *3 Pad* | *4 Anti-squeak shim*

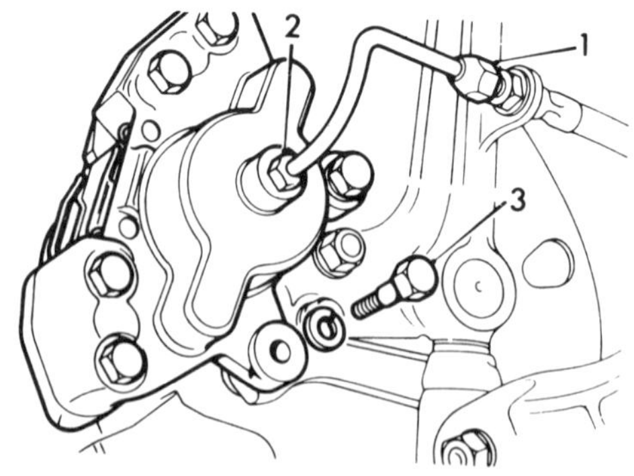

FIG.9.2. FRONT DISC BRAKE CALIPER ATTACHMENTS

1 Metal pipe union nut | *2 Metal pipe union* | *3 Securing bolt and spring washer*

back the pistons into their bores. Tighten the bleed screw and remove the bleed tube.
7 Wipe the exposed end of the pistons and in the recesses of the caliper free of dust or road dirt.
8 Refitting the pads is now the reverse sequence to removal but the following points should be noted:
a) The anti-squeak shims are fitted with the arrows pointing upwards.
b) If it is suspected that air has entered through the system during the operating described in paragraph 6, the system must be bled as described in Section 2.
9 Wipe the top of the hydraulic fluid reservoir and remove the cap. Top up and depress the brake pedal several times to settle the pads. Recheck the hydraulic fluid level.

4 Front disc brake caliper - removal and refitting

1 Apply the handbrake, chock the rear wheels, jack up the front of the car and support on firmly based stands. Remove the road wheel.
2 Wipe the top of the master cylinder reservoir, unscrew the cap and place a piece of thin polythene sheet over the top. Refit the cap. This is to stop hydraulic fluid syphoning out during subsequent operations.
3 Wipe the area around the caliper flexible hose to metal pipe union and the metal pipe to caliper connection. Unscrew the union nuts and lift away the metal pipe (Fig.9.2).
4 Undo and remove the two bolts and spring washers securing the caliper to the steering swivel. Lift the caliper from the disc.
5 Refitting the caliper is the reverse sequence to removal but the following additional points should be noted:
a) The two caliper securing bolts should be tightened to a torque wrench setting of 50 lbft (6.9 kgm).
b) Bleed the brake hydraulic system as described in Section 3.
c) Depress the brake pedal several times to reset the pads in their correct operating position.

5 Front brake disc - removal and refitting

1 Chock the rear wheels, apply the handbrake, jack up the front of the car and support on firmly based axle stands. Remove the road wheel.
2 Refer to Section 4 of this chapter and remove the caliper assembly.
3 Using a wide blade screwdriver ease off the hub grease cap.
4 Straighten the hub nut retainer locking split pin ears and extract the split pin. Remove the nut retainer andthen undo and remove the nut splined washer.
5 Withdraw the complete front hub assembly from the spindle.
6 To separate the disc from the hub first mark the relative position of the hub and disc. Undo and remove the four bolts securing the hub to the disc and separate the two parts.
7 Should the disc surfaces be grooved and a new disc not obtainable, it is permissible to have the two faces ground by an engineering works. Score marks are not serious provided that they are concentric but not excessively deep. It is however, far better to fit a disc rather than to re-grind the original one.
8 To refit the disc to the hub make sure that the mating faces are very clean and then line up the previously made alignment marks if the original parts are to be used. Secure with the four bolts which should be tightened in a progressive and diagonal manner to a final torque wrench setting of 38 - 45 lb ft (5.25 - 6.22 kg m).
9 Refitting is now the reverse sequence to removal but the following additional points should be noted:
a) Before refitting the caliper check the disc runout at a 4.75 inch (120.7mm) radius of the disc. The runout must not exceed 0.006 inch (0.152mm). If necessary remove the disc and check for dirt on the mating faces. Should these be clean reposition the disc on the hub.
b) The hub bearing end float must be adjusted as described in Chapter 11.

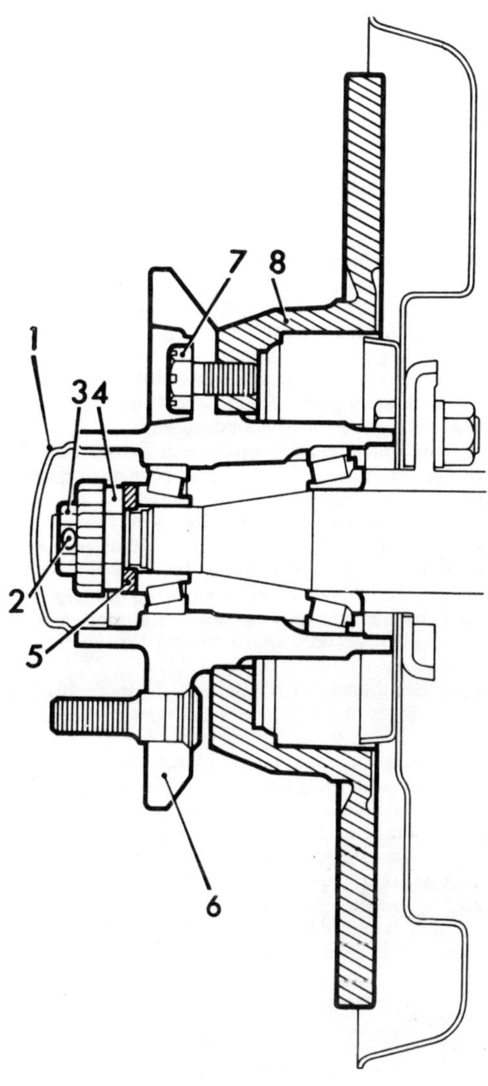

FIG.9.3. FRONT BRAKE DISC

1 Grease cap
2 Split pin
3 Nut retainer
4 Nut
5 Splined washer
6 Hub
7 Disc securing bolt
8 Disc

6 Rear drum brake shoes - inspection, removal and refitting

After high mileages, it will be necessary to fit replacement shoes with new linings. Refitting new brake linings to shoes is not considered economic, or possible, without the use of special equipment. However, if the services of a local garage or workshop having brake re-lining equipment are available there is no reason why the original shoes should not be successfully relined. Ensure that the correct specification linings are fitted to the shoes.

1 Chock the front wheels, jack up the front of the car and place on firmly based axle stands. Remove the road wheel.

2 Undo and remove the two brake drum retaining screws and carefully pull off the brake drum. If it is tight it may be tapped outwards using a soft faced hammer.

3 The brake linings should be renewed if they are so worn that the rivet heads are flush with the surface of the lining. If bonded linings are fitted, they must be renewed when the lining material has worn down to 1/16 inch (1.6mm) at its thinnest point.

4 Using a pair of pliers release the steady springs and pins from the shoes by rotating through 90o. Lift away the steady spring, pin and cup washer from each brake shoe web (Fig.9.4).

5 With a screwdriver ease the trailing shoe from its backplate anchor post and the wheel cylinder adjuster slot.

6 Lift away the brake shoes complete with return springs. It will be necessary to ease the leading shoe from the handbrake operating lever.

7 Remove the support plate from the leading shoe.

8 Lift away the adjuster from the wheel cylinder and slacken any adjustment by rotating the ratchet wheel.

9 If the shoes are to be left off for a while, do not depress the brake pedal otherwise the pistons will be ejected from the cylinders causing unnecessary work. Retain the pistons with strong elastic bands.

10 Thoroughly clean all traces of dust from the shoes, backplate and drum using a stiff brush. Do not use compressed air as it blows up dust which must not be inhaled as it is of an asbestos nature. Brake dust can cause judder or squeal and, therefore it is important to clean away all traces.

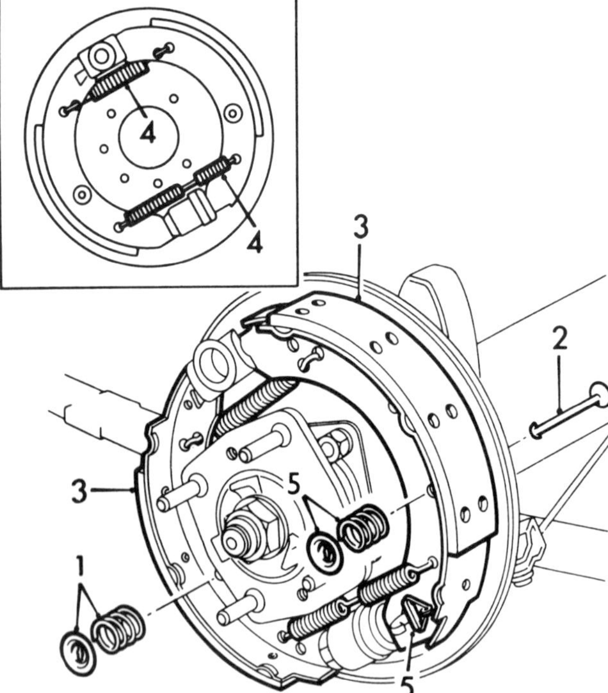

FIG.9.4. REAR DRUM BRAKE ASSEMBLY

1 Cup washer and spring
2 Steady pin
3 Brake shoe
4 Brake shoe pull-off springs
5 Shoe retaining spring and support plate

11 Check that each piston is free in its cylinder, the rubber dust covers are undamaged and in position and that there are no hydraulic fluid leaks.

12 Check that the wheel cylinder is free to move in its slot in the backplate.

13 Prior to reassembly, smear a trace of Castrol PH Brake Grease to the ends of the brake shoes, steady platforms anchor posts and the thread of the adjuster. Do not allow any grease to come into contact with the linings or rubber parts. Refit the shoes in the reverse sequence to removal. The two pull off springs should preferably be renewed every time new shoes are fitted, and must be refitted in their original web holes. Position them between the web and backplates. The return spring with the straight central portion is located next to the wheel cylinder.

14 Replace the brake drum and secure with the two retaining screws which should be tightened to a torque wrench setting of 26 - 28 lb ft (3.5 - 3.8 kg m).

15 Refit the road wheel and lower the car to the ground. Operate the handbrake several times so as to set the automatic adjuster. Road test to ensure that the brakes operate correctly.

7 Rear drum backplate - removal and refitting

For full information refer to Chapter 8, Section 3 which described removal of the axle shaft and hub assembly.

8 Master cylinder - removal and refitting

Standard model

1 Apply the handbrake and chock the front wheels. Drain the fluid from the master cylinder reservoir and master cylinder by attaching a platic bleed tube to one of the front brake bleed screws. Undo the screw one turn and then pump the fluid out into a clean glass container by means of the brake pedal. Hold the brake pedal against the floor at the end of each stroke and tighten the bleed nipple. When the pedal has returned to its normal position, loosen the bleed nipple and repeat the process until the master cylinder reservoir is empty.

2 Wipe the area around the hydraulic pipe union on the master cylinder. Undo the union nut and lift out the hydraulic pipe (Fig.9.5).

3 Undo and remove the nuts and spring washers securing the master cylinder to the pedal bracket.

4 Straighten the ears on the split pin retaining the push rod to brake pedal clevis pin, extract the split pin, lift away the plain washer and withdraw the clevis pin.

5 Lift away the master cylinder taking care not to allow any hydraulic fluid to drip onto the paintwork.

6 To refit the master cylinder position the push rod in line with the top hole in the brake pedal. Insert the clevis pin, replace the plain washer and lock with a new split pin. It is important that the master cylinder pushrod is connected to the TOP HOLE of the two holes in the brake pedal lever.

7 Replace the two nuts and spring washers that secure the master cylinder to the pedal bracket. Tighten to a torque wrench setting of 15.5 to 19.5 lb ft (1.7 to 2.1 kg m).

8 Reconnect the hydraulic pipe to the master cylinder union. Slide down the union nut and very carefully start the threads. It is easy to cross thread. Tighten the union fully.

9 Refer to Section 2 and bleed the brake hydraulic system.

Servo model

1 Drain the hydraulic fluid from the reservoir and master cylinder as described in paragraph 1 in the previous sub section.

2 Wipe the area around the hydraulic pipe union on the master cylinder. Undo the union nut and lift out the hydraulic pipe.

3 Undo and remove the two nuts and spring washers that secure the master cylinder to the servo unit.

4 Lift away the master cylinder taking care not to allow any hydraulic fluid to drip onto the paintwork.

5 Refitting is the reverse sequence to removal. Refer to paragraphs 8 and 9 in the previous sub-section for additional information.

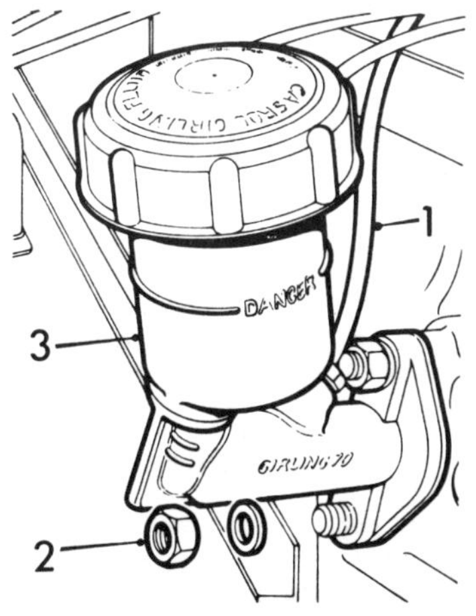

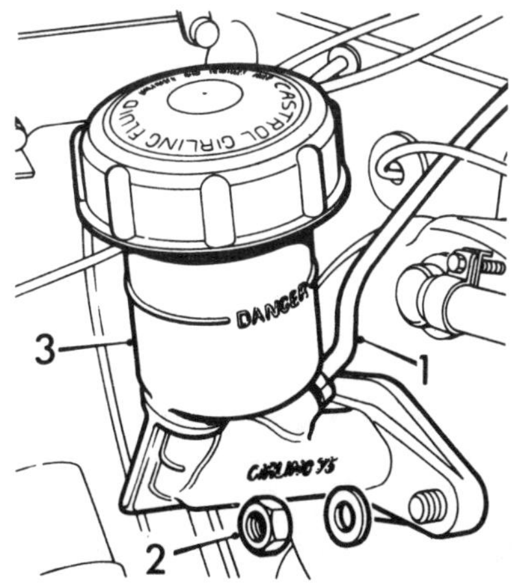

FIG.9.5. BRAKE MASTER CYLINDER ATTACHMENTS:
NON–SERVO; LEFT. SERVO; – RIGHT

1 Hydraulic pipe *2 Securing nut and spring washer* *3 Master cylinder*

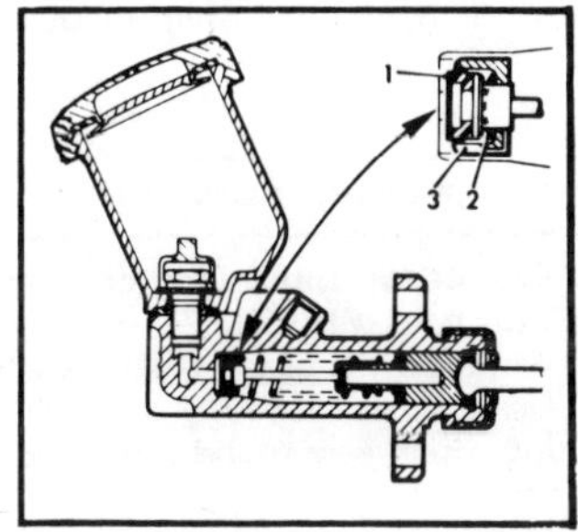

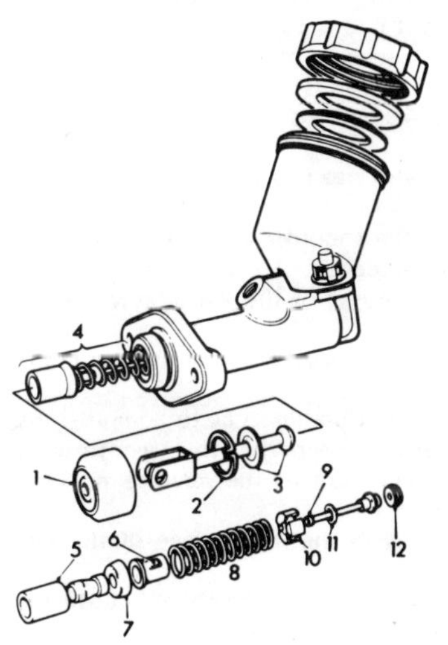

FIG.9.6. BRAKE MASTER CYLINDER COMPONENT PARTS

1 Rubber boot
2 Circlip
3 Pushrod and dished washer
4 Piston assembly
5 Piston
6 Thimble
7 Piston seal
8 Spring
9 Valve
10 Valve spacer
11 Curved washer
12 Valve seal

Inset: Section through whole master cylinder plus valve assembly
1 Seal *2 Dished washer* *3 Valve spacer*

9 Master cylinder - dismantling and reassembly

If a replacement master cylinder is to be fitted, it will be necessary to lubricate seals before fitting to the car as they have a protective coating when originally assembled. Remove the blanking plug from the hydraulic pipe union seating. Ease back and remove the plunger dust cover. Inject clean hydraulic fluid into the master cylinder and operate the piston several times so the fluid will spread over all the internal working surfaces.

If the master cylinder is to be dismantled after removal, proceed as follows:

1 Ease back the dust cover from the end of the master cylinder body. Using a pair of pointed pliers contract and lift out the circlip. Withdraw the pushrod and dished washer (Fig.9.6).
2 Carefully withdraw the complete piston assembly from the master cylinder bore. If this is difficult apply a low air pressure jet to the hydraulic pipe outlet connection.
3 With a small screwdriver lift the thimble leaf and separate the piston from the thimble.
4 Using the fingers remove the piston seal from the piston.
5 Compress the spring and remove the valve stem through the elongated hole in the thimble.
6 Lift away the thimble from the spring.
7 Remove the valve spacer and curved washer from the valve stem.
8 Carefully remove the valve seal from the valve head.
9 Thoroughly wash all parts in Girling Cleaning Fluid or methylated spirits.
10 Examine the bore of the cylinder carefully for any signs of scores or ridges. If this is found to be smooth all over, new seals can be fitted. If there is any doubt of the condition of the bore, then a new master cylinder must be fitted.
11 If examination of the seals shows them to be apparently oversize or swollen, or very loose on the piston or valve suspect oil contamination in the system. Ordinary lubricating oil will swell these rubber seals, and if one is found to be swollen it is reasonable to assume that all seals in the braking system will need attention.
12 All components should be assembled wet by dipping in clean brake fluid.
13 Fit the valve seal to the valve head so that the smallest diameter is on the valve head.
14 Fit the curved washer to the shoulder of the valve stem so that the domed side is to the shoulder.
15 Fit the valve spacer with the legs of the spacer towards the curved washer.
16 Locate the spring centrally on the valve spacer and insert the thimble into the spring.
17 Carefully push the end of the thimble so as to compress the spring against the valve spacer and insert the valve stem through the elongated hole of the thimble. Locate the valve stem in the centre of the thimble.
18 Fit the seal to the piston with the flat surface of the seal against the piston.
19 Insert the small end of the piston into the thimble until the thimble leaf engages under the shoulder of the piston.
20 Carefully insert the piston assembly into the master cylinder bore making sure the seal is not rolled or nipped as it enters the bore.
21 Fit the pushrod with the dished washer into the cylinder bore and retain in position with the circlip. Make sure the circlip is fully seated into its locating groove. Smear the pushrod and master cylinder bore of the dust cover with Girling Rubber Grease and refit the dust cover.
22 The master cylinder is now ready for refitting to the car.

10 Rear drum brake wheel cylinder - removal and refitting

1 If hydraulic fluid is leaking from the brake wheel cylinder, it will be necessary to dismantle it and replace the seal. Should brake fluid be found running down the side of the wheel or if it is noted that a pool of liquid forms alongside one wheel and the level in the master cylinder has dropped, it is indicative of seal failure.
2 Remove the brake drum and brake shoes as described in Section 5.
3 Wipe the top of the brake master cylinder reservoir and unscrew the cap. Place a piece of thin polythene sheet over the top of the reservoir and replace the cap.
4 Using an open ended spanner, carefully unscrew the hydraulic pipe connection union to the rear of the wheel cylinder. Note that the feed pipe from the left hand and right hand wheel cylinder locates in the lower opening (Fig.9.7).
5 Again using an open ended spanner undo and remove the bridge feed pipe from the right hand wheel cylinder.
6 Extract the split pin and lift away the washer and clevis pin that connects the handbrake cable yoke to the wheel cylinder operating lever.
7 Ease off the rubber boot from the rear of the wheel cylinder
8 Using a screwdriver carefully draw off the retaining plate and spring plate from the rear of the wheel cylinder.
9 The wheel cylinder may now be lifted away from the brake backplate. Detach the handbrake lever from the wheel cylinder.
10 To refit the wheel cylinder first smear the backplate where the wheel cylinder slides with a little Castrol PH Grease. Refit the handbrake lever on the wheel cylinder ensuring that it is the correct way round. The spindles of the lever must engage in the recess on the cylinder arms.
11 Slide the spring plate between the wheel cylinder and backplate. The retaining plate may now be inserted between the spring plate and wheel cylinder taking care the pips of the spring plate engage in the holes of the retaining plate.
12 Replace the rubber boot and reconnect the handbrake cable yoke to the handbrake lever. Insert the clevis pin, head upwards, and plain washer. Lock with a new split pin.
13 Refitting the brake shoes and drum is the reverse sequence to removal. Adjust the brakes as described in Section 6 and finally bleed the hydraulic system following the instructions in Section 2.

11 Rear drum brake wheel cylinder - overhaul

1 Ease off the rubber dust cover protecting the open end of the cylinder bore (Fig.9.8).
2 Withdraw the piston from the wheel cylinder body.
3 Using fingers carefully remove the piston seal from the piston noting which way round it is fitted. (Do not use a screwdriver as this could scratch the piston).
4 Inspect the inside of the cylinder for score marks caused by impurities in the hydraulic fluid. If any are found the cylinder will require renewal. NOTE: If the wheel cylinder is to be renewed always ensure that the replacement is exactly similar to the one removed.
5 If the cylinder is sound, thoroughly clean it out with fresh hydraulic fluid.
6 The old rubber seal will probably be swollen and visibly worn so it must be discarded. Smear the new rubber seal with hydraulic fluid and fit it to the piston so that the small diameter is towards the piston.
7 Carefully insert the piston and seal into the bore making sure the fine edge lip does not roll or become trapped.
8 Refit the dust cover engaging the lip with the groove in the outer surface of the wheel cylinder body.

12 Front disc brake caliper - overhaul

1 Extract the two pad retaining pin spring clips and withdraw the two retaining pins (Fig.9.9).
2 Lift away the brake pads and anti-squeak shims noting which way round the shims are fitted.
3 Temporarily reconnect the caliper to the hydraulic system and support its weight. Do not allow the caliper to hang on the flexible hose, but support its weight. Using a small G clamp hold

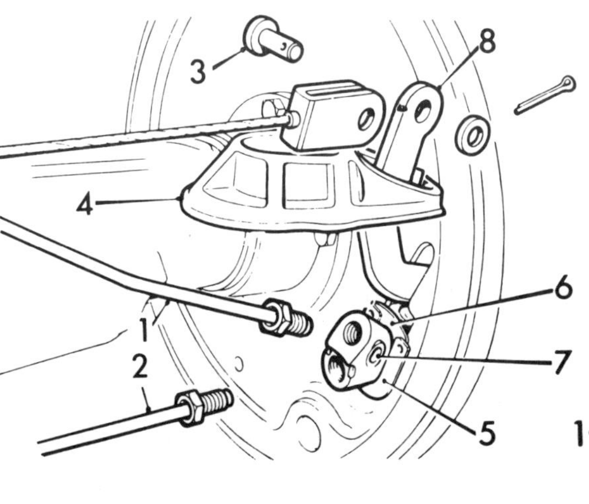

FIG.9.7. REAR DRUM BRAKE WHEEL CYLINDER ATTACHMENTS

1 Main hydraulic feed pipe
2 Bridge feed pipe
3 Clevis pin with plain washer and split pin
4 Rubber boot
5 Retaining plate
6 Spring plate
7 Wheel cylinder
8 Wheel cylinder operating lever

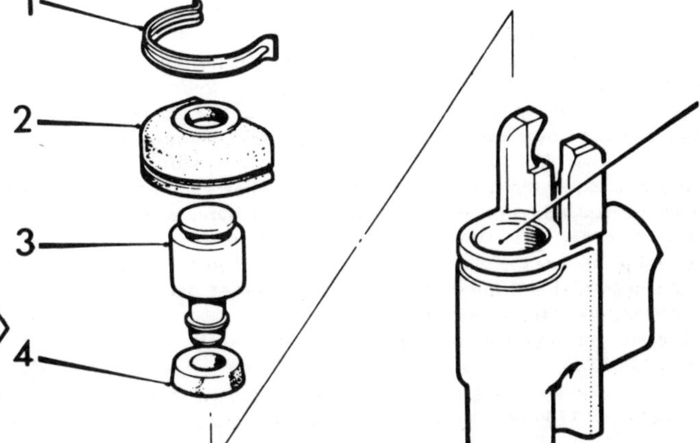

FIG.9.8. REAR DRUM BRAKE WHEEL CYLINDER COMPONENT PARTS

1 Clip
2 Dust cover
3 Piston
4 Seal
5 Wheel cylinder body

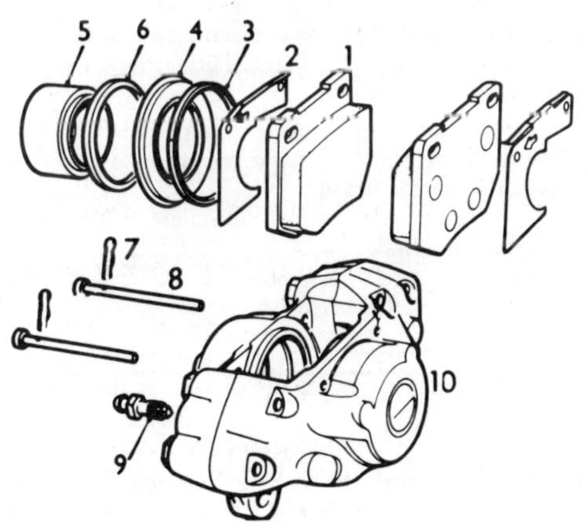

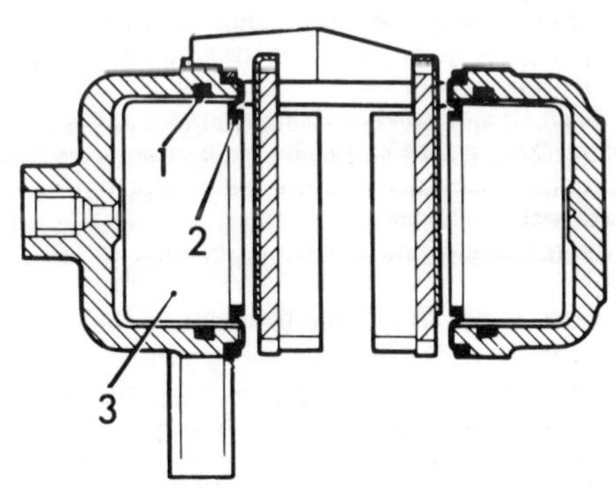

FIG.9.9. FRONT DISC BRAKE CALIPER COMPONENT PARTS

1 Pad
2 Anti-squeak shim
3 Dust cover retaining ring
4 Dust cover
5 Piston
6 Sealing ring
7 Spring clip
8 Retaining pin
9 Bleed screw
10 Caliper body

Inset: Correct fitted position of piston seal and dust cover

1 Piston seal 2 Dust cover 3 Piston

the piston in the mounting half of the caliper. Carefully depress the fotbrake pedal with the bleed nipple open so as to bleed the system, and then close the niple. Depress the fotbrake again and this will push the piston in the rim half of the caliper outwards. Release the dust cover retaining ring and the cover. Depress the fotbrake again until the piston has been ejected sufficiently to continue removal by hand. It is advisable to have a container or tray available to catch any hydraulic fluid once the piston is removed.

4 Using a tapered woden rod or an old plastic knitting needle, carefully extract the fluid seal from its bore in the caliper half.

5 Remove the G clamp from the mounting half piston. Temporarily refit the rim half piston and repeat the operations in paragraphs 3 and 4 of this section.

6 Thoroughly clean the internal parts of the caliper using only Girling Cleaning Fluid or methylated spirits. Any other fluid cleaner will damage the internal seals, between the two halves of the caliper. DO NOT SEPARATE THE TWO HALVES THE CALIPER.

7 Inspect the caliper bores and pistons for signs of scoring which if evident a new assembly should be fitted.

8 To reassemble the caliper, first wet a new fluid seal with Castrol Girling Brake Fluid and carefully insert it into its groove in the rim half of the caliper seating, ensuring that it is correctly fitted. Refit the dust cover into its special groove in the cylinder.

9 Release the bleed screw in the caliper one complete turn. Coat the side of the piston with hydraulic fluid and with it positioned squarely in the top of the cylinder bore, ease the piston in until approximately 5/16 inch (7.94mm) is left protruding. Engage the outer lip of the dust cover in the piston grove and push the piston into the cylinder as far as it will go. Fit the dust cover retaining ring.

10 Repeat the operations in paragraphs 8 and 9 for the mounting half of the caliper.

11 Fit the pads and anti-squeak shims into the caliper and retain in position with the two pins and spring clips.

12 The caliper is now ready for refitting.

13 Handbrake cable - adjustment

1 Refer to Section 6 and adjust the rear brakes.

2 Chock the front wheels and completely release the handbrake. Pull up the handbrake four clicks on the ratchet.

3 Jack up the rear of the car and support on firmly based stands.

4 Check the cable adjustments by attempting to rotate the rear wheels. If this is possible the cable may be adjusted as described in the subsequent paragraphs.

5 Refer to Fig.9.10 and slacken the adjuster locknut.

6 Turn the adjustment nut clockwise whilst the outer cable is held with an open ended spanner until the correct adjustment is obtained. Retighten the locknut.

7 Release the handbrake and check that the rear wheels can be rotated freely.

8 Lower the rear of the car to the ground.

14 Handbrake cable - removal and refitting

1 Slacken the two adjustment nuts securing the cable to its support bracket.

2 Straighten the ears, extract the split pin locking the clevis pin retaining the inner cable yoke to the handbrake lever. Lift away the plain washer and withdraw the clevis pin (Fig.9.11).

3 Repeat the previous paragraphs sequence for the clevis pin on both rear wheel cylinder operating levers.

4 Undo and remove the bolt and spring washer that secures the handbrake cable clip to the axle casing.

5 Undo and remove the trunnion retaining nut and spring washer.

6 Slacken the nut securing the compensating levers to the bracket.

7 Slacken the nut securing the cables to the compensating lever and remove the cables.

8 Refitting the cables is the reverse sequence to removal. It will be necessary to adjust the handbrake as described in Section 13 of this chapter.

15 Handbrake lever assembly - removal and refitting

1 Draw back the floor covering from around the handbrake lever. Undo and remove the four self tapping screws retaining the handbrake lever gaiter to the floor panel.

2 Straighten the ears and extract the split pin retaining the handbrake cable to lever clevis pin. Lift away the plain washer and withdraw the clevis pin.

3 Slide the gaiter up the handbrake. Undo and remove the two nuts, spring washers and bolts that secure the handbrake lever assembly to its mounting bracket. Lift away the handbrake lever assembly.

4 Refitting the handbrake lever assembly is the reverse sequence to removal. Lubricate all pivots with Castrol GTX.

16 Brake pedal assembly - removal and refitting

1 Refer to Chapter 12 and remove the complete instrument panel and the front parcel tray.

2 Refer to Chapter 3 and remove the throttle pedal.

3 Refer to Chapter 5 and remove the clutch master cylinder.

4 Wipe the top of the brake master cylinder and remove the cap. Place a piece of thin piece of polythene over the top of the reservoir and refit the cap. This is to prevent the hydraulic fluid syphoning out during subsequent operations.

5 Disconnect the brake master cylinder fluid pipe from the four way connector on the bulkhead.

6 Slacken the clip and detach the vacuum hose from the servo unit connector if a brake servo unit is fitted.

7 Make a note of the cable connections on the ignition coil. Detach the cables and remove the igntion coil.

8 Undo and remove the nuts, bolts, spring and plain washers securing the pedal housing assembly to the bulkhead (Fig.9.12).

9 Partially withdraw the pedal assembly and disconnect the electrical connections at the stop light switch.

10 Carefully pull the throttle and speedometer cable through their grommets in the pedal assembly.

11 The pedal and housing assembly may now be lifted away from inside the car.

12 Detach the return spring from thebrake and clutch pedals (Fig.9.13).

13 Undo and remove the locknut and plain washer retaining the brake pedal pivot pin. Lift away the throttle pedal stop noting which way round it is fitted.

14 Withdraw the clutch pedal complete with pivot pin and finally remove the brake pedal.

15 Refitting the pedal assembly is the reverse sequence to removal. Lubricate all pivots with Castrol GTX.

17 Brake servo unit - description

A vacuum servo unit can be fitted into the brake hydraulic circuit in series with the master cylinder, to provide power assistance to the driver when the brake pedal is depressed.

The unit operates by vacuum obtained from the induction manifold and comprises basically a booster diaphragm and a non-return valve.

The servo unit and hydraulic master cylinder are connected together so that the servo unit piston rod acts as the master cylinder pushrod. The driver's braking effort is transmitted through another pushrod to the servo unit piston and its built in control system. The servo unit piston does not fit tightly into the cylinder, but has a strong diaphragm to keep its edges in constant contact with the cylinder wall so assuring an air tight seal between the two parts. The forward chamber is held under

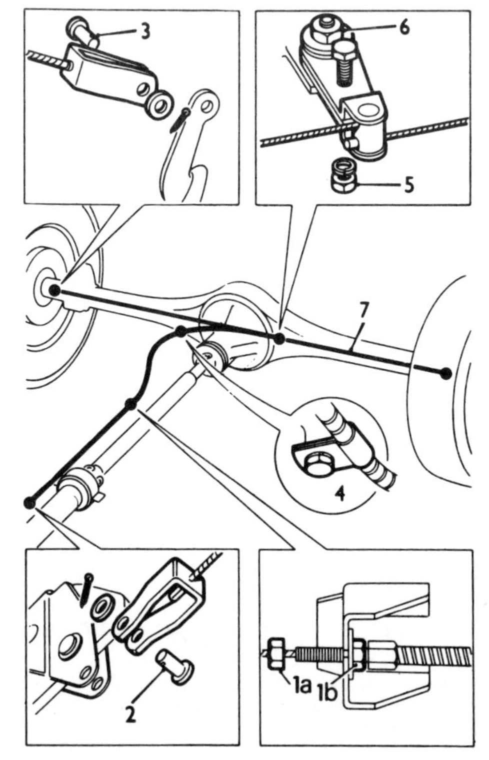

FIG.9.10. HANDBRAKE CABLE ATTACHMENT PIVOTS

1a Locknut
1b Adjustment nut
2 Clevis pin, plain washer and split pin
3 Clevis pin, plain washer and split pin
4 Handbrake cable clip
5 Retaining nut and spring washer
6 Trunnion retaining nut and spring washer
7 Rear cable

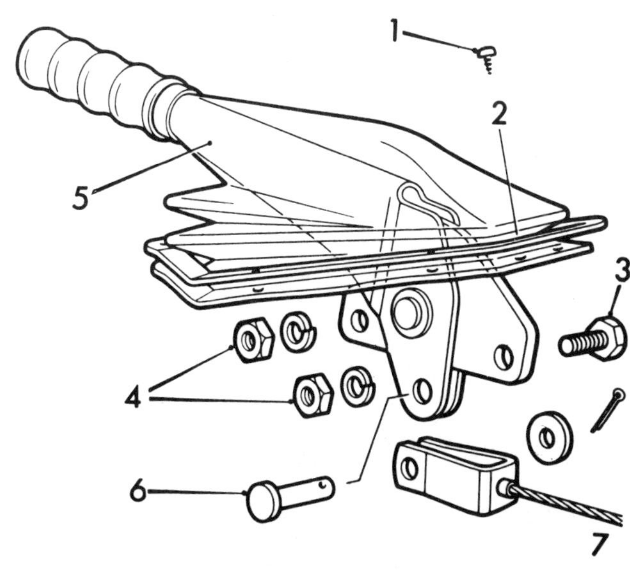

FIG.9.11. HANDBRAKE LEVER ATTACHMENTS

1 Self-tapping screw
2 Gaiter and metal plate
3 Mounting bolt
4 Nut and spring washer
5 Handbrake lever
6 Clevis pin with plain washer and split pin
7 Handbrake cable

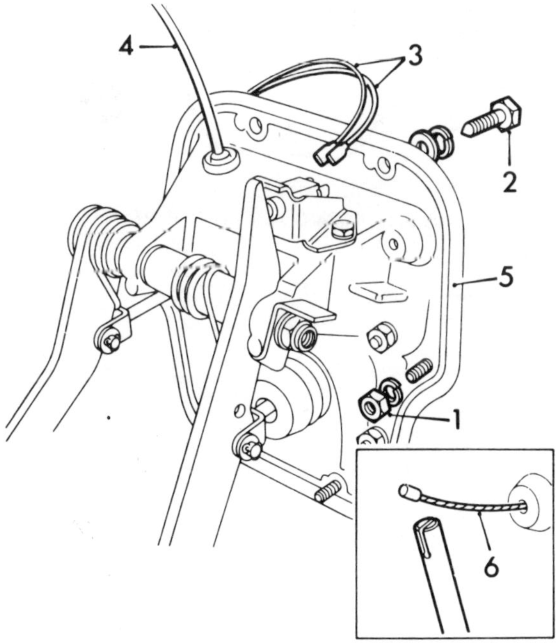

FIG.9.12. PEDAL MOUNTING BRACKET ATTACHMENTS

1 Bracket retaining nut and spring washer
2 Bracket retaining bolt with spring and plain washer
3 Stop light cables
4 Speedometer cable
5 Pedal mounting bracket
6 Inset: Throttle cable attachment to pedal

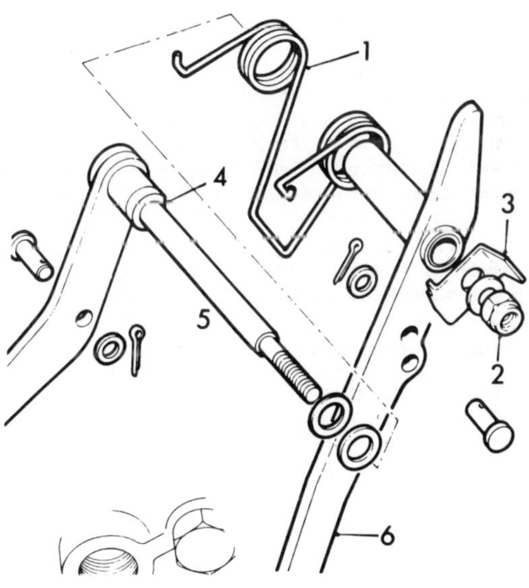

FIG.9.13. BRAKE AND CLUTCH PEDAL COMPONENTS

1 Return spring
2 Locknut and plain washer
3 Throttle pedal stop
4 Clutch pedal
5 Pivot pin
6 Brake pedal

vacuum conditions created in the inlet manifold of the engine and, during periods when the brake pedal is not in use, the controls open a passage to the rear chamber so placing it under vacuum. When the brake pedal is depressed, the vacuum passage to the rear chamber is cut off and the chamber opened to atmospheric pressure. The consequent rush of air pushes the servo piston forward in the vacuum chamber and operates the main pushrod to the master cylinder. The controls are designed so that assistance is given under all conditions and, when the brakes are not required, vacuum in the rear chamber is established when the brake pedal is released. Air from the atmosphere entering the rear chamber is passed through a small air filter.

18 Brake servo unit - removal and refitting

1 Refer to Section 8 and remove the brake master cylinder.
2 Slacken the hose clip and detach the vacuum hose from the servo connector.
3 Refer to Chapter 12 and remove the front parcel tray.
4 Detach the throttle cable from the throttle pedal (Fig.9.14).
5 Undo and remove the two nuts and spring washers that secure the throttle pedal bracket. Lift away the throttle pedal and bracket.
6 Straighten the ears of the split pin retaining the servo to brake pedal push rod clevis pin. Extract the split pin, lift away the plain washer and withdraw the clevis pin.
7 Undo and remove the four nuts and spring washers that secure the servo unit to the mounting bracket. Lift away the servo unit.
8 Refitting the servo unit is the reverse sequence to removal. It is important that the servo operating rod is attached to the BOTTOM hole of the two holes in the brake pedal lever. Bleed the brake hydraulic system as described in Section xx.

19 Brake servo unit - air filter renewal

Under normal operating conditions the vacuum servo unit is very reliable and does not require overhaul except possibly at very high mileages. In this case it is far better to obtain a service exchange unit, rather than repair the original.

However, the air filter may be renewed and fitting details are given. This will not however, repair any fault.

1 Pull back the dust cover (Fig.9.14) and slide up the push rod.
2 Using a screwdriver ease out the end cap and then with a pair of scissors cut off the old air filter.
3 Make a diagonal cut through the new air filter element and fit over the pushrod. Hold in position and refit the end cap.
4 Reposition the dust cover on the servo unit body.

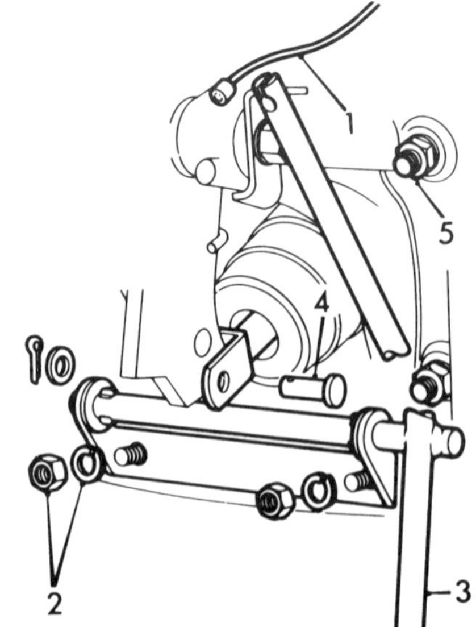

FIG.9.14. BRAKE SERVO UNIT ATTACHMENT – CAR INTERIOR

1 Throttle cable
2 Throttle pedal bracket securing nut and spring washer
3 Throttle pedal
4 Clevis pin with plain washer and split pin
5 Servo unit securing nut and spring washer

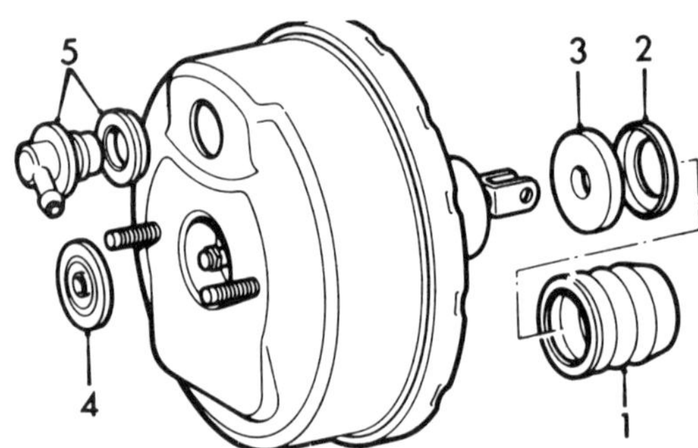

FIG.9.15. SERVO AIR FILTER RENEWAL

1 Dust cover
2 End cap
3 Filter
4 Front seal
5 Non-return valve and grommet

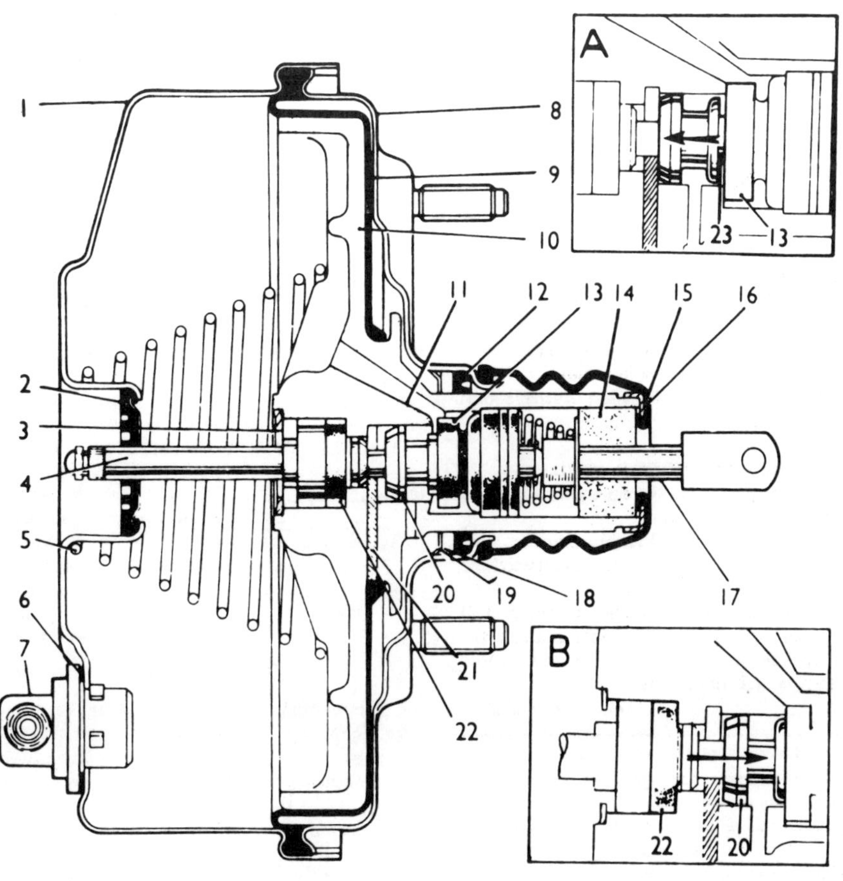

FIG.9.16. GIRLING SUPERVAC SERVO UNIT – IN SECTION

1 Front shell
2 Seal and plate assembly
3 Retainer (sprag washer)
4 Pushrod (hydraulic)
5 Diaphragm return spring
6 'O' ring
7 Non-return valve
8 Rear shell
9 Diaphragm
10 Diaphragm plate
11 Vacuum port
12 Seal
13 Control valve
14 Filter
15 Dust cover
16 End cap
17 Valve operating rod assembly
18 Bearing
19 Retainer
20 Control piston
21 Valve retaining plate
22 Reaction disc
23 Atmospheric port

Insets: A Control valve closed, control piston moved forward - atmospheric port open.
B Pressure from diaphragm plate causes reation disc to extrude, presses back control piston and closes atmospheric port.

26. Fault diagnosis

Symptom	Reason/s	Remedy
PEDAL TRAVELS ALMOST TO FLOORBOARDS BEFORE BRAKES OPERATE		
Leaks and air bubbles in hydraulic system	Brake fluid level too low	Top up master cylinder reservoir. Check for leaks.
	Wheel cylinder or caliper leaking	Dismantle wheel cylinder or caliper, clean fit new rubbers and bleed brakes.
	Master cylinder leaking (bubbles in master cylinder fluid)	Dismantle master cylinder, clean, and fit new rubbers. Bleed brakes.
	Brake flexible hose leaking	Examine and fit new hose if old hose leaking Bleed brakes.
	Brake line fractured	Replace with new brake pipe. Bleed brakes.
	Brake system unions loose	Check all unions in brake system and tighten as necessary. Bleed brakes.
Normal wear	Linings over 75% worn	Fit replacement shoes and brake linings.
BRAKE PEDAL FEELS SPRINGY		
Brake lining renewal	New linings not yet bedded-in	Use brakes gently until springy pedal feeling leaves.
	Brake drums or discs badly worn and weak or cracked	Fit new brake drums or discs.
	Master cylinder securing nuts loose	Tighten master cylinder securing nuts. Ensure spring washers are fitted.
BRAKE PEDAL FEELS SPONGY AND SOGGY		
Leaks or bubbles in hydraulic system	Wheel cylinder or caliper leaking	Dismantle wheel cylinder or caliper, clean, fit new rubbers, and bleed brakes.
	Master cylinder leaking (bubbles in master cylinder reservoir)	Dismantle master cylinder, clean, and fit new rubbers and bleed brakes. Replace cylinder if internal walls scored.
	Brake pipe line or flexible hose leaking	Fit new pipe line or hose.
	Unions in brake system loose	Examine for leaks, tighten as necessary.
BRAKES UNEVEN & PULLING TO ONE SIDE		
Oil or grease leaks	Linings and brake drums or discs contaminated with oil, grease, or hydraulic fluid	Ascertain and rectify source of leak, clean brake drums, fit new linings.
	Tyre pressures unequal	Check and inflate as necessary.
	Brake backplate caliper or disc loose	Tighten backplate caliper or disc securing nuts and bolts.
	Brake shoes or pads fitted incorrectly	Remove and fit shoes or pads correct way round.
	Different type of linings fitted at each wheel	Fit the linings specified all round.
	Anchorages for front or rear suspension loose	Tighten front and rear suspension pick-up points including spring locations.
	Brake drums or discs badly worn, cracked or distorted	Fit new brake drums or discs.
BRAKES TEND TO BIND, DRAG, OR LOCK-ON		
Incorrect adjustment	Brake shoes adjusted too tightly	Slacken off rear brake shoe adjusters two clicks.
	Handbrake cable over-tightened	Slacken off handbrake cable adjustment.
	Master cylinder pushrod out of adjustment giving too little brake pedal free movement	Reset to specifications.
Wear or dirt in hydraulic system or incorrect fluid	Reservoir vent hole in cap blocked with dirt	Clean and blow through hole.
	Master cylinder by-pass port restricted - brakes seize in 'on' position	Dismantle, clean, and overhaul master cylinder. Bleed brakes.
	Wheel cylinder seizes in 'on' position	Dismantle, clean and overhaul wheel cylinder. Bleed brakes.
Mechanical wear	Drum brake shoe pull-off springs broken, stretched or loose	Examine springs and replace if worn or loose.
Incorrect brake assembly	Drum brake shoe pull-off springs fitted wrong way round, omitted, or wrong type used	Examine, and rectify as appropriate.

Chapter 10 Electrical system

Contents

Specifications

12 volt negative earth type

Battery	Lucas A9, A11, A13 Exide 6UTP7 – BR, 6UTP9 – BR, 6UTPZ11 – BR	
Capacity at 20 hr rate/minimum fast charge time		
A9	40 amp : 1½ hours	
A11	50 amp : 1½ hours	
A13	60 amp : 1 hour	
6UTP7 – BR	30 amp : 1½ hours	
6UTP9 – BR	40 amp : 1½ hours	
6UTPZ11 – BR	50 amp : 1½ hours	
Alternator	Lucas 16ACR	
Output at 14 volts and 6,000 rpm	34 amps	
Maximum permissible rotor speed	12,500 rpm	
Stator phases	3	
Rotor poles	12	
Rotor winding resistance	4.33 ohms $\pm$ 5% at $20^{o}C$ ($68^{o}F$)	
Brush length (new)	0.5 inch (12.6 mm)	
Brush spring tension	7 to 10 oz.f. (198 to 283 gm.f.) with brush face flush with brush box.	
Control unit	Integral with alternator	
Starter motor	Lucas M418G inertia or 2M100 pre-engaged	
	M418G	**2M100**
Lock torque	17 lb.f.ft. (2.35 kg.fm) with 420 amp load	14.4 lb.f.ft. (2.02 kg.f.m.) with 463 amp load
Torque at 1000 rpm	8 lb.f.ft. (1.11 kg.f m) with 320 amp load	7.3 lb.f.ft. (1.02 kg.f.m.) with 300 amp load
Light warning current	45 amp at 7,400-8,500 rpm	40 amp at 6,000 rpm

Brush spring tension	36 oz.f. (1.02 kg.f.)	36 oz.f. (1.02 kg.f.)
Brush length minimum	0.313 inch (7.938 mm)	0.375 inch (9.5 mm)
Solenoid pre-engaged type:		
Closing coil resistance	–	0.25 to 0.27 ohms
Holding coil resistance	–	0.76 to 0.80 ohms
Wiper motor	Lucas 14W (two speed)	
Armature endfloat	0.004 to 0.008 inch (0.1 to 0.21 mm)	
Light running current: normal speed	1 to 5 amp	
high speed	2.0 amp	
Light running speed:		
normal speed	46 to 52 rpm	
high speed	60 to 70 rpm	

Replacement bulb	**Watts**	**Part Number**
Headlamp	60/45	GLU 101
Sidelamp	6	GLB 989
Front flasher	21	GLB 382
Stop, tail lamp	6/21	GLB 380
Rear flasher	21	GLB 382
Number plate	5	GLB 501
Interior	6	GLB 254
Panel and warning	2.2	37H 2139
Reverse lamp (when fitted)		BFS 272
Luggage compartment lamp (when fitted)		GLB 254
Automatic transmission selector (when fitted)		88–625625

1 General description

The electrical system is of the 12 volt type and the major components comprise, a 12 volt battery of which the negative terminal is earthed, a Lucas alternator which is fitted to the front right hand side of the engine and is driven from the pulley on the front of the crankshaft, and a starter motor which is mounted on the rear right hand side of the engine.

The battery supplies a steady amount of current for the ignition, lighting and other electrical circuits, and provides a reserve of electricity when the current consumed by the electrical equipment exceeds that being produced by the alternator.

The battery is charged by a Lucas 16 ACR alternator and information will be found in Section 6.

When fitting electrical accesories to cars with a negative earth system it is important, if they contain silicone diodes or transistors, that they are connected correctly, otherwise serious damage may result to the component concerned. Items such as radios, tape recorders, electronic tachometer, automatic dipping, parking lamp and anti-dazzle mirrors should all be checked for correct polarity.

It is important that the battery positive earth lead is always disconnected if the battery is to be boost charged or if any body and most mechanical repairs are to be carried out, using electric arc welding equipment. Serious damage can be caused to the more delicate instruments, specially those containing semi--conductors.

2 Battery - removal and replacement

1 The battery is in a special carrier fitted on the right hand wing valance of the engine compartment. It should be removed once every three months for cleaning and testing. Disconnect the positive and then the negative leads from the battery terminals by slackening the clamp retaining nuts and bolts or by unscrewing the retaining screws if terminal caps are fitted instead of clamps.

2 Unscrew the clamp bar retaining nuts, and lower the clamp bar to the side of the battery. Carefully lift the battery from its carrier. Hold the battery vertical to ensure that none of the electrolyte is spilled.

3 Replacement is a direct reversal of this procedure. NOTE: Replace the negative lead before the positive lead and smear the terminals with petroleum jelly (vaseline) to prevent corrosion. NEVER use an ordinary grease as applied to other parts of the car.

3 Battery - maintenance and inspection

1 Normal weekly battery maintenance consists of checking the electrolyte level of cell to ensure that the separators are covered by ¼ inch of electroyte. If the level has fallen, top up the battery using distilled water only. Do not overfill. If the battery is overfilled or any electrolyte spilled, immediately wipe away excess as electrolyte attacks and corrodes any metal it comes into contact with very rapidly.

2 If the battery is of the Lucas 'Pacemaker' design a special topping up procedure is necessary as follows:

a) The electrolyte levels are visible through the translucent battery case or may be checked by fully raising the vent cover and tilting to one side. The electrolyte level in each cell must be kept such that the separator plates are just covered. To avoid flooding the battery must not be topped up within half an hour of it having been charged from any source other than from the generating system fitted to the car.

b) To top up the levels in each cell, raise the vent cover and pour distilled water into the trough until all the rectangular filling slots are full of distilled water and the bottom of the trough is just covered. Wipe the cover seating grooves dry and press the cover firmly into position. The correct quantity of distilled water will automatically be distributed to each cell.

c) The vent must be kept closed at all times except when being toped up.

3 If the battery has the Auto-fill device fitted, a special topping up sequence is required. The white balls in the Auto-fill battery are part of the automatic topping up device which ensures correct electrolyte level. The vent chamber should remain in position at all times except when topping up or taking specific gravity readings. If the electrolyte level in any of the cells is below the bottom of the filling tube top up as follows:

a) Lift off the vent chamber cover.

b) With the battery level, pour distilled water into the trough until all the filling tubes and trough are full.

c) Immediately replace the cover to allow the water in the

trough and tubes to flow into the cells. Each cell will automatically receive the correct amount of water.

4 As well as keeping the terminals clean and covered with petroleum jelly, the top of the battery, and especially the top of the cells, should be kept clean and dry. This helps to prevent corrosion and ensures that the battery does not become partially discharged by leakage through dampness and dirt.

5 Inspect the battery securing nuts, battery clamp plate, tray and battery leads for corrosion (white fluffy deposits on the metal which are brittle to touch). If any corrosion is found, clean off the deposit with ammonia and paint over the clean metal with an anti-rust, anti-acid paint.

6 At the same time inspect the battery case for cracks. If a crack is found, clean and plug it with one of the proprietary compounds marked by such firms as Holts for this purpose. If leakage through the crack has been excessive then it will be necessary to refill the appropriate cell with fresh electrolyte as described later. Cracks are frequently caused at the top of the battery case by pouring in distilled water in the middle of winter AFTER instead of BEFORE run. This gives the water no chance to mix with the electrolyte and so the former freezes and splits the battery case.

7 If topping up becomes excessive and the case has been inspected for cracks that could cause leakage, but none are found, the battery is being overcharged and the voltage regulator will have to be checked and reset.

8 With the battery on the bench at the three monthly interval check, measure the specific gravity with a hydrometer to determine the state of charge and condition of the electrolyte. There should be very little variation between the different cells and, if a variation in excess of 0.025 is present, it will be due to either:

a) Loss of electrolyte from the battery at some time caused by spillage or a leak, resulting in a drop in the specific gravity of the electrolyte when the efficiency was replaced with distilled water instead of fresh electrolyte.

b) An internal short circuit caused by buckling of the plates or similar malady pointing to the likelihood of total battery failure in the near future.

9 The specific gravity of the electrolyte for fully charged conditions at the electrolyte temperature indicated, is listed in Table A. The specific gravity of a fully discharged battery at different temperatures of the electrolyte is given in Table B.

TABLE A

Specific gravity - battery fully charged

1.268 at 100°F or 38°C electrolyte temperature
1.272 at 90°F or 32°C electrolyte temperature
1.276 at 80°F or 27°C electrolyte temperature
1.280 at 70°F or 21°C electrolyte temperature
1.284 at 60°F or 16°C electrolyte temperature
1.288 at 50°F or 10°C electrolyte temperature
1.292 at 40°F or 4°C electrolyte temperature
1.296 at 30°F or -1.5°C electrolyte temperature

TABLE B

Specific gravity - battery fully discharged

1.098 at 100°F or 38°C electrolyte temperature
1.102 at 90°F or 32°C electrolyte temperature
1.106 at 80°F or 27°C electrolyte temperature
1.110 at 70°F or 21°C electrolyte temperature
1.114 at 60°F or 16°C electrolyte temperature
1.118 at 50°F or 10°C electrolyte temperature
1.122 at 40°F or 4°C electrolyte temperature
1.126 at 30°F or -1.5°C electrolyte temperature

4 Battery - electrolyte replenishment

1 If the battery is in a fully charged state and one of the cells maintains a specific gravity reading which is 0.025 or lower than the others and a check of each cell has been made with a voltage meter to check for short circuits (a four to seven second test should give a steady reading of between 1.2 and 1.8 volts), then it is likely that electrolyte has been lost from the cell with the low reading at some time.

2 Top up the cell with a solution of 1 part sulphuric acid to 2.5 parts of water. If the cell is already fully topped up draw some electrolyte out of it with a pipette. The total capacity of each cell is approximately 1/3 pint.

3 When mixing the sulphuric acid and water NEVER ADD WATER TO SULPHURIC ACID – always pour the acid slowly onto the water in a glass container. IF WATER IS ADDED TO SULPHURIC ACID IT WILL EXPLODE.

4 Continue to top up the cell with the freshly made electrolyte and to recharge the battery and check the hydrometer readings.

5 Battery charging

1 In winter time when a heavy demand is placed on the battery, such as when starting from cold, and much electrical equipment is continually in use, it is a good idea to occasionally have the battery fully charged from an external source at a rate of 3.5 to 4 amps.

2 Continue to charge the battery at this rate until no further rise in specific gravity is noted over a four hour period.

3 Alternatively, a trickle charger, charging at the rate of 1.5 amps can be safely used overnight.

4 Special rapid 'boost' charges which are claimed to restore the power of the battery in 1 to 2 hours are most dangerous unless they are thermostatically controlled as they can cause serious damage to the battery plates through overheating.

5 While charging the battery note that the temperature of the electrolyte should never exceed 100°F.

6 Alternator - general description

The Lucas 16 ACR series alternator is fitted as standard to models covered by this manual. The main advantage of the alternator lies in its ability to provide a high charge at low revolutions. Driving slowly in heavy traffic with a dynamo invariably means no charge is reaching the battery. In similar conditions even with the wipers, heater, lights and perhaps radio switched on, the Lucas 16 ACR alternator will ensure a charge reaches the battery.

An important feature of the alternator is a built in output control regulator, based on 'thick film' hybrid integrated micro-circuit technique, which results in this alternator being a self contained generating and control unit.

The system provides for direct connection of a charge light, and eliminates the need for a field switching relay and warning light control unit, necessary with former systems.

The alternator is of the rotating field ventilated design and comprises pricipally a laminated stator on which is wound a star connected 3 phase output winding, a twelve pole rotor carrying the field windings - each end of the rotor shaft runs in ball race bearings which are lubricated for life, natural finish aluminium dicast end brackets, incorporating the mounting lugs, a rectifier pack for converting the AC output of the machine to DC for battery charging, and an output control regulator.

The rotor is belt driven from the engine through a pulley keyed to the rotor shaft. A pressed steel fan adjacent to the pulley draws cooling air through the machine. This fan forms an integral part of the alternator specification. It has been designed to provide adequate air flow with a minimum of noise, and to withstand the high stresses associated with maximum speed. Rotation is clockwise viewed on the drive end. Maximum

Rectification of alternator output is achieved by six silicone diodes housed in a rectifier pack and connected as a 3 phase full wave bridge. The rectifier pack is attached to the outer face of the slip ring end bracket and contains also three 'field' diodes, at normal operating speeds, rectified current from the stator output windings flows through these diodes to provide self excitation of the rotor field, via brushes bearing on face type slip rings.

The slip rings are carried on a small diameter moulded drum attached to the rotor shaft outboard of the rotor shaft axle, while the outer ring has a mean diameter of ¾ inch. By keeping the mean diameter of the slip rings to a minimum, relative speeds between brushes and rings, and hence wear, are also minimal. The slip rings are connected to the rotor field winding by wires carried in grooves in the rotor shaft.

The brush gear is housed in a moulding screwed to the outside of the slip ring end bracket. This moulding thus encloses the slip ring and brush gear assembly, and together with the shielded bearing, protects the assembly against the entry of dust and moisture.

The regulator is set during manufacture and requires no further attention. Briefly the 'thick film' regulator comprises resistors and conductors screen printed onto a 1 inch square aluminium substrate. Mounted on the substrate are Lucas semi-conductors consisting of three transistors, a voltage reference diode and a field recirculation diode, and two capacitors. The internal connections between these components and the substrate are made by Lucas patented connectors. The whole assembly is 1/16 inch thick and is housed in a recess in an aluminium heat sink, which is attached to the slip ring end bracket. Complete heamatic sealing is achieved by a silicone rubber encapsulent to provide enviromental protection.

Electrical connections to external circuits are brought out to Lucar connector blades, these being grouped to accept a moulded connector socket which ensure correct connections.

7 Alternator - routine maintenance

1 The equipment has been designed for the minimum amount of maintenance in service, the only items subject to wear being the brushes and bearings.

2 Brushes should be examined after 60,000 miles (100,000 km) and renewed if necessary. This is a job best left to the local BLMC garage or auto-electrical engineering works.

3 The bearings are pre-packed with grease for life, and should not require any further attention.

4 For full information on fan belt adjustment and alternator removal see Chapter 2.

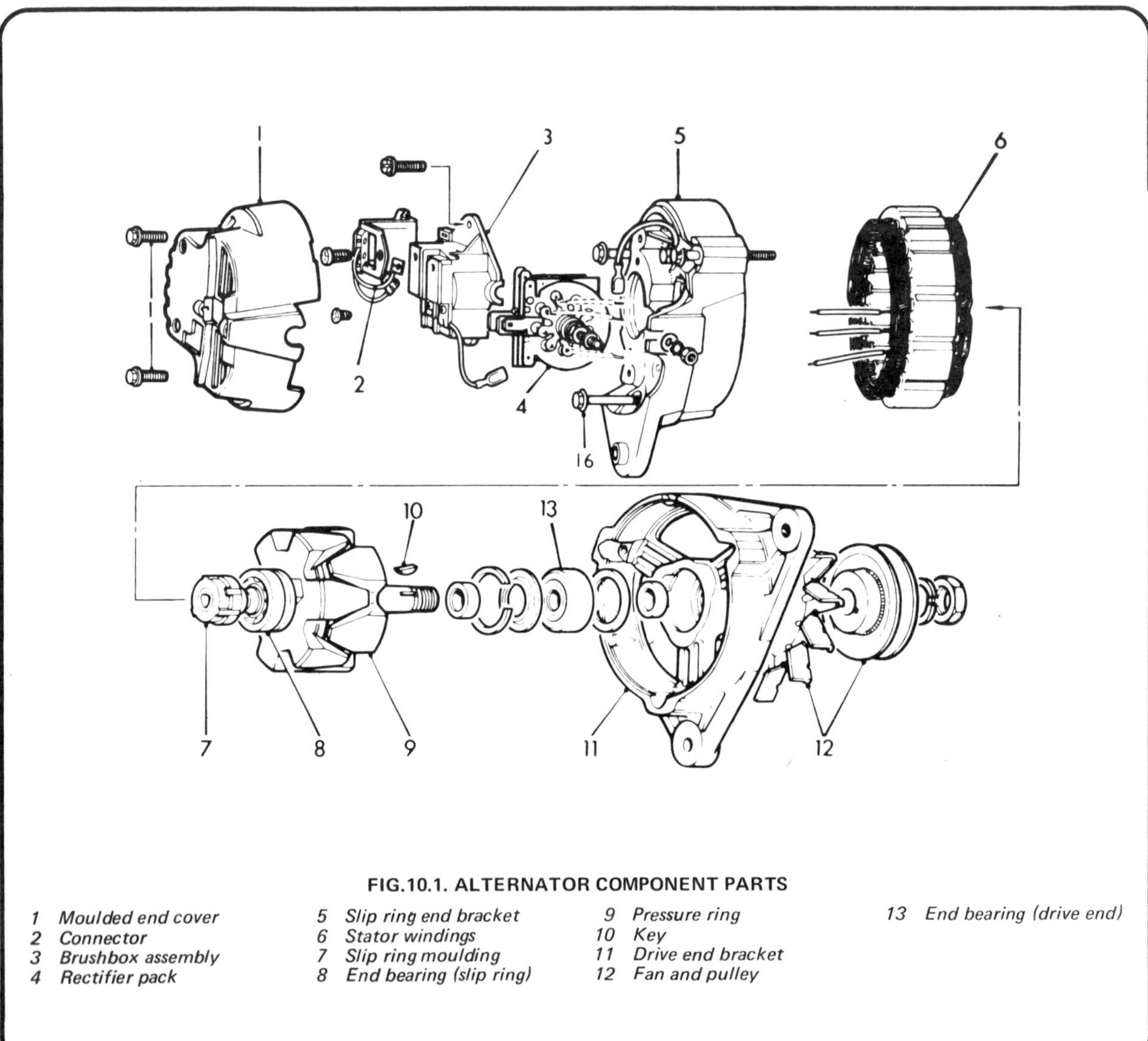

FIG.10.1. ALTERNATOR COMPONENT PARTS

1 Moulded end cover
2 Connector
3 Brushbox assembly
4 Rectifier pack
5 Slip ring end bracket
6 Stator windings
7 Slip ring moulding
8 End bearing (slip ring)
9 Pressure ring
10 Key
11 Drive end bracket
12 Fan and pulley
13 End bearing (drive end)

8 Starter motor - general description

One of two types of starter motor have been fitted to the 1.8 Marina models., an inertia or pre-engaged type.

Both starter motors are interchangeable and engage with a common flywheel starter ring gear. The relay for the inertia starter motor is mounted next to the ignition coil whereas the pre-engaged type has the solenoid switch on the top of the motor.

The principle of operation of the inertia type starter motor is as follows: When the igntion switch is turned, current flows from the battery to the starter motor solenoid switch which caused it to become energized. Its internal plunger moves inwards and closes an internal switch so allowing full starting current to flow from the battery to the starter motor. This creates a powerful magnetic field to be induced into the field coils which causes the armature to rotate.

Mounted on helical spines is the drive pinion which, because of the sudden rotation of the armature, is thrown forwards along the armature shaft and so into engagement with the flywheel ring gear. The engine crankshaft will then be rotated until the engine starts to operate on its own and, at this point, the drive pinion is thrown out of mesh with the flywheel ring gear.

The pre-engaged starter motor operates by a slightly different method but still using end face commutator brushes instead of brushes located on the side of the commutator.

The method of engagement on the pre-engaged starter differs considerably in that the drive pinion is brough into mesh with the starter ring gear before the main starter current is applied.

When the ignition is switched on, current flows from the battery to the solenoid which is mounted on the top of the starter motor body. The plunger in the solenoid moves inwards so causing a centrally pivoted lever to move in such a manner that the forked end pushes the drive pinion into mesh with the starter ring gear. When the solenoid plunger reaches the end of its travel, it closes an internal contact and full starting current flows to the stator field coils. The armature is then able to rotate the crankshaft so starting the engine.

A special one way clutch is fitted to the starter drive pinion so that when the engine just fires and starts to operate on its own, it does not drive the starter motor.

9 Starter motor (M418G) - testing on engine

1 If the starter motor fails to operate, then check the condition of the battery be turning on the headlamps. If they glow brightly for several seconds and then gradually dim, the battery is in an uncharged condition.

2 If the headlamps glow brightly and it is obvious that the battery is in good condition then check the tightness of the battery wiring connections (and in particular the earth lead from the battery terminal to its connection on the body frame).Check the tightness of the connections at the relay switch and at the starter motor. Check the wiring with a voltmeter for breaks or shorts due to failure of insulation.

3 If the wiring is in order then check that the starter motor switch is operating. To do this, press the rubber covered button in the centre of the relay switch located next to the igntion coil if it is working the starter motor will be heard to 'click' as it tries to rotate. Alternatively check it with a voltmeter.

4 If the battery is fully charged, with wiring in order, and the switch working but the starter motor fails to operate then it will have to be removed from the car for examination. Before this is done, however, ensure that the starter pinion has not jammed in mesh with the flywheel. Check by turning the square end of the armature shaft with a spanner. This will free the pinion if it is stuck in engagement with the flywheel teeth.

10 Starter motor (M418G) - removal and replacement

1 Disconnect the positive and then the negative terminals from the battery. Also disconnect the starter motor cable from the terminal on the starter motor end cover.

2 Undo and remove the bolt and spring washer and the nut and spring washer that secure the starter motor to the engine back-plate.

3 Lift the starter motor away by manipulating the drive gear out from the ring gear area and then from the engine compartment.

4 Refitting is the reverse sequence to removal. Make sure that the starter motor cable, when secured in position by its terminal retaining nut does not touch any part of the body or power unit which could damage the insulation.

FIG.10.2. STARTER MOTOR REMOVAL

1 Cable terminal nut *2 Securing bolt*

11 Starter motor (M418G) - dismantling and reassembly

Such is the reliability of starter motors generally and the difficulty is undertaking an effective repair without special equipment any dismantling and overhaul work is best left to an auto electrician. However, the drive gear can be dismantled from this type of starter motor easily if this, solely, is at fault. An exploded component illustration, Fig.10.3, is given to show just how a starter motor would dismantle.

1 To dismantle the starter motor drive, first use a press or large valve spring compressor to push the retainer clear of the circlip which can then be removed. Lift away the retainer and main spring.

2 Slide off the remaining parts with a rotary action of the armature shaft.

3 It is most important that the drive gear is completely free from oil, grease and dirt. With the drive gear removed, clean all parts thoroughly in paraffin. Under no circumstances oil the drive components. Lubrication of the drive components could easily cause the pinion to stick.

4 Reassembly of the starter motor drive is the reverse sequence to dismantling. Use a press or the large valve spring compressor to compress the spring and retainer sufficiently to allow a new circlip to be fitted to its groove on the shaft.

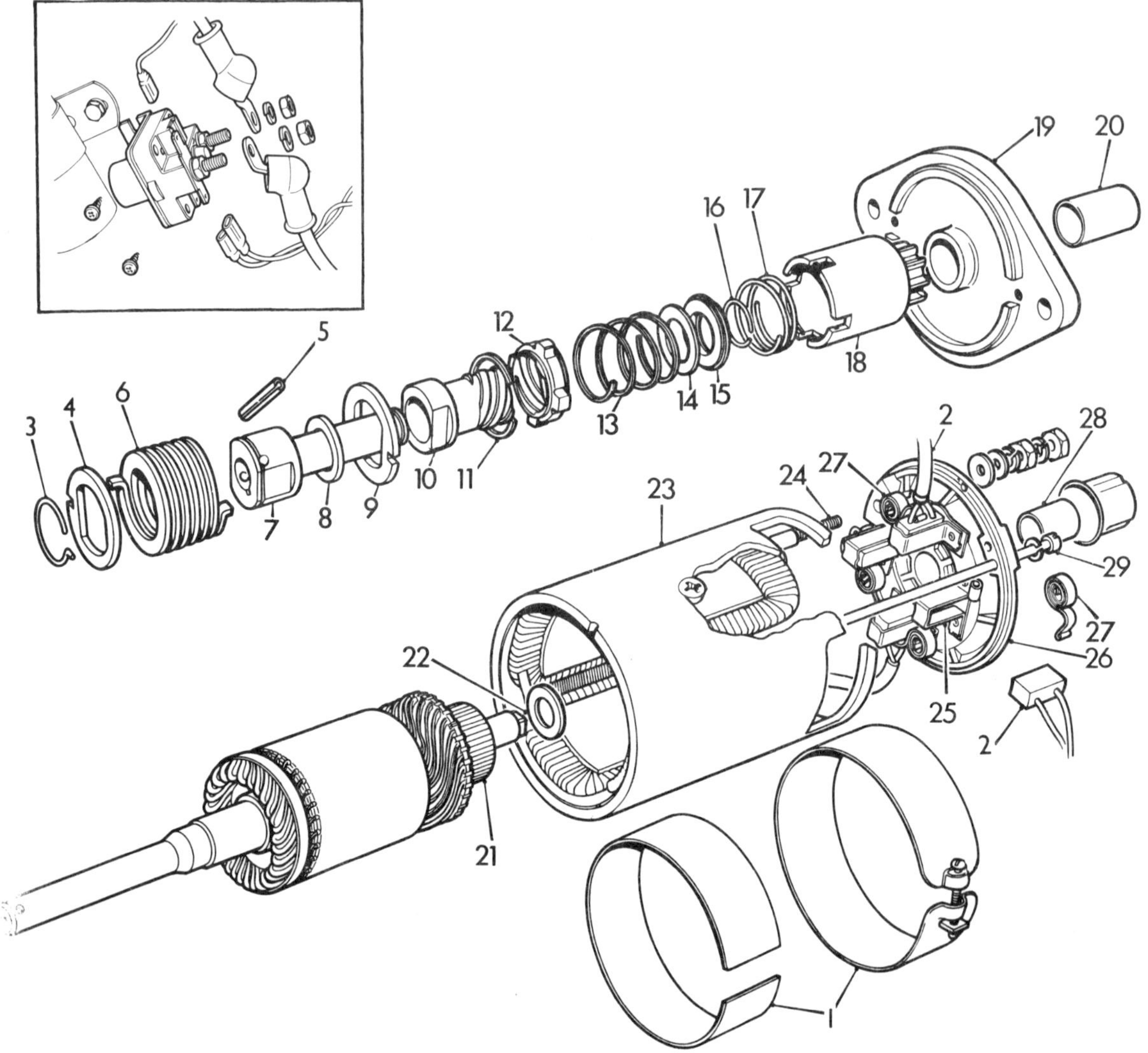

FIG 10.3 M4189 STARTER MOTOR COMPONENT PARTS, PLUS SOLENOID

1 Seal (left), cover band right
2 Brushes
3 Retaining ring
4 Front anchor plate
5 Spiral pin
6 Main spring
7 Centre sleeve
8 Fibre thrust washer
9 Rear anchor plate
10 Screwed sleeve
11 Retaining ring
12 Control nut
13 Restraining spring
14 Thrust washer
15 Locating collar
16 Retaining ring
17 Spring
18 Pinion end barrel
19 Drive end bracket
20 Driving end bush
21 Armature
22 Spacer
23 Body
24 Terminal post
25 Brush holder
26 Commutator end bracket
27 Brush tension spring
28 Bush
29 Through bolt
Inset: Solenoid component fixings

12 Starter motor (2M100 pre-engaged) - testing on engine

The testing procedure is basically similar to the inertia engagement type as described in Section 9. However, note the following instructions before finally deciding to remove the starter motor.

Ensure that the pinion gear has not jammed in mesh with the flywheels due either to a broken solenoid spring or dirty pinion gear splines. To release the pinion, engage a low gear and, with the ignition switched off, rock the car backwards and forwards which should release the pinion from mesh with the ring gear. If the pinion still remains jammed the starter motor must be removed for further examination.

13 Starter motor (2M100 - pre-engaged) - removal and replacement

1 Disconnect the positive and then the negative terminals from the battery.

2 Make a note of the electrical connections at the rear of the solenoid and disconnect the top heavy duty cable. Also release the two Lucar terminals from the rear of the solenoid. There is no need to undo the lower heavy duty cable at the rear of the solenoid.

3 Undo and remove the bolt and spring washer, and nut and spring washer which hold the starter motor in place and lift away upwards.

4 Replacement is a straightforward reversal of the removal sequence. Check that the electtrical cable connections are clean and firmly attached to their respective terminals.

14 Starter motor (2M100 - pre-engaged) - dismantling and reassembly

See Section 11 concerning the difficulty in effective repairs on the inertia starter motor. The pre-engaged is of similar complexity and should be left totally in the hands of an auto electrician.

Again an exploded component illustration is given, Fig.10.4 to show how this type of starter motor would dismantle.

15 Starter motor solenoid - removal and replacement

1 For safety reasons disconnect the battery.

2 Carefully ease back the rubber cover to gain access to the terminals (see Fig.10.3).

3 Make a note of the Lucar terminal connections and detach these connections.

4 Undo and remove the heavy duty cable terminal connection nuts and spring washers. Detach the two terminal connectors.

5 Undo and remove the two retaining screws and lift away the solenoid.

6 Refitting is the reverse sequence to removal.

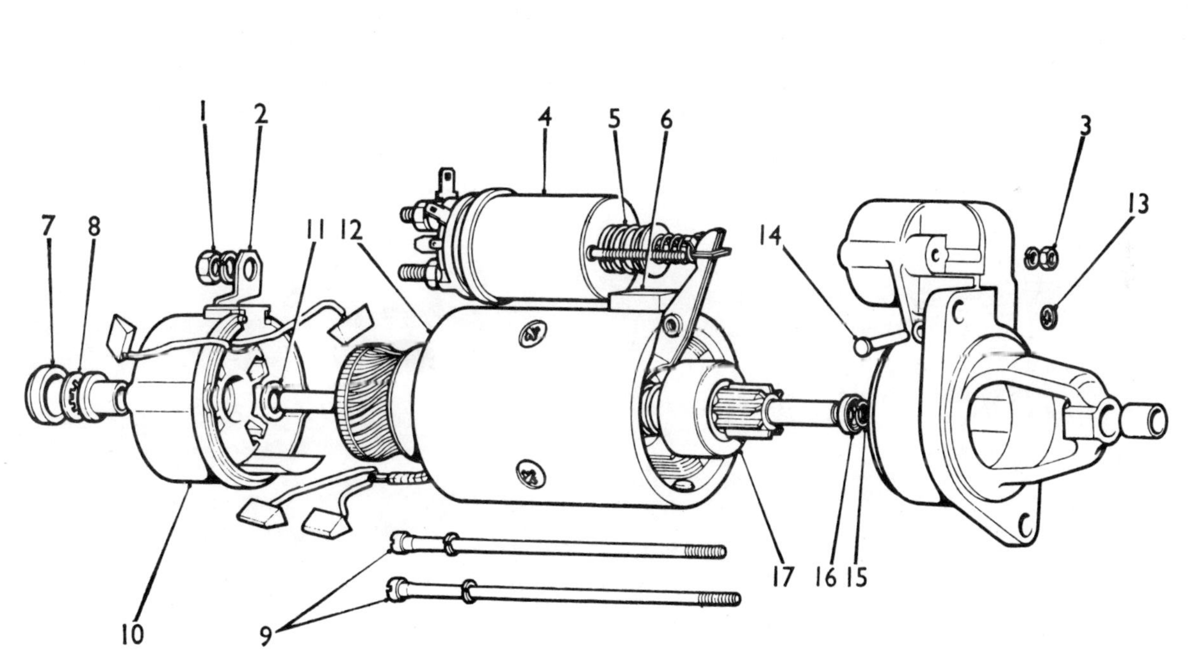

FIG.10.4. 2M100 PRE-ENGAGED STARTER MOTOR COMPONENT PARTS

1 *Connecting link securing nut*
2 *Connecting link*
3 *Solenoid to drive end bracket securing nut*
4 *Solenoid*
5 *Solenoid plunger and return spring*
6 *Rubber block*
7 *End cap seal*
8 *Armature shaft retaining ring (spire nut)*
9 *Through bolts*
10 *Commutator end cover*
11 *Thrust washer*
12 *Yoke*
13 *Retaining ring (spire nut)*
14 *Pivot pin*
15 *Thrust collar jump ring*
16 *Thrust collar*
17 *Roller clutch drive*

16 Flasher unit and circuit - fault tracing and rectification

The flasher unit located as shown in Fig.10.5 is enclosed in a small metal container and is operated only when the ignition is on by the composite switch mounted on the right hand side of the steering column.

If the flasher unit fails to operate, or works either very slowly or very rapidly, check out the flasher indicator circuit as described below, before assuming there is a fault in the unit itself.

1 Examine the direction indicator bulbs front and rear for broken filaments.

2 If the external flashers are working but the internal flasher warning lights on or both sides have ceased to function, check the filaments and replace as necessary.

3 With the aid of the wiring diagram check all the flasher circuit connections if a flasher bulb is sound but does not work.

4 In the event of total indicator failure check fuse A3 - A4.

5 With the ignition switched on, check that current is reaching the flasher unit by connecting a voltmeter between the 'plus' or 'B' terminal and earth. If this test is positive, connect the 'plus' or 'B' terminal and the 'L' terminal and operate the flasher switch. If the flasher bulb lights up the flasher unit itself is defective and must be replaced as it is not possible to dismantle and repair it.

6 To remove the flasher unit first disconnect the battery. Make a note of the electrical cable terminal positions and detach the two terminal connections. The unit may now be pulled out from its holder.

7 Refitting the flasher unit is the reverse sequence to removal.

17 Windscreen wiper arms - removal and replacement

1 Before removing a wiper arm, turn the windscreen wiper switch on and off to ensure the arms are in their normal parked position with the blades parallel with the bottom of the windscreen.

2 To remove the arm, pivot the arm back and pull the wiper arm head off the splined drive, at the same time easing back the clip with a screwdriver.

3 When replacing an arm, place it so it is in the correct relative parked position and then press the arm head onto the splined drive until the retaining clip clicks into place.

18 Windscreen wiper mechanism - fault diagnosis and rectification

Should the windscreen wipers fail, or work very slowly then check the terminals for loose connections, and make sure the insulation of the external wiring is not broken or cracked. If this is in order, then check the current the motor is taking by connecting up an ammeter in the circuit and turning on the wiper switch. Consumption should be between 1 to 5 amps for normal speed or 2 amps for high speeds.

If no current is passing, check the A3 - A4 fuse. If the fuse has blown, replace it after having checked the wiring to the motor and other electrical circuits serviced by this fuse for short circuits. Further information will be found in Section 40. If the fuse is in good condition, check the wiper switch. Should the wiper take a very high current, check the wiper blades for freedom of movement. If this is satisfactory check the wipe motor and drive cable for signs of damage. Measure the end float which should be between 0.002 - 0.008 inch (0.051 - 0.203mm). The end float is set by the thrust screw. Check that excessive friction in the cable connecting tubes, caused by too small a curvature, is not the cause of the high current consumption.

If the motor takes a very low current, ensure that the battery is fully charged. Check the brush gear after removing the commutator yoke assembly, and ensure that the brushes are free to move. If necessary, renew the tension springs. If the brushes are very worn they should be replaced with new ones. The armature may be checked by substitution.

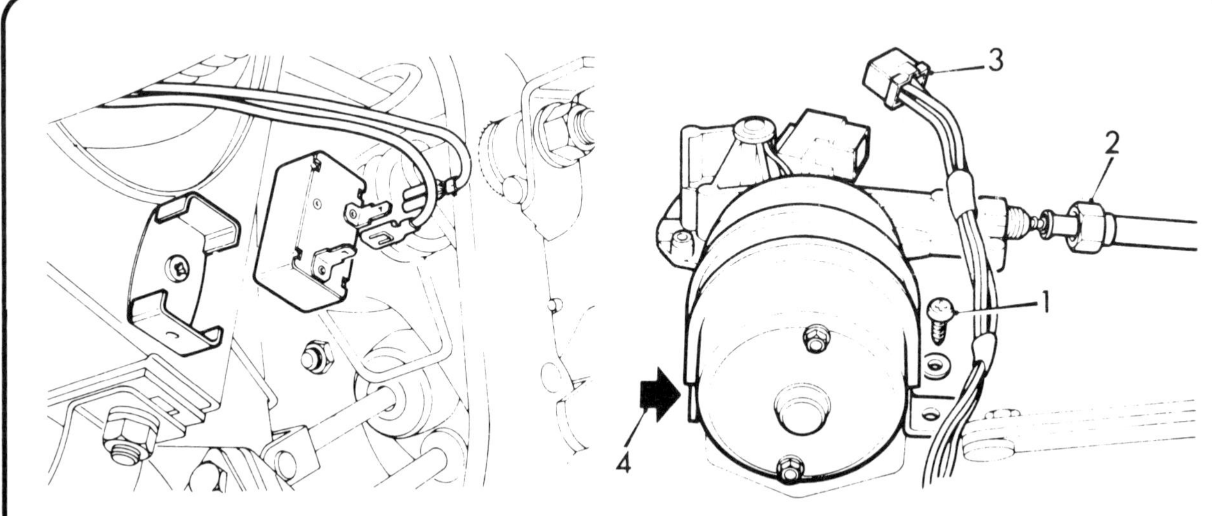

FIG.10.5. FLASHER UNIT FIXING ABOVE THE BRAKE/CLUTCH PEDALS

FIG.10.6. WINDSCREEN WIPER MOTOR REMOVAL

1 Clamp retaining screw
2 Drive tube securing nut
3 Electric cable plug
4 Clamp band

19 Windscreen wiper blades - changing wiping arc

If it is wished to change the area through which the wiper blades move, this is simply done by removing each arm in turn from each splined drive, and then replacing it on the drive in a slightly different position.

20 Windscreen wiper motor - removal and replacement

1 Refer to Section 17 and remove the wiper arms and blades.
2 Undo and remove the screw and plain washer that secures the wiper motor clamp to the body valance. Release the clamp and rubber moulding by pressing the clamp band into the release slot (Fig.10.6).
3 Undo the wiper drive tube securing nut and slide the nut down the tube.
4 Next disconnect the electrical cable plug from the motor socket.
5 Lift the motor clear of the body valance whilst at the same time pulling the inner cable from the tube.
6 Refitting the wiper motor and inner cable is the reverse sequence to removal. Take care in feeding the inner cable through the outer tube and engaging the inner cable with each wiper wheelbox spindle. Lubricate the inner cable with Castrol LM Grease.

21 Windscreen wiper motor - dismantling, inspection and reassembly

The only repair which can be effectively undertaken by the do it yourself mechanic to a wiper motor is brush replacement. Anything more serious than this will mean either exchanging the complete motor or having a repair done by an auto electrician. Spare part availability is really the problem. Brush replacement is described here.
1 Refer to Fig.10.7 and remove the four gearbox cover retaining screws and lift away the cover. Release the circlip and flat washer securing the connecting rod to the crankpin on the shaft and gear. Lift away the connecting rod followed by the second flat washer.
2 Release the circlip and flat washer securing the shaft and gear to the gearbox body.
3 De-burr the gear shaft and lift away the gear making careful note of the location of the dished washer.
4 Scribe a mark on the yoke assembly and gearbox to ensure correct reassembly and unscrew the two yoke bolts from the motor yoke assembly. Part the yoke assembly including armature from the gearbox body. As the yoke assembly has residual magnetism ensure that the yoke is kept well away from metallic dust.
5 Unscrew the two screws securing the brush gear and the terminal and switch assembly and remove both the assemblies.
6 Inspect the brushes for excessive wear. If the main brushes are worn to a limit of 3/16 inch (4.76mm) or the narrow section of the third brush is worn to the full width of the brush fit a new brush gear assembly. Ensure that the three brushes move freely in their boxes.
7 Reassembly at this stage is a straight reversal of disassembly.

22 Wheelboxes and drive cable tubes - removal and replacement

1 Refer to Section 20 and remove the windscreen wiper motor.
2 Refer to Chapter 12 and remove the instrument panel.
3 Refer to Chapter 12 and remove the glovebox.
4 Refer to Section 17 and remove the windscreen wiper arms.
5 Undo and remove the nuts that secure the wheelboxes to the body. Lift away the shaped spacer from each wheelbox (Fig.10.8).
6 Slacken the two nuts that clamp the two wheelbox plates on the glovebox side. Carefully pull out the drive tube from the wheelbox.
7 Carefully remove the free drive tube and its grommet through the glovebox opening.
8 Lift away the two wheelbox units through the instrument panel opening.
9 Recover the spacer and washer from each wheelbox unit.
10 Refitting the wheelboxes and drive cable tubes is the reverse sequence to removal.

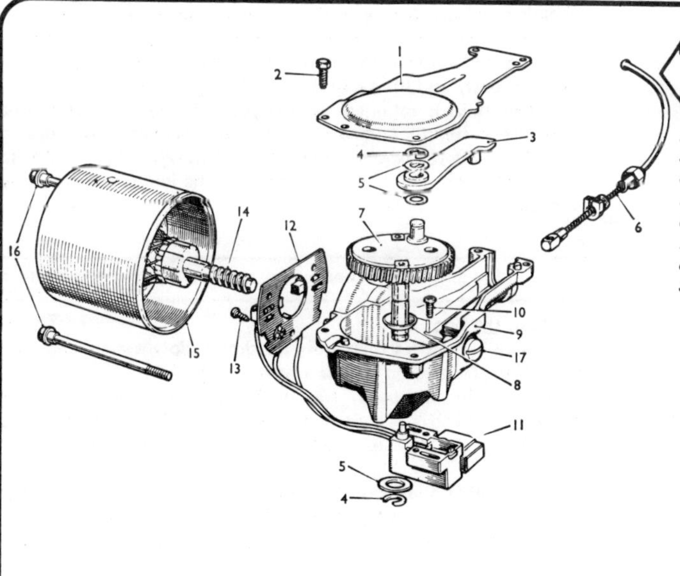

FIG.10.7. LUCAS 14W TWO SPEED WIPER MOTOR COMPONENT PARTS

1 Gearbox cover
2 Screw for cover
3 Connecting rod
4 Circlip
5 Plain washers
6 Cross head
7 Shaft and gear
8 Dished washer
9 Gearbox
10 Screw for limit switch
11 Limit switch assembly
12 Brush gear
13 Screw for brush gear
14 Armature
15 Yoke assembly
16 Yoke bolts
17 Armature thrust screw

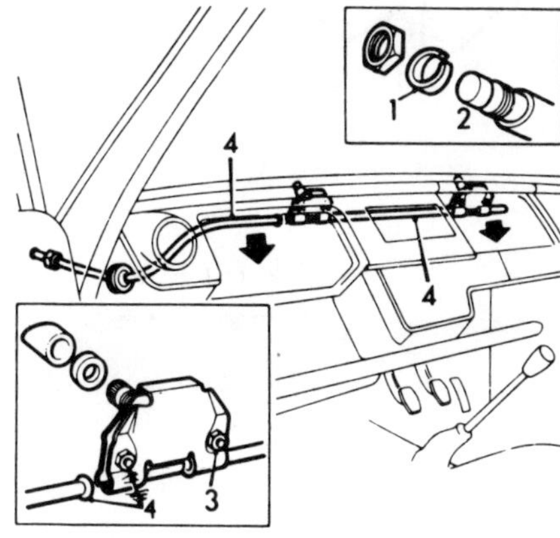

FIG.10.8. WINDSCREEN WIPER RACK AND WHEELBOX ASSEMBLY

1 Wheelbox securing nut
2 Shaped spacer
3 Wheelbox plates securing nut
4 Drive tube

23 Horns - fault tracing and rectification

1 If a horn works badly or fails completely, first check that the wiring leading to it for short circuits and loose connections. Also check that the horn is firmly secured and that there is nothing lying on the horn body.
2 The horn is protected by the A1 - A2 fuse and if this has blown the circuit should be checked for short circuits. Further information will be found in Section 40.
3 The horn should never be dismantled, but it is possible to adjust it. This adjustment is to compensate for wear of the moving parts only and will not affect the tone. To adjust the horn proceed as follows:
a) There is a small adjustment screw on the broad rim of the nearly opposite the two terminals (See Fig.10.9). Do not confuse this with the large screw in the centre.
b) Turn the adjustment screw anti-clockwise until the horn just fails to sound. Then turn the screw a quarter of a turn clockwise which is the optimum setting.
c) It is recommended that if the horn has to be reset in the car, the A1 - A2 fuse should be removed and replaced with a piece of wire, otherwise the fuse will continually blow due to the high current required for the horn in continual operation.
d) Should twin horns be fitted, the horn which is not being adjusted be disconnected while adjustments of the other takes place.

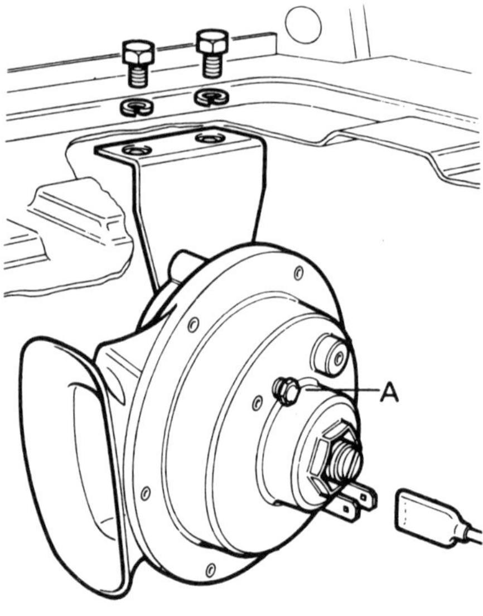

FIG.10.9. THE HORN
A Adjustment screw

24 Headlight units - removal and replacement

1 Sealed beam (or renewable bulb) light units are fitted.
2 The method of gaining access to the light unit for replacement is identical for all types of light units and bulbs.
3 Undo and remove the four screws that secure the top of the front grille to the body panel.
4 Carefully lift the grille outwards and upwards so releasing it from its locating holes in the body.
5 Undo and remove the three securing screws and lift away the headlamp rim.
6 Sealed beam unit: Disconnect the plug from the rear of the light unit and lift away the light unit.

Spring clip bulb holder: Disconnect the plug from the bulb holder and release the spring clip from the reflector. Lift away the bulb.

Cap tye bulb holder: Push and turn the cap anti-clockwise. Lift off the cap and withdraw the bulb.

7 Refitting in all cases is the reverse sequence to removal. Where a bulb is fitted make sure that the locating clip or slot in the bulb correctly registers in the reflector.

25 Headlight beam - adjustment

The headlights may be adjusted for both vertical and horizontal beam positions by the two screws, these being shown in Fig.10.10. For vertical movement screw (7) should be used and horizontal movement screw (8).

They should be set so that a full or high beam, the beams are set slightly below parallel with a level road surface. Do not forget that the beam position is affected by how the car is normally loaded for night driving, and set the beams with the car loaded to the position.

Although this adjustment can be set approximately at home, it is recommended that this be left to a local garage who will have the necessary equipment to do the job more accurately.

26 Side and front flasher bulbs - removal and replacement

1 Undo and remove the two screws securing the lamp lens to the lamp body and lift away the lenses (Fig.10.11).
2 Either bulb is retained by a bayonet fixing, so to remove a bulb push in slightly and rotate in an anti clockwise direction.
3 Refitting is the reverse sequence to removal. Take care not to tighten the two lens retaining screws as the lenses can be easily cracked.

27 Stop, tail and rear flasher bulbs - removal and replacement

1 Open the boot lid.
2 The bulb holders may now be drawn downwards and rearwards into the luggage compartment (Fig.10.12).
3 Two bulbs are used, the inner one being of the double filament type and are retained in position by a bayonet fixing. To remove a bulb, push in slightly and rotate in an anti clockwise direction.
4 The double filament bulb has offset pins on the bayonet fixing so it is not possible to fit it the wrong way round.
5 Refitting is the reverse sequence to removal.

28 Number plate light bulb - removal and replacement

1 The lenses may be removed by depressing and turning through 90o lift away the lenses (Fig.10.13).
2 Carefully pull on the bulb and it will be released from its holder. It will be noticed that capless bulbs are used.
3 Refitting is the reverse sequence to removal.

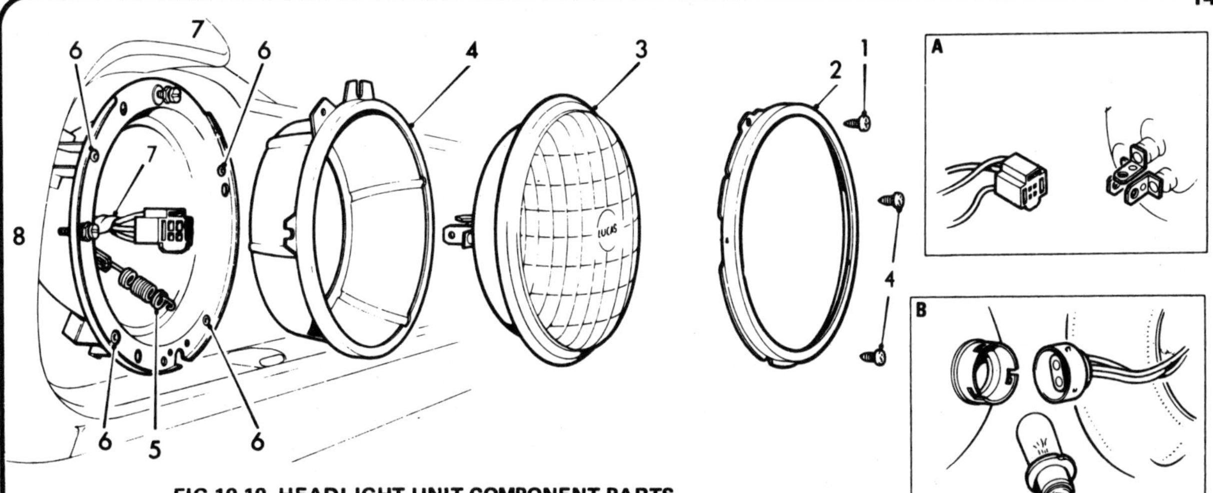

FIG.10.10. HEADLIGHT UNIT COMPONENT PARTS

1 Rim securing screws
2 Rim
3 Light unit
4 Inner shell
5 Inner shell tensioning spring
6 Snap rivets
7 Vertical adjustment screw
8 Horizontal adjustment screw
A Sealed beam light unit connection
B Cap type bulb holder
C Spring clip bulb holder

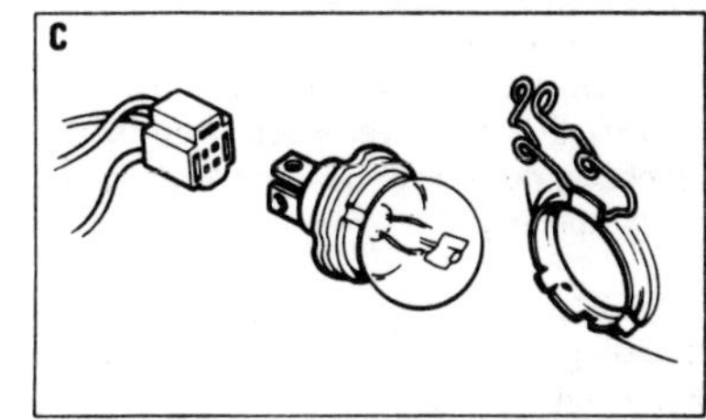

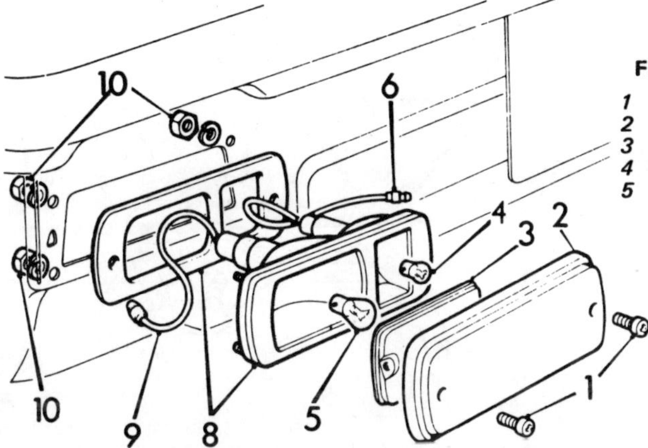

FIG.10.11. SIDE AND FRONT FLASHER ASSEMBLY

1 Lens securing screws
2 Lens - plain
3 Lens - coloured
4 Sidelamp bulb
5 Flasher bulb
6 Sidelamp connection
7 Light assembly body
8 Rubber seal
9 Flasher connection
10 Light assembly retaining nuts

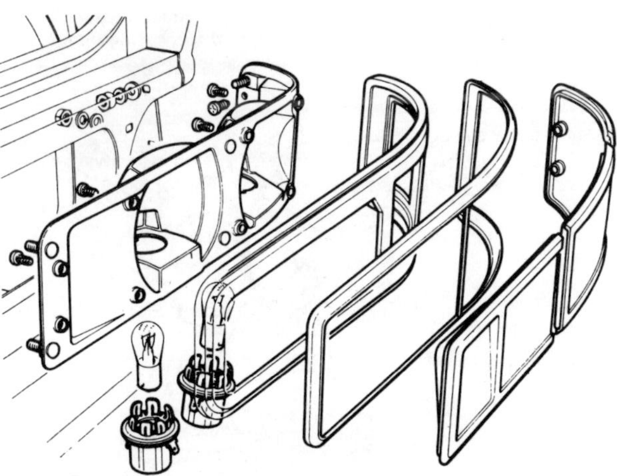

FIG.10.12. STOP, TAIL AND REAR FLASHER ASSEMBLY

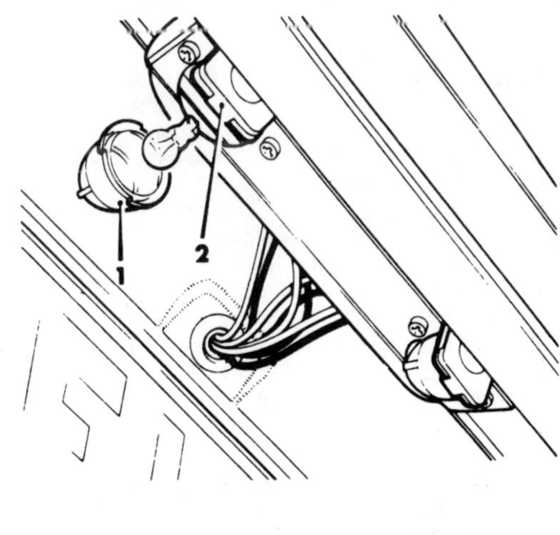

FIG.10.13. REAR NUMBER PLATE LIGHTS

1 Lens *2 Fixing clip*

29 Panel illumination lamp bulb - removal and replacement

1 Disconnect the battery.
2 Refer to Chapter 12 and remove the instrument panel.
3 Pull out the bulb holder from the rear of the panel giving access to the bulb (Fig.10.14).
4 Carefully pull on the bulb and it will be released from its holder. It will be noticed that capless bulbs are used.
5 Refitting is the reverse sequence to removal.

30 Ignition, starter, steering lock switch - removal and replacement

1 Disconnect the battery.
2 Undo and remove the four screws that secure the switch cowls. Lift the cowls from over the switch stalks.
3 Detach the multi-pin plug from the electrical leads to the switch assembly at the harness socket (Fig.10.15).
4 Undo and remove the one screw that retains the switch assembly in the lock housing.
5 Slide the switch assembly from the lock housing.
6 Refitting is the reverse sequence to removal. Make sure that the locating peg on the switch correctly registers in the groove in the lock housing.

31 Headlight dip/flasher, horn, direction indicator switch removal and replacement

1 Disconnect the battery.
2 Refer to Chapter 12 and remove the steering wheel.
3 Detach the multi-pin plug from the electrical leads to the switch assembly at the harness socket located under the facia (Fig.10.16).
4 Slacken the switch clamp tightening screw located on the underside of the switch and ease the switch assembly from the steering column.
5 Refitting the switch assembly is the reverse sequence to removal. Make sure that the lug on the inner diameter of the switch locates in the slot in the outer steering column as shown in 'B' Fig.10.17 and also that the striker dog on the nylon switch centre is in line with and towards the switch stalk 'A'.

32 Lighting switch - removal and replacement

1 Disconnect the battery.
2 Withdraw the choke control as far as possible (manual choke only).
3 Undo and remove the two crosshead screws retaining the finisher, and move the finisher up the choke control knob as far as possible (Fig.10.18).
4 Make a note of the two cable connections at the rear of the switch and detach the two terminals.
5 To remove the switch it is necessary to compress four little clips, two each side of the switch body and then draw the switch forwards from the panel. Although a U shaped tool is desirable to do this it is possible for one person to compress the clips whilst a second person pulls the switch forwards.
6 Refitting the lighting switch is the reverse sequence to removal.

33 Heater fan switch - removal and replacement

1 Disconnect the battery.
2 Carefully pull off the two heater control knobs.
3 Undo and remove the three crosshead screws securing the finisher. Lift away the finisher.
4 Make a note of the two cable connections at the rear of the switch and detach the two terminals.

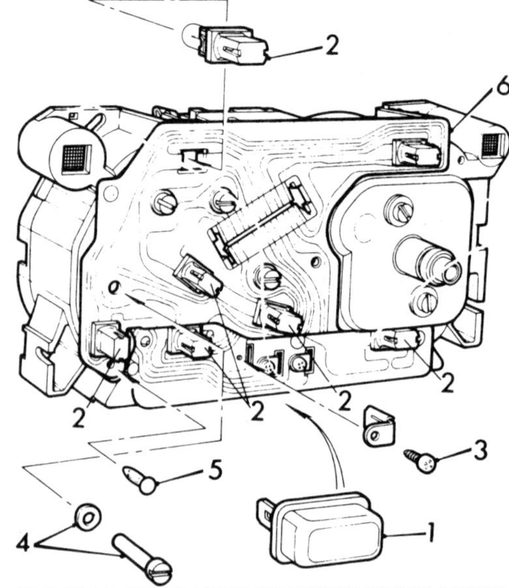

FIG.10.14. REAR VIEW OF INSTRUMENT PANEL

1 *Voltage stabilizer*
2 *Light bulb holders in situ*
3 *Tab connector retaining screw*
4 *Sleeve screw and washer*
5 *Plastic retaining peg*
6 *Printed circuit*

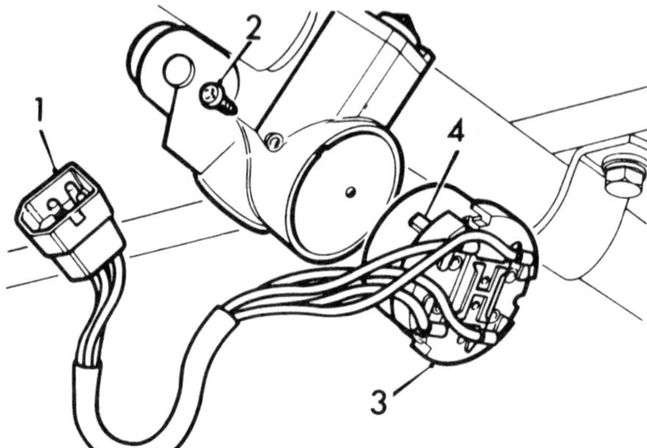

FIG.10.15. COMBINED IGNITION, STARTER AND STEERING LOCK SWITCH

1 *Multi pin plug*
2 *Switch assembly retaining screw*
3 *Switch assembly*
4 *Locating peg*

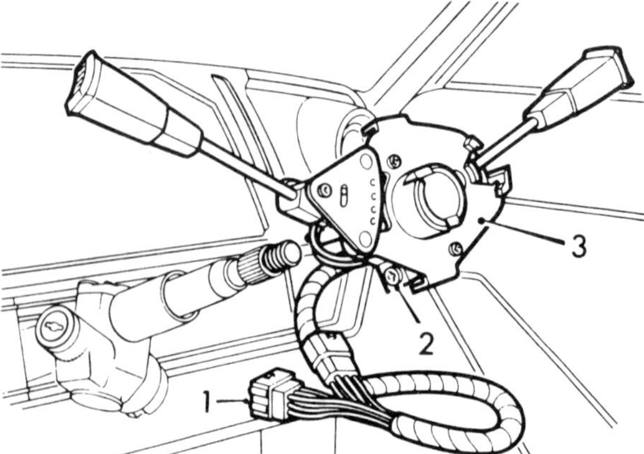

FIG.10.16 COMBINATION SWITCH ATTACHMENTS

1 *Multi pin plug*
2 *Switch clamp screw*
3 *Switch assembly*

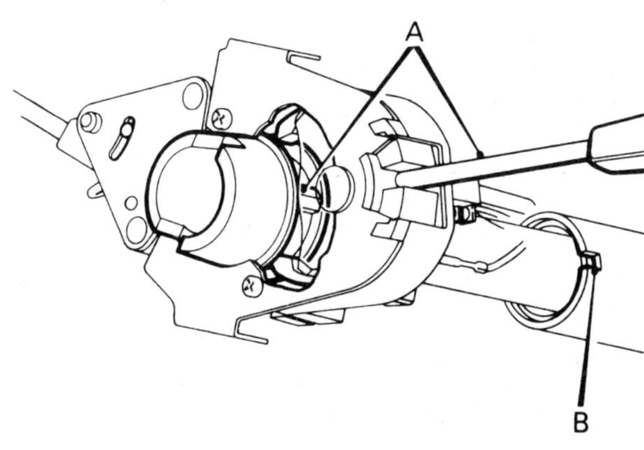

FIG.10.17. COMBINATION SWITCH ALIGNMENT

5 To remove the switch it is necessary to compress four little clips, two each side of the switch body and then draw the switch forwards from the panel. Although a U shaped tool is desirable to do this it is possible for one person to compress the clips whilst a second person pulls the switch forwards.
6 Refitting the heater fan switch is the reverse sequence to removal.

34 Stop light switch - removal and replacement

1 Make a note of the two cable connections at the rear of the switch located on the top of the brake pedal mounting bracket. Detach the two terminals (Fig.10.19).
2 Undo and remove the two bolts and spring washers securing the switch mounting bracket to the brake pedal mounting bracket. Lift away the switch and bracket.
3 Straighten the ears of the switch locking split pin and withdraw the split pin.
4 The switch may now be unscrewed from its mounting bracket.
5 Refitting the stop light switch is the reverse sequence to removal. It is however, necessary to adjust the position of the switch when refitting to its mounting bracket.
6 Screw the switch into its mounting bracket until one complete thread of the switch housing is visible on the pedal side of the bracket. Lock with a new split pin.

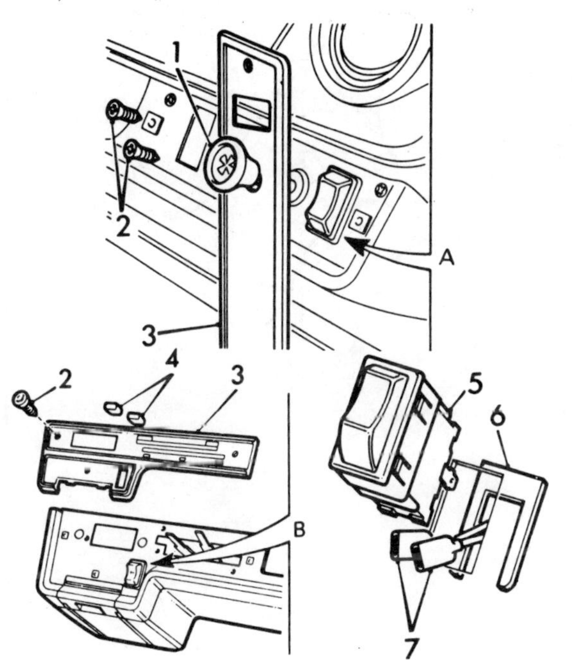

FIG.10.18. LIGHTING SWITCH (A) AND HEATER FAN SWITCH (B) REMOVAL

1 Cable control
2 Finisher retaining screw
3 Finisher
4 Heater control knob
5 Switch
6 'U' shape metal tool to compress switch clips
7 Switch terminal connectors

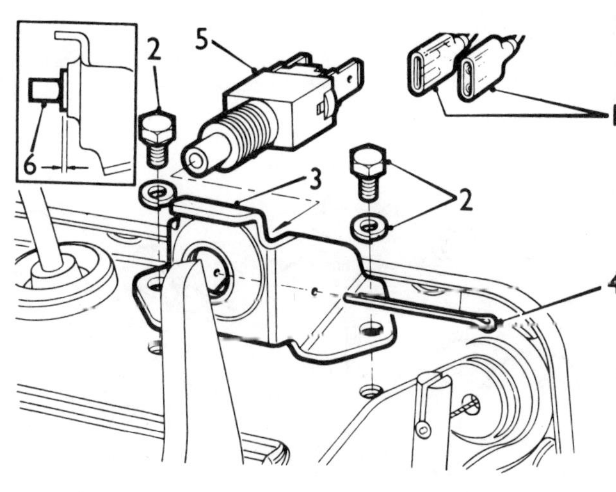

FIG.10.19. STOP LIGHT SWITCH REMOVAL

1 Switch terminal connections
2 Switch bracket securing screw and spring washer
3 Bracket
4 Split pin
5 Switch
6 Switch adjustment

35 Instrument panel printed circuit - removal and replacement

1 Refer to Chapter 12 and remove the instrument panel.
2 Withdraw the voltage stabilizer from the rear of the instrument panel printed circuit.
3 Withdraw the warning light and panel light bulb holders from the speedometer and gauges.
4 Undo and remove the three screws securing the voltage stabiliser tag connectors to the rear of the instrument panel printed circuit. Lift away the tag connector.
5 Undo and remove the four long sleeve screws and shaped washers that secure the gauge units to the rear of the instrument panel.
6 Very carefully ease out the five plastic pegs securing the printed circuit to the rear of the instrument panel. Lift away the printed circuit.
7 Refitting the printed circuit is the reverse sequence to removal.

36 Gauge units - removal and replacement

1 This section is applicable for the removal of either the fuel gauge or temperature gauge.
2 Refer to Chapter 12 and remove the instrument panel.
3 Undo and remove the four screws and washers that secure the instrument pack to the instrument panel.
4 Undo and remove the four long sleeve screws and shaped washers that secure the gauge units to the rear of the instrument panel.
5 Spring back the three clips that retain the instrument glass and panel.
6 Undo and remove the three screws that secure the instruments face plate.
7 Lift away the fuel gauge and/or temperature gauge.
8 Refitting the gauge units is the reverse sequence to removal.

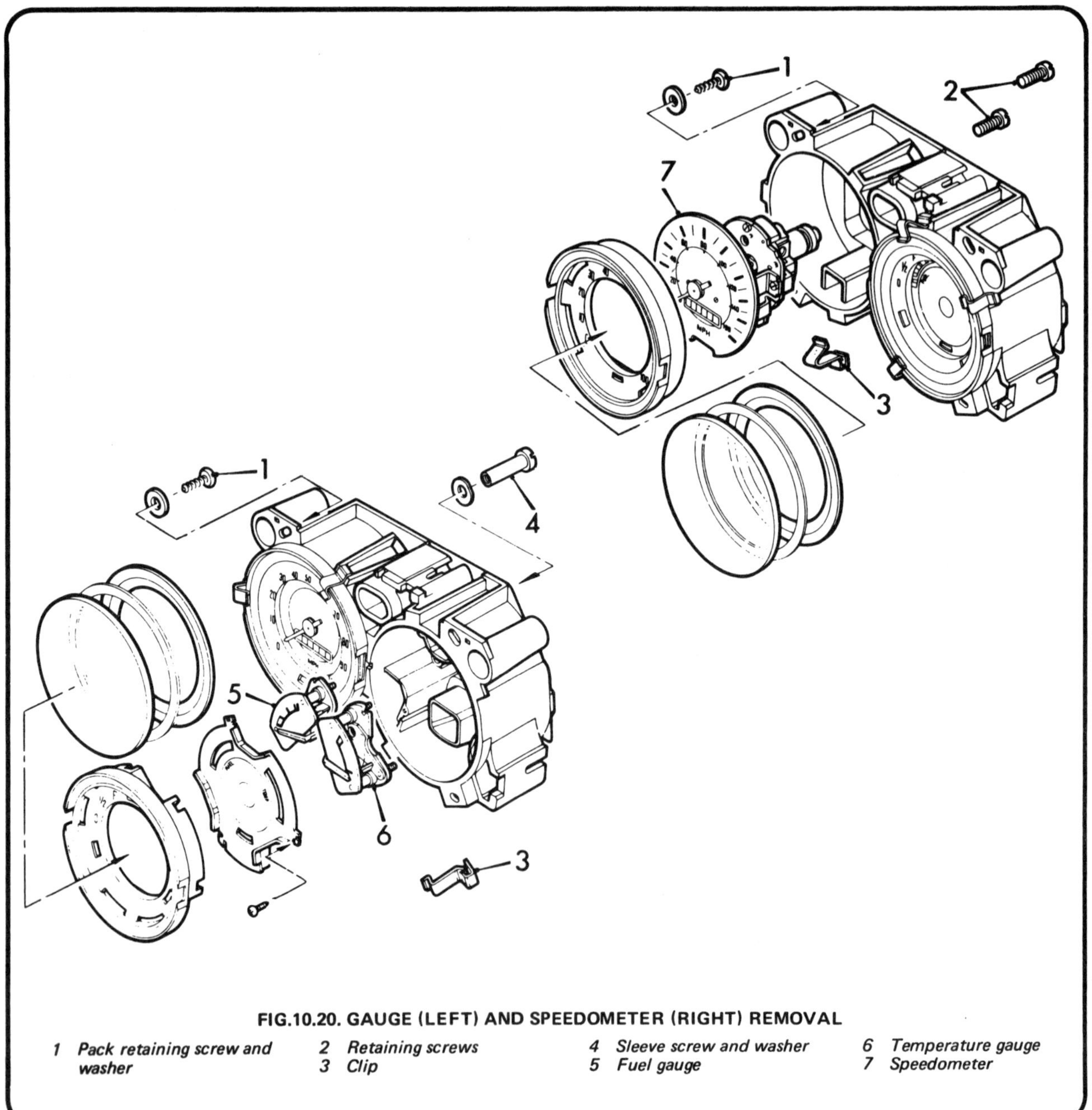

FIG.10.20. GAUGE (LEFT) AND SPEEDOMETER (RIGHT) REMOVAL

1 Pack retaining screw and washer *2 Retaining screws* *3 Clip* *4 Sleeve screw and washer* *5 Fuel gauge* *6 Temperature gauge* *7 Speedometer*

37 Speedometer - removal and replacement

1 Refer to Chapter 12 and remove the instrument panel.
2 Undo and remove the four screws and washers that secure the instrument pack to the instrument panel. Lift away the instrument pack.
3 Undo and remove the two screws that secure the speedometer in position.
4 Spring back the three clips that retain the instrument glass and bezel. Lift away the speedometer head.

38 Voltage stabilizer - removal and replacement

1 The voltage stabilizer is a push fit into the rear of the instrument panel printed circuit board.
2 Before removal, as a safety precaution disconnect the battery.
3 Carefully pull the voltage stabilizer from the rear of the printed circuit.
4 Refitting is the reverse sequence to removal. Note that the terminals of the stabilizer are offset, so it cannot be fitted the wrong way round.

39 Instrument operation - testing

The bi-metal resistance equipment for the fuel thermal type temperature gauges comprises an indicator head and transmitter with the unit connected to a common voltage stabilizer. This item is fitted because the method of operation of the equipment is voltage sensitive, and a voltage stabilizer is necessary to ensure a constant voltage supply at all times.

Special test equipment is necessary when checking correct operation of the voltage stabilizer, fuel gauge and temperature gauge so, if a fault is suspect, the car must be taken to the local BLMC garage who will have this equipment.

There are, however, several initial checks that can be carried out without the use of this equipment and should be performed as follows:

1 Connect a 0 - 20 voltmeter across the A3 fuse box terminal and a good earth on the car body.
2 Switch on the ignition and note the reading on the meter. It should be approximately 12 volts.
3 Start the engine and run at a fast idle speed of between 1000 and 1100 rpm. The ignition warning light should be out and the meter registering between 12 and 14 volts.
4 Next make sure that the instrument panel wiring multi connector plug is correctly fitted to the back of the panel.
5 Finally the wiring harness to the multi connector plug should be checked for continuity and all instrument earth connections checked for tightness.

40 Fuses

The fuse box is located inside the car behind the facia panel just above the parcel shaft and is attached to the inner body panel on the steering wheel side of the car.

Fuse A1 - A2: This has a 35 amp rating and protects the equipment which operates independant of the ignition switch. These include, interior lamp, horn-push, headlamp flasher and luggage compartment lamp (if fitted). When fitting accessories which are required to operate independantly of the ignition circuit connect to the terminal marked '2'.

Fuse A3 - A4: This has a 35 amp rating and protects the circuits which operate only when the ignition is switched on. These include, flashing direction indicators, windscreen wiper motor, brake stop warning lamps, reverse lamps (when fitted), and heated backlight (when fitted). When fitting accessories which are required to operate only when the ignition is switched on, connect to the terminal marked '4'.

A line fuse located in a cylindrical fuse holder adjacent to the instrument wiring connector near the fuse box protects the rear and number plate light bulbs.

A second line fuse located adjacent to the heater blower motor switch protects the heater blower motor. This fuse is accessible from behind the centre facia panel.

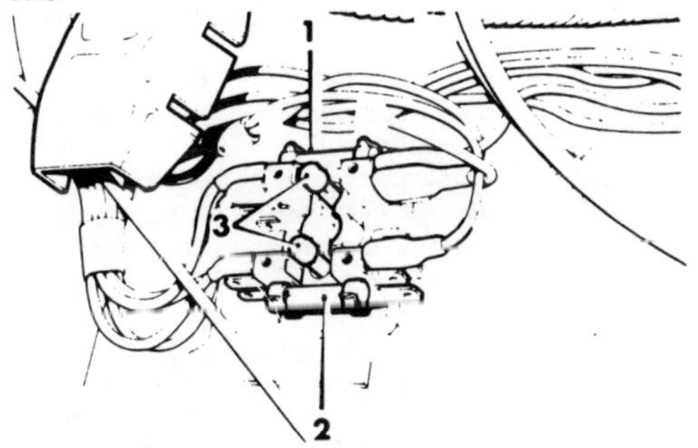

FIG.10.21. FUSE BOX

1 Fuse A1 (left end) – A2 (right end)
2 Fuse A3 (left end) – A4 (right end)
3 Spare fuses

49. Fault diagnosis

Symptom	Reason/s	Remedy
STARTER MOTOR FAILS TO TURN ENGINE		
No electricity at starter motor	Battery discharged	Charge battery.
	Battery defective internally	Fit new battery.
	Battery terminal leads loose or earth lead not securely attached to body	Check and tighten leads.
	Loose or broken connections in starter motor circuit	Check all connections and check any that are loose.
	Starter motor switch or solenoid faulty	Test and replace faulty components with new
Electricity at starter motor: faulty motor	Starter motor pinion jammed in mesh with ring gear	Disengage pinion by turning squared end of armature shaft.
	Starter brushes badly worn, sticking, or brush wires loose	Examine brushes, replace as necessary, tighten down brush wires.
	Commutator dirty, worn, or burnt	Clean commutator, recut if badly burnt.
	Starter motor armature faulty	Overhaul starter motor, fit new armature.
	Field coils earthed	Overhaul starter motor.

Symptom	Reason/s	Remedy
STARTER MOTOR TURNS ENGINE VERY SLOWLY		
Electrical defects	Battery in discharged condition	Charge battery.
	Starter brushes badly worn, sticking, or brush wires loose	Examine brushes, replace as necessary, tighten down brush wires.
	Loose wires in starter motor circuit	Check wiring and tighten as necessary.
STARTER MOTOR OPERATES WITHOUT TURNING ENGINE		
Dirt or oil on drive gear	Starter motor pinion sticking on the screwed sleeve	Remove starter motor, clean starter motor drive.
Mechanical damage	Pinion or ring gear teeth broken or worn	Fit new gear ring, and new pinion to starter motor drive.
STARTER MOTOR NOISY OR EXCESSIVELY ROUGH ENGAGEMENT		
Lack of attention or mechanical damage	Pinion or ring gear teeth broken or worn	Fit new ring gear, or new pinion to starter motor drive.
	Starter drive main spring broken	Dismantle and fit new main spring.
	Starter motor retaining bolts loose	Tighten starter motor securing bolts. Fit new spring washer if necessary.
BATTERY WILL NOT HOLD CHARGE FOR MORE THAN A FEW DAYS		
Wear or damage	Battery defective internally	Remove and fit new battery.
	Electrolyte level too low or electrolyte too weak due to leakage	Top up electrolyte level to just above plates.
	Plate separators no longer fully effective	Remove and fit new battery.
	Battery plates severely sulphated	Remove and fit new battery.
	Drive belt slipping	Check belt for wear, replace if necessary, and tighten.
	Battery terminal connections loose or corroded	Check terminals for tightness, and remove all corrosion.
	Short in lighting circuit causing continual battery drain	Trace and rectify.
	Regulator unit not working correctly	Check setting, clean, and replace if defective.
IGNITION LIGHT FAILS TO GO OUT, BATTERY RUNS FLAT IN A FEW DAYS		
Dynamo not charging	Drive belt loose and slipping, or broken	Check, replace, and tighten as necessary.
	Brushes worn, sticking, broken or dirty	Examine, clean, or replace brushes as necessary.
	Brush springs weak or broken	Examine and test. Replace as necessary.
	Commutator dirty, greasy, worn, or burnt	Clean commutator and undercut segment separators.
	Armature badly worn or armature shaft bent	Fit new or reconditioned armature.
	Contacts in light switch faulty	By-pass light switch to ascertain if fault is in switch and fit new switch as appropriate.
Or alternator not charging		Seek professional advice from BLMC garage.
WIPERS		
Wiper motor fails to work	Blown fuse	Check and replace fuse if necessary.
	Wire connections loose, disconnected, or broken	Check wiper wiring. Tighten loose connections.
	Brushes badly worn	Remove and fit new brushes.
	Armature worn or faulty	If electricity at wiper motor remove and overhaul and fit replacement armature.
	Field coils faulty	Purchase reconditioned wiper motor.
Wiper motor works very slow and takes excessive current	Commutator dirty, greasy, or burnt	Clean commutator thoroughly.
	Drive to wheelboxes too bent or unlubricated	Examine drive and straighten out severe curvature. Lubricate.
	Wheelbox spindle binding or damaged	Removal, overhaul, or fit replacement.
	Armature bearings dry or unaligned	Replace with new bearings correctly aligned.
	Armature badly worn or faulty	Remove, overhaul, or fit replacement armature.
Wiper motor works slowly and takes little current	Brushes badly worn	Remove and fit new brushes.
	Commutator dirty, greasy, or burnt	Clean commutator thoroughly.
	Armature badly worn or faulty	Remove and overhaul armature or fit replacement.
Wiper motor works but wiper blades remain static	Driving cable rack disengaged or faulty	Examine and if faulty, replace.
	Wheelbox gear and spindle damaged or worn	Examine and if faulty, replace.
	Wiper motor gearbox parts badly worn	Overhaul or fit new gearbox.

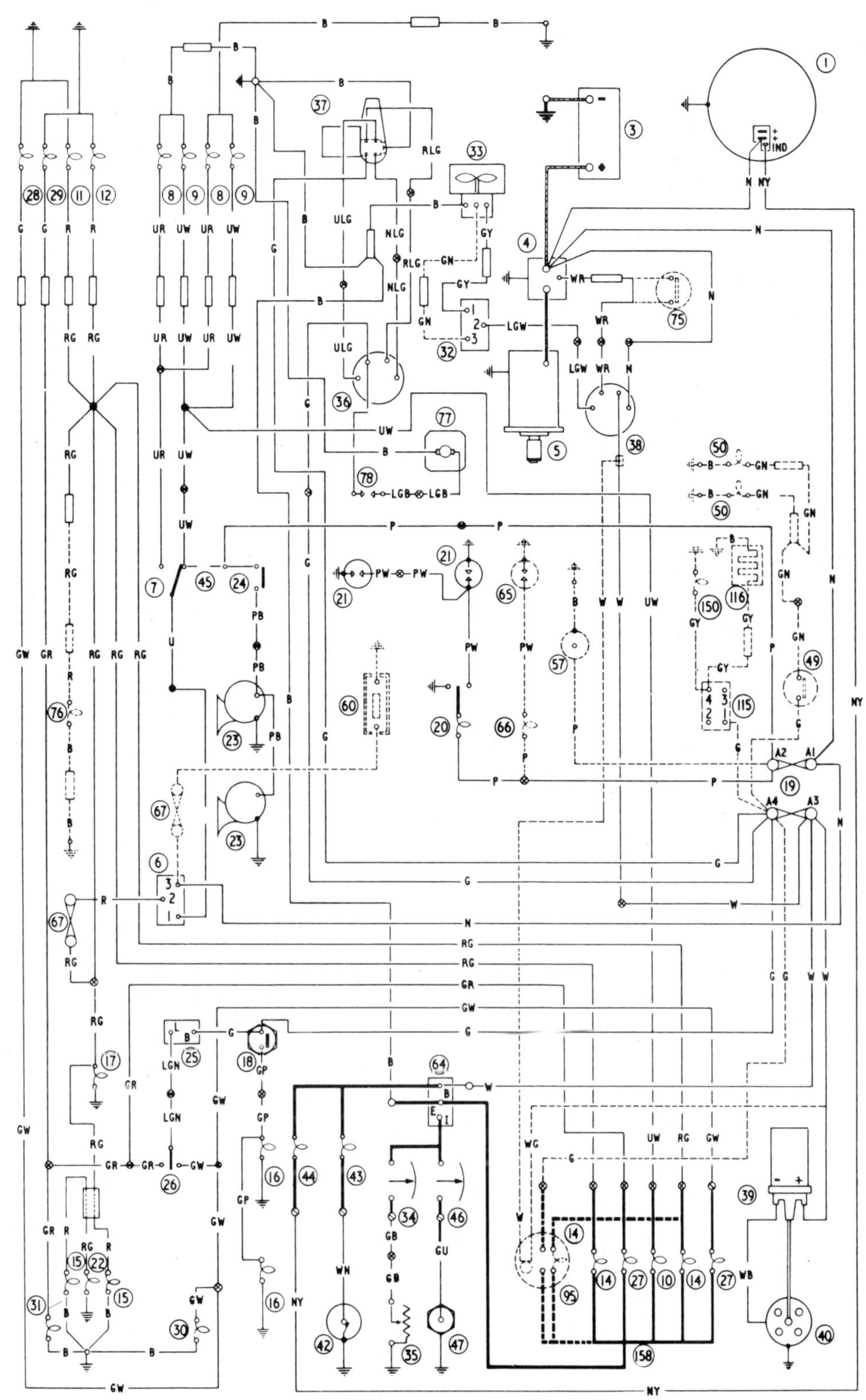

THEORETICAL WIRING DIAGRAM FOR ALL MODELS

The coding is given on page 154

WIRING DIAGRAM CODING

1 Alternator
2 Control box
3 Battery
4 Starter solenoid
5 Starter motor
6 Lighting switch
7 Dip switch
8 Headlamp high beam
9 Headlamp low beam
10 Main beam warning lamp
11 RH sidelamp
12 LH sidelamp
14 Panel lamps
15 Number plate lamps
16 Stop lamps
17 RH tail lamp
18 Stop lamp switch
19 Fuse unit
20 Interior light
21 Door switch
22 LH tail lamp
23 Horns
24 Horn - push
25 Flasher unit
26 Direction indicator switch
27 Direction indicator warning light
28 RH front flasher
29 LH front flasher
30 RH rear flasher
31 LH rear flasher
32 Heater switch
33 Heater motor
34 Fuel gauge
35 Fuel gauge tank unit
36 Wiper switch
37 Wiper motor
38 Ignition switch
39 Ignition coil
40 Distributor
42 Oil pressure switch
43 Oil pressure warning light
44 Ignition warning light
45 Headlamp flasher switch
46 Water temperature gauge
47 Water temperature transmitter
49 Reverse lamp switch (if fitted)
50 Reverse lamps (if fitted)
57 Cigar lighter (if fitted)
60 Radio (if fitted)
64 Voltage stabilizer
65 Boot light switch (if fitted)
66 Boot lamp (if fitted)
67 Line fuse
75 Automatic gearbox safety switch (if fitted)
76 Automatic gearbox quadrant lamp (if fitted)
77 Electric screen washer motor
78 Electric screen washer switch
95 Tachometer (if fitted)
115 Rear window demist switch (if fitted)
116 Rear window demist unit (if fitted)
150 Rear window demist warning light (if fitted)
158 Printed circuit instrument panel

CABLE COLOUR CODE

N	*Brown*	*P*	*Purple*	*W*	*White*
U	*Blue*	*G*	*Green*	*Y*	*Yellow*
R	*Red*	*LG*	*Light Green*	*B*	*Black*
		O	*Orange*		

When a cable has two colour code letters the first denotes the main colour and the second denotes the tracer colour

Chapter 11 Suspension and steering

Contents

Specifications

Front suspension	Independant by torsion bar with lever type shock absorbers
King pin inclination	7½% positive
Camber angle	0° 50′ positive
Castor angle	2° positive, early produced cars 5°
Hub bearing end float	0.001 to 0.005 in (0.025 - 0.0127mm)
Swivel pin link lower bush finished diameter	0.688 ± 0.0005 in (17.48 ± 0.013mm)
Trim height:	
Normal	25 3/8 ± 1/4 inch (7.715 ± 0.064mm)
With new torsion bars	+ 5/16 inch (7.94mm)
Rear suspension	Semi elliptic leaf spring with telescopic shock absorbers
Saloon	
Number of spring leaves	2
Width of leaves	2 inches (50.0mm)
Gauge of leaves	0.3 to 0.164 in (7.62 - 0.076mm)
Working load	270 lb (122.7 kg)
Estate	
Type	Heavy duty rating
Front wheel alignment	1/16 in (1.6mm) toe in
Pinion bearing pre-load	0.001 to 0.003 inch (0.025 to 0.076mm)
Oil capacity of rack and pinion	1/3 pint (190 cm^3)
Rack travel	6.5 in (16.5cm)
Rack travel - either side of centre	3.25 in (8.25 cm)
Pinion rotations, full rack travel	3.98 turns
Pinion pre-load	0.001 -0.003 in (0.025 - 0.76mm)
Shims available	0.002 in (0.050mm) 0.005 in (0.127mm) 0.010 in (0.1254mm) 0.060 in (1.524mm)
Cover gasket thickness	0.010 in (0.254 mm)
Yoke clearance	0.002 - 0.005 in (0.050 - 0.127mm)
Shims available	0.002 in (0.050mm) 0.010 in (0.254mm) 0.005 in (0.127mm)
Cover gasket thickness	0.010 in (0.254mm)
Ball pin centre dimension (ball pins screwed to tie rod equal amount)	43.7 in (1109.98 mm)
Wheels	4 stud pressed steel 13 in x 4½

Saloon tyre fitment: Standard	5.20 x 13 cross ply			
: Optional	145 x 13 radial ply			
Tyre pressures	Normal load		Heavy load	
	Front	Rear	Front	Rear
Cross ply tyres	26 lb/sq.in. (1.8kg/cm^2)	28 lb/sq.in. (2.0kg/cm^2)	28 lb/sq.in. (2.0kg/cm^2)	30 lb/sq.in. (2.1kg/cm^2)
Radial tyres	24 lb/sq.in. (1.6kg/cm^2)	26 lb/sq.in. (1.8kg/cm^2)	26 lb/sq.in. (1.8kg/cm^2)	28 lb/sq,in. (2.0kg/cm^2)

Estate tyre fitment: Standard	155 x 13 radial			
: Optional	165 x 70 radial			
Tyre pressures	Normal load		Heavy load	
	Front	Rear	Front	Rear
	26 lb/sq.in (1.8kg/cm^2)	28 lb/sq.in. (2.0kg/cm^2)	26 lb/sq.in. (1.8kg/cm^2)	32 lb/sq.in. 2.25kg/cm^2)
Maximum payload	900 lb (408 kg)			

TORQUE WRENCH SETTING

Front susupension	lb ft	kg m
Ball pin retainer locknut	70 - 80	9.6 - 11.0
Eyebolt nut	50 - 54	6.9 - 7.4
Torsion bar reaction lever lockbolt	22	3.0
Reaction pad nut	35 - 40	4.8 - 5.5
Shock absorber retaining nuts	26 - 28	3.5 - 3.8
Tie rod fork nut	48 - 55	6.6 - 7.6
Tie rod to fork	22	3.0
Caliper bracket or dust shield bolts	35 - 42	4.8 - 5.8
Rear suspension		
Upper shackle pin nuts	28	3.9
Spring eye bolt nuts	40	5.5
Spring 'U' bolt nuts	40	5.5
Shock absorber to spring bracket	28	3.9
Shock absorber to body bracket	28	3.9
Steering		
Rack clamp bracket nuts	20 - 22	2.77 - 3.04
Tie rod ball pin nuts	20 - 24	2.77 - 3.3
Flexible joint pinch bolt nut	6 - 8	0.4 - 0.5
Pinion end cover retaining bolts	12 - 15	1.6 - 2.0
Pinion pre load	15 (lb in)	0.17
Rack yoke cover bolts	12 - 15	1.6 - 2.0
Tie rod housing locknut	33 - 37	4.6 - 5.6
Tie rod ball spheres pre load	32 - 52 (lb in)	0.37 - 0.6
Steering column mounting bolts	14 - 18	1.94 - 2.49
Flexible joint coupling bolts	20 - 22	2.77 - 3.04
Steering column lock shear screw	14	1.94
Steering wheel nut	43 - 50	6.1 - 6.9
Tie rod locknuts	35 - 40	4.8 - 5.5

1 General description

The component parts of the right hand side front suspension unit are shown in Fig.11.I. Although the left hand side front suspension is identical in principle some parts are handed and therefore not interchangeable.

Attached to the hub is the road wheel as is also the brake disc, these being retained by countersunk screws or bolts. The hub rotates on two opposed tapered roller bearings mounted on the swivel pin stub axle and is retained on the stub axle by a nut. Also attached to the swivel pin is the brake drum backplate or disc brake dust shield.

The shock absorbers is attached to the body and its arm carries at the outer end the ball joint for the swivel pin top attachement. Its arm therefore acts as an uper suspension wishbone. The bottom end of the steering swivel screws into the lower link which is mounted between the outer ends of the lower arms. This link is mounted on a pivot pin so that the suspension is able to move in a vertical manner. Horizontal movement of the suspension is controlled by a tie rod assembly. The inner ends of the lower arms are free to pivot about an eye bolt and the rear arm is spline attached to the torsion bar. The rear of the torsion bar is attached to the body so that both the body weight and road shocks are taken by the torsion bar.

Rear suspension is by semi elliptic leaf springs, the springs being mounted on rubber bushed shackle pins. Double acting telescopic hydraulic shock absorbers are fitted to absorb road shocks and damp spring oscillations.

A rack and pinion steering is used. The steering wheel in splined to the upper inner column which in turn is connected to the lower column by a flexible coupling. A second flexible coupling connects the lower column to the steering gearbox pinion. The pinion teeth mesh with those machined in the rack so that rotation of the pinion moves the rack from one side of the housing to the other. Located at either end of the rack are tie rods and ball joints which are attached to the suspension swivel pin steering arms.

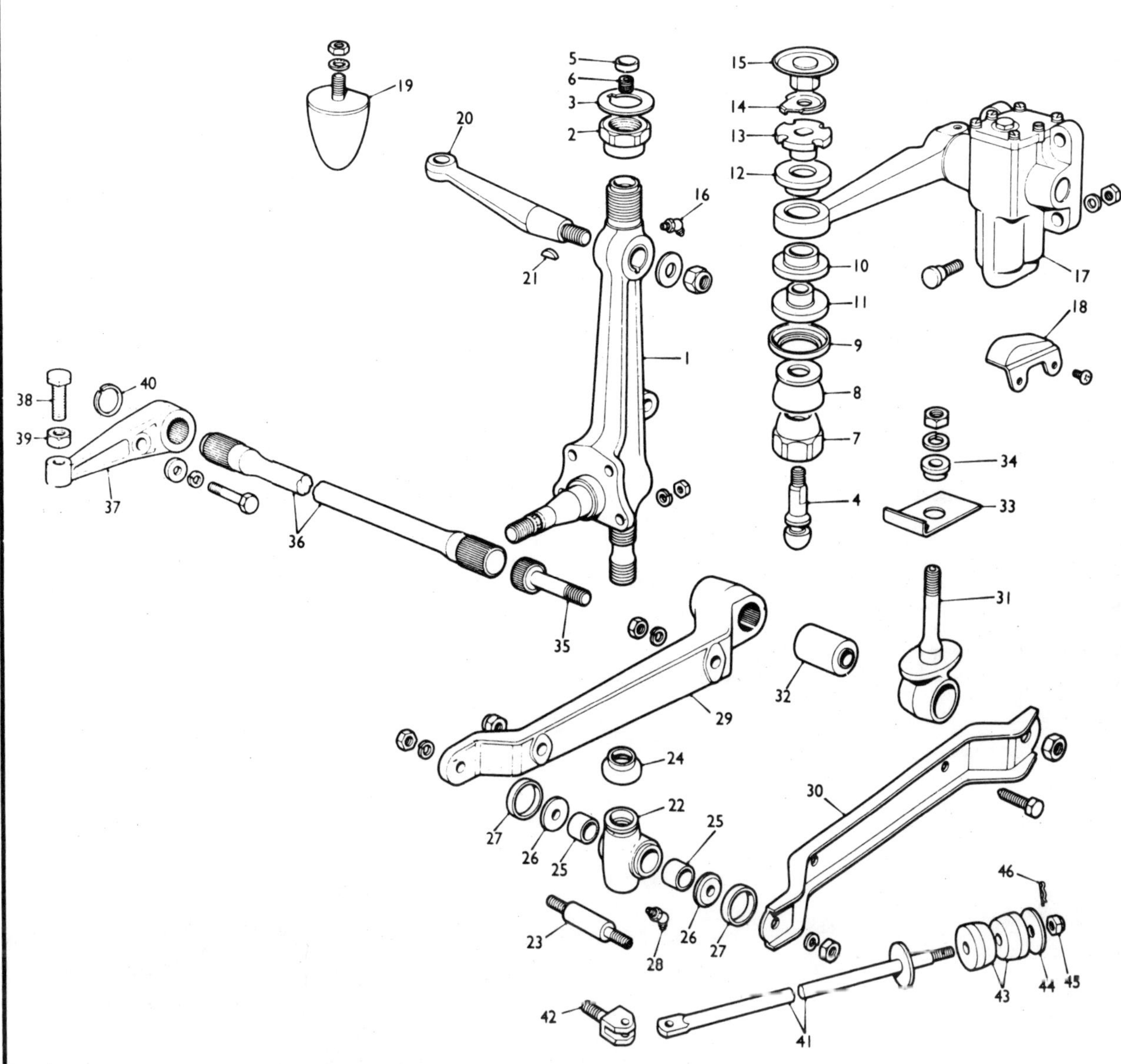

FIG 11.1 FRONT SUSPENSION COMPONENT PARTS

1 Swivel pin and stub axle-RH
2 Locknut for ball pin
3 Tab washer for ball pin
4 Ball pin
5 Seat for ball pin
6 Spring for ball pin
7 Retaining nut for ball pin
8 Dust cover for retaining nut
9 Clip for dust cover
10 Lower bush
11 Housing for lower bush
12 Upper bush
13 Housing for upper bush
14 Tab washer
15 Reaction pad
16 Grease nipple
17 Front shock absorber RH
18 Bump rubber for shock absorber
19 Rebound rubber
20 Steering lever RH
21 Key for lever
22 Lower link for swivel pin RH
23 Fulcrum pin for link
24 Rubber seal for link
25 Bush for link
26 Thrust washer for link
27 Sealing ring
28 Grease nipple for lower link
29 Lower arm - rear
30 Lower arm - front
31 Eyebolt
32 Bush for eyebolt
33 Reinforcement plate
34 Bush for plate
35 Serrated bolt
36 Torsion bar
37 Lever to torsion bar
38 Adjusting screw
39 Locknut
40 Circlip for torsion bar
41 Tie rod
42 Fork for tie rod
43 Pad for tie rod
44 Plain washer
45 Nut
46 Retaining clip for tie rod

2 Front hub bearings - removal and refitting

1 Jack up the front of the car and support on firmly based axle stands.
2 Remove the wheel trim and the road wheels.
3 Refer to Chapter 9 and remove the disc brake caliper.
4 Using a wide blade screwdriver carefully ease off the grease cap.
5 Straighten the split pin ears and extract the split pin. Lift away the nut retainer and then undo and remove the hub nut. Withdraw the splined washer. The hub may now be drawn from the axle stub.
6 Remove the outer bearing cone.
7 Using a screwdriver ease out the oil seal noting that the lip is innermost. Lift away the inner bearing cone.
8 If the bearings are to be renewed carefully drift out the bearing cups working from the inside of the hub.
9 Thoroughly wash all parts in paraffin and wipe dry using a non fluffy rag.
10 Inspect the bearings for signs of rusting, pitting or overheating. If evident, a new set of bearings must be fitted.
11 Inspect the oil seal journal face of the stub axle shaft for signs of damage. If evident, either polish with fine emery tape or if very bad a new stub axle will have to be fitted.
12 To reassemble, if new bearings are to be fitted, carefully drift in the new bearing cups using a piece of tube of suitable diameter. Make sure they are fitted the correct way round with the tapers facing outwards.
13 Work some high melting point grease into the inner bearing cone and fit it into the hub.
14 Smear a new oil seal with a little Castrol GTX and fit it with the lip innermost using a tube of suitable diameter. The final fitted position should be flush with the flange of the hub.
15 Fit the hub to the axle stub. Work some high melting point grease into the outer bearing cone and fit it into the hub.
16 Refit the splined washer and nut.
17 It is now necessary to adjust the hub bearing end float and full information will be found in Section 3 of this chapter.
18 Refit the grease cap, road wheel and wheel trim. Lower the front of the car to the ground.

3 Front hub bearings - adjustment

1 Jack up the front of the car and suport on firmly based axle stands.
2 Remove the wheel trim, road wheel and grease cap.
3 Straighten the split pin ears and extract the split pin. Lift away the hub nut retainer.
4 Back off the hub nut and spin the hub. Whilst it is spinning tighten the nut using a torque wrench set to 5 lb ft (9.69 kg m).
5 Stop the hub spinning and slacken the nut. Tighten the nut again but this time finger tight only.
6 Position the nut retainer so that half the split pin hole is covered by one of the arms of the retainer.
7 Slacken the nut and retainer until the split pin hole is fully uncovered.
8 Fit a new split pin and lock by opening the ears of the split pin and bending circumferentially around the nut retainer.
9 Fit the grease cap and replace the road wheel and wheel trim.
10 It will be observed that the end float setting achieved can cause a considerable amount of movement when the tyre is 'rocked'. Do not reduce the end float any further provided it has been set correctly as described. The bearings must not on any account be pre-loaded.

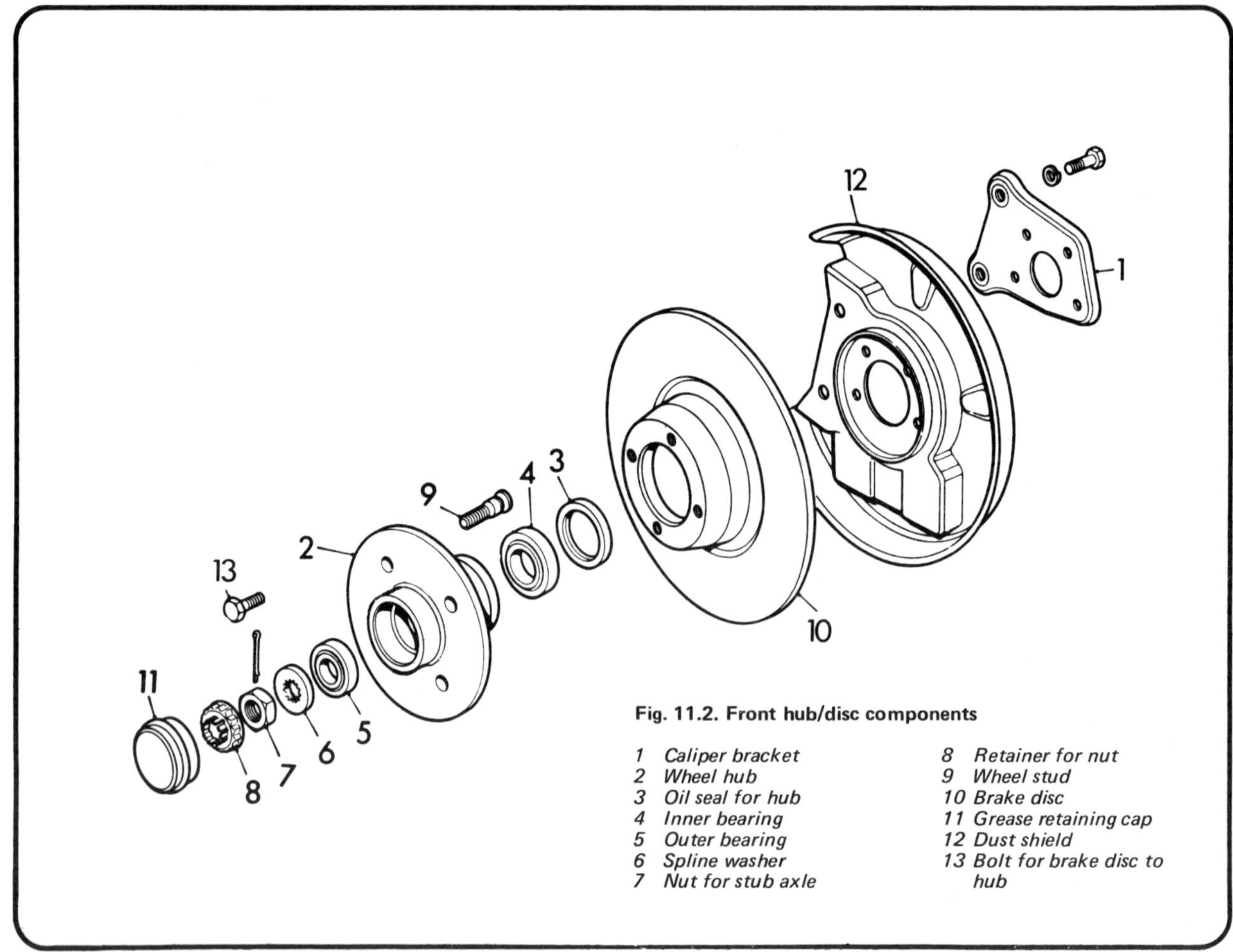

Fig. 11.2. Front hub/disc components

1 Caliper bracket
2 Wheel hub
3 Oil seal for hub
4 Inner bearing
5 Outer bearing
6 Spline washer
7 Nut for stub axle
8 Retainer for nut
9 Wheel stud
10 Brake disc
11 Grease retaining cap
12 Dust shield
13 Bolt for brake disc to hub

Length. 13ft 11 5/8" Width 5ft 4 7/8" Height 4ft 8 3/8"

Kerb Wieght: 2172 lbs. 985 kg.

Sump Capacity 6·375 pints. 3-8 litres.

Sparging Plugs. Champion N-9Y.

Size. 14 mm.

Gap. 0·024 – 0·026 in

Tyres. 155x13 radial. or 165x70 radial. Normal. Front 26. Rear 28. Heavy load. F 26 R 32.

Contanct breaker gap, 0·014 – 0·016

Condenser capacity, 0.18 – 0·24 m.fd.

Maximum payload. 900 lb. 408 kg.

Blow off pressure of exp in tank cap. 15 lbs in2.

Fan Belt Tension. 0.5 in.

Cooling System Capacity (with Heater) 9 pints.

Tappets, valve Rocker Clearance. 0·013 ins.

	Watts	Part No.
Headlamp	60/45	GLU 101.
Side lamp.	6.	GLB 989.
Front Flasher. Rear Flasher	21.	GLB 382.
Stop, tail lamp.	6/21.	GLB 380.
Number Plate.	5	GLB 501.
Interior	6.	GLB 254.
Reverse lamp		BFS 272.
Panel and Warning.	2·2.	37H 2139.

4 Lower suspension arm - removal and refitting

1 Jack up the front of the car and suport on firmly based axle stands. Suitably support the suspension unit under the rear lower arm.
2 Remove the wheel trim and the road wheel.
3 Undo and remove the nut and spring washer from the eye bolt pin.
4 Undo and remove the front nut and spring washer from the swivel lower link pin.
5 Undo and remove the nut, bolt and spring washer retaining the tie rod to the tie rod fork.
6 Undo and remove the nut retaining the tie rod fork to the lower suspension arms. Lift away the fork.
7 Undo the nut, bolt and spring washer that clamps the front and rear lower arms together.
8 The front lower suspension arm may now be lifted away.
9 Refer to Section 10 and remove the torsion bar.
10 Withdraw the eyebolt pin and then undo and remove the rear nut and spring washer from the swivel lower link pin.
11 The rear lower suspension arm may now be lifted away.
12 Refitting the lower suspension arm assembly is the reverse sequence to renewal, but the following additional points should be noted:

a) Tighten the rod fork nut to a torque wrench setting of 48 - 55 lb ft (6.6 - 7.7 kg m).
b) Tighten the tie rod to fork nut to a torque wrench setting of 22 lb ft (30 kg m).

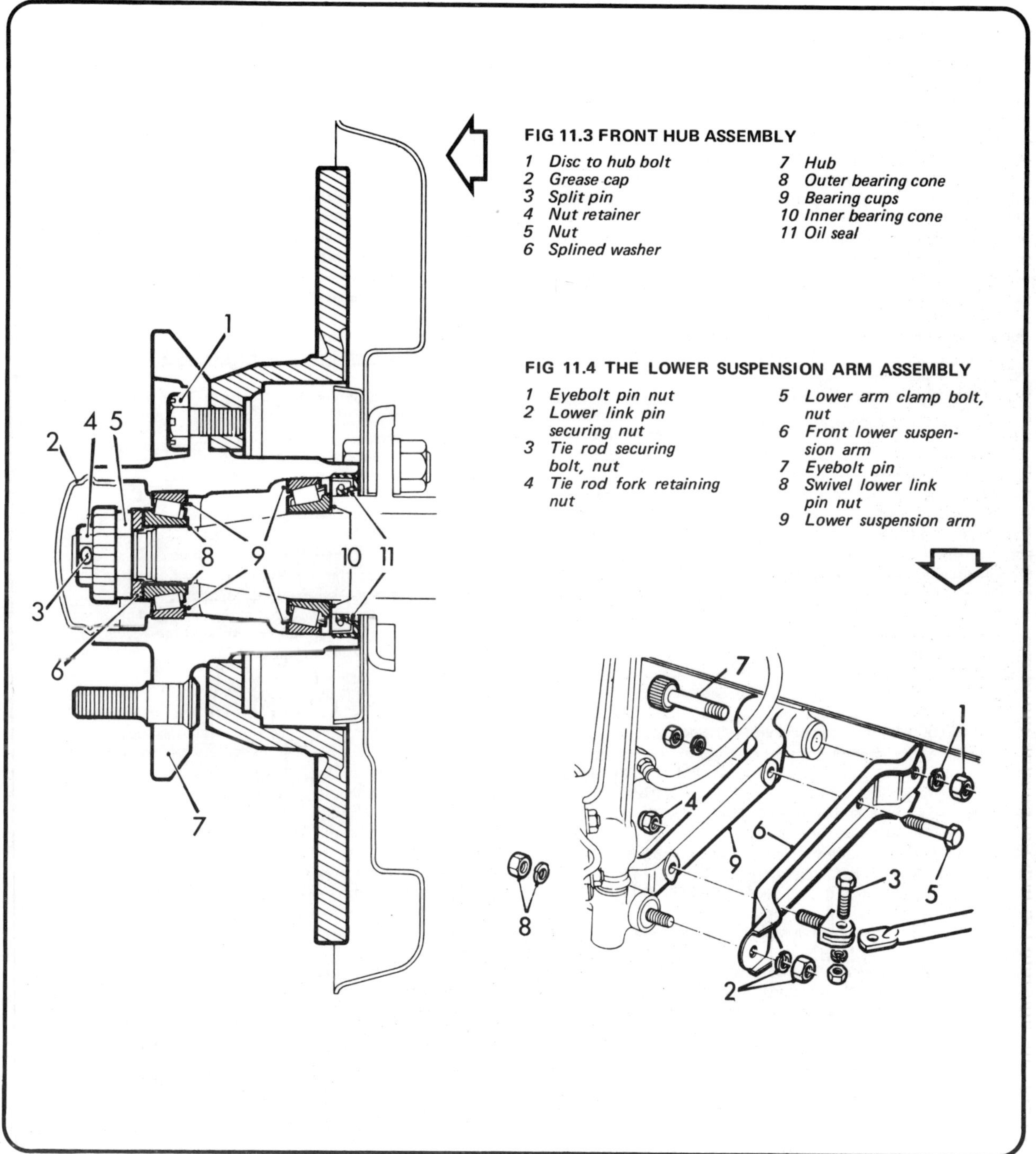

FIG 11.3 FRONT HUB ASSEMBLY

1 Disc to hub bolt
2 Grease cap
3 Split pin
4 Nut retainer
5 Nut
6 Splined washer
7 Hub
8 Outer bearing cone
9 Bearing cups
10 Inner bearing cone
11 Oil seal

FIG 11.4 THE LOWER SUSPENSION ARM ASSEMBLY

1 Eyebolt pin nut
2 Lower link pin securing nut
3 Tie rod securing bolt, nut
4 Tie rod fork retaining nut
5 Lower arm clamp bolt, nut
6 Front lower suspension arm
7 Eyebolt pin
8 Swivel lower link pin nut
9 Lower suspension arm

5 Shock absorber - removal and refitting

1 Jack up the front of the car and support on firmly based axle stands. Suitably support the lower suspension arm.
2 Remove the wheel trim and road wheel.
3 Unlock the reaction pad nut. Using a mole wrench hold the upper bush housing and remove the nut (Fig.11.5).
4 Lift away the lock washer, upper bush housing and upper bush.
5 Raise the shock absorber arm. Undo and remove the four nuts and plain washers that secure the shock absorber to its mounting.
6 Lift away the shock absorber.
7 Test the operation of the shock absorber by topping up the leve if necessary and then moving the shock arm up and down. If the action is weak or jerky then either the unit is worn or air has entered the operating cylinders. Move the arm up and down ten times and if the performance has not improved a new shock absorber must be obtained.
8 Inspect the shock absorber arm bushes for wear. If evident, obtain new bushes.
9 Refitting the shock absorber is the reverse sequence to removal, but the following additional points should be noted:
a) Always use a new reaction pad lockwasher.
b) Tighten the reaction pad nut to a torque wrench setting of 35 - 40 lb ft (4.8 - 5.5 kg m).
c) Tighten the shock absorber retaining nuts to a torque wrench setting of 26 - 28 lb ft (3.5 - 3.8 kg m).

6 Swivel pin - removal and refitting

1 Refer to Section 5 and follow the instructions given in paragraphs 1 - 4 inclusive.
2 Raise the shock absorber arm.
3 Wipe the top of the brake master cylinder reservoir. Remove the cap and place a piece of thick polythene over the top. Refit the cap. This is to stop syphoning of fluid during subsequent operations.
4 Wipe the area around the flexible brake hose connection at the body mounted bracket. Hold the flexible hose metal end nut and undo and remove the metal pipe union nut. Undo and remove the flexible hose securing nut and star washer and draw the flexible hose from the bracket.
5 Undo and remove the lower link pin rear nut and spring washer.
6 The swivel pin assembly may now be lifted away.
7 Refitting the swivel pin assembly is the reverse sequence to removal.

7 Swivel pin ball joint - removal and refitting

1 Refer to Section 5 and follow the instructions given in paragraphs 1 - 4 inclusive.
2 Raise the shock absorber arm.
3 Remove the dust cover and retaining clip.
4 Unlock the tab washer and using an open ended spanner hold the locknut. With a ring spanner undo the ball pin retainer.
5 Lift away the ball pin, ball seat and spring. Finally remove the tab washer and locknut.
6 To reassemble first obtain a new tab washer. Pack the ball pin retainer with Castrol LM Grease.
7 Fit the tab washer and locknut and then replace the ball seat and spring. Refit the ball pin and its retainer.
8 Fully slacken the locknut and tighten the ball retainer until the torque required to produce articulation of the ball pin is 32 - 52 lb in (0.38 - 0.56 kg cm).
9 Hold the ball retainer against rotation and tighten the locknut to a torque wrench setting of 70 - 80 lb ft (9.6 - 11.0 kg m). Ideally a special tol is required for this but may be judged by using a spare nut and bolt held in the vice so that the degree of tightness may be felt.
10 Lock the retainer and the locknut with the tab washer.
11 Reassembly is now the reverse sequence to removal.

8 Lower swivel pin link - removal and refitting

1 Jack up the front of the car and support on firmly based axle stands. Suitably support the rear lower suspension arm.
2 Remove the wheel trim and road wheel.
3 Refer to Chapter 3 and remove the disc brake caliper.
4 Using a wide blade screwdriver carefully ease off the grease cap.
5 Straighten the split pin ears and extract the split pin. Lift away the nut retainer and then undo and remove the hub nut. Withdraw the splined washer.
6 The hub may now be drawn from the axle stub.
7 Wipe the top of the brake master cylinder reservoir. Remove the cap and place a piece of thin polythene over the top. Refit the cap. This is to stop syphoning of fluid during subsequent operations.
8 Wipe the area around the flexible brake hose connection at the body mounted bracket. Hold the flexible hose metal end nut and undo and remove the metal pipe union nut.
9 Undo and remove the flexible hose securing nut and star washer and draw the flexible hose from the bracket.
10 Undo and remove the four nuts, bolts and spring washers securing the dust shield and caliper bracket to the swivel pin. Lift away the dust shield and caliper bracket.
11 Refer to Section 4 and remove the lower suspension arm.
12 Undo and remove the remaining nut and spring washer from the lower link pin.
13 Swing the swivel pin forwards and remove the rubber sealing rings and thrust washers from the lower link.
14 Withdraw the lower link pin.
15 Unscrew and remove the lower link from the swivel pin.
16 Thoroughly wash all parts in paraffin and wipe dry using a non fluffy rag.
17 Check for excessive wear across the thrust faces and in the threaded bore. If wear is excessive a new swivel link must be obtained.
18 Check the lower link bushes for wear and if this is evident new bushes should be fitted by a BLMC garage as it has to be ream finished. If an expanding reamer and micrometer are available however the old bushes should be drifted out. Further instructions are given in paragraphs 22 and 23.
19 Inspect the thrust washers for signs of damage or wear which, if evident, new thrust washers must be obtained.
20 Remove the grease nipple and ensure that both it and its hole are free from obstruction.
21 Obtain a new set of rubber sealing rings.
22 If new bushes are to be fitted these should be drifted or pressed in so that the oil grove is located as shown in Fig.11.7. The bush oil grove blank ends should be towards the outside edge of the link.
23 Using the expanding reamer line ream the new bushes to a finished size of 0.688 $\pm$ 0.013 mm).
24 Place the swivel pin link and seal on the swivel pin and screw on the link. Engage the seal on the recessed shoulder of the link and screw the link fully onto the swivel pin.
25 Unscrew the link one complete turn.
26 Reassembly is now the reverse sequence to removal, but the following additional points should be noted:
a) The caliper bracket and dust shield retaining bolts should be tightened to a torque wrench setting of 35 - 42 lb ft (4.8 - 5.8 kg m).
b) Refer to Section 3 and adjust the front hub bearing endfloat.

9 Eye bolt bush - removal and refitting

1 Refer to Section 10 and remove the torsion bar.
2 Undo and remove the nut and spring washer from the eyebolt

3 Withdraw the eyebolt pin.
4 Draw the suspension assembly clear of the eyebolt.
5 Undo and remove the nut, spring washer and spacer from the eyebolt.
6 Lift away the eyebolt and, if fitted, the reinforcement plate.
7 The bush may be removed with pieces of suitable diameter tube and pressing it out in a bench vice.
8 To fit a new bush lubricate its outer surface with a little soapy water and press it in using the reverse procedure to removal.
9 Refitting the eyebolt is the reverse sequence to removal, but the following additional points should be noted:
a) It is not necessary to fit the reinforcement plate when a later type eyebolt is being used. This is identifiable by having a 2.5 inch (63 mm) elliptical diameter.
b) The eyebolt retaining nut should be tightened to a torque wrench setting of 50 - 54 lb ft (6.9 - 7.4 kg m).

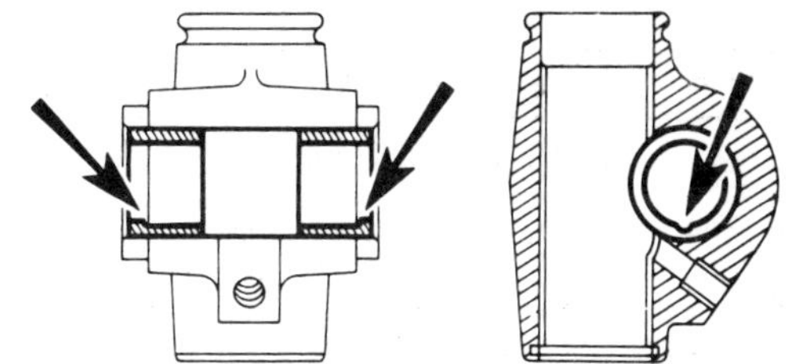

FIG 11.7 CORRECT POSITION OF BUSH OIL GROOVE

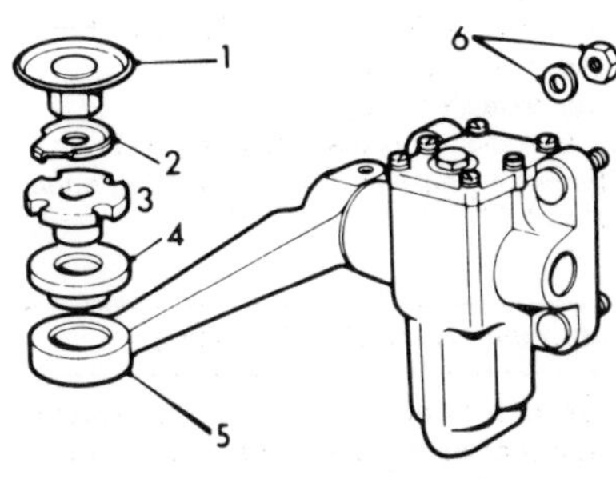

FIG 11.5 FRONT SHOCK ABSORBER REMOVAL

1 Reaction pad nut
2 Lockwasher
3 Upper bush housing
4 Upper bush
5 Shock absorber arm

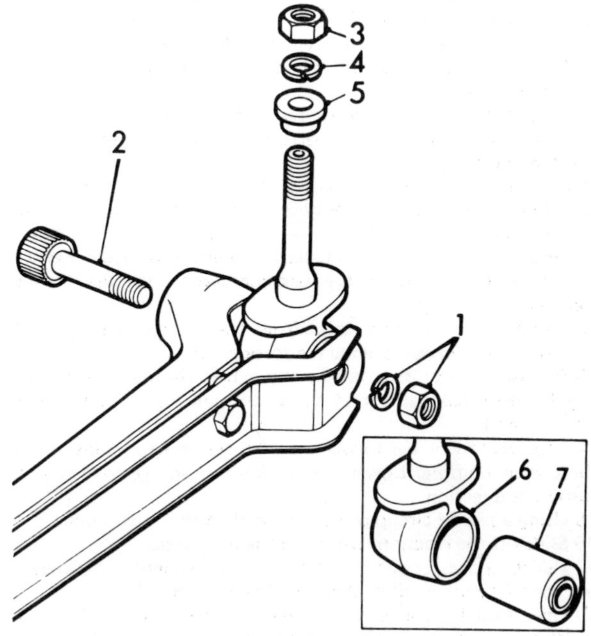

FIG 11.8 EYEBOLT BUSH REMOVAL

1 Eyebolt pin nut and spring washer
2 Bolt
3 Nut
4 Spring washer
5 Spacer
6 Eyebolt
7 Bush

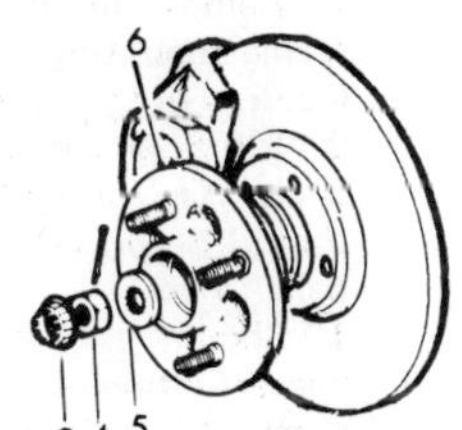
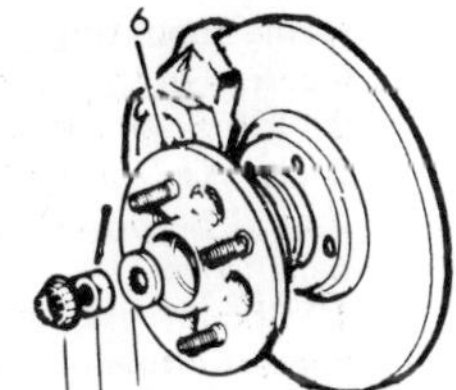

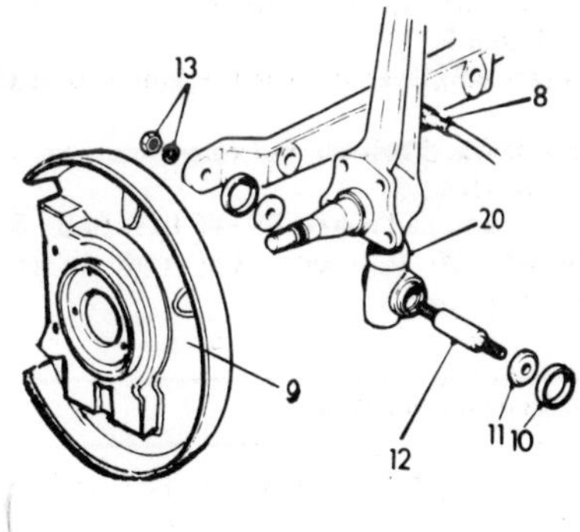

FIG 11.6 LOWER SWIVEL PIN LINK REMOVAL

1 Lower link bushes
2 Grease cap
3 Nut retainer and split pin
4 Nut
5 Splined washer
6 Hub
7 Mudshield retaining bolt and spring washer
8 Brake hydraulic hose
9 Disc brake mudshield
10 Sealing ring
11 Thrust washer
12 Lower link pin
13 Link pin securing nut and spring washer
14 Lower link

10 Torsion bar - removal and refitting

1 Unscrew and remove the grease nipple from the swivel pin lower link.
2 Place a wooden block 8 inch (200 mm) thick on the floor under the lower suspension arm as near as possible to the disc brake dust shield as shown in Fig.11.9.
3 Jack up the front of the car. Remove the wheel trim and road wheel.
4 Carefully lower the car until the weight of the suspension is placed on the woden block.
5 Unlock the reaction pad nut. Using a mole wrench or 'C' spanner hold the upper bush housing and remove the nut.
6 Remove the upper bush housing and the upper bush.
7 Raise the shock absorber arm clear of the ball pin and lift away the lower bush.
8 Undo and remove the steering rack rod ball pin nut.
9 Using a universal ball joint separator release the ball pin from the steering lever.
10 Jack up the front of the car so as to relieve the torsion bar load and yet the lower suspension arm is still just resting on the wooden block.
11 Undo and remove the bolt, spring washer and special washer that secures the torsion bar reaction lever onto the chassis member.
12 Remove tne reaction lever from the chassis member and move the lever forwards along the torsion bar.
13 Release the nut that retains the eybolt through the chassis member and make sure that the suspension lowers itself by ½ inch (12mm).
14 Ease the torsion bar forwards until it clears the shoulder from the chassis housing. Lower the torsion bar and remove it in a rearwards direction.
15 Using a pair of circlip pliers remove the torsion bar circlip.
16 Slide off the reaction lever from the torsion bar.
17 Refitting the torsion bar is the reverse sequence to removal but the following additional points should be noted:
a) Once a torsion bar has been fitted and used on one side of the car it must not under any circumstances be used on the other side. This is because a torsion bar becomes handed once it has been in use. Torsion bars are only interchangeable when new.
b) Do not fit a torsion bar that is corroded or deeply scored as this will affect its reliability and in bad cases cause premature failure.
c) The reaction lever adjustment screw must be set to the mid-way position of its travel and the locknut tightened before re-fitting.
d) Tighten the eyebolt nut to a torque wrench setting of 50 - 54 lb ft (6.9 - 7.4 kg m).
e) Tighten the reaction lever to chassis member bolt to 22 lb ft (3.0 kg m).
f) Tighten the track rod ball pin nut to a torque wrench setting of 2.6 lb ft (3.3 kg m).
g) Tighten the reaction pad nut to 35 - 40 lb ft (4.8 - 5.5 kg m).
18 Refer to Section 25 and adjust the front suspension trim height if necessary.

11 Tie rod - removal and refitting

1 Jack up the front of the car and support on firmly based axle stands.
2 Remove the wheel trim and road wheel.
3 Using a pair of pliers remove the tie rod spring clip from the end of the tie rod.
4 Undo and remove the locking nut and large plain washer.
5 Slide off the rubber outer pad.
6 Undo and remove the nut, spring washer and bolt that secures the tie rod to the fork end.
7 Remove the rubber inner pad from the tie rod.
8 Undo and remove the nut that secures the rod fork and lift away the fork from the lower suspension arm.
9 Refitting the tie rod is the reverse sequence to removal but the following additional point should be noted:
a) Inspect the two rubber pads and if they show signs of oil contamination, cracking or perishing obtain and fit a new pair of pads.
b) The tie rod to fork nut should be tightened to a torque wrench setting of 22 lb ft (3.0 kg m).
c) Tighten the rod fork nut to a torque wrench setting of 48 - 55 lb ft (6.6 - 7.6 kg m).

12 Rear hub assembly - removal and refitting

1 Chock the front wheel, jack up the rear of the car and place on firmly based axle stands.
2 Remove the wheel trim and road wheel. Apply the handbrake.
3 Undo and remove the axle shaft nut and washer.
4 Release the handbrake and referring to Chapter 9, back off the brake adjuster. Remove the two countersunk screws that retain the brake drum and pull off the brake drum. If it is tight tap the circumference with a soft faced hammer.
5 Using a universal puller and suitable thrust block pull the hub from the end of the axle shaft.
6 Remove the axle shaft key.
7 Refitting the rear hub assembly is the reverse sequence to removal. The axle shaft nut must be tightened to a torque wrench setting of 85 lb ft (11.7 kg m).

13 Rear road spring - removal and refitting

1 Refer to Section 14 and remove the road spring shackle plate.
2 Jack up the rear of the car and support on firmly based axle stands located under the main longitudinal chassis numbers. Support the weight of the axle on the side which the spring is to be removed.
3 Undo and remove the shock absorber locknut, plain nut and plain washer. Note the location of the lower bush in the shock absorber lower mounting plate and remove the lower bush.
4 Undo and remove the nut, spring washer and bolt that secures the front spring eye to the body mounted brackets.
5 Undo and remove the four nuts from the two 'U' bolts.
6 Carefully lower the spring and its mountings.
7 Remove the shock absorber mounting plate followed by the spring mounting plates and mounting rubbers. Note the fitted location of the spring mounting wedge.
8 Lift away the two 'U' bolts.
9 If the spring bushes are worn or have deteriorated they should be pressed out using suitable diameter tubes and a large bench vice.
10 Should the spring have considerably weakened or failed neccessitating the fitting of a new one, rear springs must be renewed in pairs and not singly as the remaining spring will have settled slightly. Unless the springs have the same performance and characteristics road holding can be adversely affected.
11 Refitting the road spring is the reverse sequence to removal, but the following additional points should be noted:
a) Tighten the upper shackle pin nuts to a torque wrench setting of 28 lb ft (3.9 kg m).
b) Tighten the spring eye bush bolt nuts to a torque wrench setting of 40 lb ft (5.5 kg m).
c) Tighten the 'U' bolt nuts to a torque wrench setting of 14 lb ft (1.9 kg m).
d) Tighten the shock absorber to spring bracket retaining nut to a torque wrench setting of 28 lb ft (3.9 kg m) and then secure by tightening the locknut.

14 Rear rod spring shackles - removal and refitting

1 Chock the front wheels, jack up the rear of the car and place on firmly based axle stands located under the main longitudinal

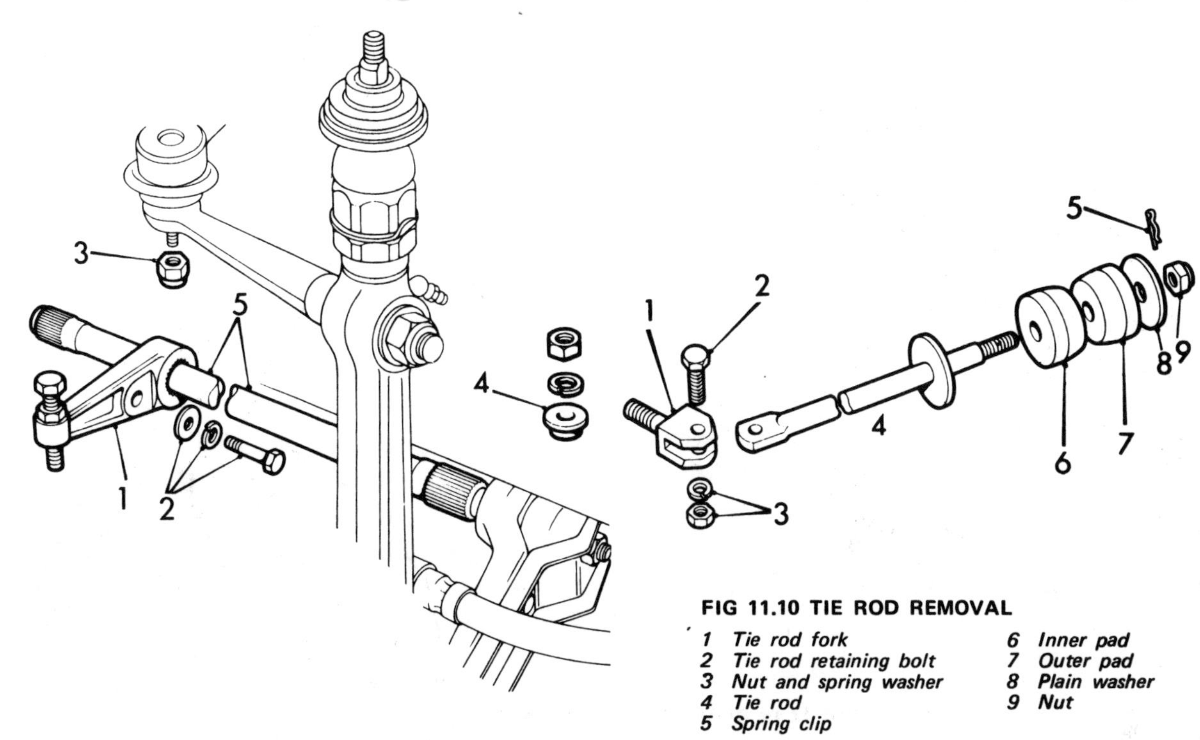

FIG 11.10 TIE ROD REMOVAL

1 Tie rod fork
2 Tie rod retaining bolt
3 Nut and spring washer
4 Tie rod
5 Spring clip
6 Inner pad
7 Outer pad
8 Plain washer
9 Nut

FIG 11.9 TORSION BAR REMOVAL

1 Reaction lever
2 Reaction lever retaining bolt, spring and special washer
3 Track rod ball pin nut
4 Eyebolt retaining nut and bush
5 Torsion bar

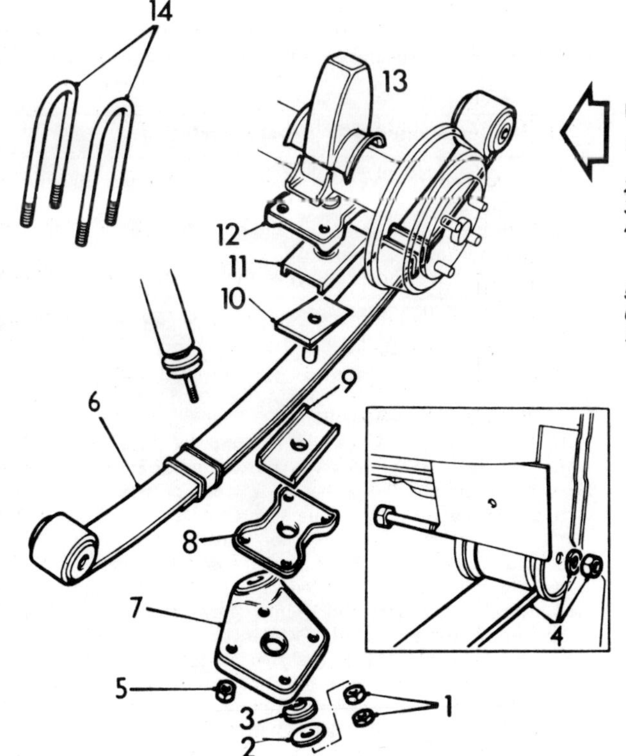

FIG 11.11 REAR SPRING REMOVAL

1 Shock absorber retaining nut and locknut
2 Plate washer
3 Lower bush
4 Forward spring eyebolt securing nut and spring washer
5 'U' bolt nut
6 Spring assembly
7 Shock absorber mounting plate
8 Spring mounting plate (lower)
9 Rubber pad
10 Wedge
11 Rubber pad
12 Spring mounting plate (upper)
13 Rubber bump stop
14 'U' bolts
15 Inset: drifting in new shackle bush

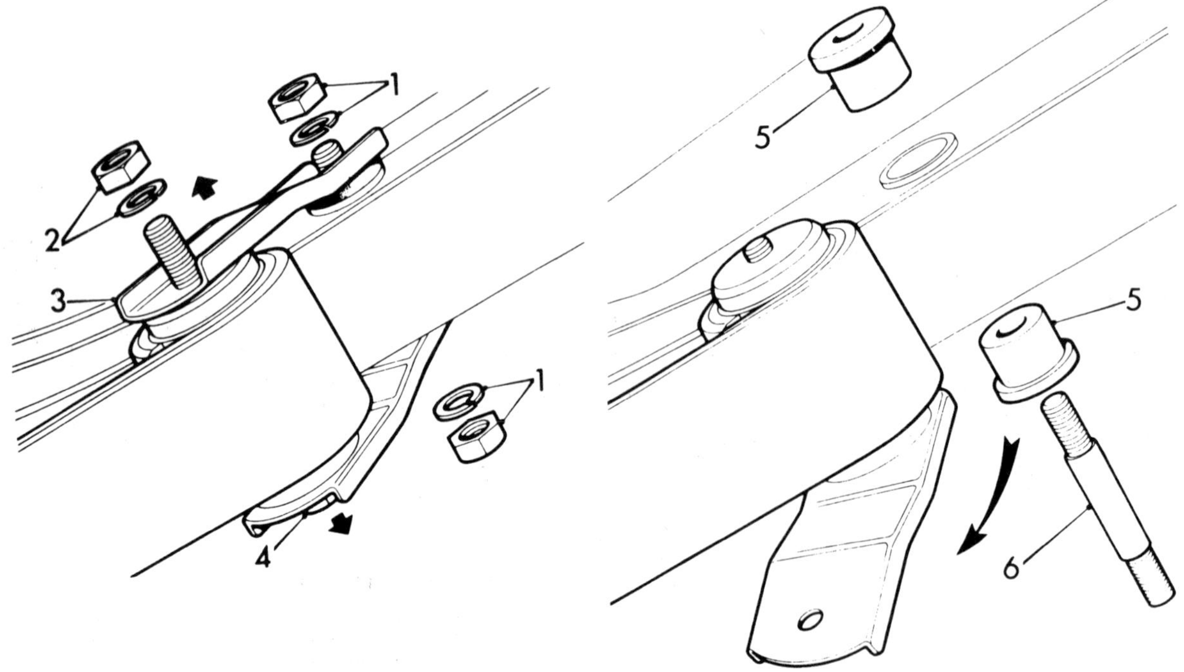

FIG 11.12 REAR SPRING SHACKLE

1 Upper shackle pin securing nut and spring washer
2 Lower spring shackle bolt securing nut and spring washer
3 Inner shackle plate
4 Shackle bolt
5 Upper shackle bushes
6 Upper shackle pin

chassis members.

2 Remove the wheel trim and road wheel.

3 Undo and remove the nut and spring washer on each side of the upper shackle pin.

4 Undo and remove the nut and spring washer from the spring bush bolt.

5 Lift away the inner shackle plate.

6 Using a suitable diameter parallel pin punch partially drift out the spring bolt and then release the outer plate from the upper pin (Fig.11.12).

7 Remove the upper shackle pin and lift away the two half bushes.

8 Inspect the bushes for signs of deterioration or oil contamination which, if evident, new bushes should be obtained.

9 Refitting is the reverse sequence to removal, but the following additional points should be noted:

a) Tighten the upper shackle pin nuts to a torque wrench setting of 28 lb ft (3.9 kg m).

b) Tighten the spring eye bush bolt nut to a torque wrench setting of 40 lb ft (5.5 kg m).

15 Bump stop - removal and refitting

1 Chock the front wheels, jack up the rear of the car and place on firmly based axle stands located under the main longitudinal chassis members.

2 Remove the wheel trim and road wheel.

3 Support the weight of the axle on the side to be worked upon.

4 Undo and remove the shock absorber locknut, plain nut, and plain washer. Note the location of the lower bush in the shock absorber mounting bracket and lift away the lower bush.

5 Undo and remove the four 'U' bolt nuts.

6 Lift away the shock absorber mounting plate and spring locating bracket and rubber.

7 Lift away the bump stop and two 'U' bolts.

8 Refitting the bump stop rubber is the reverse sequence to removal but the following additional points should be noted:

a) Check the condition of the spring mounting rubber and if its condition has deteriorated a new mounting rubber should be obtained and fitted.

b) The shock absorber to spring bracket retaining nut should be tightened to a torque wrench setting of 28 lb ft (3.9 kg m).

16 Rear shock absorber - removal and refitting

1 Undo and remove the shock absorber lower locknut and retaining nut.

2 Lift away the plain washer and note the position of the lower bush. Lift away the lower bush.

3 Contract the shock absorber thereby detaching it from the mounting bracket.

4 Note the position of the upper bush and then lift it away followed by the plain washer.

5 Undo and remove the nut, spring washer and bolt that fixes the upper part of the shock absorber to the body bracket. Lift away the shock absorber.

6 To test the shock absorber alternatively compress and extend it throughout its full movement. If the action is jerky or weak, it is an indication that either it is worn or there is air in the hydraulic cylinder. Continue to compress and extend it and if the action does not become more positive a new shock absorber should be obtained. If the shock absorber is showing signs of leaking it should be discarded as it is not possible to overhaul it.

7 Check the bushes and if they show signs of deterioration a new set of rubbers should be obtained.

8 Refitting the shock absorber is the reverse sequence to removal but the following additional points should be noted:

a) Tighten the shock absorber to body bracket retaining bolt nut to a torque wrench setting of 28 lb ft (3.9 kg m).

b) The shock absorber to spring bracket should be tightened to a torque wrench setting of 28 lb ft (3.9 kg m), and then locked with the locknut.

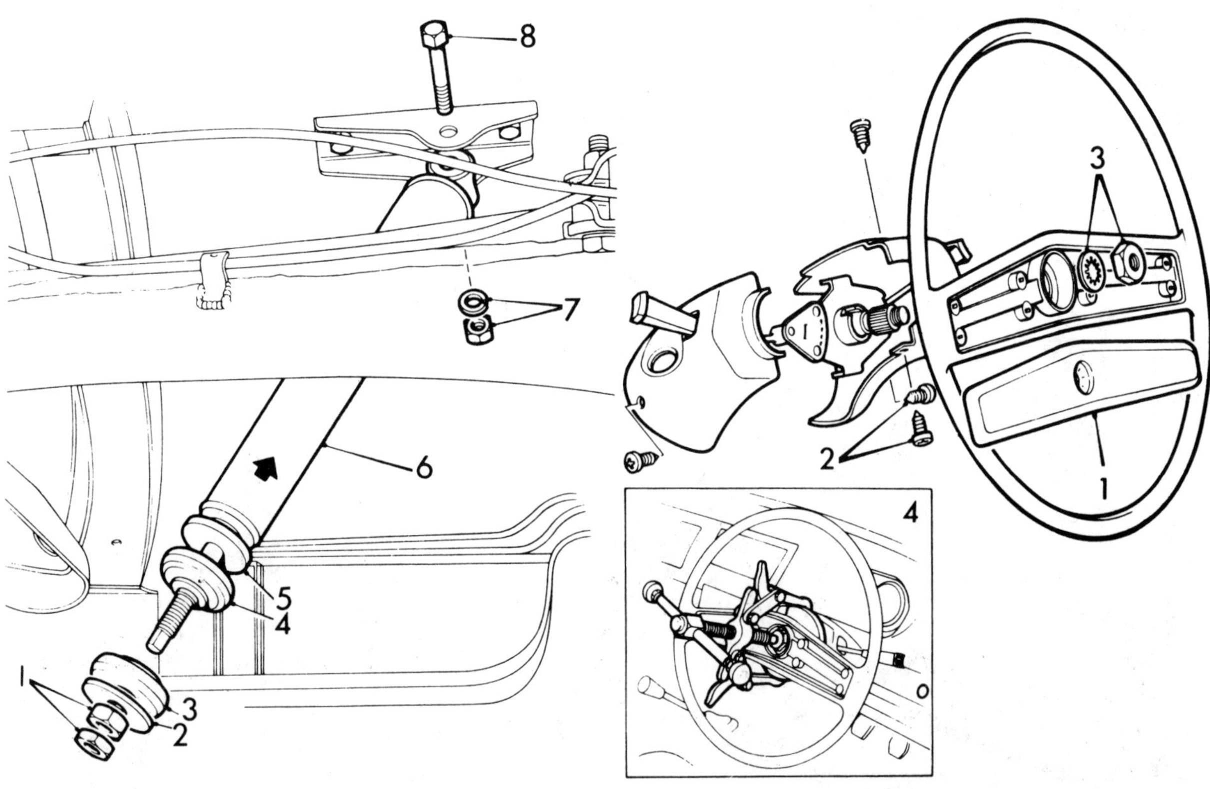

FIG 11.13 REAR SHOCK ABSORBER REMOVAL

1 Shock absorber retaining nut and locknut
2 Plate washer
3 Lower bush
4 Upper bush
5 Plate washer
6 Shock absorber
7 Upper mounting bolt securing nut and spring washer
8 Upper mounting bolt

FIG 11.14 STEERING WHEEL REMOVAL

1 Safety pad
2 Switch cowl securing screw
3 Steering wheel securing nut and shakeproof washer
4 Using a universal puller to remove steering wheel

17 Steering wheel - removal and refitting

1 Using a knife carefully prise the safety pad from the centre of the steering wheel.
2 Undo and remove the five self tapping screws that secure the switch cowls. Lift away the cowls from over the switch arms.
3 Undo and remove the nut and shakeprof washer that secures the steering wheel to the upper inner column.
4 With a centre punch mark the relative positions of the steering wheel hub and inner column so that they may be refitted in the same position as they were prior to removal.
5 With the palms of the hands behind the spokes and near to the centre hub, thump the steering wheel from the steering inner column splines. If it is very tight it will be necessary to use a universal puller fitted with long feet and a suitable thrust block.
6 Refitting the steering wheel is the reverse sequence to removal, but the following additional points should be noted:
a) The steering wheel securing nut should be tightened to a torque wrench setting of 43 - 50 lb ft (6.0 - 6.9 kg m).
b) When refitting the safety pad to the centre of the steering wheel the pins at each end of the pad must be located and inserted first. This will make sure that the width between the safety pad and steering wheel is equally spaced on either side of the pad.

18 Steering column top bush - removal and refitting

1 Refer to Section 17 and remove the steering wheel.
2 Slacken the screw that retains the combined switch mechanism and lift the switch mechanism from over the top of the inner column.
3 Using a screwdriver ease the top bush from the inside of the outer column.
4 To refit the top bush first align the slits in the column bush with the depression in the outer column and ensure that the chamfered end of the bush enters the column first.
5 Using a suitable diameter metal drift carefully drive the top bush into position.
6 Refitting the combined switch mechanism and steering wheel is now the reverse sequence to removal.

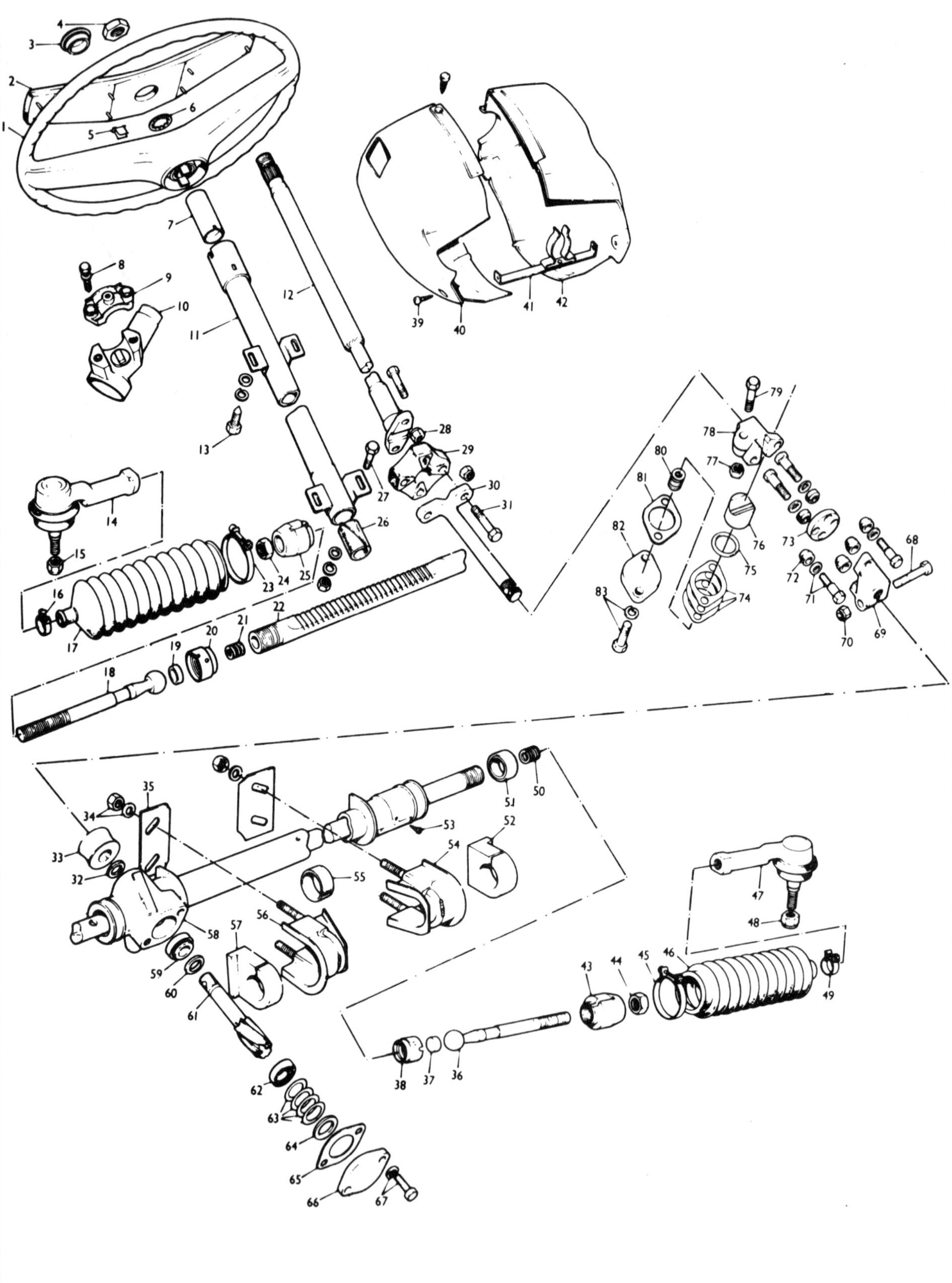
1
2
3
4
5
6
7
8
9
10
11
12
13
14
15
16
17
18
19
20
21
22
23
24
25
26
27
28
29
30
31
32
33
34
35
36
37
38
39
40
41
42
43
44
45
46
47
48
49
50
51
52
53
54
55
56
57
58
59
60
61
62
63
64
65
66
67
68
69
70
71
72
73
74
75
76
77
78
79
80
81
82
83

19 Steering column lock and ignition starter switch housing - removal and refitting

1 Refer to Section 17 and remove the steering wheel.
2 Refer to Chapter 12 and remove the lower facia panel.
3 Refer to Chapter 12 and remove the instrument panel.
4 Locate the multi pin terminal connector on the end of the wiring harness to the column lock and ignition starter switch and disconnect the cable connection.
5 Using either a drill or a drill and 'easy out' stud extractor remove the two special shear screws.
6 Lift away the clamp plate and the steering lock.
7 To refit offer up the steering column lock and ignition switch and clamp plate so that the indent in the top of the column is lined up with the clamp plate grub screw.
8 Lightly tighten the two new shear screws and the one grub screw.
9 Check the operation of the lock to ensure that it operates correctly.
10 Slowly tighten the two shear bolts until the heads shear at the waited point. This will normally occur at a torque wrench setting of 14 lb ft (1.94 kg m).
11 Reassembly is now the reverse sequence to removal.

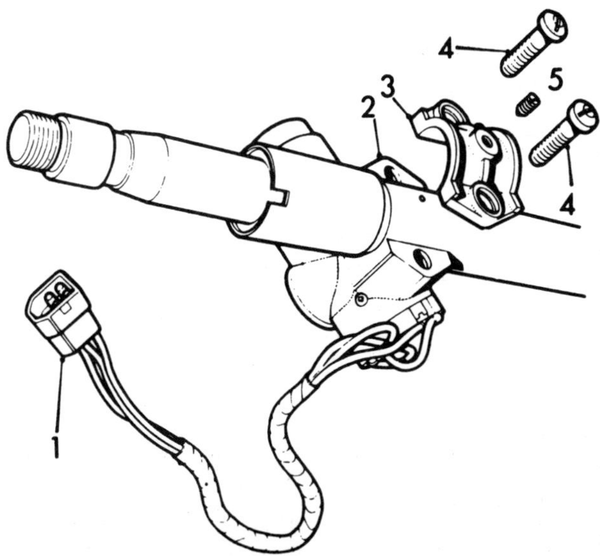

FIG 11.16 STEERING COLUMN LOCK AND IGNITION STARTER SWITCH HOUSING REMOVAL

1 Multi-pin connector
2 Steering lock housing
3 Clamp plate
4 Shear bolts
5 Grub screw

FIG.11.15. RACK AND PINION STEERING ASSEMBLY

1 Steering wheel
2 Safety pad
3 Motif
4 Nut
5 Clip-safety pad to wheel
6 Shakeproof washer
7 Bush-upper
8 Shear bolt-steering lock
9 Clamp plate
10 Steering lock
11 Column outer - upper
12 Column inner - upper
13 Screw - spring and plain washer
14 Tie-rod end
15 Nut - self-locking
16 Clip - small
17 Rack seal
18 Tie-rod
19 Ball seat
20 Locknut
Thrust spring
22 Rack
23 Clip - large
24 Locknut
25 Ball housing
26 Lower bush
27 Bolt - plain and spring washer
28 Nut
29 Flexible coupling
30 Column - lower
31 Bolt
32 Pinion oil seal
33 Sealing washer
34 Nut and plain washer
35 Locating plate
36 Tie-rod
37 Ball seat
38 Locknut
39 Screw
40 Cowl half
41 Cowl support
42 Cowl half
43 Ball housing
44 Locknut
45 Clip - large
46 Rack seal
47 Tie-rod end
48 Nut - self-locking
49 Clip - small
50 Thrust spring
51 Rack bearing
52 Rack mounting rubber
53 Screw - rack bearing
54 Rack clamp
55 Sealing rubber
56 Rack clamp
57 Rack mounting rubber
58 Pinion housing
59 Pinion bearing
60 Washer
61 Pinion
62 Pinion bearing
63 Shim
64 Shim - .60 in. (1.524 mm)
65 Shim gasket - .010 in. (0.254 mm)
66 End cover
67 Bolt and spring washer
68 Bolt
69 Flexible joint - half
70 Nut
71 Shouldered bolt
72 Rubber bush
73 Joint plate
74 Shim
75 'O' ring
76 Support yoke
77 Nut
78 Flexible joint - half
79 Bolt
80 Thrust spring
81 Joint
82 End cover
83 Bolt and spring washer

20 Steering column universal joint coupling - removal and refitting

1 Refer to Section 21 and remove the upper steering column.
2 Undo and remove the pinch bolt and nut that secures the lower column to the rack pinion.
3 Lift away the lower steering column assembly.
4 Undo and remove the pinch bolt and nut that secures the lower column to the flexible joint.
5 Unlock and remove the four shouldered bolts from the flexible joint.
6 Lift away the rubber washers noting that the conical face mates with the countersunk face of the joint plate.
7 Lift away the plain washers from each of the four shouldered bolts.
8 Undo and remove the two nuts and bolts that retain the flexible coupling to the lower steering column.
9 Inspect the flexible couplings for signs of deterioration which if evident a new coupling must be obtained.
10 Refitting the couplings is the reverse sequence to removal. The flexible joint coupling bolts should be tightened to a torque wrench setting of 20 - 22 lb ft (2.77 - 3.04 kg m). If a new coupling has been fitted it will be necessary to break the band that compresses the coupling.

21 Upper steering column - removal and refitting

1 Refer to Section 17 and remove the steering wheel.
2 Refer to Chapter 12, and remove the lower facia panel.
3 Refer to Chapter 12 and remove the instrument panel.
4 Disconnect the multi pin,connector on the end of the wiring harness to the switch mechanism at the harness connector.
5 Slacken the screw that retains the combined switch mechanism and lift the switch mechanism from over the top of the inner column.
6 Disconnect the multi pin connector on the end of the wiring harness to the ignition switch at the harness connection.
7 Undo and remove the two nuts and bolts that secure the uper column to the flexible coupling.
8 Undo and remove the two screws, plain and spring washers that secure the column to the uper support bracket.
9 Undo and remove the two locknuts, plain and spring washers that attach the column to the lower support bracket bolts.
10 Lift away the upper steering column.
11 To refit the upper steering column first engage the steering lock.
12 Centralise the steering rack by making sure the front wheels are in the straight ahead position.
13 Refitting is now the reverse sequence to removal but the following additional points should be noted:
a) The steering column mounting bolts should be tightened to a torque wrench setting of 20 - 22 lb ft (2.77 - 3.04 kg m).
b) The flexible joint coupling bolts should be tightened to a torque wrench setting of 20 - 22 lb ft (2.77 - 3.04 kg m).
c) If a new flexible coupling has been fitted it will be necessary to break the band that compresses the coupling. Lift away the band.

22 Steering rack and pinion - removal and refitting

1 Refer to Chapter 12 and remove the lower facia panel.
2 Refer to Chapter 12 and remove the instrument panel.
3 Disconnect the steering column combined switch mechanism and ignition switch connections at the wiring harness multi pin connectors.
4 Undo and remove the two screws, plain and spring washers securing the steering column to the upper support bracket.
5 Undo and remove the two locknuts, plain and spring washers that secure the steering column to the lower support bracket.
6 Undo and remove the pinch bolt and nut securing the flexible joint to the steering rack pinion.
7 The steering column assembly may now be lifted away.
8 Carefully pull off the two heater rain water vent tubes from the front of the bulkhead.
9 Jack up the front of the car and support with firmly based axle stands located under the two longitudinal chassis members.
10 Undo and remove the nut that secures each tie rod ball pin end. Using a universal ball joint separator detach the tie rod ball pin ends from the steering levers.
11 Undo and remove the two nuts and plain washers securing each rack clamp bracket to the bulkhead. Make a note of the fitted position of the packing strip relative to the body panel. Lift away the packing strip.
12 The clamp brackets and rubber inserts may now be removed. The rubber inserts have slots cut in them to enable them to be removed from the rack tube.
13 The rack assembly may now be lifted from the car through the wheel arch opening.
14 Lift away the pinion seal from over the end of the pinion.
15 Refitting the steering rack and pinion assembly is the reverse sequence to removal, the following additional points should be noted:
a) Check the pinion seal and the two clamp bracket rubber inserts for signs of oil contamination or deterioration. If evident new rubbers must be obtained.
b) The rack clamp nuts should be tightened to a torque wrench setting of 20 - 22 lb ft (2.77 - 3.04 kg m).
c) The tie rod ball pin nuts should be tightened to a torque wrench setting of 20 - 24 lb ft (3.3 kg m).
d) Tighten the lower flexible joint pinch bolt to a torque wrench setting of 6 - 8 lb ft (0.4 - 0.5 kg m).
16 It will now be necessary to check and reset the front wheel alignment. Further information will be found in Section 24.

23 Steering rack and pinion - dismantling, overhaul and re-assembly

1 Wash the outside of the rack and pinion assembly in paraffin or Gunk and wipe dry with a non fluffy rag.
2 Slacken off the two tie rod end locknuts nad unscrew the two tie rod ends as completele assemblies.
3 Unscrew and remove the two locknuts from the ends of the tie rods.
4 Slacken the rack seal clips at either end of the rack assembly body. Remove the clips and two rack seals.
5 Using a small chisel carefully ease out the locknut indent from each of the ball joint housings.
6 Using two mole wrenches or one mole wrench and a soft metal drift hold the locknut and unscrew the ball joint housing from each end of the rack. Lift away the tie rods.
7 Recover the ball cup and spring from each end of the rack.
8 Using a small chisel carefully ease out the locknut indent from the rack. Unscrew the locknuts.
9 Undo and remove the rack bearing pan head retaining screw located in the rack tub end as opposed to the pinion housing.
10 The bearing may now be removed from the rack housing.
11 Undo and remove the two bolts and spring washers that secure the rack yoke cover plate.
12 Lift away the cover plate, shims and joint washer.
13 Recover the rack support yoke from the pinion housing.
14 Remove the 'O' ring and thrust spring from the support yoke.
15 Undo and remove the two bolts and spring washers that secure the pinion and cover plate. Lift away the cover plate, shims and joint washers.
16 Carefully push out the pinion and the lower bearing. Note which way round the bearing is fitted.
17 The steering rack may now be withdrawn from the rack tube. Note which way round the rack is fitted in the rack tube.
18 Using a soft metal drift, tap out the upper pinion bearing and its washer. Note which way round the bearing is fitted.
19 Recover the pinion shaft oil seal from the pinion housing.
20 The steering rack assembly is now fully dismantled. Clean all

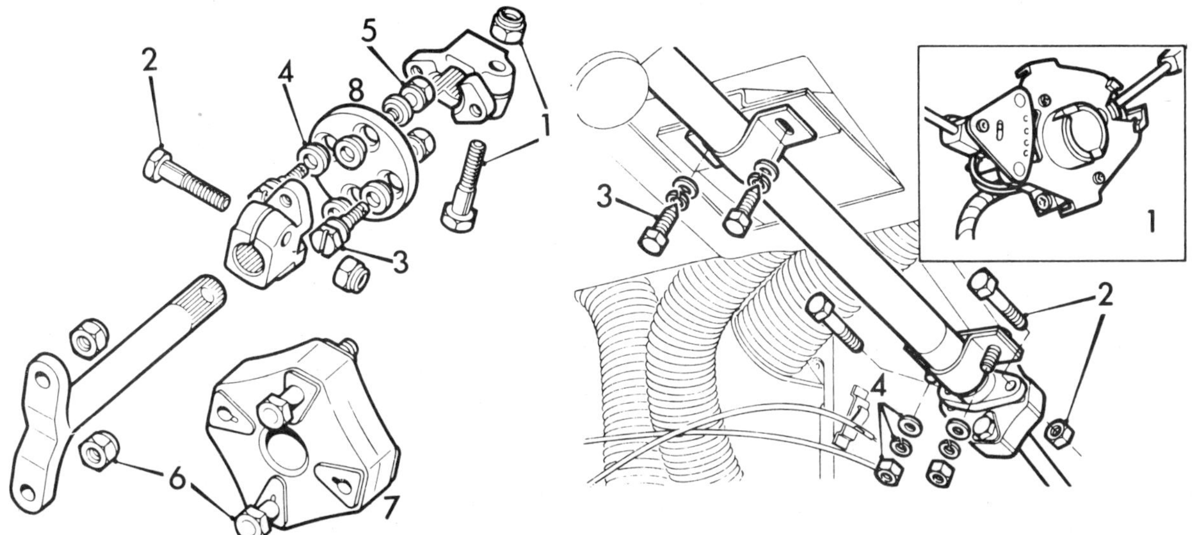

FIG 11.17 STEERING COLUMN UNIVERSAL JOINT COUPLINGS

1 Pinch bolt and locknut (upper)
2 Pinch bolt and locknut (lower
3 Flexible joint shouldered bolt
4 Conical rubber washers
5 Plain washer
6 Flexible coupling securing locknut and bolt
7 Flexible coupling (upper)
8 Joint plate

FIG 11.18 UPPER STEERING COLUMN REMOVAL

1 Combination switch
2 Upper column to flexible coupling bolt and locknut
3 Column to upper support bracket, bolt, plain and spring washer
4 Column to lower support bracket securing nut spring and plain washer

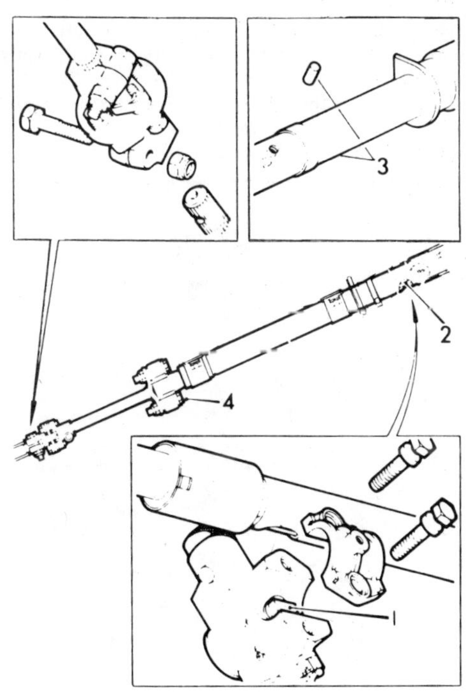

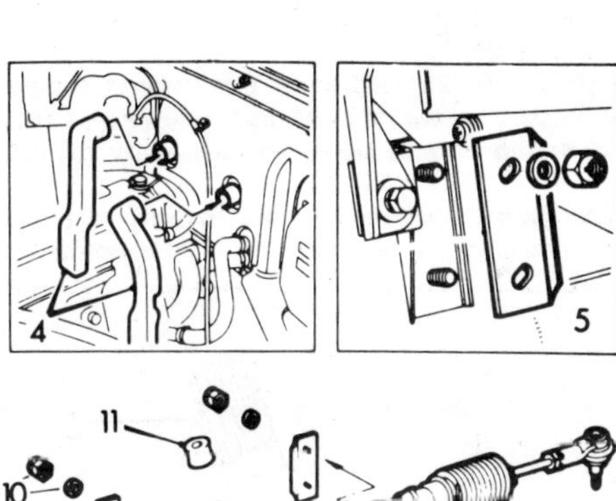

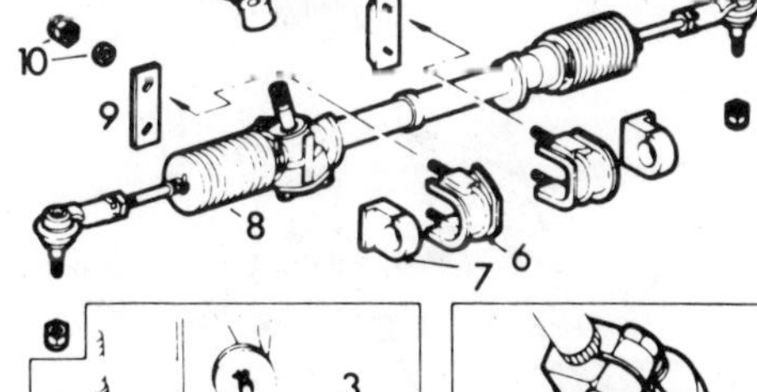

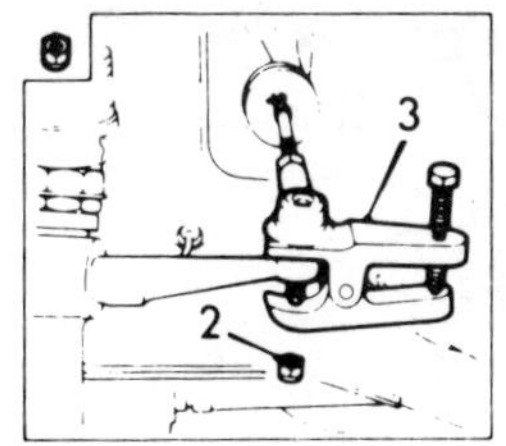

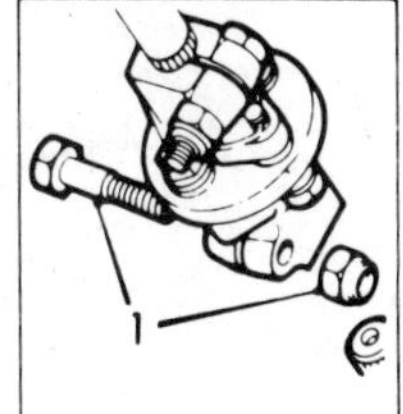

FIG 11.19 UPPER STEERING COLUMN ATTACHMENTS

1 Steering lock engagement sector
2 Slot in column
3 Steering rack centralisation
4 Lower universal coupling

FIG 11.20 STEERING RACK REMOVAL

1 Pinch bolt and locknut
2 Tie rod ball pin nut
3 Universal joint separator
4 Heater drain tubes
5 Rack clamp bracket packing strip
6 Rack clamp bracket
7 Rubber insert
8 Rack and pinion assembly
9 Plate
10 Bracket securing nut and spring washer
11 Pinion seal

parts in paraffin and wipe dry with a non fluffy rag.
21 Thoroughly inspect the rack and pinion teeth for signs of wear, cracks or damage. Check the ends of the rack for wear especially where it moves in the bushes.
22 Examine the rubber gaiters for signs of cracking, perishing or other damage which if evident new gaiters must be obtained.
23 Inspect the ball ends and housing for wear which if evident new parts will be necessary. Any other parts that show wear or damage must be renewed.
24 To reassemble first fit a new rack bearing into the rack housing so that the flats of the bearing are positioned offset to the bearing retaining screw hole.
25 Using a 0.119 inch (3.00mm) diameter drill located in the retaining screw hole drill through the bearing. Clear away any swarf from the bearing and the housing.
26 Apply some non hardening oil resistant sealing compound to the bush retaining screw and refit the screw.
27 It is very important that the screw does not protrude into the bore of the bearing. Should this condition exist the end of the screw must be filed flat.
28 Fit the pinion washer to the pinion followed by the upper bearing. The thrust face must face towards the pinion washer.
29 Carefully fit the rack into the rack housing the correct way round as noted during dismantling.
30 Insert the pinion into the housing and then centralise the rack relative to the rack housing. Fit a peg into the centre locating hole.
31 Position the pinion making sure the groove in the pinion serrations is facing and also parallel with the rack teeth.
32 Refit the lower bearing with the thrust face facing towards the pinion.
33 Replace the bearing shims and make sure that the bearing shim pack stands proud of the pinion housing. If necessary add new shims to achieve this condition.
34 Refit the pinion housing end cover but without the paper gasket. Secure in position with the two bolts and spring washers. The two bolts should only be tightened sufficiently to nip the end cover.
35 Using feeler gauges measure the gap between the pinion housing and the end cover. Make a note of the measurement.
36 Undo and remove the two pinion housing end cover securing bolts and spring washers. Lift away the end cover.
37 Adjust the number of shims in the end pack so as to obtain a 0.011 to 0.013 inch (0.279 - 0.330 mm) gap. A range of shims is available for this adjustment. Details may be found in the specifications at the beginning of this chapter.
38 It is important that the 0.060 inch (1.524 mm) shim is positioned next to the joint washer. Refit the shim pack, joint washer and end cover.
39 Apply a little non hardening oil resistant sealing compound to the end cover securing bolts. Fit the two bolts and spring washers and tighten to a torque wrench setting of 12 - 15 lb ft (1.6 - 2.0 kg m).
40 Carefully fit a new pinion oil seal.
41 Refit the damper yoke, cover plate gasket and cover plate.
42 Replace the cover bolts and spring washers and gradually tighten these in a progressive manner whilst turning the pinion to and fro through 180o until it is just possible to rotate the pinion between the finger and thumb.
43 Using feeler gauges measure the gap between the cover the the housing.
44 Remove the cover and reassemble this time including the damper spring, a new 'O' ring oil seal and shims to the previous determined measurement plug 0.002 - 0.005 inch (0.05 - 0.13mm).
45 Tighten the bolts that secure the yoke cover to a torque wrench setting of 12 - 15 lb ft (1.6 - 2.0 kg m).
46 Screw a new ball housing locknut onto each end of the rack to the limits of the thread.
47 Insert the two thrust springs into the ends of the rack.
48 Fit each tie rod into its ball housing and locate the ball cup against the thrust spring.
49 Slowly tighten the two ball housings until the tie rod is just niped.
50 Using a mole wrench and a soft metal drift carefully tighten the locknut onto the ball housing. Again check that the tie rod is still pinched.
51 Next slacken the ball housing back by one eigth of a turn to allow full articulation of the tie rods.
52 Fully tighten the locking ring to the housing. Whilst this is

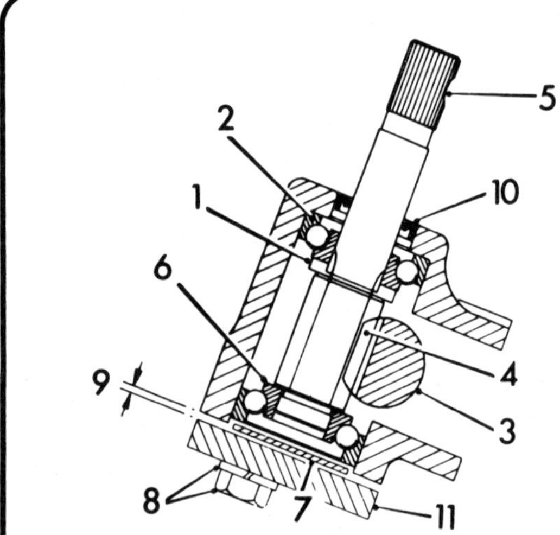

FIG 11.21 PINION END CROSS SECTION

1 Pinion washer
2 Upper bearing
3 Rack
4 Pinion teeth
5 Pinion
6 Lower bearing
7 Shims
8 Bolt and spring washer
9 Gap measurement
10 Pinion shaft oil seal
11 End cover

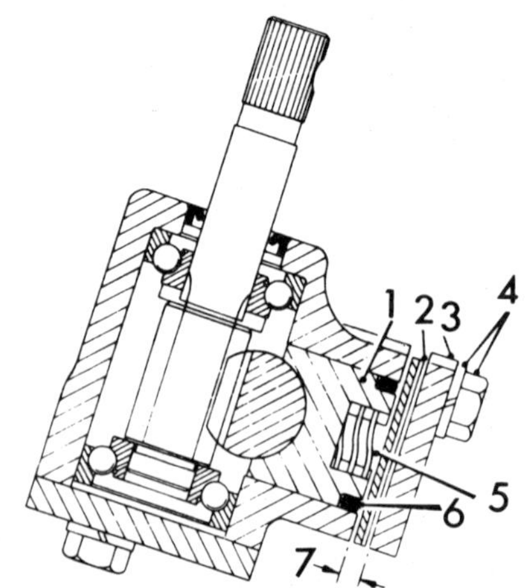

FIG 11.22 DAMPER COVER SHIM THICKNESS

1 Damper yoke
2 Shims and gasket
3 Cover plate
4 Bolt and spring washer
5 Damper spring
6 'O' ring seal
7 Gap measurement

being done make sure the housing does not turn.

53 Using a centre punch or blunt chisel drive the ball housing edge of the locking ring into the locking slots of the ball housing and opposite into the locking slot of the rack.

54 Replace the two rack rubber seals and secure with the large clips to the housing. Position the two small clips and tighten on the pinion end.

55 Refit the tie rod locknuts and then screw on each tie rod end by an equal amount until the dimension between the two ball pin centres is 43.7 inches (110.9cm). Tighten the locknuts sufficiently to prevent this initial setting being lost during refitting.

56 Using a squirt type oil can insert 2/3 pint (0.19 litre) of recommended grade oil through the pinion seal. Finally position the small seal clip and lightly tighten.

24 Front wheel alignment

The front wheels are correctly aligned when they are turning in at the front 1/16 inch (1.6mm). It is important that this measurement is taken on a centre line drawn horizontally and parallel to the ground through the centre line of the hub. The exact point should be in the centre of the sidewall of the tyre and not on the wheel rim which could be distorted and therefore give inaccurate readings.

The adjustment is effected by loosening the locknut on each tie rod ball joint and also slackening the rubber gaiter clip holding it to the tie rod, both tie rods then being turned equally until the adjustment is correct.

This is a job best left to a BLMC garage, as accurate alignment requires the use of special equipment. If the wheels are not in alignment, tyre wear will be heavy and uneven, and the steering be stiff and unresponsive.

25 Front suspension trim height - adjustment

Before checking the front rim height of the car it must be prepared by removing the contents of the boot with the exception of the spare wheel. Ideally there should be two gallons of petrol in the tank. Check and adjust the tyre pressure as necessary.

Stand the car on a level surface and measure the vertical distance between the underside of the wheel arch and the floor, this distance being taken through the centre line of the hub.

This height measurement should be 25 3/8 + 1/4 inch (7.715 + 0.064mm) when the vehicle has been in service for a short while. However if new torsion bars are fitted this dimension must be increased by 5/16 inch (7.94mm) to allow for initial settling.

Coarse Adjustment

This is applicable when there is a need to adjust the trim height by more than ¾inch (19.05mm) up or 1¼ inch (31.75mm) down.

1 Apply the handbrake and chock the rear wheels. Jack up the front of the car and place on firmly based axle stands located under the front chassis members.

2 Remove the wheel trim and the road wheel.

3 Hold the upper bush housing with a mole wrench and unlock the reaction pad nut. Unscrew and remove the nut.

4 Lift away the lock washer, upper bush housing and the upper bush.

5 Undo and remove the steering track rod ball pin nut and using a universal ball joint separator detach the ball pin from the steering lever.

6 Raise the shock absorber arm and support the weight of the suspension on a wod block. The assembly must not be allowed to hang on the brake flexible hydraulic hose.

7 Mark the relative position of the torsion bar lever and car body with a scriber. Do not mark the torsion bar.

8 Ease the lever forwards out of mesh with the torsion bar splines and reposition it one spline up or down.

9 Reassembling is now the reverse sequence to removal. It will now be necessary to make the final fine adjustment.

Fine adjustment

1 Remove the adjustment lever lock bolt spring washer and spacer.

2 Slacken the adjuster screw locknut and turn the adjuster screw in a clockwise direction to increase the height trim or anti-clockwise to decrease the trim height. Retighten the locknut.

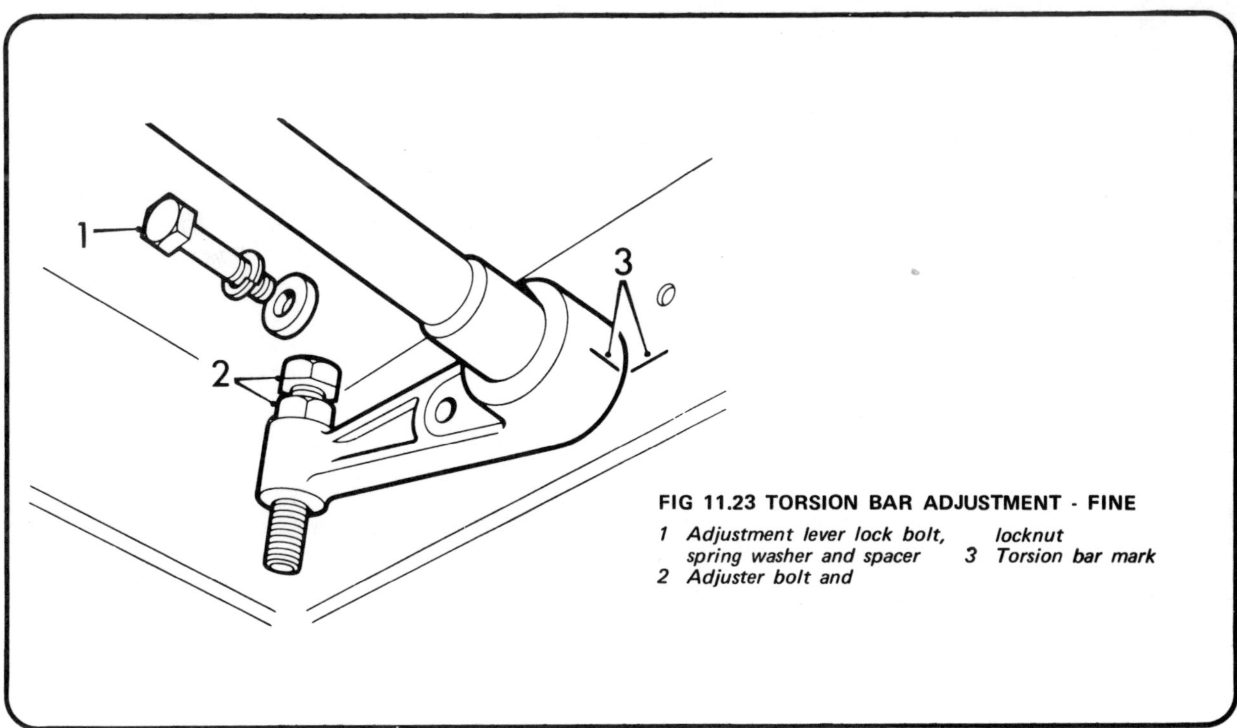

FIG 11.23 TORSION BAR ADJUSTMENT - FINE

1 Adjustment lever lock bolt, spring washer and spacer
2 Adjuster bolt and locknut
3 Torsion bar mark

26. Fault diagnosis

Symptom	Reason/s	Remedy
STEERING FEELS VAGUE, CAR WANDERS AND FLOATS AT SPEED		
General wear or damage	Tyre pressures uneven	Check pressures and adjust as necessary.
	Shock absorbers worn	Test, and replace if worn.
	Steering gear ball joints badly worn	Fit new ball joints.
	Suspension geometry incorrect	Check and rectify.
	Steering mechanism free play excessive	Adjust or overhaul steering mechanism.
	Front suspension and rear suspension pick-up points out of alignment or badly worn	Normally caused by poor repair work after a serious accident. Extensive rebuilding necessary.
	Front suspension lacking grease	Check condition and grease or replace worn parts and re-grease.
STIFF AND HEAVY STEERING		
Lack of maintenance or accident damage	Tyre pressures too low	Check pressures and inflate tyres.
	No grease in steering rack	Top up steering rack.
	No grease in steering ball joints	Replace.
	Front wheel toe-in incorrect	Check and reset toe-in.
	Suspension geometry incorrect	Check and rectify.
	Steering gear incorrectly adjusted too tightly	Check and re-adjust steering gear.
	Steering column badly misaligned	Determine cause and rectify (usually due to bad repair after severe accident damage and difficult to correct).
WHEEL WOBBLE AND VIBRATION		
General wear or damage	Wheel nuts loose	Check and tighten as necessary.
	Front wheels and tyres out of balance	Balance wheels and tyres and add weights as necessary.
	Steering ball joints badly worn	Replace steering gear ball joints.
	Hub bearings badly worn	Remove and fit new hub bearings.
	Steering gear free play excessive	Adjust and overhaul steering gear.
	Front torsion bars weak or broken	Inspect and renew as necessary.

Chapter 12 Bodywork and underframe

Contents

1 General description

The combined body and underframe is of all welded construction. This makes a very strong and torsionally rigid shell.

The Marina steel 1.8 is two or four doors, with a fifth rear door on the Estate. The door hinges are securely bolted to both the door and body. The drivers door is locked from the outside by means of a key and all other doors may be locked from the inside.

The toughened safety glass is fitted to all windows; the windscreen has a specially toughened 'zone' in front of the driver. In the event of the windscreen shattering this 'zone' breaks into much larger pieces than the rest of the screen thus giving the driver much better vision than would otherwise be possible.

The front seats are of the adjustable bucket type whilst the rear seat is a bench seat, without a central arm rest.

For occupant safety all switches and controls are suitably recessed or positioned so that they cannot cause body harm. Provision is made for the fitting of either static or automatic seat belts.

The instruments are contained in two dials located above the steering column. A heater and ventilation system is fitted incorporating a full flow system with outlet ducts at instrument panel level.

2 Maintenance - body and chassis

1 The condition of the bodywork is of considerable importance as it is on this in the main that the second-hand value of the car will mainly depend. It is much more difficult to repair neglected bodywork than to renew mechanical assemblies. The hidden portions of the body, such as the wheel arches, the underframe and the engine compartment are equally important, although obviously not requiring such frequent attention as the immediately visible paintwork.

2 Once a year, or every 12,000 miles, it is advisable to visit a garage equipped to steam clean the body. This will take about 1½ hours. All traces of dirt and oil will be removed and the underside can then be inspected carefully for rust, damaged hydraulic pipes, frayed electrical wiring and similar maladies. The car should be greased on completion of this job.

3 At the same time the engine compartment should be cleaned in a similar manner. If steam cleaning facilities are not available, then brush 'Gunk' or a similar cleaner over the whole of the engine, and engine compartment, with a stiff brush, working it well in where there is an accumulation of oil and dirt. Do not paint the ignition system, and protect it with oily rags when the 'Gunk' is washed off. As the 'Gunk' is washed away it will take with it all traces of oil and dirt, leaving the engine looking clean and bright.

4 The wheel arches should be given particular attention, as under sealing can easily come away here, and stones and dirt thrown up from the road wheels can soon cause the paint to chip and flake, and so allow rust to set in. If rust is found, clean down the bare metal with wet and dry paper. Paint on an anti-corrosive coating such as 'Kurust', or if preferred red lead, and renew the undercoating and top coat.

5 The bodywork should be washed once a week or when dirty. Thoroughly wet the car to soften the dirt, and then wash the car down with a soft sponge and plenty of clean water. If the surplus dirt is not washed off very gently it will in time wear the paint as surely as wet and dry paper. It is best to use a hose if this is available. Give the car a final wash down and then dry with a soft chamois leather to prevent the formation of spots.

6 Spots of tar and grease thrown up from the road can be removed by a rag dampened in petrol.

7 Once every three months, give the bodywork and chromium trim a thoroughly good wax polish. If a chromium cleaner is used to remove rust on any of the cars plated parts, remember that any cleaner also removes part of the chromium so use only when absolutely necessary.

3 Maintenance - upholstery and carpets

1 Remove the carpets or mats, and thoroughly vacuum clean the interior of the car every three months, or more frequently if necessary.

2 Beat out the carpets and vacuum clean them if they are very dirty. If the upholstery is soiled apply an upholstery cleaner with a damp sponge and wipe off with a clean dry cloth.

4 Body repairs - minor

1 Major damage must be repaired by a specialist body repair shop but there is no reason why you cannot successfully beat out, repair, and respray minor damage yourself. The essential items which the owner should gather together to ensure a really professional job are:-

a) A plastic filler such as Holts 'Cataloy'.

b) Paint whose colour matches exactly that of the bodywork, either in a can for application by a spray gun, or in an aerosol can.

c) Fine cutting paste.

d) Medium and fine grade wet and dry paper.

2 Never use a metal hammer to knock out small dents as the blows tend to scratch and distort the metal. Knock out the dent with a mallet or rawhide hammer and press on the underside of the dented surface a metal dolly or smoth woden block roughly contoured to the normal shape of the damaged area.

3 After the worst of the damaged area has been knocked out, rub down the dent and surrounding area with medium wet and dry paper and thoroughly clean away all traces of dirt.

4 The plastic filler comprises a paste and hardener which must be thoroughly mixed together. Mix only a small portion at a time as the paste sets hard within five to fifteen minutes depending on the amount of hardener used.

5 Smooth on the filler with a knife or stiff plastic to the shape of the damaged portion and allow to thoroughly dry – a process which takes about six hours. After the filler has dried it is likely that it will have contracted slightly so spread on a second layer of filler if necessary.

6 Smooth down the filler with fine wet and dry paper wrapped round a suitable block of wood and continue until the whole area is perfectly smoth and it is impossible to feel where the filler joins the rest of the paintwork.

7 Spray on from an aerosol can, or with a spray gun, an anti-rust undercoat, smooth down with wet and dry paper and then spray on two coats of the final finishing using a circular motion.

8 When thoroughly dry polish the whole area with a fine cutting paste to smooth the resprayed areas into the remainder of the wing and to remove the small particles of spray paint which will have settled round the area.

9 This will leave the wing looking perfect with not a trace of the previous dent.

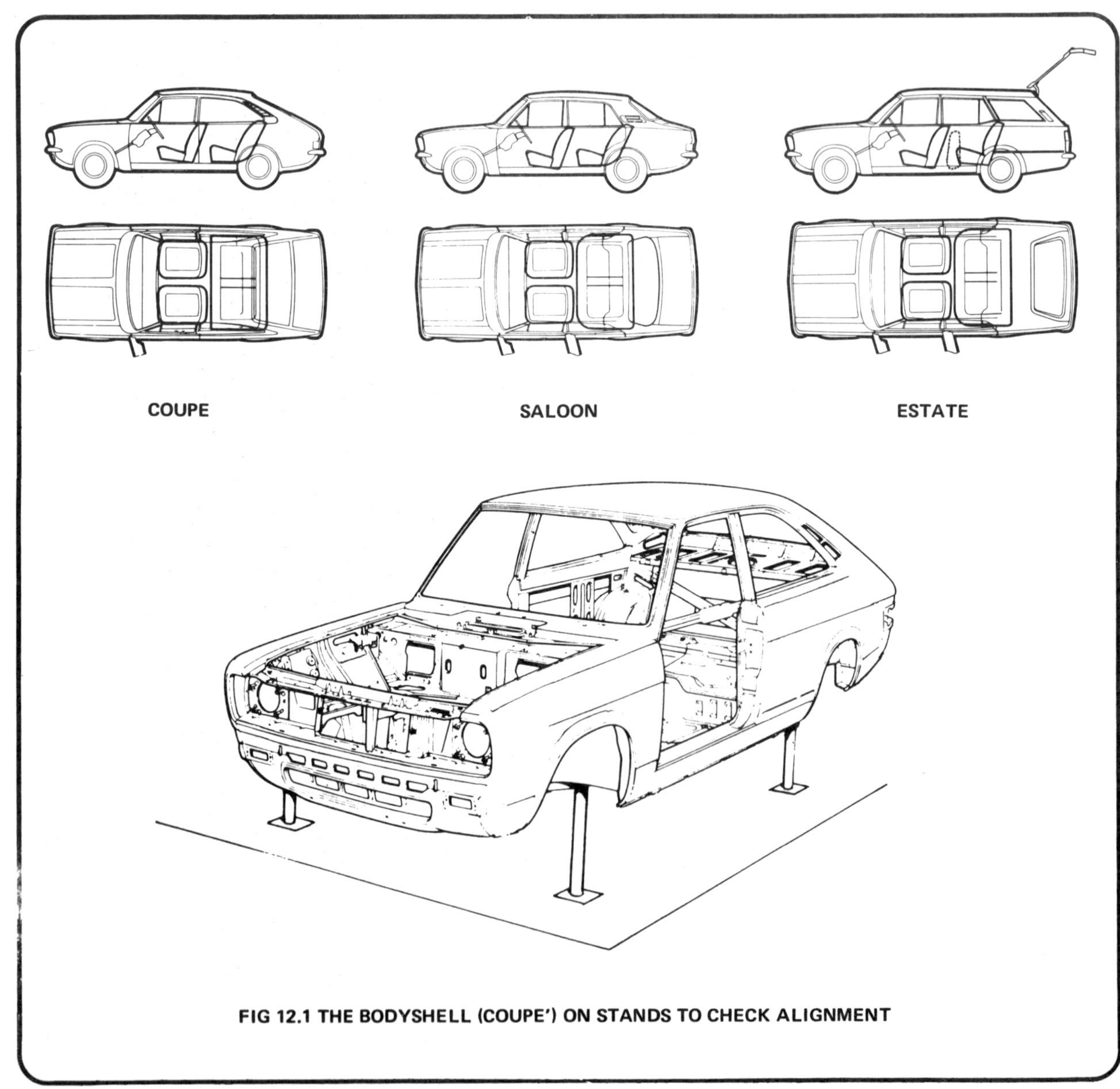

FIG 12.1 THE BODYSHELL (COUPE') ON STANDS TO CHECK ALIGNMENT

5 Body repairs - major

1 Because the body is built on the monocoque principle and is integral with the underframe, major damage must be repaired by specialists with the necessary welding and hydraulic straightening equipment.
2 If the damage is severe, it is vital that on completion of the repair the chassis is in correct alignment. Less severe damage may also have twisted or distorted the chassis although this may not be visible immediately. It is therefore always best on completion of repair to check for twist and squareness to make sure all is well.
3 To check for twist, position the car on a clean level floor, place a jack under each jacking point, raise the car and take off the wheels. Raise or lower the jacks until the sills are parallel with the ground. Depending where the damage occurred, using an accurate scale, take measurements at the suspension mounting points and if comparable readings are not obtained it is an indication that the body is twisted.
4 After checking for twist, check for squareness by taking a series of measurements on the floor. Drop a plumb line and bob weight from various mounting points on the underside of the body and mark these points on the floor with chalk. Draw a straight line between each point and measure and mark the middle of each line. A line drawn on the floor starting at the front and finishing at the rear should be quite straight and pass through the centres of the other lines. Diagonal measurements can also be made as a check for squareness.

6 Maintenance - locks and hinges

Once every 6,000 miles (10,000 km) or 6 months the door, bonnet and boot hinges should be oiled with a few drops of engine oil from an oil can. The door striker plates can be given a thin smear of grease to reduce wear and ensure free movement.

7 Door rattles - tracing and rectification

The most common cause of door rattles is a misaligned, loose or worn striker plate but other causes may be:
1) Loose door handles, window winder handles or door hinges.
2) Loose, worn or misaligned door lock components.
3) Loose or worn remote control mechanism.
Or a combination of these.
2 If the striker catch is worn as a result of door rattles renew it and adjust as described later in this Chapter.
3 Should the hinges be badly worn then they must be renewed.

8 Door - removal and refitting

1 Refer to Section 10 and remove the door trim panel.
2 Working inside the door mark the outline of the stiffener plate at each hinge position (Fig.12.2). An assistant should now take the weight of the door.
3 Undo and remove the locknuts and plain washers that secure the door to the hinge.
4 Lift away the stiffener plates and finally the door.
5 Refitting the door is the reverse sequence to removal. Should it be necessary to adjust the position of the door in the aperture leave the locknuts slightly loose and reposition the door by trial and error. Fully tighten the locknuts.

9 Door hinge - removal and refitting

1 Refer to Section 22 and remove the front parcel tray.
2 Using a wide blade screwdriver carefully ease back the side trim panel door seal and then the trim panel.
3 If the rear door hinges are to be removed, using a wide blade screwdriver ease back the 'B' post door seals. Undo and remove the carpet finisher retaining screws, slide the front seat forward and ease the trim panel retaining clips from the 'B' post. Hinge the trim panel up at the PVC lining crease. This will give access to the door hinge retaining nuts.
4 Undo and remove the locknuts and plain washers securing each hinge (Fig.12.2). Lift away the stiffener plates and finally the door hinges.
5 Refitting the door hinge is the reverse sequence to removal.

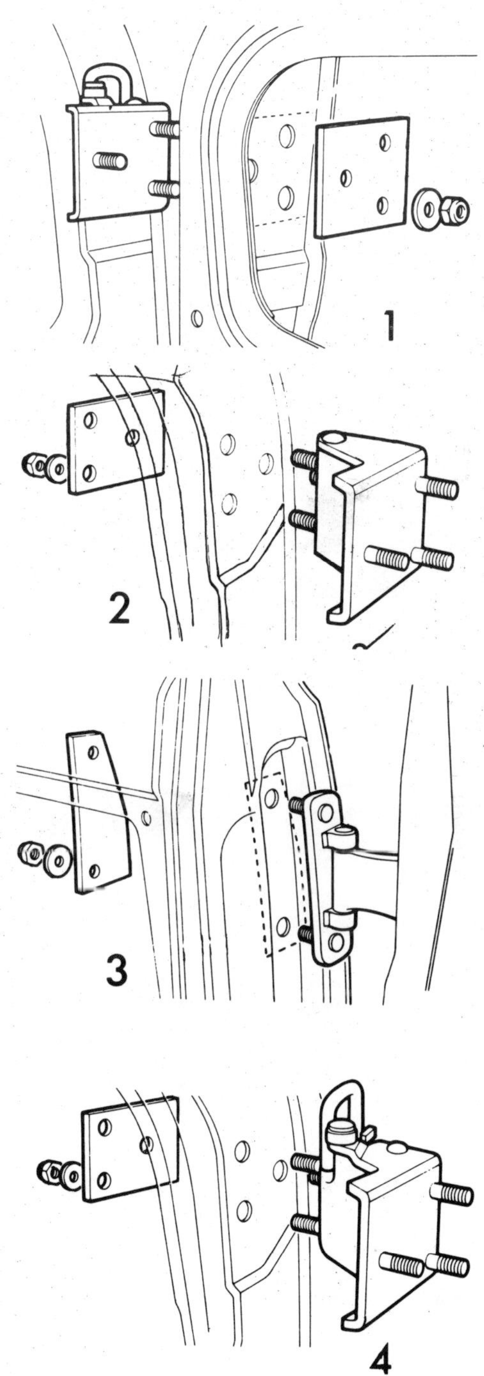

FIG 12.2 FRONT AND REAR DOOR HINGE ASSEMBL

1 Top front door
2 Bottom front door
3 Top rear door
4 Bottom rear door

10 Door trim panel and capping - removal and refitting

1 Wind the window up fully and note the position of the handle.
2 Undo and remove the screw and spacer that secures the window regulator handle. Lift away the handle (Fig.12.3).
3 Undo and remove the two screws that retain the arm rest. Lift away the arm rest.
4 With a screwdriver carefully slide the upper and lower bezels from the remote control door handle (photo).
5 With a wide blade screwdriver or knife inserted between the trim panel and door carefully ease the trim panel clips from the door. Lift away the trim panel.
6 Should it be necessary to remove the trim capping, undo and remove the screws and shaped washers and unclip the trim capping from the door.
7 Refitting is the reverse sequence to removal. If the capping has been removed make sure that the door glass seal and wiper strip are correctly positioned.

11 Door exterior handle - removal and refitting

1 It is important to check that if the door lock is not operating correctly that the cause is not due to maladjustment. Full information on this will be found in Section 12.
2 Refer to Section 10 and remove the door trim.
3 Undo and remove the two nuts or screws, plain and shakeproof washers. Lift away the clamp bracket.
4 Front door: Disconnect the private lock control rod clip from the locking bar cross shaft. Carefully unclip and detach the screwed rod at the exterior handle release lever.
5 Rear door only: Disconnect the screwed rod at the cross lever

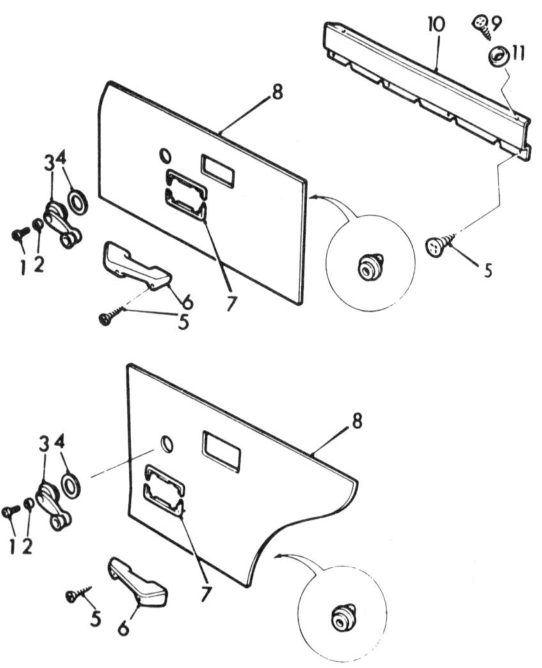

FIG 12.3 DOOR TRIM PANEL AND CAPPING

1 Screw
2 Spacer
3 Window regulator handle
4 Bezel
5 Screw
6 Rim rest
7 Upper and lower bezel
8 Trim panel
9 Screw
10 Coupling
11 Shaped washer

but do not alter the rod adjustment.
6 Lift away the hand assembly.
7 Refitting is the reverse sequence to removal. Lubricate all moving parts with Castrol GTX.

12 Door lock adjustment

Four adjustments may be made to the door locks and it will usually be found that any malfunction of a lock is caused by incorrect adjustment.

Exterior handle

1 Refer to Section 10 and remove the trim panel.
2 Close the door and partially operate the exterior release lever. Check that there is free movement of the lever before the point is reached where the transfer lever and its screwed rod move.
3 Operate the exterior release lever fully and check that the latch disc is released from the door striker before the lever is fully open.
4 To adjust, disconnect the screwed rod and screw in or out to achieve the correct setting.

Remote control

1 Refer to Section 10 and remove the trim panel.
2 Undo and remove the screw and slacken the control retaining screws.
3 Move the remote control assembly towards the latch unit. Retighten the retaining screws and make sure that the operating lever is against its stop 'A' (Fig.12.4 or 12.5).

Safety locking lever

Refer to Section 10 and remove the trim panel.

Front

1 Disconnect the long lock rod from the safety locking lever and then the short rod from the locking bar. Push the locking bar against its stop 'B' and move the safety locking lever to the locked position.
2 Refit the long rod in the safety locking lever and then press in the legs of the clip. Adjust the short rod so as to fit into the rod bush in the locking bar.
3 Release the safety locking lever and make sure that the operating lever is quite free to operate.

Rear

1 Disconnect the long lock rod from the safety locking lever and then the short lock rod from the locking lever.
2 Press the free wheeling operating lever against the stop 'D' and position the safety locking lever in the locked position.
3 Reconnect the long lock rod to the safety locking lever. Push in the legs of the clip and adjust the short rod to fit into the rod bush in the locking lever.
4 Release the safety locking lever and ensure that the operating tab aligns with the striker pin of the latch disc release lever.

Door striker

1 It is very important that the latch disc is in the open position. Also do not slam the door whilst any adjustment is being made otherwise damage may result.
2 Slacken the striker plate retaining screws until it is just sufficient to allow the door to close and latch.
3 Push the door inwards or pull it outwards without operating the release lever until the door is level with the body and aperture.
4 Open the door carefully and with a pencil round the striker plate to act as a datum.
5 Place the striker accurately by trial and error until the door can be closed easily without signs of lifting, dropping or rattling.
6 Close the door and make sure that the striker is not positioned too far in by pressing on the door. It should be possible to press the door in slightly as the seals are compressed.
7 Finally tighten the striker plate retaining screws.

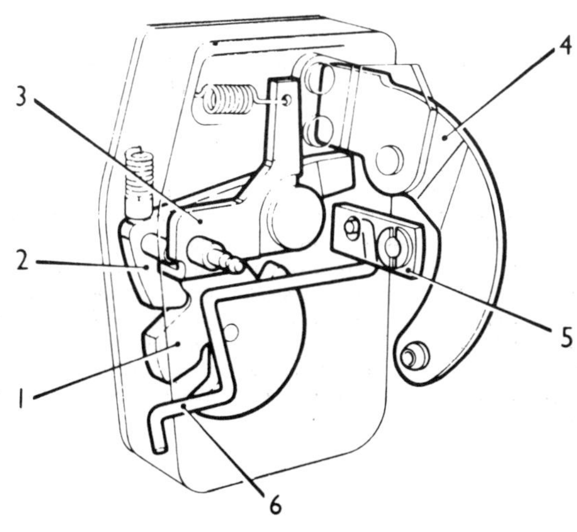

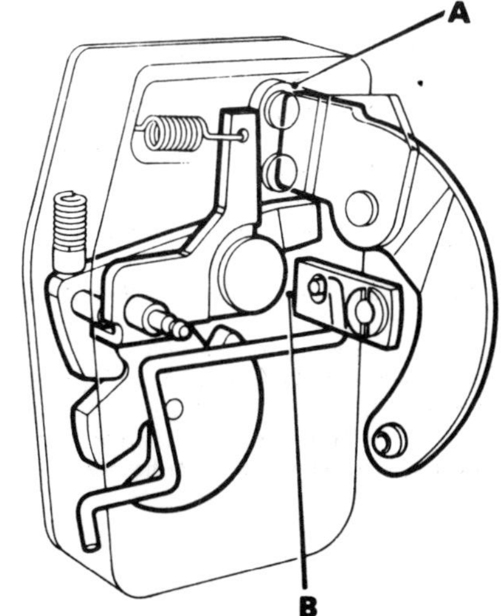

FIG 12.4 FRONT DOOR LOCK MECHANISM

1 Latch disc 2 Latch disc release lever 3 Cross control lever 4 Operating lever 5 Locking bar 6 Locking bar cross shaft Positive stop A Positive stop B

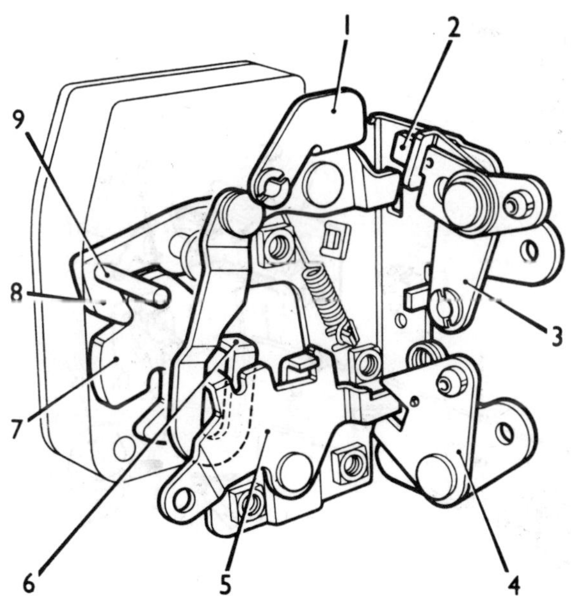

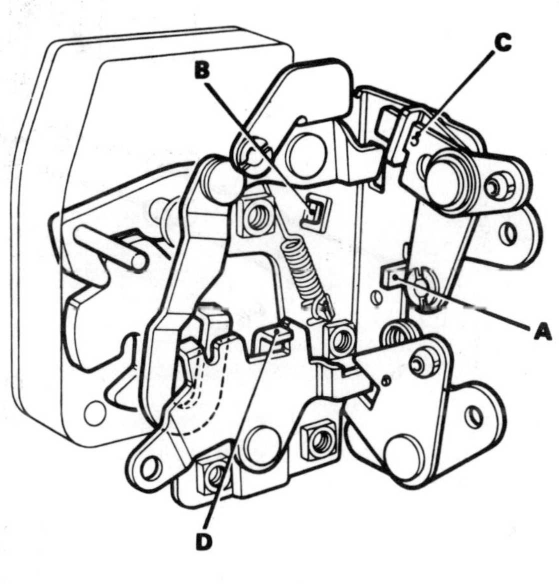

FIG 12.5 REAR DOOR LOCK MECHANISM

1 Cross lever 2 Child safety intermediate lever 3 Operating lever 4 Locking lever 5 Free wheel actuating lever 6 Operating tab 7 Latch disc 8 Latch disc release lever 9 Striker pin Positive stop B and C Positive stop A Positive stop D

13 Door remote control handle - removal and refitting

It is important to check that if the door lock is not operating correctly that the cause is not due to maladjustment. Full information on this will be found in Section 12.

2 Refer to Section 10 and remove the door trim.

3 Undo and remove the three screws, shakeproof and plain washers that secure the remote control.

4 Undo and remove the lock screw.

5 Detach the long remote control lock rod from the safety locking lever.

6 Detach the remote control release rod from the operating lever.

7 Lift away the remote control assembly.

8 Front door only: Undo and remove the screw and plain washer that secures the glass channel. Detach the exterior handle transfer lever from the lifting stud of the cross control lever.

9 Rear door only: Detach the exterior handle screwed rod from the cross lever.

10 Detach the remote control release rod from the operating lever of the disc lock front door or free wheel assembly - rear door.

11 Detach the lock rod clip from the lock bar cross shaft.

12 Front door only: Detach the short lock rod from the locking bar.

13 Rear door only: Detach the short lock rod from the free wheel locking lever.

14 Using a pencil mark the position of the disc latch body on the door. Undo and remove the four screws that secure the disc latch and the free wheel from the rear door.

15 With a pencil mark the position of the door pillar and remove the two screws retaining the striker plate assembly. The striker plate may now be lifted away. The tapped stiffener plate is retained inside the door 'B' post by fan retaining tags.

16 Refitting the door remote control assembly is the reverse sequence to removal. Lubricate all moving parts with Castrol GTX.

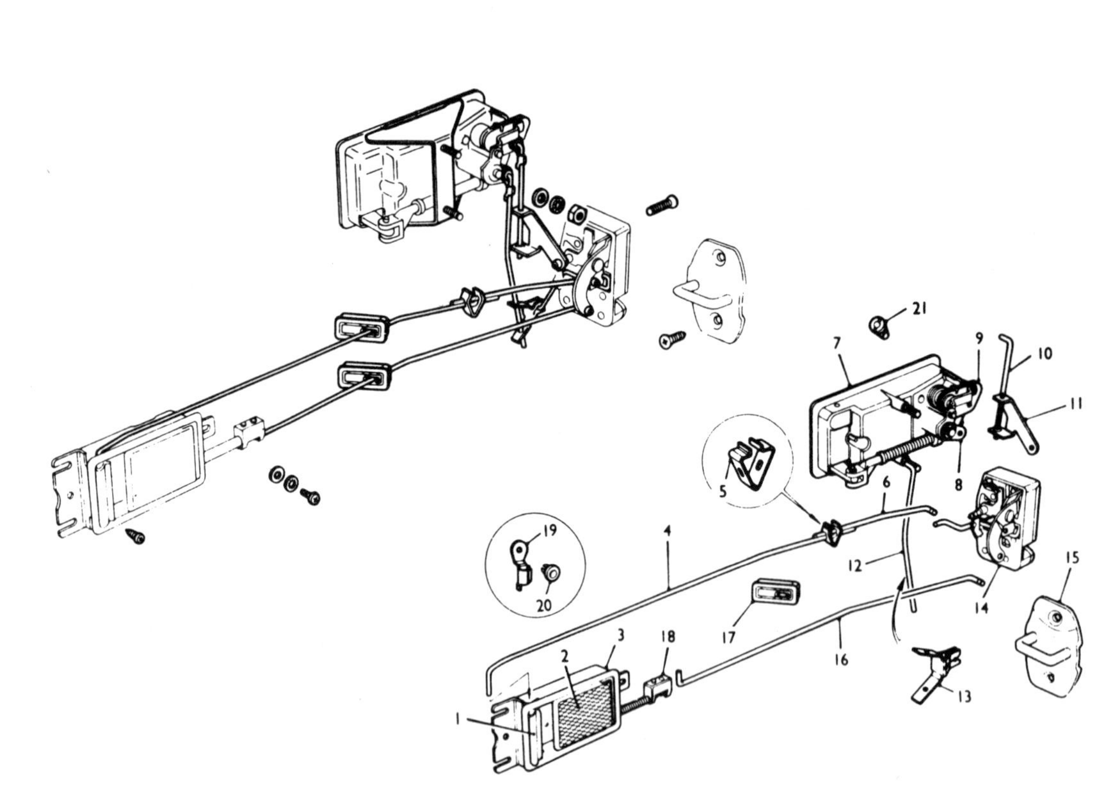

FIG 12.6 FRONT DOOR LOCK COMPONENT PARTS

1 Safety locking lever
2 Remote release handle
3 Remote control assembly
4 Remote lock rod-long
5 Remote lock rod clip
6 Remote lock rod-short
7 Outside handle
8 Lock barrel free wheel lever
9 Outside handle release lever
10 Screwed rod
11 Transfer lever
12 Lock rod (outside handle)
13 Lock rod clip
14 Disc lock assembly
15 Lock striker
16 Remote release rod
17 Door rod guide
18 Retaining clip
19 Rod clip
20 Rod bush
21 Rod bush (cross control lever)

14 Door private lock - removal and refitting

1 Refer to Section 11 and remove the door exterior handle.
2 Using a small screwdriver carefully remove the circlip and lift away the spring and special washers (Fig.12.8).
3 The lock barrel may now be removed.
4 Refitting is the reverse sequence to removal.

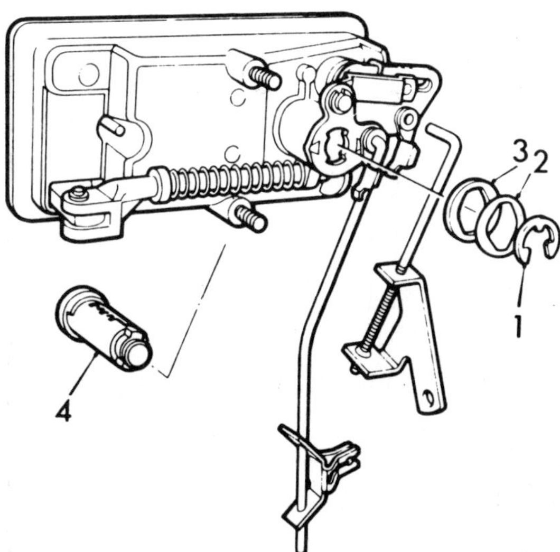

FIG 12.8 DOOR PRIVATE LOCK ASSEMBLY REMOVAL

1 Circlip
2 Spring washer
3 Shaped washer
4 Lock barrel

15 Door glass - removal and refitting

1 Refer to Section 10 and remove the door trim.
2 Lower the window until the glass regulator channel appears in the door inner aperture.
3 Undo and remove the four screws and spring washers that secure the regulator and lift away the regulator (Fig.12.9).
4 Front door: Carefully lower the glass to the bottom of the door.
5 Rear door: Raise the glass fully.
6 If the capping is fitted this should next be removed. Undo and remove the screws and shaped washers. Unclip the trim capping from the door.
7 Using a screwdriver carefully so as not to damage the paintwork spring off the six clips that retain the glass wiper strip. Lift away the wiper strip.
8 Carefully remove the window channel rubber by easing it out of the door glass aperture.
9 Using a drill of suitable diameter remove the 'pop' rivet that retains the top of the centre window channel.
10 Undo and remove the screw and plain washer that retains the bottom of the centre window channel.
11 The window channel may now be removed by turning it through 90° and aligning the narrowest section with the glass aperture in the door.
12 Remove the door fixed or opening quarter light whichever is fitted, and its sealing rubber.
13 The window glass may now be lifted out of the glass aperture.
14 Finally remove the regulator channel and its protective rubber from the glass.
15 Refitting the door glass is the reverse sequence to removal. If a new glass is to be fitted make sure that the regulator channel is refitted centrally on the door glass. Lubricate all moving parts with Castrol GTX.

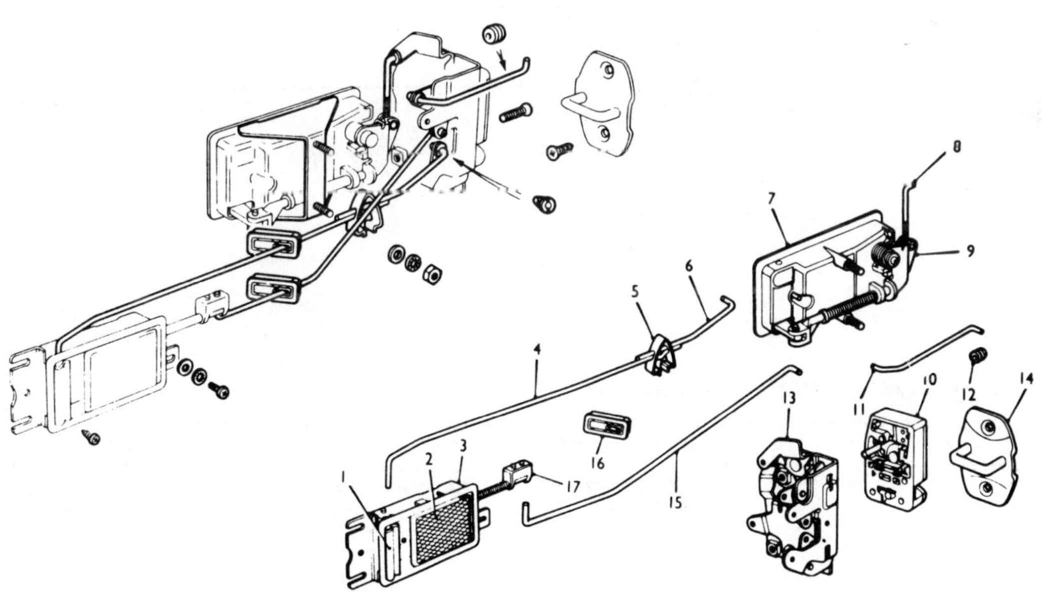

FIG 12.7 REAR DOOR LOCK COMPONENT PARTS

1 Safety locking lever
2 Remote release lever
3 Remote control assembly
4 Remote lock rod-long
5 Remote lock rod clip
6 Remote lock rod-short
7 Outside handle
8 Screwed rod
9 Outside handle release lever
10 Disc lock assembly
11 Child safety lever rod
12 Door grommet
13 Free-wheel assembly
14 Lock striker
15 Remote release rod
16 Door rod guide
17 Retaining clip
18 Rod bush

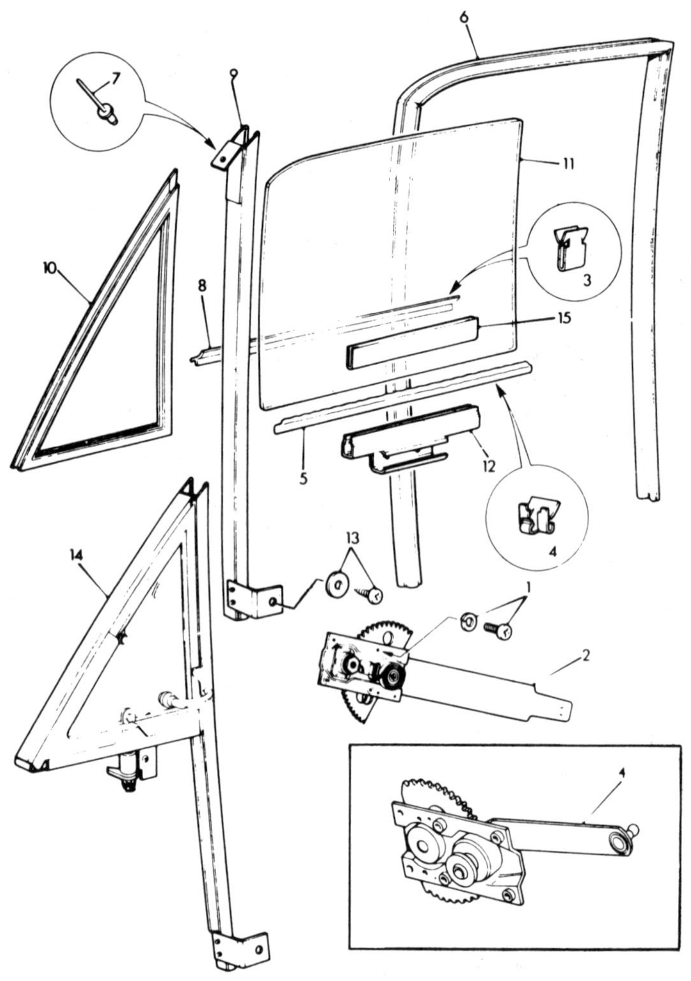

FIG 12.9 DOOR GLASS ASSEMBLY REMOVAL

1 Regulator securing bolt and spring washer
2 Regulator
3 Clip
4 Clip
5 Glass wiper strip
6 Window channel rubber
7 'Pop' rivet
8 Glass outer weatherstrip
9 Window channel
10 Quarter light sealing rubber
11 Door glass
12 Regulator channel
13 Channel securing screw and plain washer
14 Opening quarter light assembly
15 Protective rubber
Inset 'A' shows rear regulator

16 Bonnet - removal and refitting

1 Open the bonnet and support on its stay.
2 With a pencil mark the outline of the hinge on the bonnet to assist correct refitting. If the hinge is to be removed also mark the inner panel as well.
3 An assistant should now take the weight of the bonnet. Undo and remove the bonnet to hinge retaining bolts, spring and plain washers at both hinges. Carefully lift away the bonnet over the front of the car (Fig.12.10).
4 Refitting is the reverse sequence to removal. Alignment in the body may be made by leaving the securing bolts slightly loose and repositioning by trial and error. The securing bolts must not be overtightened as they could damage the outer bonnet panel.

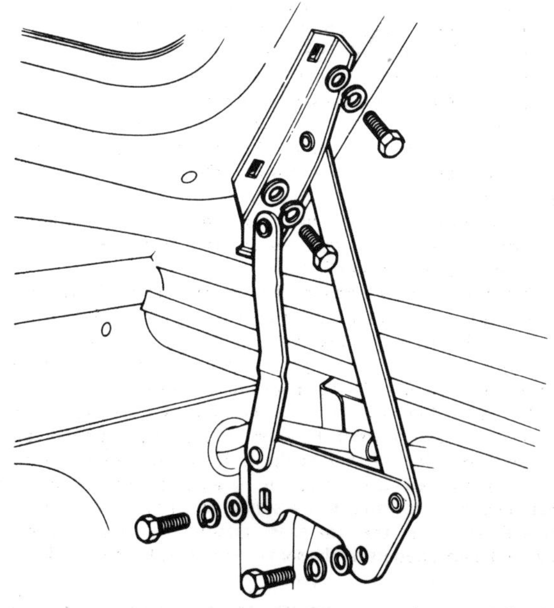

FIG 12.10 BONNET HINGE ASSEMBLY

17 Bonnet lock - removal and refitting

1 Open the bonnet and support it on its stay.
2 Slacken the nut and detach the release cable from the trunnion located at the lock lever (Fig.12.11).
3 Detach the release cable and its clip from the bonnet lock.
4 Undo and remove the three bolts, plain and shakeproof washers securing the bonnet lock. Lift away the bonnet lock.
5 Undo and remove the two bolts, plain and shakeproof washers that secure the locking pin assembly to the underside of the bonnet.
6 Detach the return spring and remove the rivet that secures the safety catch.
7 Refitting is the reverse sequence to removal. It is now necessary to adjust thelock pin assembly until a clearance of 2 inches (50.8mm) exists ('A' Fig.12.11) between the thimble and bonnet panel.
8 Carefully lower the bonnet and check the alignment of the pin thimble with the lock hole. If misaligned slacken the fixing bolts and move the assembly slightly. Retighten the fixing bolts.
9 Close the bonnet and check its alignment with the body wing panels. If necessary reposition the lock pin assembly.
10 The bonnet must contact the rubber stops. To adjust the position of the stops, screw in or out as necessary.
11 Lubricate all moving parts and finally check the bonnet release operation.

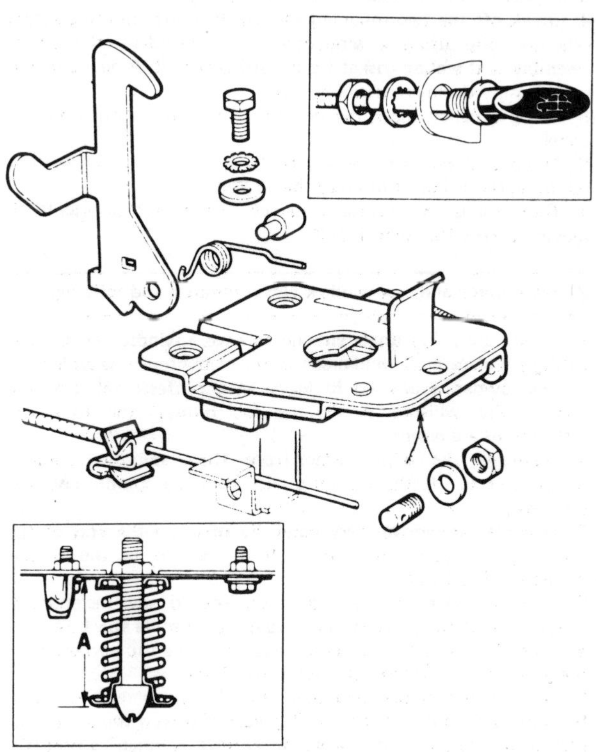

FIG 12.11 BONNET LOCK ASSEMBLY

18 Bonnet lock control cable - removal and refitting

1 Open the bonnet and support on its stay.
2 Slacken the nut and detach the release cable from the trunnion located at the lock lever (Fig.12.11).
3 Detach the release cable and its clip from the bonnet lock (photo).
4 Release the outer control cable from its snap clamp and then unscrew and remove the screw that secures each clip to the wing valance. Lift away the two clips.
5 Undo and remove the nut and shakeproof washer that secures the outer cable to the body side bracket mounted below the facia panel.
6 Carefully withdraw the control cable assembly through the body grommet.
7 Refitting is the reverse sequence to removal. It is however, necessary to adjust the inner cable. Push the release knob in fully and make sure that the lock release lever is not pre-loaded by the release cable.
8 There must be a minimum movement of 0.5 in (12.7mm) prior to the release of the bonnet. To adjust, slacken the cable trunnion nut and re-adjust the cable so that the bonnet is released within 0.5 to 2.0 in (12.7 to 50.8mm) of cable movement.

19 Boot lid hinge and tail gate - removal and refitting

1 Open the lid and using a pencil mark the position of the hinge relative to the luggage compartment lid.
2 Undo and remove the four bolts, spring and plain washers that secure the hinges to the lid. Lift away the lid over the back of the car. For this operation it is desirable to have the assistance of a second person.
3 To remove the hinge undo and remove the two nuts, plain and spring washers that secure each hinge to the body bracket. Lift away the hinge (Fig.12.12).
4 Refitting is the reverse sequence to removal but if adjustment is necessary leave the bolts securing the hinge to the lid slack.
5 Close the lid and adjust the position to ensure correct trim spacing. Open the lid and tighten the hinge bolts. Do not over-tighten as they could damage the outer lid panel.
6 The tail gate of the Estate is removed by undoing the hinge bolts or the tailgate itself. Have an assistant hold the tail gate in the open position so that as the bolts are removed it will still remain supported. Do not forget to scribe round the hinges so that they can be refitted in a similar position. Refitting a new tailgate will mean that the exact positioning when closed will have to be adjusted using the same method as for a slide door.

20 Boot lid lock and tailgate lock - removal and refitting

1 Using a pencil mark the outline of the lock catch plate on the lid under panel.
2 Undo and remove the three bolts, spring and plain washers that secure the lock catch (Fig.12.13).
3 Slacken the locknut and unscrew the spindle. Lift away the shakeproof washer, spindle striker and spring.
4 Break off the two retaining ears of the barrel housing spring retaining clip using a screwdriver and withdraw the barrel assembly and sealing gasket from outside the lid. A new clip will be necessary during reassembly.
5 Using a pencil mark the outline of the striker on the body panel.
6 Undo and remove the two bolts, spring and plain washers retaining the striker. Lift away the striker.
7 Refitting is the reverse sequence to removal. Lubricate all moving parts with Castrol GTX.

21 Windscreen and rear window glass - removal and refitting

If you are unfortunate enough to have a windscreen shatter, fitting a replacement windscreen is one of the few jobs which the average owner is advised to leave to a professional. For the owner who whishes to do the job himself the following instructions are given:
1 Remove the wiper arms from their spindles using a screwdriver to lift the retaining clip from the spindle end and pull away.
2 Using a screwdriver very carefully prise up the end of the finisher strip and withdraw it from its slot in the rubber moulding (Fig.12.14).
3 The assistance of a second person should now be enlisted, ready to catch the glass when it is released from its aperture.
4 Working inside the car, commencing at one top corner, press the glass and ease it from its rubber moulding.
5 Remove the rubber moulding from the windscreen aperture.
6 Now is the time to remove all pieces of glass if the screen has shattered. Use a vacuum cleaner to extract as much as possible. Switch on the heater boots motor and adjust the controls to 'Screen defrost' but watch out for flying pieces of glass which might be blown out of the ducting.
7 Carefully inspect the rubber moulding for signs of splitting or deterioration. Clean all traces of sealing compound from the rubber moulding and windscreen aperture flange.
8 To refit the glass, first apply sealer between the rubber and glass.

FIG 12.12 BOOT LID HINGE

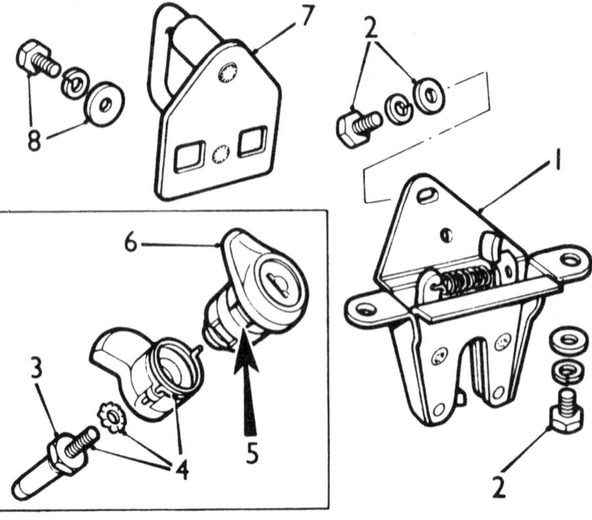

FIG 12.13 BOOT LOCK ASSEMBLY

1 Lock catch plate
2 Bolt, spring and plain washer
3 Locknut
4 Shakeproof washer, spindle and spring
5 Barrel housing spring
6 Lock barrel assembly
7 Striker
8 Bolt, spring and plain washer

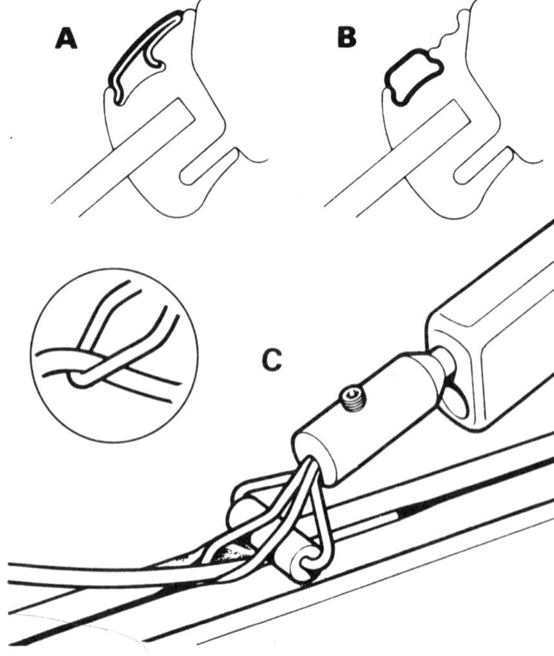

FIG 12.14 GLASS REMOVAL AND REFITTING

A and B Profile of two types of finisher strip in place
C Type of tool necessary to replace finisher

9 Press a little 'Dum Dum' onto four or five inches of the body flange on either side of each corner.
10 Apply some 'Bostik' mastic sealer to the body flange.
11 With the rubber moulding correctly positioned on the glass it is now necessary to insert a piece of cord about 16 ft long all round the outer channel in the rubber surround which fits over the windscreen aperture flange. The two free ends of the cord should finish at either top or bottom centre and overlap each other by a minimum of 1 ft.
12 Offer the screen up to the aperture and get an assistant to press the rubber surround hard against the body flange. Slowly pull one end of the cord moving round the windscreen so drawing the lip over the windscreen flange on the body. If necessary use a piece of plastic or tapered wood to assist in locating the lip on the windscreen flange.
13 The finisher strip must next be fitted to the moulding and for this a special tool is required. An illustration of this tool is shown in Fig.12.14 and a handyman should be able to make up an equivalent using netting wire and a woden file handle.
14 Fit the eye of the tool into the groove and feed in the finisher strip.
15 Push the tool around the complete length of the moulding, feeding the finisher into the channel as the eyelet opens it. The back half beds the finisher into the moulding.
16 Clean off traces of sealer using turpentine.

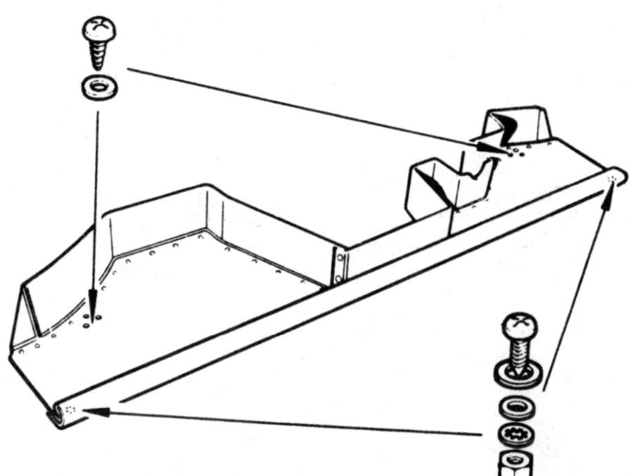

FIG 12.15 PARCEL SHELF ATTACHMENTS

22 Parcel tray - removal and refitting

1 Refer to Fig.12.15 and undo and remove the screw and plain washer.
2 Undo and remove the nut, shakeproof washer, bolt and plain washer.
3 Remove the parcel tray from the inside of the car taking care not to damage the headlining or interior trim.
4 Refitting the parcel tray is the reverse sequence to removal.

23 Facia panel - removal and refitting

1 Refer to Section 32 and remove the instrument panel.
2 Refer to Section 25 and remove the glovebox.
3 Refer to Section 24 and remove the lower facia panel.
4 Undo and remove the six nuts, spring and plain washers that secure the facia to the windscreen lower panel (Fig.12.16).
5 Undo and remove the three bolts that secure the facia panel to the lower rail.
6 Undo and remove the four bolts, plain and spring washers that secure the two outer brackets to the lower rail.
7 Undo and remove the two bolts, spring and plain washers that secure the upper steering column bracket.
8 Slacken the two nuts that secure the lower steering column bracket and remove the facia panel from the inside of the car taking care not to damage the headlining or interior trim.
9 Refitting the facia panel is the reverse sequence to removal.

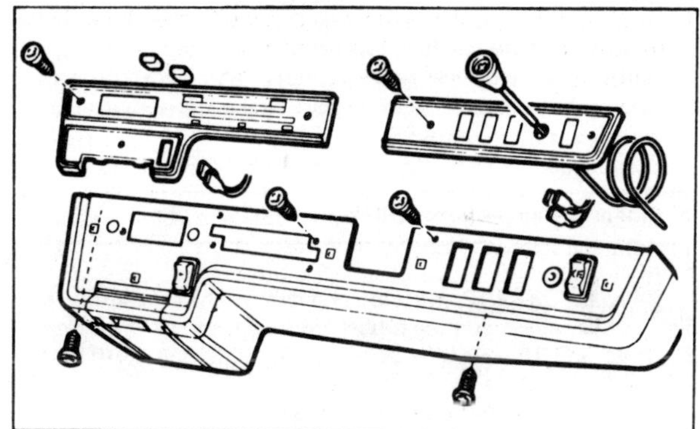

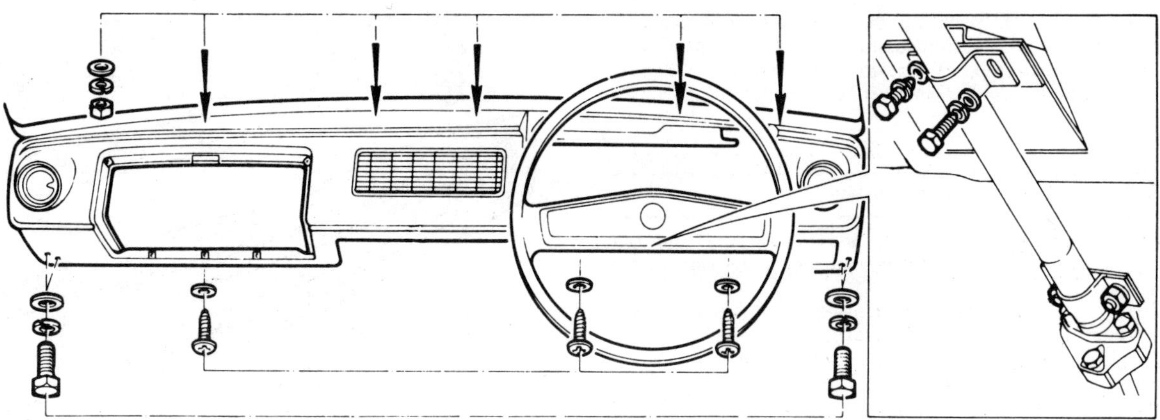

FIG 12.16 FACIA PANEL ASSEMBLY - INSET: LOWER FACIA PANEL ASSEMBLY

24 Lower facia panel - removal and refitting

1 Open the bonnet and slacken the choke control cable clamp at the carburettor. Detach the control cable and pull out the choke control knob and inner cable.
2 Undo and remove the two self tapping screws that secure the right hand switch trim panel. Lift away the panel.
3 Undo and remove the three self tapping screws that secure the left hand switch trim panel. Lift away the panel.
4 Undo and remove the two screws that secure the heater controls.
5 Undo and remove the three screws that retain the facia lower panel.
6 Undo and remove the two self tapping screws that secure the facia lower panel brackets to the upper facia panel.
7 Carefully draw the panel forwards and make a note of the electrical cable connections at the rear of the heater and lighting switches. Detach the cable connectors from the rear of the switches.
8 The choke control outer cable and facia lower panel may now be lifted away from the inside of the car.
9 Refitting is the reverse sequence to removal.

25 Glovebox - removal and refitting

1 Open the glovebox lid. Undo and remove the three screws that secure the hinge and lower the lid (Fig.12.17).
2 Undo and remove the two screws that retain the glovebox compartment. Lift away the glovebox.
3 Undo and remove the two screws that secure the glovebox lid catch. Lift away the catch and spacer plates.
4 Refitting is the reverse sequence to removal.

26 Bumpers - removal and refitting

Front

1 Refer to Fig.12.18 and undo and remove the bolt, spring and plain washer and mounting rubber from each end of the bumper.
2 Undo and remove the bolts, spring and plain washer that secures each support bracket to the body.
3 Lift away the front bumper assembly.
4 Undo and remove the bolts, spring and plain washers securing each bracket to the bumper.
5 Refitting is the reverse sequence to removal.

Rear

The sequence for removing the rear bumper is basically identical to that for the front bumper with the exception that before the bumper support brackets are released, the electric cables to the number plate light must be disconnected.

27 Radiator grille - removal and refitting

1 Refer to Fig.12.19 and undo and remove the four self tapping screws and plain washers that secure the case to the body (photo).
2 The grille and case may now be lifted upwards and forwards away from the front of the car (photo).
3 To detach the grille from the case undo and remove the self tapping screws and the plain washers.
4 Refitting is the reverse sequence to removal. Make sure that the rubber inserts are correctly positioned in the body panel cut-out and the locating pegs of the case are located in the centre of the rubber inserts.

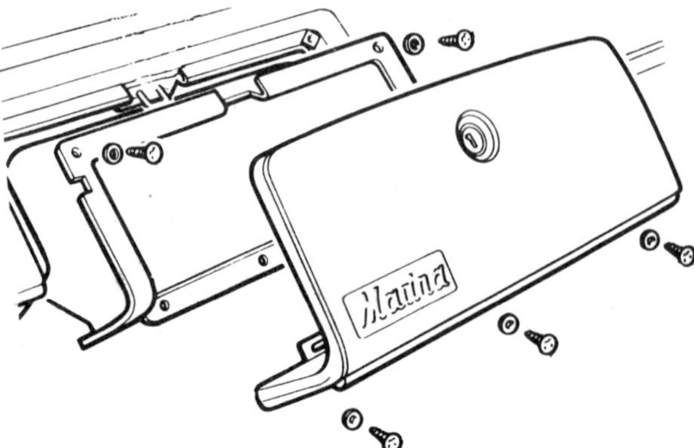

FIG 12.17 GLOVEBOX LID

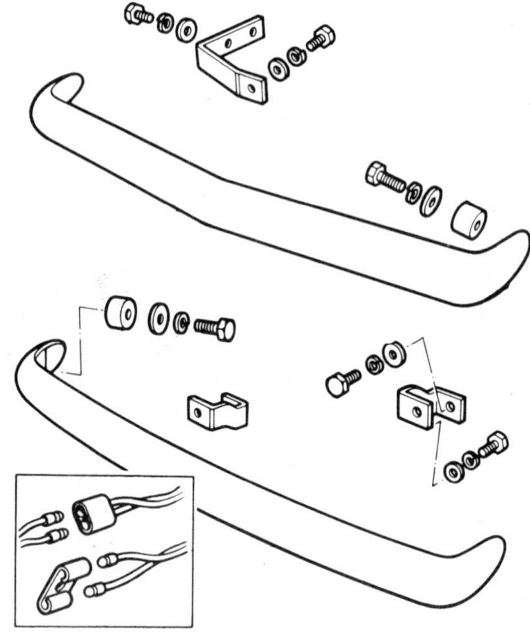

FIG 12.18 BUMPER ASSEMBLIES

Top Front
Bottom Rear (with number plate light connection)

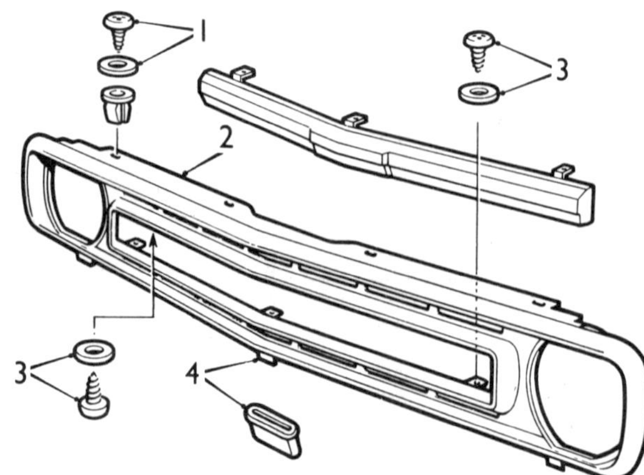

FIG 12.19 RADIATOR GRILLE ASSEMBLY

28 Heater unit - removal and refitting

1 Refer to Section 24 and remove the lower facia panel.
2 Refer to Section 32 and remove the instrument panel.
3 Detach the demister duct tubes from the heater.
4 Refer to Chapter 2, Section 2 and completely drain the cooling system.
5 Slacken the two heater hose clips located at the front of the bulkhead and remove the two hoses (Fig.12.20).
6 Pull off the two plenum chamber drain tubes located at the front of the bulkhead.
7 Undo and remove the nut and spring washer that holds the top of the heater unit to the bulkhead.
8 Undo and remove the two bolts, spring and plain washers that hold the heater side brackets to the bulkhead.
9 Detach the heater motor cable terminals from the wiring harness connector.
10 Place some plastic sheeting on the floor to prevent water damaging the carpeting. Draw the top of the heater unit rearwards to clear the upper fixing stud.
11 Pull the lower section of the heater rearwards until the heater unit is tilted so that it can be removed from under the facia support rail in front of the passengers position. Lift away from inside the car.
12 Refitting is the reverse sequence to removal but there are several additional points to be noted to ensure a satisfactory and watertight job.
13 Undo and remove the three self tapping screws that secure the air intake grille to the bulkhead top panel. Lift away the grille.
14 Place the heater in the car and lift into position engaging the top stud with the hole in the bulkhead. Refit the securing spring washer and nut but leave lose.
15 Working through the air intake grille hole carefully work the seal over the grille housing panel. Always fit a new seal if the condition of the original one is suspect.

29 Heater fan and motor - removal and refitting

1 Refer to Section 28 and remove the heater unit.
2 Undo and remove the heater plenum chamber securing self tapping screws and lift away the plenum chamber (Fig.12.21).
3 Undo and remove the three nuts and plain washers that secure the motor and fan assembly to the heater body. Lift away the motor.
4 If it is necessary to remove the fan, note which way round on the motor spindle it is fitted and remove the spring clip on the fan boss. Lift away the fan.
5 Refitting the heater fan and motor is the reverse sequence to removal. Before fitting a new motor always test it by placing the cable terminals on the battery terminals.

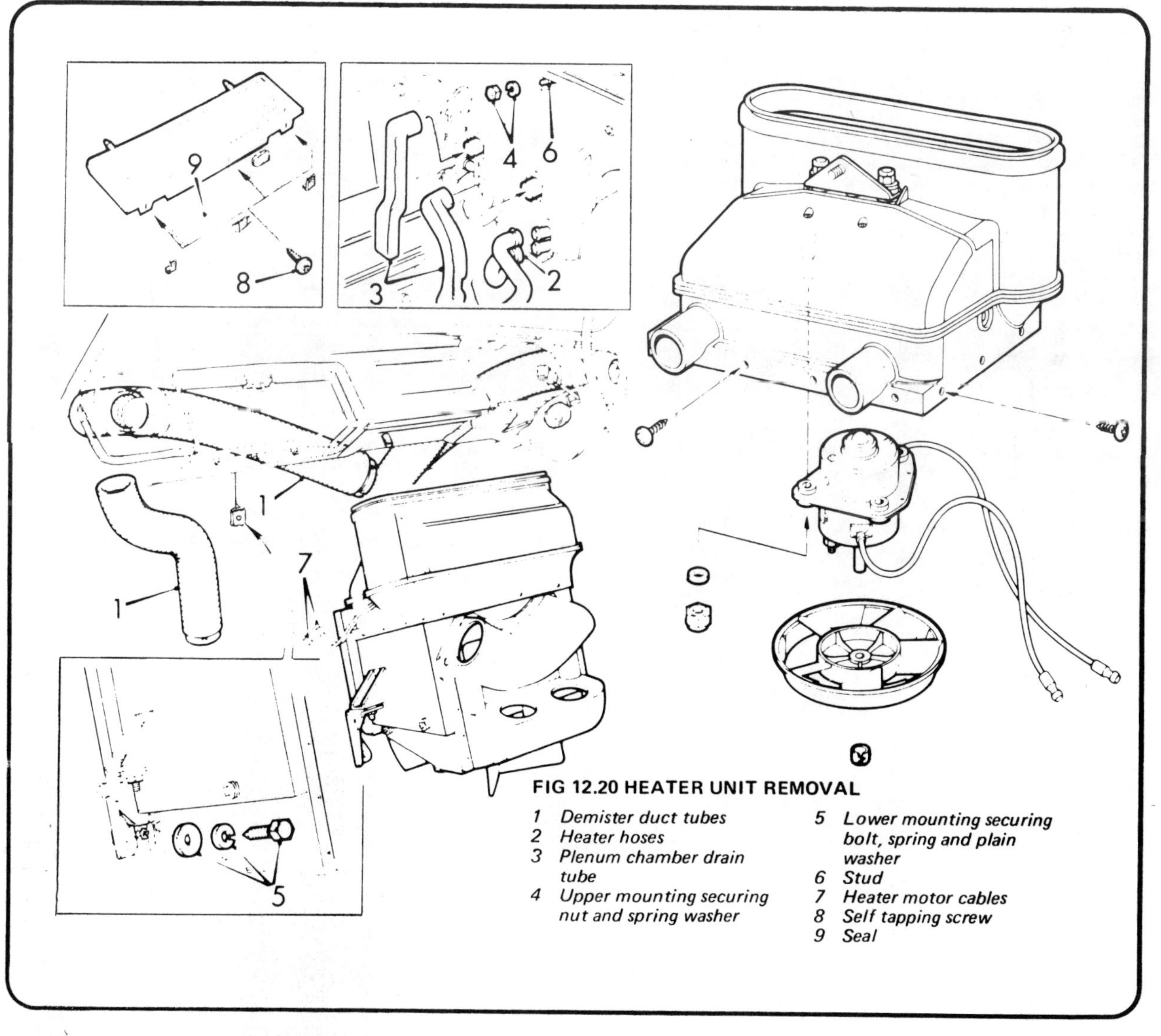

FIG 12.20 HEATER UNIT REMOVAL

1 Demister duct tubes
2 Heater hoses
3 Plenum chamber drain tube
4 Upper mounting securing nut and spring washer
5 Lower mounting securing bolt, spring and plain washer
6 Stud
7 Heater motor cables
8 Self tapping screw
9 Seal

30 Heater matrix - removal and refitting

1 Refer to Section 28 and remove the heater unit.
2 Carefully remove the packing rubber from the forward end of the heater unit.
3 Undo and remove the screws securing the matrix cover plate to the heater body. Lift away the cover plate.
4 The heater matrix may now be slid out from its location in the heater body.
5 If the matrix is leaking or blocked follow the instructions given in Chapter 2, Section 2.
6 Refitting the heater matrix is the reverse sequence to removal.

31 Windscreen demister duct - removal and refitting

1 Refer to Section 32 and remove the instrument panel.
2 Refer to Section 25 and remove the glovebox.
3 Detach the tubes from the demister duct (Fig.12.22).
4 Working under the facia undo and remove the two nuts, shakeproof and plain washers that secure the duct in position.
5 Carefully raise the duct finisher to clear the bolts and lift away the duct.
6 Refitting the duct is the reverse sequence to removal.

32 Instrument panel - removal and refitting

1 Undo and remove the four crosshead screws, spring and plain washers that secure the instrument panel to the facia. Note that the two longest screws are located above the instruments (Fig.12.23).
2 Draw the instrument panel away from the facia panel.
3 Press the release lever on the speedometer cable connector and detach the speedometer cable.
4 Disconnect the electrical multi pin connector from the rear of the instrument panel. Completely lift away the instrument panel.
5 Refitting the instrument panel is the reverse sequence to removal.

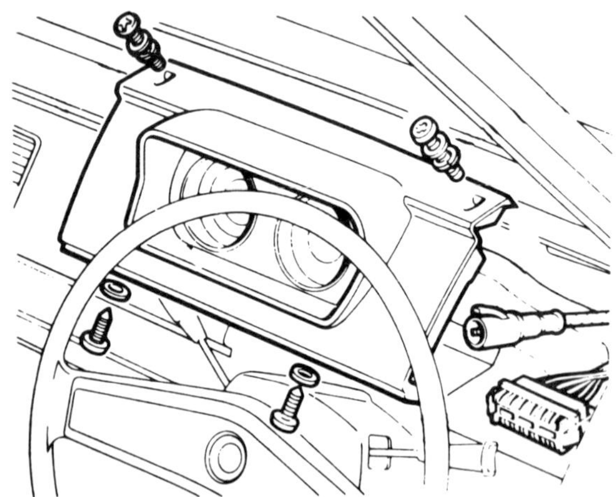

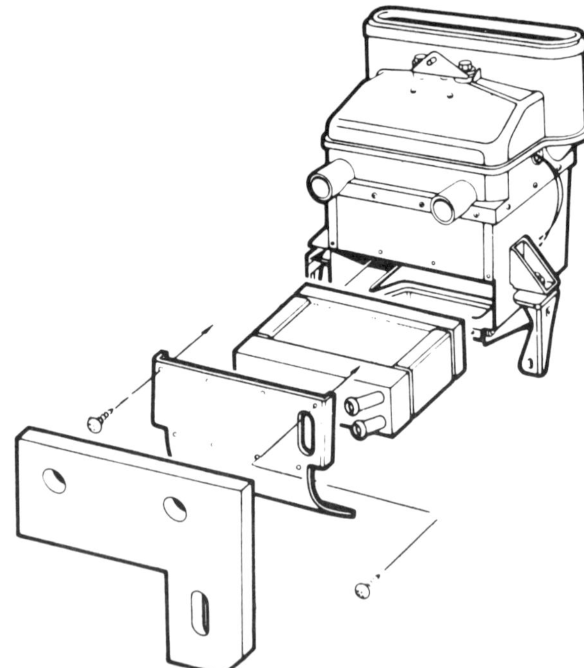

FIG 12.21 HEATER FAN AND MATRIX

Top - fan motor and blades
Bottom - heater radiator matrix

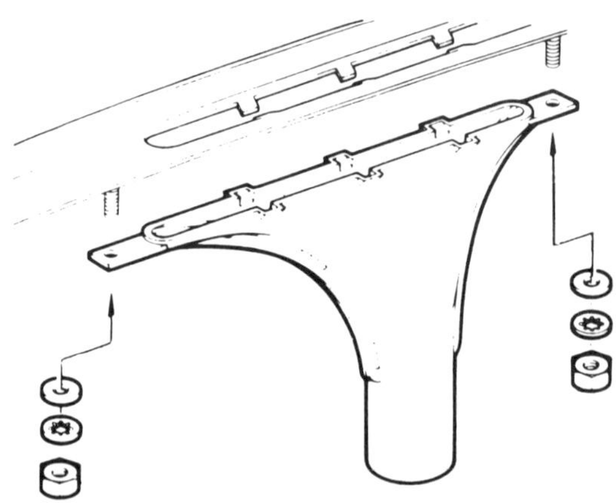

FIG 12.22 WINDSCREEN DEMISTER DUCT

FIG 12.23 INSTRUMENT PANEL REMOVAL

Chapter 13 Supplement

Contents

Specifications for U.S.A.

The specifications of the Marina differ from those given in earlier Chapters in the following respects:

Engine

Type	18V 659 M	
Torque SAE net	87 lb f. ft at 2,750 rpm	
Power SAE net	68.5 hp at 5,000 rpm	
Compression ratio	8 : 1	

Carburettor

Make and type	Single SA HIF 6	
Needle	BBE or BBQ (cold air intake)	
Emissions control	Air pump and exhaust port injection	

Fuel system

Tank capacity	11 gallons	
Idling speed	850 rpm	
Exhaust gas analysis at idle	CO less than 2.0%	

Ignition system

Timing to be set stroboscopically	12° BTDC at 1,500 rpm (vacuum pipe removed)	
Spark plug gap	0.035 in	(0.89 mm)

Lights

Side marker lights
Reverse light

Tyres	155 x 13 Radial ply	
Windows	Tinted glass (laminated windscreen)	
Overall length	2 door - 166.12 in	4 door - 169.12 in
width	2 door - 64.61 in	4 door - 64.81 in
Approximate weight	2 door - 2,156 lb	4 door - 2,193 lb

1 Introduction

1 This chapter deals with differences on some Marina models compared with the basic Morris Marina 1.8 which was the subject of Chapters 1-12. These differences are found in particular on the Austin Marina for North America.
2 The differences between the Morris Marinas for the home market and the Austins mainly concern the emissions control equipment needed to meet the USA regulations. These fall into three main groups. The SU carburettor is of the HIF type to give tighter control over mixture. This is used in conjunction with ignition timing retarded at idle so a wider throttle opening is needed, the stronger combustion giving less carbon monoxide and unburned hydrocarbons. Then there is the air injection system to blow into the exhaust ports to complete burning of the CO and HC to carbon dioxide (CO^2) and water (H^2O). Finally there is the fuel vapour control system connected to the absorption canister.
3 There are other minor variations. Yellow turn indicators used in Europe, are red for the USA. There is the useful brake pressure warning light. The combined lap and diagonal one piece seat belts almost universal in Europe are replaced by two part separate lap and shoulder belts.
4 Because of the additions the engine suffers, in common with other manufacturers' engines both piston and wankel, reduced power and increased fuel consumption, coupled with production of a higher grand total of exhaust gasses. The European regulations for exhaust control are not so extreme as those of the USA. Modifications that can in the future be expected for Europe include the adoption of the emissions control HIF carburettor for a wider market. Because such changes are tending to be introduced at short notice and without formal change of the car model title, the sections of this chapter may prove to be of wider application in the future.
5 In particular the tetra ethyl lead additives in petrol have been reduced in Europe from what was allowed before. The amount still allowed, and the amount still allowed in the USA, should be sufficient to allow the Marina engine to run the normal mileages without attention to the valves. The lead is put in the fuel to raise the octane rating, so ensure knock free combustion, but the lead also acts as a lubricant for the valve seat. Therefore in the Routine Maintenance, the testing of compression is recommended as a more frequent task. If local regulations reduce the amount of lead in the petrol then it is suggested that the compression tests in section 14 be done more frequently until it is established that the car is running happily on the new fuel.
5 The sections in this chapter are arranged in the order corresponding to that in which the subjects were covered in Chapters 1 – 12.

2 Routine maintenance: Austin Marina

1 There are additions to the routine maintenance tasks scheduled at the beginning of the book to suit the special fitments of the Austin version.
2 **6,000 miles (10,000 km).**
Check the tension of the air pump belt. See Section 7:4.
3 **12,000 miles (20,000 km).**
a) Replace the air filter element on the air pump.
b) Replace the air filter in the fuel vapour absorption canister.
c) Replace the fuel line filter.
d) If forced to use low lead fuel, test the compression at the end of the car's first 12,000 miles.
4 **18,000 miles (30,000 km).**
Test the compression. See Section 14. If one cylinder varies from the others by more than 5% remove the cylinder head and grind in the valves. Whilst doing this do the air injection servicing which would otherwise be done at 24,000 miles.
5 **24,000 miles (40,000 km).**
Service the air injection system, as detailed in Section 8. Check the air pump pressure, and if it is low, dismantle it. Remove the valves and check them. Remove the air supply manifold from the head and check its air flow, and that the exhaust port injectors are clear. Renew the air pump 'V' belt.
6 **50,000 miles (80,000 km).**
Replace the complete absorption canister.
7 Note that there is no filter in the oil filler cap on cars with absorption canisters, so the 12,000 mile task to replace it does not apply.

3 HIF 6 carburettors

1 The Austin Marina has full emissions control equipment, and this includes carburettors of the HIF 6 model, instead of the HS6 described in Chapter 3. These are still worked on the same basic principle of the SU, with dashpots holding pistons to regulate the amount of air and needles to control the fuel flow from the jet. From above they look much the same.
2 But there is no float chamber beside the piston. Instead this is concentric with the jet, and gives the bottom of the carburettor a fatter shape. Placing the float chamber centrally limits fuel level changes when braking, accelerating or cornering.
3 The jet is held in place by a horizontal arm. This is made of a bi-metal spring, so will vary the jet height to give compensation for temperature changes. These would otherwise give mixture variation due to fuel vicosity altering. This jet mounting arm is connected through a pivot to a lever. The lever is moved by a screw in the side of the carburettor body to adjust the mixture. The screw head may be hidden under a seal.
4 The rich mixture needed for cold starting is provided by a special jet. This has a progressive control to allow partial enrichment and is worked by turning a cam lever on the carburettor side opposite to that having the mixture control screw. This lever has the cam so that as it is moved to enrich the mixture the cam will push up the fast idle screw to open the throttle. The valve that controls this cold start mixture is a hollow inner core that is twisted within a cylindrical sleeve to bring a hole in it in line with one in the sleeve.
5 An emulsion bypass passage runs from the jet bridge to the throttle. At small throttle openings unevaporated fuel drops will be drawn along this passage, and mixed better with this faster travelling air. To match this slot there is a passage cut out of the base of the piston. When fitting a needle its base should be flush with this slot.
6 The HIF 6 has an over-run valve in the throttle disc, and the spring biased needle described in Chapter 3/17.
7 Mixture setting is much the same as described in Chapter 3/18. The engine response is similar. There are two differences. Instead of turning the jet adjusting nut on the bottom, the side screw is used; and this works the jet through the bi-metal spring. Before making an adjustment which means undoing any seal check you will not be breaking any regulation.
8 The initial setting after dismantling is to screw the jet up as far as it will go. Then start turning the screw clockwise. Note when the jet starts to move down, and thereafter screw two turns.
9 If the idle throttle setting has been lost, unscrew the throttle stop screw till the throttle is completely shut. Then screw it in again one complete turn. Screw in the fast idle screw till it is close to, but not touching, the cam on the choke mechanism.
10 Start up and warm up.
11 Once the engine is warmed up the fast idle screw should be adjusted to give 1200 rpm. Push in the choke control, and adjust the throttle stop screw to give the correct idle speed. The idle speed is:
a) Normally 500 rpm.
b) At 850 rpm for emissions control engines with air pumps.
12 Now adjust the mixture. A vacuum gauge can be very useful and is expensive. It also allows other engine tests to be made, so is worthwhile. This meter should be tapped into the inlet manifold. It must have its own tapping and not use temporarily one of the others, as their disconnection could upset the carburation and ruin the adjustment. The most accurate setting can

FIG.13.1 THE AUSTIN MARINA 1.8 ENGINE

1 *Air pump*
2 *It's air cleaner*
3 *Non return check valve to the air manifold*
4 *Gulp valve*
5 *Brake pressure warning switch*
6 *Fuel vapour absorption canister*
7 *Two way valve for air cleaner hot or cold intake*
8 *crank case fume pipe to carburettor*
9 *Tapping for engine pre-heater.*

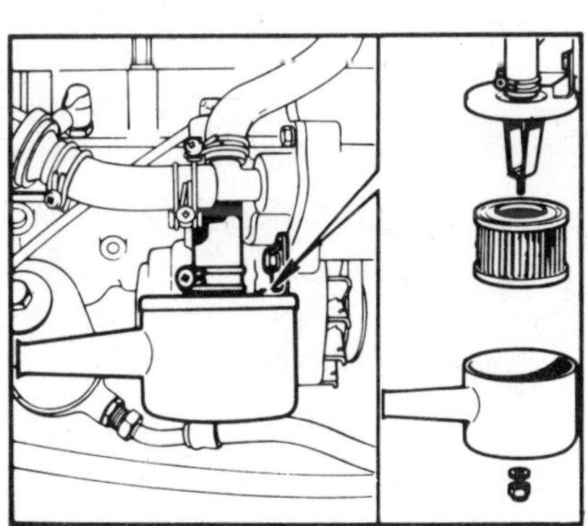

Fig.13.2 The air cleaner on the air pump

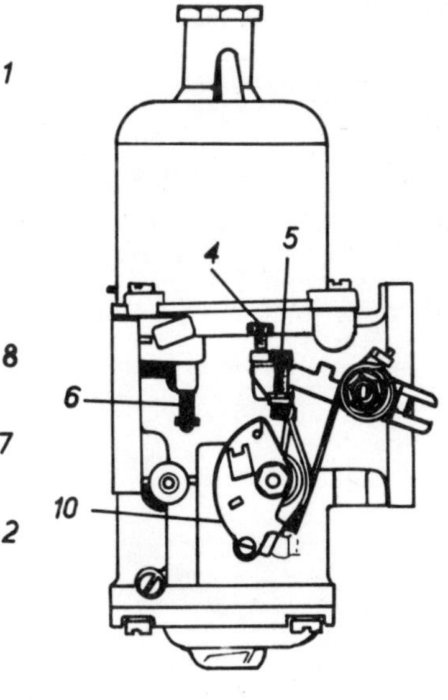

FIG.13.3 THE HIF CARBURETTOR

1 *Dashpot*
2 *Jet adjusting screw*
3 *Float chamber*
4 *Throttle stop screw*
5 *Fast idle screw*
6 *Piston lifting pin*
7 *Fuel inlet*
8 *Float chamber vent*
9 *Ignition connection. (blanked off for some markets)*
10 *Cold start cam*
11 *Crankcase fume connection*

be achieved using an exhaust gas analyser, and this may be essential to meet local regulations.

13 To weaken the mixture screw the screw out (anti-clockwise). As the screw is coupled through the spring there may be some lag in the movement of the jet. Tap the carburettor body to encourage it to find its new position. Also note where the mixture seems best when screwing in one direction; count the ¼ turns of the screw, going on past the correct position, and then coming back again still counting the distance the screw has been turned back to try and note the correct position: This is half way between the two positions which make the engine slow down because of mixture too weak and too rich.

14 The correct setting for the jet can be found from a combination of engine speed, which should be as fast as possible and if a vacuum gauge is being used the highest but steady reading, and listening to the exhaust note. The exhaust note should be smooth. If it is haphazardly irregular accompanied by a burping noise, with the engine still running fairly fast if the weakness is not extreme, a weak mixture is indicated. This can be confirmed by lifting the piston about 1/8th of an inch with the lifting device on the side of the carburettor, or a very fine screwdriver; the engine should immediately slow down and will be very liable to stall. If the mixture is too rich the idle will tend to be slow, accompanied by a rythmic irregular sound from the exhaust. Lifting the piston about 1/8th of an inch will result in the engine speeding up. Readings on a vacuum gauge with a weak mixture will be fairly high, but with fluctuation, whilst for a rich mixture the needle will show a low reading with rhythmic fluctuations. Moving the jet a ¼ turn of the adjusting screw from the correct setting should give an indication of weak or rich mixture. It is best to err in the direction of weakness; when the air cleaners are fitted there is slight enrichment of the mixture.

15 Finally having got the mixture correct recheck that the idle speed is still correct.

16 If at times the engine does not seem to respond to adjustment of the mixture correctly, blip the throttle a few times to clear the petrol that will collect in the inlet manifold, and burn soot off the spark plugs.

17 Replace the air cleaners.

18 On the road it might be found that the mixture has been set a trace rich or weak. Richness is apparent by the car idling well when cool; but when hot becoming lumpy and after a few seconds slower and more and more uneven. A weak mixture is indicated by a liability to stall when coming down to idling speed; if only slightly weak there will be a hesitation, slow idle, ragged, which then steadies and speeds up to a smooth correct idle. If the mixture appears to be wrong try a correction of ¼ of a turn only at a time, on the jet adjusting screw.

19 It is not practical to fine tune the carburettors by referring to the colour of the exhaust, as the colour will depend upon the driving conditions immediately before it is examined. But on a long journey, immediately on halting, an indication of whether the mixture is rich or weak can be got by the paleness of the tail pipe. This will indicate, not that readjustment of the setting of the carburettor jet nut is needed but whether a richer or weaker needle is needed. The carburettor must be set for the correct idle. If not giving the right mixture on the road then a different needle is needed.

4 Carburettor heater

1 The carburettor on cars for certain markets has a heater. This is an electrical element connected to the carburettor throat and the dash pot. This improves driveablility when cold, particularly on cars with emissions control equipment, that otherwise might be temperamental. It can also prevent carburettor icing.

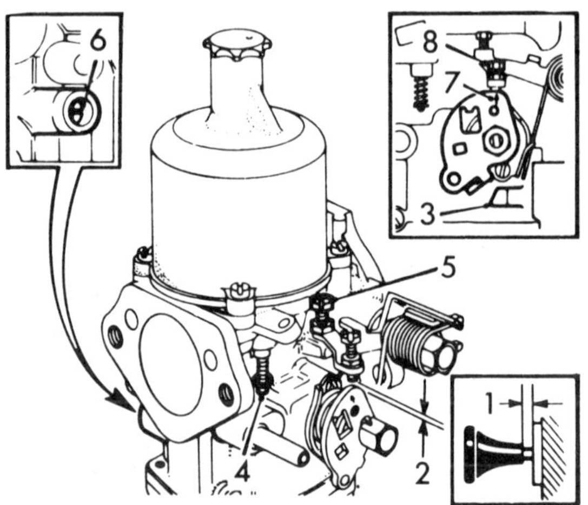

FIG.13.4 THE HIF CONTROLS

There should be 1/16 in movement (1) before the choke control starts moving the carburettor lever. There should be a small clearance (2) between the lever cam when on its stop (3) and the fast idle screw (8). Fine adjustment is done when choke pulled till arrow (7) is lined up with screw. Also shown is the piston lifting pin (4), throttle stop screw (5), and round the other side, the mixture screw (6).

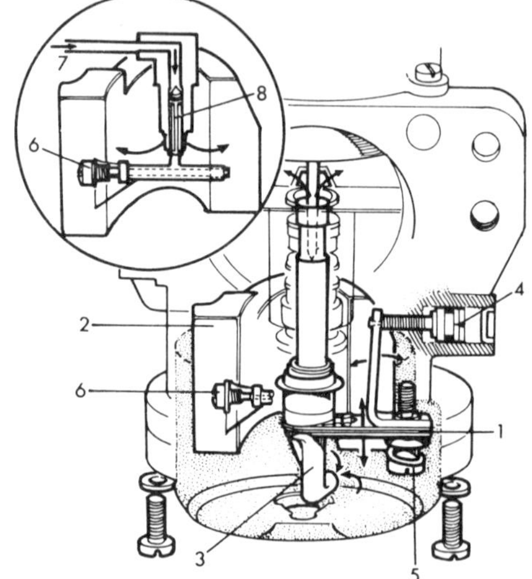

FIG.13.5 THE HIF CONCENTRIC FLOAT CHAMBER

1 Bimetal jet lever. 2 Float. 3 Jet. 4 Adjusting screw. 5 Jet lever pivot. 6 Float pivot. 7 Fuel inlet. 8 Needle valve.

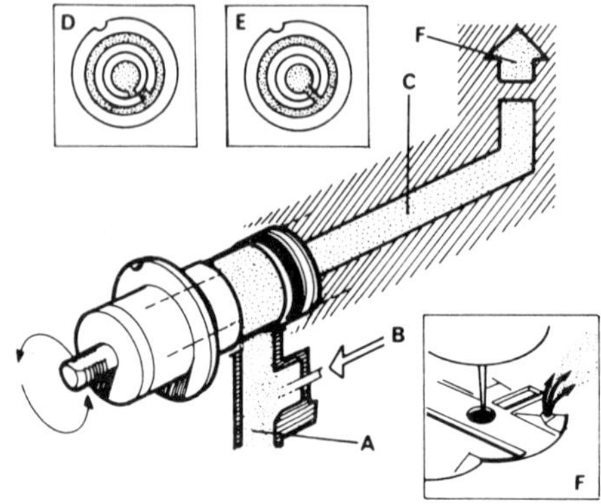

FIG.13.6 THE COLD START DEVICE OF THE HIF

Fuel enters at A, is emulsified with air at B, controlled by the setting of the spool, (inset at D and E), to pass along a passage C to come out in the air steam to the throttle at F.

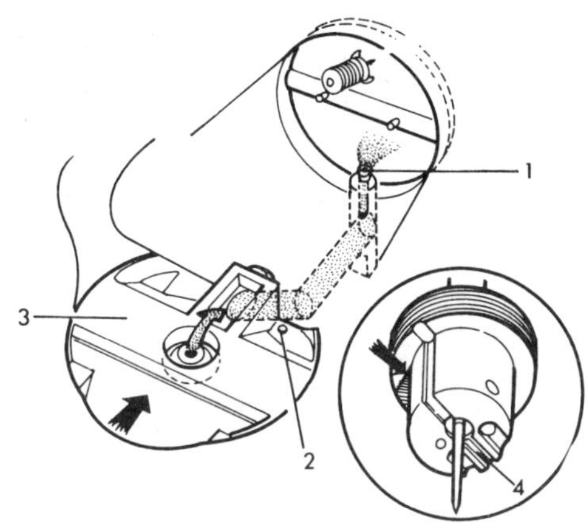

FIG.13.7 ON THE HIF A BY-PASS IDLE SYSTEM IS USED

1 The fuel outlet at the throttle. 2 Passage along the carburettor. 3 Jet bridge. 4 Slot in piston.

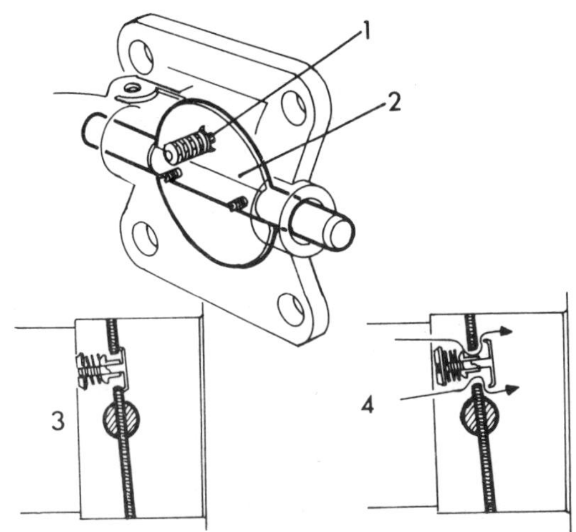

FIG.13.8 THROTTLE OF EMISSIONS CONTROLLED CARBURETTORS

Over-run valve (1) in throttle disc (2). The valve shut (3) and blown open on over-run (4).

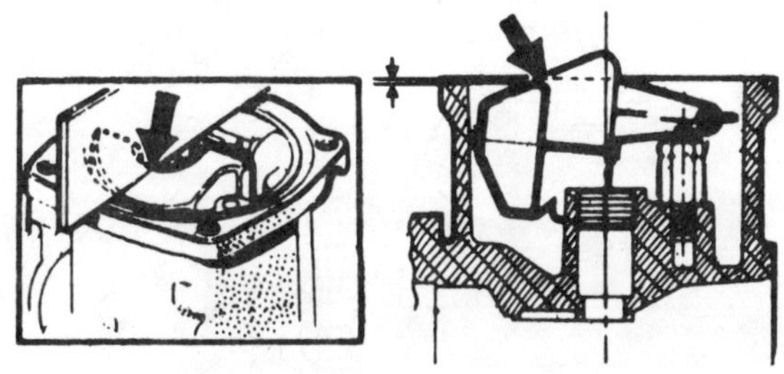

Fig.13.9 To check the float setting on the HIF the carburettor must be removed. The point arrowed should be 0.04 in ± .02 (1.0 mm ± 0.5) below float chamber face

Fig.13.10 The speed response of the engine to adjustment of the mixture.

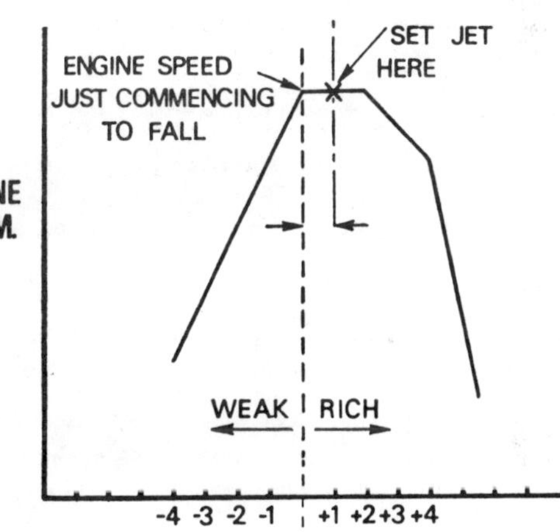

5 Carburettor hot air intake

1 In conjuction with the heater of the carburettor, the air is drawn into the aircleaner by two possible routes. When cold the air comes from a shield round the exhaust manifold. When hot it comes in direct from the front of the car. The 'T' junction where these two intakes join is controlled by a temperature sensitive disc valve. It is advisable to check this valve does move over. If it jams in the hot position driveability when cold will suffer. If jammed in the cold position, engine performance will be reduced.

6 Crankcase emissions control

1 All engines now have a control system for removing fumes from the crankcase of the engine, to be burnt in the combustion chamber.

2 Fumes are drawn from the engine at the side tappet chest and led round the front, then to the carburettors, to a tapping close to the dashpot piston, where the depression is constant valve, and so a valve is unnecessary. The air supply to this breathing system comes normally through the oil filler cap in the rocker cover. This has a small hole to restrict the air flow, and a filter to clean it.

3 Systems that have a carburettor fuel evaporative loss control have a normal sealed oil filler cap, and instead draw air from the fuel absorption canister. The air flow from the canister goes to the rocker cover, through a union which incorporates a restrictor hole.

4 The crankcase emission control can be tested as follows. With the engine idling undo the oil filler cap. This will allow an unrestricted flow of air into the engine, so its speed should increase, and there be signs of a weak mixture.

7 Exhaust emission control (exhaust port air injection)

1 An air injection system is fitted on cars going to North America. This blows air into the exhaust ports to burn off any hydrocarbons that come from the cylinders, which would otherwise be unwelcome emissions. An air pump driven by a rubber belt from the engine draws air through an air cleaner and delivers it to an air supply manifold along the cylinder head. Drillings pass through the cylinder head to each exhaust port. A check valve in the air delivery pipe to the manifold prevents blow back of high pressure exhaust to the air pump, and in the

Fig.13.11 The air cleaner removed to show the fuel line filter (Black arrow). The white arrow points to the crankcase fume pipe, which is just this side of the gulp valve

Fig.13.12 The HIF carburettor with the heater round the dash pot. The mixture adjustment is made by the sealed screw that moves the jet, low down on the body. Beside the carburettor is the gulp valve (white arrow), with its small pipe from the manifold to trigger it.

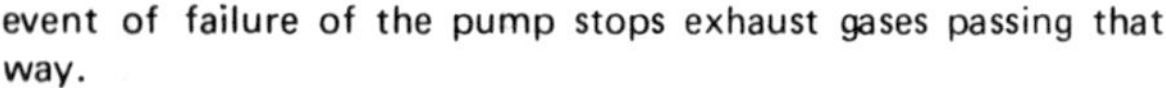

Fig.13.13 The air pump belt is tightened by moving the pump on pivot (1) after slackening its nut and that on the slide (2)

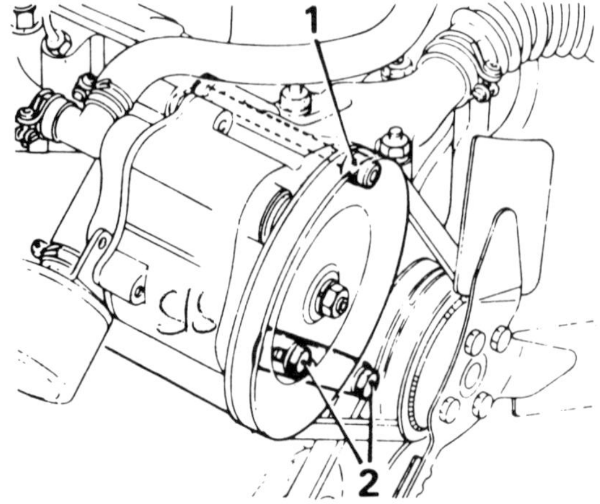

event of failure of the pump stops exhaust gases passing that way.

2 When slowing down with the engine on over-run the air pump also supplies air to the inlet manifold through a gulp valve.

3 The pump is a rotary vane type driven by a belt from the water pump pulley. The belt is tensioned by moving the pump away from the engine block in a similar manner to a generator adjusting the fanbelt. The air cleaner has a renewable element filter. The pump has a relief valve to allow excessive air pressure to blown off to atmosphere.

4 The drive belt tension should allow a total deflection of ½ inch under hand pressure at the midway point of the run of the belt between the pulleys.

8 Air injection servicing

1 The air pump should be tested with the engine running at 1000 rpm.

2 Disconnect the gulp valve air supply hose at the gulp valve and plug it, to prevent any escape of air from the pump. Disconnect the hose from the air supply manifold, and put a pressure gauge on it. The air pump should give a gauge reading of not less than 2.75 lb in^2. A low reading is likely to be due to three causes:

a) The air cleaner might be blocked. Fit a new element and recheck.

b) The relief valve might not be seating correctly. Check this by blanking off the valve, and renew if it is faulty.

c) The pump may need servicing.

3 To overhaul the pump remove it from the engine and proceed as follows:

a) Remove the four port-end cover bolts and take off the cover.

b) Remove the four screws securing the rotor bearing end plate and remove the end plate. Lift out the vanes and take the carbon strips and springs from the rotor.

c) Clean all the components with a lint free cloth.

d) Repack the bearings with ANDOK 260.

e) Renew worn or damaged vanes.

f) Fit new carbons. Note that the slots which carry the carbon and springs are the deeper ones, and the carbons are fitted with the chamfered edge to the inside.

g) Reassemble in reverse order. The underside of the heads of the screws retaining the rotor bearing end plate must be smeared with a locking compound like 'Locktite'.

4 Check the relief valve. Speed the engine up until the valve blows off. This should give a gauge reading of between 4.5 and 6.5 lb/sq in. It is difficult to detect when the valve blows off. Do not try to sense this by putting a finger between the valve and the driving pulley. Adhesive tape can be put over the blow off hole to form an orifice from which the flow of air can be felt.

5 **Check valve.** The air supply pipe being already removed from the check valve, remove the valve itself from the air manifold: Hold the air manifold connection to prevent that twisting, and unscrew the check valve. Blow through the valve by mouth, in each direction in turn. Air should only pass through the valve when blown from the side of the air supply hose connection. If air passes in the wrong direction renew the check valve. Do not use air blast for this test. When refitting to the air manifold hold the latter's connection to prevent it twisting whilst screwing in and tightening the check valve.

6 **Gulp valve.** The gulp valve cures sudden enrichment of the mixture following the closing of the throttle after running on full power. The fuel will continue to flow out of the carburettor slightly longer than will the air after the throttle is closed, as it is heavier. The gulp valve is connected to the inlet manifold. It has

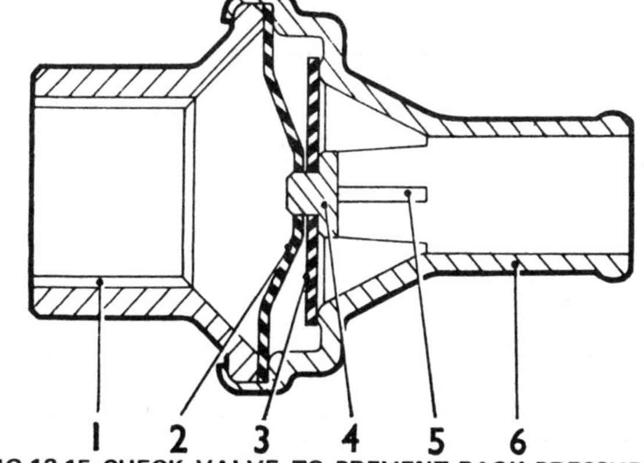

FIG.13.15 CHECK VALVE TO PREVENT BACK PRESSURE REACHING THE AIR PUMP

1 *Air manifold connection*
2 *Diaphragm*
3 *Valve*
4 *Valve pilot*
5 *Guide*
6 *Air supply from pump*

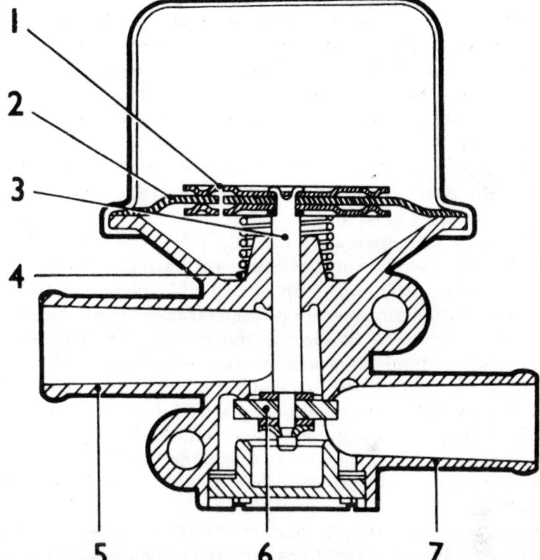

FIG.13.16 GULP VALVE: ALLOWS THE PUMP TO GIVE A GULP OF AIR TO THE INLET MANIFOLD FOR A SHORT TIME AFTER SUDDEN THROTTLE CLOSURE

1 *Metering balance orifice*
2 *Diaphragm*
3 *Valve spindle*
4 *Return spring*
5 *Inlet manifold connection*
6 *Valve*
7 *Air pump connection*

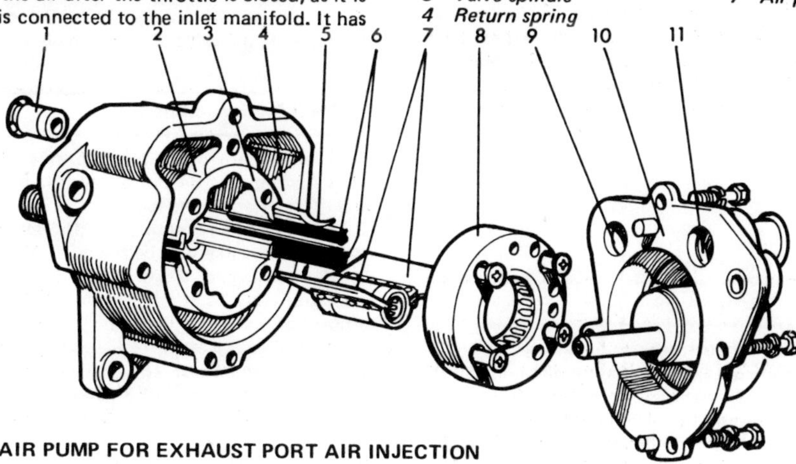

FIG.13.14 THE AIR PUMP FOR EXHAUST PORT AIR INJECTION

1 *Relief valve*
2 *Inlet chamber*
3 *Rotor*
4 *Outer chamber*
5 *Springs*
6 *Carbons*
7 *Vanes*
8 *Rotor bearing-end plate*
9 *Outlet port*
10 *Port-end cover*
11 *Inlet port*

a valve which will feed the manifold depression on throttle closure. There is a small hole in the disc on the valve which will normally equalise pressure both sides, and so the spring can maintain the valve in the closed position, and so the gulp valve is shut. On sudden closure of the throttle the sharp increase of manifold depression is felt on one side of the valve, and will open it. The small hole will not have time to act. As the valve is open, air from the air pump is allowed to enter the inlet manifold and so weaken the mixture. In a few moments the pressure will become equal on both sides of the valve and it will close it again.

7 To test the gulp valve.

a) Disconnect the air supply hose from the air pump to the valve.

b) Connect a vacuum gauge with a T connection to the disconnected end of the gulp valve air hose.

c) Start the engine and run it at idling speed.

d) With a finger close the open connection on the gauge T piece, and check that a zero gauge reading is shown for at least 15 seconds. As the idle speed is constant the gulp valve should be closed, and so no reading registered on the gauge. Do not increase the engine speed above an idle during this test.

e) Now open the throttle, allow the engine to speed up, and then shut it sharply. As the engine speed falls the gauge should register a vacuum. Remove the finger from the end of the pipe to release the vacuum, and then repeat the test a number of times. The gauges should register a vacuum on this method. If it does not renew the gulp valve.

8 Inlet manifold depression limit valve. There is a small valve in the throttle disc to limit the manifold depression under overrun conditions. (See Fig.13.8).

9 To check this disconnect the gulp valve pipe from the inlet manifold. Connect a vacuum gauge to the union on the inlet manifold. Warm the engine up at fast idle speed and until the normal operating temperature is reached. Speed the engine up to 3,000 rpm, and then release the throttle quickly. The vacuum gauge reading should immediately rise to between 20.5 and 22 inches Hg. If the vacuum is greater than this the throttle disc limit valve will not be functioning; a new disc with valve must then be fitted, after which the carburettor requires retuning.

10 Air manifold and injectors. To check the air flow:

a) Disconnect the air manifold from the cylinder head connections.

b) Slacken the air supply hose at the check valve, rotate the manifold till the pipes point upwards and retighten the hose clip.

c) Run the engine (at idle only) and check:

Air comes out of all the pipes, and equally from each.

Exhaust gases blow from each of the injectors in the cylinder head vacated by the air pipes.

d) Be careful not to displace the injectors in the cylinder head as they may be free.

e) If an injector is blocked turn the engine over till that exhaust valve is shut. Using a hand drill to ensure a light touch, pass a 1/8 inch drill through the injector bore, taking care not to touch the exhaust valve stem at the other end. Blow out the carbon through the injector before turning the engine over again.

9 Fuel line filter

In markets where the exhaust emission control system is fitted, a fuel line filter is added to ensure that no dirt impedes its operation. The filter should be serviced, by direct replacement, every 12,000 miles. It is removed by releasing the clip holding it to the exhaust manifold shield and pulling off the flexible pipes. Ensure the replacement is fitted the right way round. After fitting the new filter run the engine for a few minutes and check for leaks.

10 Absorption canister

1 To prevent fumes being emitted by fuel as it evaporates either from the tank or the carburettor float chamber their breathers are plumbed in to an absorptive canister. This has a charcoal body into which fuel vapour is absorbed whilst the engine is switched off. When the engine is next run the fuel vapour absorbed is sucked into the engine by the air breathing system, and burned.

2 The air filter located in the bottom section of the canister must be renewed every 12,000 miles. This filter protects not only the absorption canister, but also the engine breathing system.

3 The filter is replaced as follows. Disconnect the air vent tube (1) (Fig.13.20) from the base of the canister. Then disconnect from the top the two vapour pipes (2) and the purge pipe (3), and finally unscrew the mounting clip nut and bolt (4), taking care to catch the spacer that is in the clamp, and lift away the canister.

4 The air filter may be removed by unscrewing the bottom end cap (5) of the canister which will then expose the filter (6). Lift it out and throw it away: Wipe inside the cap with a non-fluffy rag, and fit a new filter pad, followed by the cap.

5 Remount the canister in the clip, and reconnect the pipes. The purge pipe to the engine valve rocker cover must be fitted to the centre connection on the top of the canister.

6 In time the canister looses its ability to absorb, so at 50,000 miles the complete canister must be renewed.

11 Anti run-on valve

1 Using the car on low octane fuel and with the lean mixtures required to meet anti-pollution standards makes the engine liable to run-on by self ignition after switching off. This puts great stress on the engine. It will try to run backwards, and there may be blow back through the carburettor.

2 The anti run-on valve cuts off fuel to the carburettor jet when the ignition is switched off. So though combustion chamber temperature might be so high running-on would have otherwise occurred, the engine will quickly and smoothly stop.

3 The valve is on the right front of the engine compartment near the absorption canister. A pipe comes to it from the inlet manifold. Another goes to the absorption canister to connect to the line going to the float chamber air vent. The valve is operated by an electric solenoid. This solenoid is live when the ignition is switched off, but there is oil pressure in the engine. Immediately after the ignition is switched off the engine will be still turning so there will be oil pressure. The anti-run on valve opens, and connects full inlet manifold suction to the carburettor float chamber air space using the air vent piping. This stops fuel flow to the jet so the engine stops. Oil pressure then drops, and switches off the valve. So the engine is ready to start again.

12 Fault finding - emissions

1 The addition of emission control adds some new hazards to fault finding. Yet do not always blame them; the usual old ones will most often be the fault.

2 Erratic running, with poor driveability, if not a conventional defect is most likely to be the gulp valve.

3 If the engine stops after short periods it may be fuel starvation due to a blockage in the air lines to or from the absorption canister. This can be checked by quickly taking off the fuel filler cap as the engine fails, to listen for an intake of air.

4 If enrichment of the mixture is needed to get a correct exhaust emission reading there is likely to be an air leak to the crankcase, either on the engine itself, or the breather system piping.

5 If the exhaust temperature seems excessive check the air injectors for air throughput.

6 Leaks can often be located by listening with a plastic pipe

Fig.13.17 The right front of the Austin Marina engine showing: 1 Absorption canister. 2 Vapour pipe from fuel tank. 3 Vapour pipe from carburettor float chamber. 4 Purge pipe to engine. 5 Anti-run-on valve which is connected to the air inlet at the bottom of the canister, and to the inlet manifold. 6 Air pump air cleaner. The white arrows point to two of the air injectors

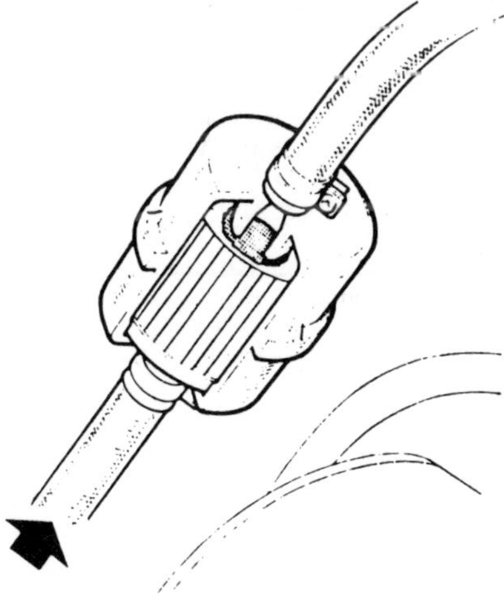

Fig.13.18 The fuel line filter

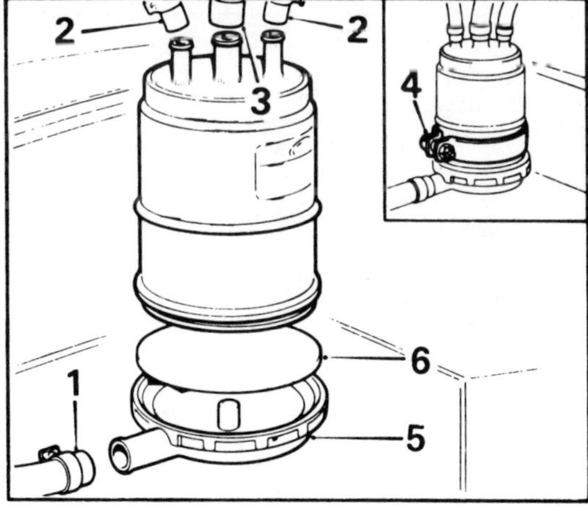

FIG.13.19 ABSORPTION CANISTER

1 Air intake from anti-run-on valve
2 Vapour pipes from tank and float chamber
3 Purge pipe to engine rocker box
4 Clamp
5 Screwed bottom cover
6 Replaceable filter pad

with metal pipe at the end.

7 If the air pump is suspected of noise, run the engine with its belt removed to listen for the difference. Doing this also shows you how the characteristics of the engine are affected by loss of the air output from the pump, and enables you on another occasion to recognise symptoms better.

13 Ignition timing

1 The specifications at the begining of this chapter call for the setting of the ignition by stroboscope. Because of the special ignition timing to limit emissions, the characteristics of the ignition automatic advance are critical, so the timing MUST be set with the engine running, and using a stroboscope.

2 If the timing has been completely lost in dismantling, set it first by the static method described in Chapter 4/10, to 5° Before Top Dead Centre. This will allow the engine tobe started.

3 Disconnect the ignition suction pipe in the case of cars for America that specify that particular setting. Do this at the distributor end of the pipe, and plug the end of the pipe with a match stick or some such.

4 Wire up the stroboscope to the lead to No 1 cylinder's spark plug in accorance with the light maker's instructions.

5 Start up the engine, and set it to run on the fast idle setting of the choke to the engine speed in the specification. For cars without a tachometer, one will have to be connected up direct to the engine.

6 Shine the stroboscope light on the timing marks on the crankshaft pulley. Adjust the distributor till the notch on the pulley, 'frozen' by the strobe, is by the correct timing mark.

7 The stroboscope is also useful for watching the automatic ignition advance. The centrifugal advance can be seen working as the engine is sped up. The suction advance will work as the throttle is opened and shut abruptly.

14 Engine compression test

1 Cars used with the lean mixture necessary to meet some countries' regulations, and using fuel with low lead content, are liable to burn the exhaust valve seats. This applies amongst others, to North America and Germany.

2 If valve burning is detected early it can be easily rectified. Long before it is noticeable to the car it can be detected by a compression test.

3 A special gauge for this, and an assistant, will be needed. The gauges are not very expensive, and will be a useful investment. But if necessary a garage can quickly do this check.

4 Warm up the engine.

5 Remove all the spark plugs.

6 Push the rubber seal of the gauge hard against the spark plug hole in the cylinder head.

7 Get the assistant to open the throttle wide, and work the starter. The engine should be cranked for about three seconds; long enough to build up a reading on the gauge.

8 Write down the reading.

9 Relieve the pressure in the gauge, and repeat for the other cylinders.

10 If the readings are not all within 5 lb f/ in^2 of each other do the whole test again. If the second reading for a particular cylinder varies from the first, do that one again to get a better average.

11 If it is definite that there is variation of more than 5%, which is also near enough 5 lb f/in^2, between cylinders, then it indicates the valves are not seating properly, and they should be reground.

12 Should this job be necessary early in the life of the car it does not follow that it will continue to be so in the future at the same frequency. If the valves are carefully reground by hand a better seating can be obtained than by machining, and these will last better. See Chapter 1/35.

13 Note that little stress has been laid on the actual gauge readings: it is the difference between the cylinders that is important. The actual reading depends on the accuracy of the gauge, the compression ratio of the engine, and the state of wear of the piston rings. It is assumed that these all wear the same, and none are broken.

15 Brake pressure failure switch.

1 Cars for some markets, including North America, have a pressure warning switch.

2 This switch gives warning should pressure fail in one of the brake lines. The switch has a shuttle valve which normally, with brake fluid pressure equal on either side, sits centrally in the valve cylinder. Loss of pressure in one side lets the valve move over to one side and close the switch contacts.

3 Satisfactory working of the switch can be shown when bleeding the brakes.

4 Should the switch need overhaul remove it from the car first. Brake fluid ruins paint, so none must be allowed to run down in the engine compartment.

5 First drain both lines of the brakes at the bleed nipples.

6 Put a rag around the switch to catch drips.

7 Unplug the wires from the switch, undo all the pipe unions, and remove the bolt holding the valve to the car body.

8 Remove the end plug. Unscrew the plastic switch. Remove the shuttle valve, noting which way round everything goes.

9 Always use a new copper washer for the plug, and new rubbers for the piston seals.

10 After reassembly refill the system with fluid. Bleed the brakes starting with the rear. Note the working of the warning light. Then check for leaks.

16 Centralisation of brake pressure warning switch

1 During bleeding of the brakes, the loss of pressure in one of the brake systems will force the shuttle valve of the brake pressure differential warning switch over to one side. Thus after the last wheel has been bled it will be off centre, and the warning light still on. (Note some cars are wired through the ignition switch, so this must be on to check).

2 To centralise the switch proceed as follows:

3 Refit the bleed pipe to a wheel on the other pipe circuit to the last one just bled. For instance the right rear. Then an assistant should apply the brakes and hold them firmly and watch the warning light.

4 Slacken the bleed nipple. The assistant might feel pedal movement as the shuttle moves; the warning light will go out; as soon as it does shut the nipple. If the nipple is tightened too late the valve will move past centre, and the light will come on again. The procedure must then be repeated, but more quickly this time, on a brake on the other pipe circuit, ie, front right.

17 Electrical warning buzzer

1 A safety warning buzzer is fitted.

2 On entering the car, if the engine is started, and a gear engaged, but the driver or front passenger have not done up their safety belts, a buzzer in the dash will sound, and a light on the dash shine. This system is triggered by a switch on the gear selectors, the igintion switch, and for the passenger, a pad switch in the seat. It is switched off by contacts in the reel of the lap part of the seat belt.

3 On leaving the car, if the key is left in the ignition switch steering lock, the buzzer will sound when the door is opened.

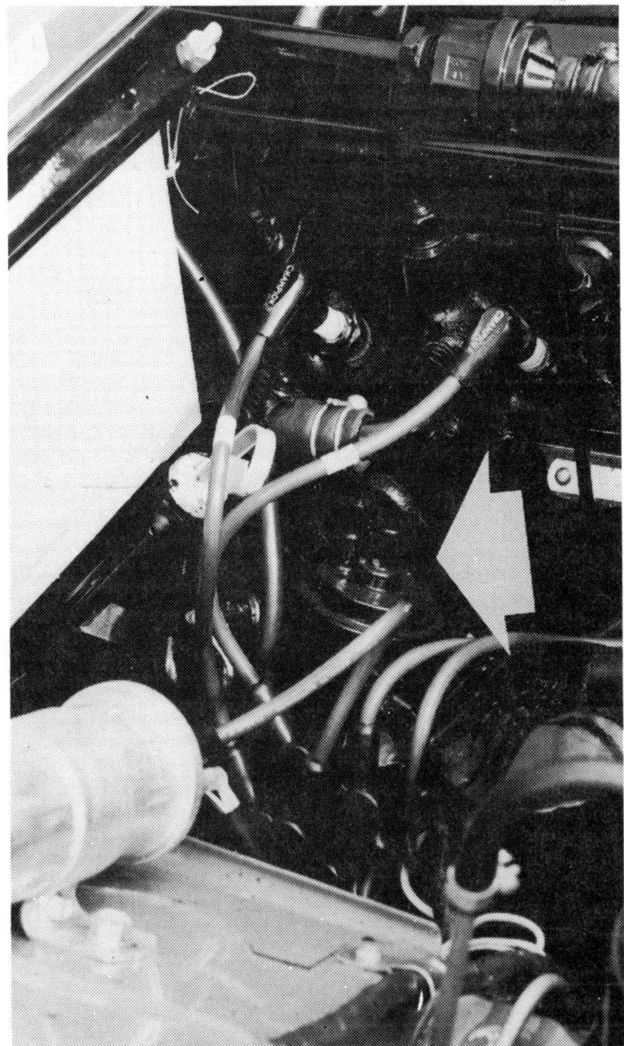

Fig.13.20 The ignition advance has a special capsule on the distributor, and this is connected to the inlet manifold, and not beside the throttle

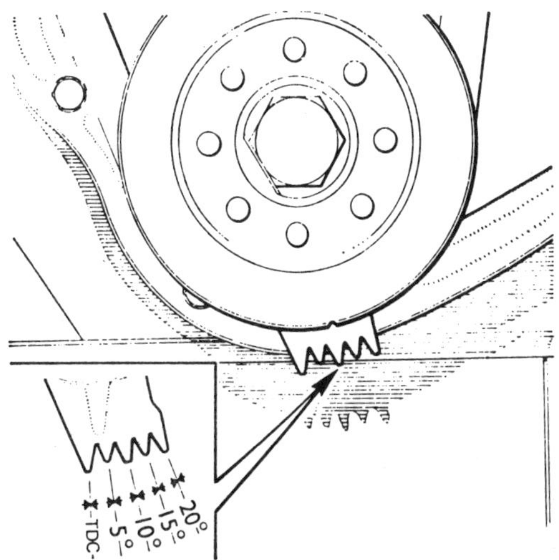

Fig.13.21 The timing marks by the crankshaft pulley.

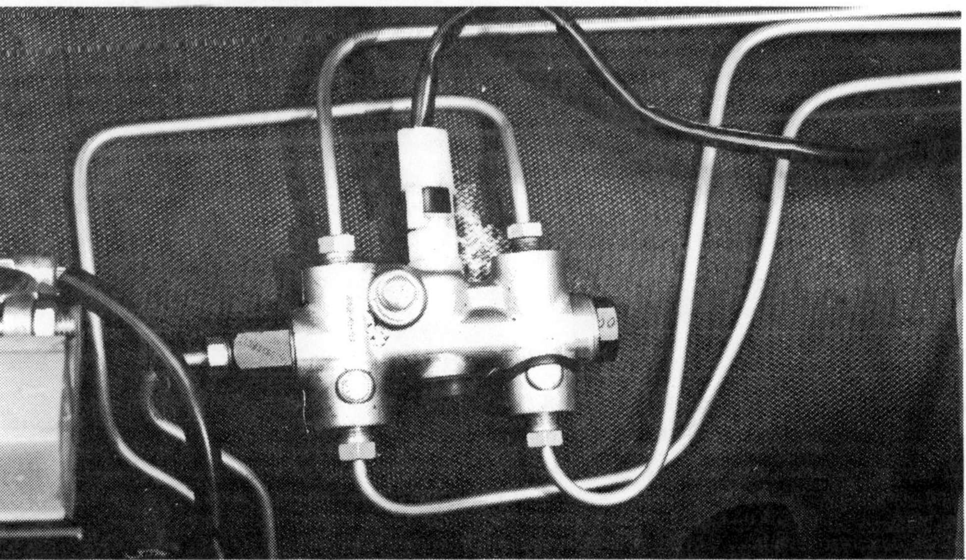

Fig.13.22 The brake pressure failure warning switch.

As this book has been written in the United Kingdom it uses the appropriate English component names. Some of these differ from those used in America. Normally this causes no difficulty. But to make sure, a glossary is printed below.

Glossary

English	American
Adjustable spanner	Crescent wrench
Anti-roll bar	Stabiliser or sway bar
Bonnet (engine cover)	Hood
Boot (luggage compartment)	Trunk
Bottom gear	1st gear
Bulkhead	Firewall
Clearance	Lash
Crownwheel	Ring gear (of differential)
Catch	Latch
Camfollower or tappet	Valve lifter or tappet
Cat's eye	Road reflecting lane marker
Circlip	Snap ring
Drop arm	Pitman arm
Drop head coupe	Convertible
Dynamo	Generator (DC)
Earth (electrical)	Ground
Estate car	Station wagon
Exhaust manifold	Header
Fault finding	Trouble shooting
Free play	Lash
Free wheel	Coast
Gudgeon pin	Piston pin or wrist pin
Gearchange	Shift
Gearbox	Transmission
Hood	Soft top
Hard top	Hard top
Half shaft	Axle shaft
Hot spot	Heat riser
Leading shoe (of brake)	Primary shoe
Layshaft (of gearbox)	Counter shaft
Mudguard or wing	Fender
Mole grips	Vise grips
Motorway	Freeway, turnpike etc
Paraffin	Kerosene
Petrol	Gas
Reverse	Back-up
Saloon	Sedan
Split cotter (for valve spring cap)	Lock (for valve spring retainer)
Split pin	Cotter pin
Sump	Oil pan
Silencer	Muffler
Steering arm	Spindle arm
Side light	Parking light
Side marker light	Cat's eye
Spanner	Wrench
Tappet	Valve lifter
Tab washer	Tank; lock
Top gear	High
Transmission	Whole drive line from clutch to axle shaft
Trailing shoe (of brake)	Secondary shoe
Track rod (of steering)	Tie rod (or connecting rod)
Windscreen	Windshield

Miscellaneous points

An 'Oil seal' is fitted to components lubricated by grease!

A 'Damper' is a 'Shock absorber': it damps out bouncing, and absorbs shocks of bump impact. Both names are correct, and both are used haphazardly.

Note that British drum brakes are different from the Bendix type that is common in America, so different descriptive names result. The shoe end furthest from the hydraulic wheel cylinder is on a pivot; interconnection between the shoes as on Bendix brakes is most uncommon. Therefore the phrase 'Primary' or 'Secondary' shoe does not apply. A shoe is said to be Leading or Trailing. A 'Leading' shoe is one on which a point on the drum, as it rotates forward, reaches the shoe at the end worked by the hydraulic cylinder before the anchor end. The opposite is a trailing shoe, and this one has no self servo from the wrapping effect of the rotating drum.

The word 'Tuning' has a narrower meaning than in America, and applies to that engine servicing to ensure full power. The words 'Service' or 'Maintenance' are used where an American would say 'Tune-up'

Metric conversion tables

Inches	Decimals	Millimetres	Millimetres to Inches		Inches to Millimetres	
			mm	Inches	Inches	mm
1/64	0.015625	0.3969	0.01	0.00039	0.001	0.0254
1/32	0.03125	0.7937	0.02	0.00079	0.002	0.0508
3/64	0.046875	1.1906	0.03	0.00118	0.003	0.0762
1/16	0.0625	1.5875	0.04	0.00157	0.004	0.1016
5/64	0.078125	1.9844	0.05	0.00197	0.005	0.1270
3/32	0.09375	2.3812	0.06	0.00236	0.006	0.1524
7/64	0.109375	2.7781	0.07	0.00276	0.007	0.1778
1/8	0.125	3.1750	0.08	0.00315	0.008	0.2032
9/64	0.140625	3.5719	0.09	0.00354	0.009	0.2286
5/32	0.15625	3.9687	0.1	0.00394	0.01	0.254
11/64	0.171875	4.3656	0.2	0.00787	0.02	0.508
3/16	0.1875	4.7625	0.3	0.01181	0.03	0.762
13/64	0.203125	5.1594	0.4	0.01575	0.04	1.016
7/32	0.21875	5.5562	0.5	0.01969	0.05	1.270
15/64	0.234375	5.9531	0.6	0.02362	0.06	1.524
1/4	0.25	6.3500	0.7	0.02756	0.07	1.778
17/64	0.265625	6.7469	0.8	0.03150	0.08	2.032
9/32	0.28125	7.1437	0.9	0.03543	0.09	2.286
19/64	0.296875	7.5406	1	0.03937	0.1	2.54
5/16	0.3125	7.9375	2	0.07874	0.2	5.08
21/64	0.328125	8.3344	3	0.11811	0.3	7.62
11/32	0.34375	8.7312	4	0.15748	0.4	10.16
23/64	0.359375	9.1281	5	0.19685	0.5	12.70
3/8	0.375	9.5250	6	0.23622	0.6	15.24
25/64	0.390625	9.9219	7	0.27559	0.7	17.78
13/32	0.40625	10.3187	8	0.31496	0.8	20.32
27/64	0.421875	10.7156	9	0.35433	0.9	22.86
7/16	0.4375	11.1125	10	0.39370	1	25.4
29/64	0.453125	11.5094	11	0.43307	2	50.8
15/32	0.46875	11.9062	12	0.47244	3	76.2
31/64	0.484375	12.3031	13	0.51181	4	101.6
1/2	0.5	12.7000	14	0.55118	5	127.0
33/64	0.515625	13.0969	15	0.59055	6	152.4
17/32	0.53125	13.4937	16	0.62992	7	177.8
35/64	0.546875	13.8906	17	0.66929	8	203.2
9/16	0.5625	14.2875	18	0.70866	9	228.6
37/64	0.578125	14.6844	19	0.74803	10	254.0
19/32	0.59375	15.0812	20	0.78740	11	279.4
39/64	0.609375	15.4781	21	0.82677	12	304.8
5/8	0.625	15.8750	22	0.86614	13	330.2
41/64	0.640625	16.2719	23	0.90551	14	355.6
21/32	0.65625	16.6687	24	0.94488	15	381.0
43/64	0.671875	17.0656	25	0.98425	16	406.4
11/16	0.6875	17.4625	26	1.02362	17	431.8
45/64	0.703125	17.8594	27	1.06299	18	457.2
23/32	0.71875	18.2562	28	1.10236	19	482.6
47/64	0.734375	18.6531	29	1.14173	20	508.0
3/4	0.75	19.0500	30	1.18110	21	533.4
49/64	0.765625	19.4469	31	1.22047	22	558.8
25/32	0.78125	19.8437	32	1.25984	23	584.2
51/64	0.796875	20.2406	33	1.29921	24	609.6
13/16	0.8125	20.6375	34	1.33858	25	635.0
53/64	0.828125	21.0344	35	1.37795	26	660.4
27/32	0.84375	21.4312	36	1.41732	27	685.8
55/64	0.859375	21.8281	37	1.4567	28	711.2
7/8	0.875	22.2250	38	1.4961	29	736.6
57/64	0.890625	22.6219	39	1.5354	30	762.0
29/32	0.90625	23.0187	40	1.5748	31	787.4
59/64	0.921875	23.4156	41	1.6142	32	812.8
15/16	0.9375	23.8125	42	1.6535	33	838.2
61/64	0.953125	24.2094	43	1.6929	34	863.6
31/32	0.96875	24.6062	44	1.7323	35	889.0
63/64	0.984375	25.0031	45	1.7717	36	914.4

1 Imperial gallon = 8 Imp pints = 1.16 US gallons = 277.42 cu in = 4.5459 litres

1 US gallon = 4 US quarts = 0.862 Imp gallon = 231 cu in = 3.785 litres

1 Litre = 0.2199 Imp gallon = 0.2642 US gallon = 61.0253 cu in = 1000 cc

Miles to Kilometres		Kilometres to Miles	
1	1.61	1	0.62
2	3.22	2	1.24
3	4.83	3	1.86
4	6.44	4	2.49
5	8.05	5	3.11
6	9.66	6	3.73
7	11.27	7	4.35
8	12.88	8	4.97
9	14.48	9	5.59
10	16.09	10	6.21
20	32.19	20	12.43
30	48.28	30	18.64
40	64.37	40	24.85
50	80.47	50	31.07
60	96.56	60	37.28
70	112.65	70	43.50
80	128.75	80	49.71
90	144.84	90	55.92
100	160.93	100	62.14

lb f ft to Kg f m		Kg f m to lb f ft		lb f/in^2 : Kg f/cm^2		Kg f/cm^2 : lb f/in^2	
1	0.138	1	7.233	1	0.07	1	14.22
2	0.276	2	14.466	2	0.14	2	28.50
3	0.414	3	21.699	3	0.21	3	42.67
4	0.553	4	28.932	4	0.28	4	56.89
5	0.691	5	36.165	5	0.35	5	71.12
6	0.829	6	43.398	6	0.42	6	85.34
7	0.967	7	50.631	7	0.49	7	99.56
8	1.106	8	57.864	8	0.56	8	113.79
9	1.244	9	65.097	9	0.63	9	128.00
10	1.382	10	72.330	10	0.70	10	142.23
20	2.765	20	144.660	20	1.41	20	284.47
30	4.147	30	216.990	30	2.11	30	426.70

Index

Printed by
J. H. HAYNES & Co. Ltd
Sparkford Yeovil Somerset
ENGLAND